Probability
and
Stochastic
Processes

Probability and Stochastic Processes

Frederick Solomon
State University of New York—Purchase

Prentice-Hall, Inc., Englewood Cliffs, New Jersey 07632

Library of Congress Cataloging-in-Publication Data

SOLOMON, FREDERICK, 1946–
    Probability and stochastic processes.

    Bibliography: p.
    Includes index.
    1. Probabilities.   2. Stochastic processes.
I. Title.
QA273.S686 1987   519.2   86-25213
ISBN 0-13-711961-5

Editorial/production supervision and
   interior design: Jean Hunter
Cover design: 20/20 Services, Inc.
Manufacturing buyer: John B. Hall

Printed in the United States of America

10 9 8 7 6 5 4 3 2 1

ISBN 0-13-711961-5 01

PRENTICE-HALL INTERNATIONAL (UK) LIMITED, *London*
PRENTICE-HALL OF AUSTRALIA PTY. LIMITED, *Sydney*
EDITORA PRENTICE-HALL DO BRASIL, LTDA., *Rio de Janeiro*
PRENTICE-HALL CANADA INC., *Toronto*
PRENTICE-HALL HISPANOAMERICANA, S.A., *Mexico*
PRENTICE-HALL OF INDIA PRIVATE LIMITED, *New Delhi*
PRENTICE-HALL OF JAPAN, INC., *Tokyo*
PRENTICE-HALL OF SOUTHEAST ASIA PTE. LTD., *Singapore*

To Louise, Benjy, and Alice

". . . and [we ought] always to search for
that which is eternal amidst the random,
everyday events."

Martin Kindder

Contents

3   CONDITIONAL PROBABILITY AND INDEPENDENCE   54

4   DISCRETE RANDOM VARIABLES   80

Contents

Preface

This text is designed for a one-semester or two-quarter course in probability theory and applications. Calculus through the techniques of integration is required for the first seven chapters. Chapter 8 requires knowledge of multiple integrals. Although matrix multiplication is used in Chapter 12, Appendix 2 explains the necessary material. In addition, numerous programs are included. These are in a simplified Pascal and only a slight exposure to programming is required.

There is much that is aesthetic in probability. Like any mathematical subject there is an "elegance" that endows the reasoning and the manipulations of symbols with a sense of logical completeness and simplicity. But there is a sense of *magic* when abstract mathematics is seen to apply validly to the "real world." To convey the intuition of the subject has been paramount in writing this book: how reasonable assumptions can be used to formulate a mathematical model which then has applications to the myriad phenomena surrounding us. One does not have to look far to see randomness and chance events. They are everywhere: in the pattern of raindrops, arrival of buses, shapes of natural objects, and so on.

Since probability is an applied subject, I have taken care to include computational ideas. A simplified version of Pascal is used to express algorithms. These are of two types: for calculations of formulas and (beginning with Chapter 7) simulations of random models. Not only is computation necessary in any specific application of probability, but the algorithmic approach provides another means by which we can gain insight into how a model works.

With the exception of Chapter 7, the first ten chapters form the core of a first course in probability. Chapter 7 on simulations can be covered as a single unit or section by section as the topics arise in the earlier chapters; for example, random number generators can be one of the first topics during the first week.

It will not be possible in one semester to cover all the material in Chapters 11 and 12. Neither of these chapters is a prerequisite for the other and can be covered independently. Chapter 11 shows how to solve for the steady state in a birth and death process in continuous time; queues are featured. Chapter 12 is the only one to require matrix multiplication; it covers Markov chains in discrete time.

Throughout the text there are optional sections which contain material at a deeper level of sophistication. If several of these are deleted, a semester course should be able to cover the first ten chapters and at least one of Chapters 11 and 12.

I have tried to convey a sense of the openness of the subject. With simulations particularly, probability affords opportunities for projects and independent work.

I would like to thank Jean Hunter and David Ostrow of Prentice-Hall for their editorial guidance, the reviewers, Professor Galen R. Shorack, the University of Washington, Professor Franklin Sheehan, San Francisco State University, and Professor Donald E. Myers, the University of Arizona, for their excellent suggestions, my family for its patience, and Monique Brion-Escher, Peter Brooks, Jason Choi, Clare Detko, Karl Dushin, Robert Koff, Susan Schroeder, William Widulski, and Robert Drummond—students who made very fine contributions to the quality of the text.

Purchase, New York   *Frederick Solomon*

Probability
and
Stochastic
Processes

The loser, when the game at dice breaks up,
lingers despondent, and repeats the throws to learn,
in grief, what made his fortune droop.

Dante, 1265–1321, The Divine Comedy

— Chapter 0

Introduction

Quite naturally we look for relationships and patterns among the variable features in the world around us: We attempt to devise *abstract models*. This means that amidst the infinity of detail in any actual situation we try to strip away the inessential and isolate those variables that are most important to the questions in which we are interested. We do this model building for two reasons: first, for the practicality of it; in applying an abstract model that accurately mirrors an aspect of reality, we are better able to control events; and second, even if a model leads to no practical consequence, understanding the model leads to a sense of insight which is felt to be valuable in its own right.

A mathematical model is one in which the variables and the relationships among them are mathematical. This means that they have a high degree of logical structure: The variables are all numerical or possibly geometric in nature.

It is an oversimplification to say that mathematical model building consists in the observation of variables, the derivation of formulas, and finally the checking of the model's predictions with reality. Rather, the model proceeds through several versions; the checking operation might suggest new variables that are relevant; the derivation of mathematical formulas might suggest new ways in which the model can be checked. The process finally stops when the model is "good enough" for the purpose to which it was intended or one runs out of time or further refinements are too complicated. But the point is that only in the very simplest situations are mathematical models completely successful. There is almost always the possibility of further revision and refinement.

1

A **random model** is one in which chance and randomness play a significant role. For example, a mathematical model for the amount of traffic on a certain highway cannot possibly assume that all the relevant variables are known; this would imply knowing whether *each* car in the entire city is on the highway. Nor is such detailed knowledge necessary. Rather, a model would make reasonable assumptions and predict the traffic up to likelihoods or various degrees of certainty. How to devise random models, how to interpret them, and how to use them are what this book is about.

Probability deals with the formulation of random models, the derivations of formulas, and the predictions based on them. Mathematical statistics deals with analyzing and revising the model in the light of actual data. For example, a question for probability is: "Given that 40 out of 100 people favor proposition A, what is the likelihood that among 10 people interviewed at random fewer than 3 will be in favor?" A corresponding question for statistics is: "Among 10 people interviewed, 3 favored proposition A. *Given* this, what conclusions can be drawn about the popularity of the proposition among the total population?"

Games of chance are millenia old. Heel bones of hooved animals which have four roughly symmetrical faces were used for the "dice." An Egyptian board game using such a bone dates to 1800 B.C. The casting of lots and other randomizing procedures were common. In the biblical story of Jonah such a device was used to determine that Jonah was responsible for the storm at sea. But there was never more than the most elementary mathematics applied.

As with many other mathematical and scientific fields, the origins of probability lie in sixteenth-century late renaissance. Although the first problems concerned odds in gambling, it is wrong to suppose that the *need* to solve such problems was behind the development of probabilistic methods. Rather, at this time there was a new spirit in the air—a sense of objectivity, an interest in applying logic to phenomena in the natural world, and a faith in our ability to discover scientific-type laws. Gambling games provided the *occasion* for the application of mathematics.

> In this treatise I had in mind foremost the enjoyment of the mathematicians and not the advantages of the players; it is our opinion that those who waste time on games fully deserve to lose their money as well.
>
> *Pierre-Remond de Montmort, 1713*

In the mid-eighteenth century probability was applied to areas other than gambling—first to demography (mortality, census tables, and population studies), then to physics, and theories of random errors of measurement. Presently, all scientific disciplines use methods developed in this text. Precisely because the applications are so varied, the subject itself must be abstract. If a queueing model applies to a waiting line at a telephone booth *as well as* cars waiting at a car wash *as well as* toys on a shelf "waiting" to be sold *as well as* radioactive atoms "waiting" to disintegrate *as well as* playing cards "waiting" to be dealt, . . . , then the model must use an abstract symbolism stripped of specific connotations.

Randomness alone can never produce a significant pattern,
for it consists in the absence of any such pattern.

M. Polanyi, Personal Knowledge: Towards a Post-
Critical Philosophy. Copyright © 1974. The Univ. of
Chicago Press. Reprinted by permission of the publisher.

— Chapter 1 —————————————————

The Language and Axioms
of Probability

1.1 WHAT IS RANDOMNESS?

In experience there are unpredictable, inexplicable features; the weather is unpredictable, so we say that it is due to randomness as though randomness were a "thing," something to be invoked for lack of a better explanation—for lack of *any* explanation, in fact. A coin is flipped. Will it land heads or will it land tails? If the *exact* force of the thumb on the coin were known and the *exact* position of the fingers and the *exact* air currents and the *exact* composition of the table, *then* one might be able to predict how the coin would land. But these things are not known and to measure them with the required degree of accuracy might well be impossible even in theory. So the *lack* of an explanation for why the coin landed as it did is summarized by the words "randomness" and "chance."

Around the year 1900 the world was felt to be deterministic, by and large. Randomness was an "epiphenomenon"—a category that *we* used to describe the world due to *our* ignorance, but not an essential aspect of the world as it actually is.

If a minute case which escapes our notice determines a considerable effect which we cannot miss, then we say that this effect is due to chance. If we had an exact knowledge of the laws of nature and the position of the universe at the initial moment, we could predict exactly the position of that same universe in a succeeding moment.

Henri Poincaré, 1912

Events in the natural world seem to have causes: Push this and that pops; slide here and that breaks over there. We say that A causes B **deterministically** when the cause A is "as recognizable" as the effect B. To explain what this means, consider this example: A hammer is swung, thereby driving in the nail. The cause (the hammer swing) was an act that took effort, that was *recognizable* in relation to the effect (nail in board). We say that the hammer swing *caused* the effect because we *saw it happen* that way. Now consider this example: Hold a pencil vertically, point downward on a table. Let go. In what direction does the pencil finally point? There is a very definite cause: Shift the angle at which the pencil is held by .01° and the pencil points in a completely different direction. The effect (the direction in which the pencil comes to rest) is "large" in comparison to the cause (the exact angle at which the pencil was originally held). In this case we say that the final direction is random.

Whether an event is random often depends on the viewpoint; it is *relative*. For example, if the bus is 5 minutes late, to the bus driver there is a perfectly well defined cause: heavy traffic on Fifteenth Street. But to the person waiting for the bus to arrive, the cause is hidden; it is not as "recognizable" as the effect—the 5-minute lateness. Thus the *same* event is seen by the bus driver as deterministically caused, but as random by the passenger.

In this way a caused event can be distinguished from a random one:

> A **random event** is a "large" or visible effect with a "small," invisible, or nonexistent cause.

Are there any events that are *really* random? Are there events *without* causes in the natural world? Or is randomness just a synonym for *lack of knowledge*? In the development of quantum physics in the 1920s it was found necessary to include randomness as an essential ingredient in the behavior of elementary particles. *When* the radium atom disintegrates is completely random; the atom simply decays at some time without *any* apparent cause whatsoever. All attempts at building a theory without randomness have failed and there is strong evidence to show that models not incorporating randomness cannot apply, in theory, to the happenings at the elementary particle level.

The remarks so far in this chapter have been philosophical. From here on we will be considering the *mathematical* theory of randomness. Whatever randomness *is*, there are certain obvious features about it that are clear to intuition. Once these are captured in a set of axioms, our subject begins. But the philosophy is still important; mathematics can be used to derive a theory, but only a more reflective attitude can reveal the *meanings* of the terms.

1.2 DEFINITION OF THE SAMPLE SPACE ASSOCIATED WITH A RANDOM EXPERIMENT

A **random experiment** is an experiment or observation which can be performed, at least in thought, any number of times under the same relevant conditions. The experiment is called "random" because the result or outcome cannot be known in complete detail by knowing the relevant conditions. Examples: Flip a coin, count the number of meteors in a half-hour interval, measure the time it takes for an object to fall from A to B, count the number of people in line at the checkout counter. . . . In flipping a coin repeatedly, each flip constitutes one experiment. *All* the conditions cannot be the same: The exact time of each flip differs. But the relevant conditions remain the same: same coin, same method of flipping. The very nature of the random experiment reveals what *outcomes* are possible. In counting the number of meteors there could be 0 or 1 or 2 or. . . . In waiting for an atom to decay, the outcome is the instant of time recorded by the Geiger counter; it could be any real number in $(0, \infty)$ and might even be ∞ if no decay is ever recorded.

Given a random experiment, the set of possible results is the **sample space**. This is not quite correct, actually. If the random experiment consists of choosing a card at random from a standard deck of 52 cards, the sample space is *not* the set of possible results; this set, after all, is the deck of cards itself. Rather the sample space is a set of *symbols*—each symbol *representing* a result. To each distinct possible result in the *real* experiment there is associated one element in the sample space. Thus there are as many elements in the sample space as there are possible results.

Given a random experiment, the sample space Ω is a set each of whose elements represents one possible result.

Example 1

Choose 1 card from a standard deck of 52 cards. What is Ω?

Solution Ω as the set representing the results might be

$$\Omega = \{AC, 2C, 3C, \ldots, KC, AD, 2D, \ldots, KD, \ldots, KS\}$$

where

AC represents ace of clubs

2C represents 2 of clubs

.

.

.

KC represents king of clubs

.

.

. ∎

Of course, there are an infinite number of ways to describe the result of the random experiment of choosing one card. All of these ways are essentially identical; the difference between one sample space and another is just in the symbolic scheme used to represent the results. Also, the sample space above would *not* be accurate if certain features we take for granted are not in fact true. For example, if your dog could possibly grab the card before you have a chance to see what it is, this would have to be included as the fifty-third result. If a coin is flipped once, then

$$\Omega = \{H, T, S, G, O\}$$

where H represents heads, T represents tails, S represents "landed on its side," G represents "rolled into the gutter and was never seen," and finally O represents "went into orbit and never returned" *if* in fact the latter cases are real possibilities.

Elements ω of the sample space are called **sample points** *or* **outcomes**.

Just as it is not possible to specify in complete detail everything about a random experiment, it is also not possible to specify *exactly* what happened. In throwing a die once, the outcome is taken to be the number showing uppermost; but *where* on the table it landed and the temperature are also parts of the result. We almost always have a good idea as to what are the *relevant* or most significant parts of the results of the random experiment; it is these that are labeled the outcome. Thus an outcome is *a complete specification of the result of the random experiment*—complete enough to be able to distinguish one result from another.

Example 2

Flip a coin twice and note the side showing uppermost on each flip. What is the sample space Ω?

Solution 1

$$\Omega_1 = \{HH, HT, TH, TT\}$$

where, for example, the outcome HT represents the event "heads on first flip, tails on the second." Thus the first letter indicates the result of the first flip and the second letter represents the result of the second flip.

Solution 2

$$\Omega_2 = \{HH, HT\ TT\}$$

where HH represents "two heads," TT represents "two tails," and HT represents "one head and one tail without specifying whether the first or the second was the head."

Both Ω_1 and Ω_2 are valid sample spaces. Ω_2 is formed by *collapsing* two outcomes in Ω_1 into one outcome in Ω_2. Which sample space is better? It depends on what questions are asked. If all we are interested in is the total number of heads, then Ω_2 is every bit as valid as Ω_1. But Ω_1 contains more detailed information than does Ω_2. ■

Example 3

Measure the temperature outside. What is the sample space?

> **Solution** Let
> $$\Omega_1 = \{-100, -99, -98, \ldots, 148, 149, 150\}$$
> $$= \{t : t \text{ is an integer and } -100 \leq t \leq 150\}$$
> $$\Omega_2 = \{t : t \text{ is a integer}\}$$
> $$\Omega_3 = \{t : t \text{ is a real number}\}$$

If the finest calibration of which the thermometer is capable is the closest degree, then Ω_1 might be suitable. Ω_2 is perhaps simpler to describe than Ω_1 and there is no harm in including sample points that cannot in reality occur. Ω_3 might be used if accuracy finer than a degree is used or if one is unwilling to specify a limit to that accuracy. Note that the event "temperature is 67°" is represented by the single sample point $\omega = 67$ if sample spaces Ω_1 or Ω_2 are used. If Ω_3 is used, this same event is represented by a set consisting of *infinitely* many real numbers:

$$\text{"temperature is 67 °"} = \{t : 66.5 \leq t < 67.5\}$$

The event "temperature is freezing" is represented by the set

$$\{t : t < 32\} \quad \blacksquare$$

"Things" that can happen as the result of a random experiment are usually composed of many outcomes and consequently are *subsets* of Ω.

> An **event** is a subset of the sample space Ω.

The **empty set** is denoted $\emptyset$; in the sample space language $\emptyset$ represents "nothing happened as the result of the random experiment." This is impossible. (Even if nothing might happen as the result of our experiment, this would have to be included as a sample point and is not represented by $\emptyset$. For example, if we wait for the bus and the bus *never* arrives, *this* possibility is an outcome and not nothing.) Something always happens as the result of the random experiment, so $\emptyset$ is also called the *impossible event*. The entire sample space Ω, on the other hand, is the *sure event* and represents the possibility that *something* happened which, of course, always happens.

Technically, an outcome is an element of the sample space Ω and an **elementary event** is a subset of Ω consiting of one outcome. Thus if $\omega \in \Omega$, then ω is an outcome, but $\{\omega\}$ is an elementary event. We will not insist on such precision of language and "outcomes" and "elementary events" will be used interchangeably, if this clarifies the ideas.

Sometimes a geometric description of the sample space is useful:

Example 4

A bus arrives at some time between time 0 and 1 hour; this time is denoted t_a. The bus departs at a time t_d between t_a and 1 hour. Let the sample space Ω be the set of ordered pairs of times (t_a, t_d). After writing a description of Ω in set terminology, plot Ω on a Cartesian coordinate system with horizontal axis t_a and vertical axis t_d. Then plot these events:

A = "arrival time after half an hour"

B = "departure time before 15 minutes"

C = "bus was in the station less than half an hour"

Solution Since both times t_a and t_d are between 0 and 1 and since the arrival time must be less than the departure time ($t_a = t_d$ if the bus passes the bus stop without stopping),

$$\Omega = \{(t_a\ t_d) : 0 \le t_a \le t_d \le 1\}$$

as depicted in Fig. 1.1.

The descriptions of the events A and B in terms of sets are

$$A = \left\{t_a \ : \frac{1}{2} < t_a \le 1\right\}$$

$$B = \left\{t_d \ : 0 \le t_d < \frac{1}{4}\right\}$$

(see Figs. 1.2, 1.3) To see how to describe C, note that "bus was in the station less than half an hour" is equivalent to

$$t_d - t_a < \frac{1}{2}$$

or

$$t_d < t_a + \frac{1}{2}$$

Event C is shown in Fig. 1.4. ∎

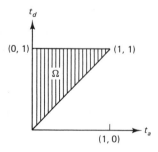

Figure 1.1 The sample space is represented by the shaded region.

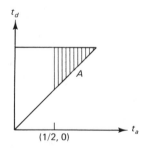

Figure 1.2

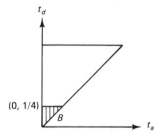

Figure 1.3

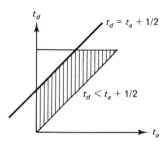

Figure 1.4 Event C is the intersection of the sample space and the region below the line $t_d = t_a + 1/2$.

PROBLEMS

In the following problems, what is the sample space corresponding to the random experiment? What are the subsets of the sample space corresponding to the events A, B, C, . . .?

1.1. Flip a coin, then roll a die. Note the result showing uppermost on each.

> A = "coin was a head and die was either a 1 or a 5"
> B = "coin resulted in heads"
> C = "die showed an even number"

1.2. Flip three coins and note the result showing uppermost on each.

> A = "first coin was a tail"
> B = "first was a tail or third was a head"
> C = "exactly one head on all three tosses"

1.3. Flip a coin; if heads was the result, roll a die; otherwise, flip another coin.

> A = "second coin resulted in tail"
> B = "a die was tossed"
> C = "an even number resulted on the die"

1.4. Observe a license plate consisting of 6 characters, the first 3 of which are digits and the last 3 of which are letters.

> A = "first letter was an X and first digit was a 7"
> B = "at least 2 A's"
> C = "all digits were 9"

1.5. Go out on a starry night and note the first time a shooting star is seen. Assume that the night is 10 hours long.

> A = "time was within 5 minutes of going out to observe"
> B = "time was between 3 and 5 hours"
> C = "never saw one"

1.6. A furnace controlled by a thermostat is monitored at each minute starting at time 1 minute. At each monitoring, whether the furnace is on or idle is noted. Assume that an infinite number of readings is obtained. Thus a typical sample point is $(O, I, I, \ldots)$, which represents the readings on, idle, idle, ...

> A = "first monitoring was on, but second was idle"
> B = "after the first 2 monitorings, the furnace was always idle"
> C = "there were exactly 2 idles in the first 4 monitorings"
> D = "at least 2 idles in the first 4 monitorings"

1.7. Alice and Benjy each arrive at an intersection at times between time 0 and time 1 hour. Let S be Alice's arrival time and T be Benjy's arrival time. (S may be less than, equal to, or greater that T.) A sample point is the ordered pair (S, T).

> A = "Alice arrived before 20 minutes"
> B = "Benjy arrived during the last 5 minutes of the hour"
> C = "Alice and Benjy both arrived in the first 15 minutes"
> D = "Alice arrived after Benjy"
> E = "Alice arrived after Benjy, but within 10 minutes of Benjy"
> F = "Alice and Benjy arrived within 15 minutes of each other"

Plot the sample space as well as each of these events on a two-dimensional coordinate system in which S is the horizontal and T the vertical axis.

1.8. Two bags of feed are bought for a bird feeder. The first is opened at time 0; it lasts a random time until t_1, at which time the second bag is opened; the second lasts a random time t_2. That is, both bags last till time $t_1 + t_2$. Assume that both t_1 and t_2 can take on any positive real value.

A = "first bag lasts at least 10 days"
B = "second bag runs out within 2 days of opening"
C = "the first and second bags *each* last more than 3 days"
D = "first lasts more than 1 day, second lasts between 2 and 5 days"
E = "both bags emptied within a week (that is, the *sum* of the times is less than 7)"
F = "both bags last (the *sum*) at least 4, but less than 10 days"
G = "both bags (the sum) last at least 5 days"
H = "both bags (the sum) last *exactly* 10 days"

Plot the sample space as well as each of these events on a two-dimensional coordinate system in which t_1 is the horizontal and t_2 the vertical axis.

1.3 REVIEW OF SET NOTATION AND OPERATIONS WITH SETS

If ω is an outcome and A is an event of a sample space Ω, we use the notation

$$\omega \in A$$

to indicate that ω is an element of A. ($\omega \notin A$ indicates that ω is not an element of A.) For A and B events (subsets of the sample space Ω, that is) the **union** of A and B is defined as the event consisting of all outcomes in either A or B or both:

$$A \cup B = \{\omega \in \Omega : \omega \in A \text{ or } \omega \in B\}$$

The **intersection** of A and B consists of those outcomes in both:

$$A \cap B = \{\omega \in \Omega : \omega \in A \text{ and } \omega \in B\}$$

Unions and intersections of more than two events can be formed. Thus

$$A \cup B \cup C = \{\omega \in \Omega : \omega \in A \text{ or } \omega \in B \text{ or } \omega \in C\}$$

is the event consisting of those outcomes in at least one of A, B, or C. More generally, if $A_1, \ldots, A_n$ are events,

$$\bigcup_{i=1}^{n} A_i = \{\omega \in \Omega : \omega \in A_i \text{ for at least one } i = 1, \ldots, n\}$$

$$\bigcap_{i=1}^{n} A_i = \{\omega \in \Omega : \omega \in A_i \text{ for all } i = 1, \ldots, n\}$$

Unions and intersections of infinitely many events $A_1, A_2, \ldots$ can also be formed.

The **complement** of an event A is the set of outcomes *not* in A. Of course, if $\omega \notin A$, implicitly we assume that ω is an outcome in the *same* sample space of which A is an event. For example, if Ω is the sample space corresponding to the temperature at noon and A is the event "freezing temperature," then the complement of A is the *set of temperatures* not in A. The *complement* is defined and denoted in set terminology by

$$A^c = \{\omega \in \Omega : \omega \notin A\}$$

Note that

$$A^{cc} = \{\omega \in \Omega : \omega \notin A^c\} = \{\omega \in \Omega : \omega \in A\} = A$$

Set **inclusion** between two events A and B is denoted

$$A \subseteq B$$

and means that every element of A is also an element of B; that is, A is a subset of B. This *includes* the possibility that $A = B$. Hence for each event A

$$A \subseteq A$$

$$\emptyset \subseteq A \subseteq \Omega$$

It is also clear that

$$A \cap B \subseteq A \subseteq A \cup B$$

For events $A \subseteq B$ we define the **difference** to be

$$B - A = \{\omega \in \Omega : \omega \in B, \text{ but } \omega \notin A\}$$

and we will only use $B - A$ if A is a subset of B. Thus

$$A^c = \Omega - A$$

and

$$\Omega^c = \Omega - \Omega = \emptyset$$

$$\emptyset^c = \Omega - \emptyset = \Omega$$

The following standard notation will be used: R^1 and R both denote the set of real numbers. R^2 denotes two-dimensional Euclidean space. The intervals determined by the real numbers $a < b$ are $[a, b] = \{x : a \leq x \leq b\}$, $(a, b] = \{x : a < x \leq b\}$, $[a, b) = \{x : a \leq x < b\}$, and $(a, b) = \{x : a < x < b\}$.

Set theory does not have to be used to build a vocabulary for probability theory. In fact, sentences could always be used. But the abstract notation of sets has two advantages: First, there is an economy of notation that vastly reduces the number of symbols in an equation; this in turn helps to provide insight into the really important features of a problem. Second, the language of sets provides a precision which ordinary English possesses only with difficulty. This allows us to look at an equation or theorem and see at a glance what it *does* say and, just as important, what it does *not* say. On the other hand, descriptions of events in terms of English sentences can always be converted to set language. In this conversion these correspondences hold:

English	Set notation
A or B	$A \cup B$
A and B	$A \cap B$
Not A	A^c
Neither A nor B	$A^c \cap B^c$
At most one of A and B	$(A \cap B)^c$

To see relations among events, **Venn diagrams** are by far the simplest way for two or three events, although they become too cumbersome for more than three. Represent events A, B, and C by overlapping regions inside an all-encompassing region labeled Ω. Then all possible intersections among A, B, C, and their complements have corresponding regions in the diagrams as shown in Fig. 1.5.

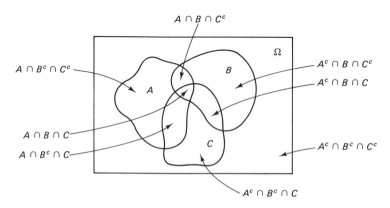

Figure 1.5 There are eight "fundamental regions" determined by the intersections of A, B, C, and their complements.

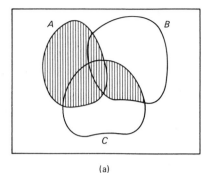
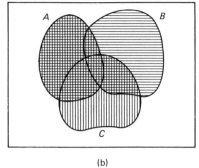

(a)   (b)

Figure 1.6

Example 5

Show that

$$A \cup (B \cap C) = (A \cup B) \cap (A \cup C)$$

Solution Using Venn diagrams, $A \cup (B \cap C)$ is the shaded area in part (a) of Fig. 1.6, whereas $(A \cup B) \cap (A \cup C)$ is the region with both horizontal and vertical stripes in part (b). ■

Finally, events $A_1, \ldots, A_n$ are called **pairwise disjoint** or simply **disjoint** if no outcome ω is in more than one A_i, that is, if

$$A_i \cap A_j = \emptyset \quad \text{for } i \neq j$$

For two events A and B this states that $A \cap B = \emptyset$.

PROBLEMS

1.9. In Problem 1.1, describe in words the events **(a)** $A \cup B$; **(b)** $B \cap C$; **(c)** A^c. What outcomes are in each of these events?

1.10. In Problem 1.4, describe in words the events **(a)** $A \cap B$; **(b)** $A \cup B$; **(c)** B^c; **(d)** $B \cap C$. What outcomes are in each of these events?

1.11. In Problem 1.7, plot these events: **(a)** $A \cap D$; **(b)** D^c; **(c)** F^c; **(d)** $C \cup F$.

1.12. In Problem 1.8, plot these events: **(a)** $A \cap B$; **(b)** $B \cap C$; **(c)** $D \cap F$; **(d)** F^c.

1.13. Prove each of these relations among events using Venn diagrams:
   (a) $B - (A \cap B) = A^c \cap B$
   (b) $(A \cup B) \cap C^c = (A \cap B^c \cap C^c) \cup (B \cap C^c)$
   (c) $(A - (A \cap B)) \cup (B - (A \cap B)) = (A \cup B) - (A \cap B)$
   (d) $(A \cup B \cup C) - (A \cap B \cap C) = ((A^c \cap B^c \cap C^c) \cup (A \cap B \cap C))^c$

1.14. Prove each of these relations among events using Venn diagrams:
   (a) If $B \subseteq A$ and $C \subseteq A$, then $A - (B \cup C) = A \cap B^c \cap C^c$
   (b) $A \cup (B^c \cap C) = (A \cup B^c) \cap (A \cup C)$
   (c) $A \cap (B \cup C^c) = (A \cap B) \cup (A^c \cup C)^c$
   (d) $(A \cup B \cup C) - (A \cup B) = A^c \cap B^c \cap C$

1.15. Use Venn diagrams to prove *DeMorgan's Laws*:

$$(A \cup B \cup C)^c = A^c \cap B^c \cap C^c$$
$$(A \cap B \cap C)^c = A^c \cup B^c \cup C^c$$

1.16 Use Venn diagrams to prove the *distributive laws*:

$$A \cup (B \cap C) = (A \cup B) \cap (A \cup C)$$
$$A \cap (B \cup C) = (A \cap B) \cup (A \cap C)$$

1.4 THE AXIOMS OF PROBABILITY

Prior to the early twentieth century, probability theory was tinged with philosophical questions. Exactly what the word "probability" referred to was not widely agreed upon. There were basically two interpretations. One held that the probability of an event indicated our subjective degree of belief in the occurrence of the event. The other interpretation tried to see probability as objective—as a part of the world independent of our specific beliefs. The subjective definition was found to be difficult to deal with and has been superseded by the **frequency interpretation**, whose best known spokesman was Robert von Mises (1883–1953), a German scientist who found refuge from Hitler's Germany in the United States.

The frequency interpretation elucidates what we *mean* when we say that the probability of an event is an indication of *how likely* it is to occur. Consider performing a random experiment repeatedly (for example, rolling a die) and suppose that A is an event (for example, "the die lands with an even number showing"). To say that the probability that A occurs is p means that we expect that A will occur in a fraction p of the total number of times the random experiment is performed *in the long run*. Suppose that the random experiment is performed N times, n of which result in the occurrence of A. Then as N becomes larger, the ratio of n to N becomes closer to p. In the language of limits

$$\lim_{N \to \infty} \frac{n}{N} = p$$

The use of the limit concept in this definition is intuitive. The *interpretation* is that *in reality* the ratio n/N becomes closer and closer to p as the number N of experiments becomes larger and larger. That it does so is not a mathematical theorem, but an observation about nature.

A computer program simulated the toss of a fair die 1000 times. (Chapter 7 develops methods for performing simulations.) The number of times the die landed showing a 1 was counted and the *frequency* of 1's was printed at the end of each series of 100 tosses. Note how the average number of flips that produce a 1 tends to the value 1/6.

Still, the frequency interpretation needs to be cast into a set of basic properties that are easy to apply to concrete situations. That is, probability theory needs a *set of axioms*. The Soviet mathematician A. N. Kolmogorov in 1933 wrote a

#(flips)	#(ones)	#(ones)/#(flips)
100	12	.12
200	30	.15
300	52	.17
400	72	.18
500	97	.194
600	104	.1733
700	125	.1786
800	140	.175
900	153	.17
1000	168	.168

monograph in which set theory was used as the language for these axioms. So successful was this approach that after more than 50 years it still forms the theoretical foundations of the entire subject.

Given an event $A \subseteq \Omega$ the probability of A is a real number $P(A)$. Since $P(A)$ is to be the fraction of times A occurs over a large number of repetitions of the experiment, $P(A)$ is between 0 and 1. $\emptyset$ is impossible and the entire sample space Ω is sure, so the probabilities of $\emptyset$ and Ω are 0 and 1, respectively. Now let A and B be *disjoint* events. Suppose that in a large number of repetitions N of the random experiment B occurs n_B times and A occurs n_A times. Since $A \cap B = \emptyset$, A and B cannot both occur at the same experiment; thus the number of times that $A \cup B$ occurs must be

$$n_{A \cup B} = n_A + n_B$$

Now for large N = number of experiments,

$$P(A \cup B) \cong \frac{n_{A \cup B}}{N} = \frac{n_A + n_B}{N} = \frac{n_A}{N} + \frac{n_B}{N} \cong P(A) + P(B)$$

and the approximate equalities will be exact in the limit as $N \to \infty$ by the intuitive frequency interpretation of probability.

To summarize in a definition:

Definition:

Let Ω be a sample space. A **probability measure** or **probability** P is an assignment of a real number $P(A)$ to each event $A \subseteq \Omega$ that satisfies these Axioms:

1. $P(\emptyset) = 0, \quad P(\Omega) = 1.$

2. $0 \leq P(A) \leq 1.$

3. For disjoint events A and B ($A \cap B = \emptyset$),
$$P(A \cup B) = P(A) + P(B)$$

Certainly, there are more properties that hold about probabilities. A few of the more theoretical ones are presented in this chapter. But the fact that Axioms 1 to 3 can be used to develop models of real applicability to random phenomena is surprising.

Basic Properties:

4. If $A \subseteq B$, then $P(B - A) = P(B) - P(A)$.

5. $P(A^c) = 1 - P(A)$.

6. If $A_1, \ldots, A_n$ are disjoint events, then

$$P\left(\bigcup_{i=1}^{n} A_i\right) = \sum_{i=1}^{n} P(A_i)$$

7. Whether A and B are disjoint or not,

$$P(A \cup B) = P(A) + P(B) - P(A \cap B)$$

The way to remember Property 6 is "the probability of a disjoint union is the sum of the probabilities."

Based on Axioms 1 to 3, here is a

Proof of Property 4.

$$B = (B - A) \cup A$$

is a *disjoint* union. Consequently, Axiom (3) implies that

$$P(B) = P((B - A) \cup A) = P(B - A) + P(A)$$

Property 4 then follows by subtracting $P(A)$:

$$P(B) - P(A) = P(B - A) \quad \blacksquare$$

Proof of Property 5. Now A and A^c are *disjoint* and their union is Ω. Thus Axioms 3 and 1 imply that

$$1 = P(\Omega) = P(A \cup A^c) = P(A) + P(A^c)$$

Subtract $P(A)$ to obtain

$$1 - P(A) = P(A^c) \quad \blacksquare$$

Proof of Property 6. Axiom 3 *is* Property 6 for $n = 2$. For $n > 2$,

$$\bigcup_{i=1}^{n} A_i = A_1 \cup \cdots \cup A_{n-1} \cup A_n = (A_1 \cup \cdots \cup A_{n-1}) \cup A_n$$

expresses the entire union as the union of *two* events which are disjoint. That is, if $A_i \cap A_n = \emptyset$ for $i = 1, \ldots, n - 1$, then $A_1 \cup \cdots \cup A_{n-1}$ and A_n are disjoint.

Consequently, Axiom 3 implies that

$$P\left(\bigcup_{i=1}^{n} A_i\right) = P(A_1 \cup \cdots \cup A_n)$$

$$= P(A_1 \cup \cdots \cup A_{n-1}) + P(A_n)$$

Now repeat this process over and over (or use **mathematical induction**).

$$P\left(\bigcup_{i=1}^{n} A_i\right) = P(A_1 \cup \cdots A_{n-1}) + P(A_n)$$

$$= P(A_1 \cup \cdots \cup A_{n-2}) + P(A_{n-1}) + P(A_n)$$

$$= \cdots$$

$$= P(A_1) + P(A_2) + \cdots + P(A_{n-1}) + P(A_n)$$

$$= \sum_{i=1}^{n} P(A_i) \quad \blacksquare$$

Proof of Property 7. From Fig. 1.7 $A \cup B$ is the union of these *disjoint* events:

$$A \cup B = (A - (A \cap B)) \cup (B - (A \cap B)) \cup (A \cap B)$$

Thus Basic Property 6 that we have just proved implies the first equality:

$$P(A \cup B) = P(A - (A \cap B)) + P(B - (A \cap B)) + P(A \cap B)$$

$$= P(A) - P(A \cap B) + P(B) - P(A \cap B) + P(A \cap B)$$

$$= P(A) + P(B) - P(A \cap B)$$

where the second equality follows from Basic Property 4.

The intuitive way to think about why Property 7 is true is to think of $A \cup B$ as the *union* of A and B, but this counts $A \cap B$ twice. Thus $P(A \cup B)$ is the sum of $P(A)$ and $P(B)$, but this adds in $P(A \cap B)$ one too many times. $\blacksquare$

Of particular importance are probabilities of events consisting of just one outcome. Thus if $\omega \in \Omega$ is an outcome, the *elementary event* $\{\omega\}$ consisting of ω is an event. Thus $P(\{\omega\})$ is real number—the probability that the random experiment resulted in outcome ω. However, for ease of notation we write $P(\omega)$ for the more complicated, but correct $P(\{\omega\})$ even though $P(\omega)$ is technically inaccurate since $P(A)$ is used only for *events* A and *outcome* ω is *not* an event; it is an outcome.

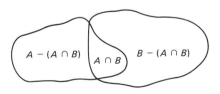

$A - (A \cap B)$ $A \cap B$ $B - (A \cap B)$

Figure 1.7

More Basic Properties

8. For events A and B, $A \subseteq B$ implies that

$$P(A) \leq P(B)$$

9. Suppose that A has n elements,

$$A = \{\omega_1, \ldots, \omega_n\}$$

Then

$$P(A) = P(\omega_1) + \cdots + P(\omega_n) = \sum_{i=1}^{n} P(\omega_i)$$

Proof of Property 8. Basic Property 4 implies that

$$P(B) = P(A) + P(B - A)$$

By Axiom 2,

$$P(B - A) \geq 0$$

Therefore,

$$P(B) \geq P(A) \qquad \blacksquare$$

Proof of Property 9. This follows from Basic Property 7 since

$$A = \{\omega_1\} \cup \{\omega_2\} \cup \cdots \cup \{\omega_n\}$$

disjointly. $\blacksquare$

Example 6

Roll a die once and note the number showing uppermost. Assuming that each outcome (one of the numbers 1 to 6) has probability 1/6 of occurring, what is the chance of an even number? Of a number larger than 1?

Solution The sample space is

$$\Omega = \{1, 2, 3, 4, 5, 6\}$$

with

$$P(\omega) = \frac{1}{6}$$

for $\omega = 1, 2, \ldots,$ or 6. Thus

$$P(\text{even result}) = P(\{2, 4, 6\}) = P(2) + P(4) + P(6) = \frac{3}{6}$$

$$P(\text{result} > 1) = 1 - P(\text{result} = 1) = 1 - \frac{1}{6} = \frac{5}{6}$$

where Property 9 was used to find the first probability and Property 5 was used for the second. ■

Example 7

Suppose that A, B, and C are events of Ω and

$$P(A) = .5, \qquad P(A \cap C) = .2, \qquad P(A \cap B^c \cap C^c) = .1, \qquad P(A \cap B \cap C) = .05$$

What is $P(A \cap B)$?

Solution The basic technique is to *decompose the entire Venn diagram into disjoint parts* and then fill in the probabilities of each of the "fundamental regions" using Axiom 3 and Property 6 that a disjoint union has probability equal to the sum. Thus the fact that $P(A \cap B^c \cap C^c) = .1$ allows us to fill in the ".1" in Figure 1.8. And $P(A \cap B \cap C) = .05$ allows us to fill in the ".05" in Fig. 1.8. The ".15" is a consequence of the fact that $A \cap C$ is the disjoint union of two events, one of which has been filled in with .05. Finally, the ".2" must be filled into the region $A \cap B \cap C^c$ since the sum of the probabilities in event A must sum to .5. Now that we have exhausted all the given information, we see from Fig. 1.8 that

$$P(A \cap B) = .2 + .05 = .25 \qquad ■$$

Example 8

Suppose that

$$\Omega = \{\omega_1, \omega_2, \omega_3, \omega_4\}$$

with

$$P(\{\omega_1, \omega_2, \omega_3\}) = \frac{1}{3}$$

$$P(\{\omega_1, \omega_2\}) = \frac{1}{6}$$

$$P(\{\omega_1, \omega_3, \omega_4\}) = \frac{5}{6}$$

Find $p_i = P(\omega_i)$ for $i = 1, 2, 3, 4$.

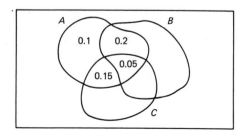

Figure 1.8

Solution The first equation implies that

$$p_1 + p_2 + p_3 = \frac{1}{3}$$

Consequently,

$$P_4 = \frac{2}{3}$$

(Why?) The first two equations imply that

$$p_3 = \frac{1}{3} - \frac{1}{6} = \frac{1}{6}$$

by subtracting the second equation from the first. Now that we know $p_4 = 2/3$, the last equation implies that

$$p_1 + p_3 = \frac{5}{6} - \frac{2}{3} = \frac{1}{6}$$

But $p_3 = 1/6$, so $p_1 = 0$. Finally, the second equation yields

$$p_2 = \frac{1}{6} \quad \blacksquare$$

1.5 THE AXIOM OF COUNTABLE ADDITIVITY (OPTIONAL)

Sometimes in applications, events that are a union of infinitely many other events arise. For example, if the number of birds arriving at a feeding station is monitored, an appropriate sample space is

$$\Omega = \{0, 1, 2, 3, \ldots\}$$

where $\omega = j$ is the event "j birds." (Of course, there is a finite limit to the number of birds, but it is convenient not to set an upper bound on ω. It will simply be the case that $P(\omega) = 0$ for ω large.) The event "more than 10 birds" has an infinite number of outcomes, as does the event "an even number of birds." For an event that has a *finite* number of outcomes, Property 9 implies that the probability of the event is the sum of the individual probabilities. Does the same result hold for an event composed of infinitely many outcomes? The answer is *no*! An additional axiom is required. Although in any real application we might be able to get away with sample spaces with only a finite number of outcomes, many random phenomena have conceptually simpler models when infinite sample spaces are used.

The ideas are rather similar to those we have already considered. In a completely rigorous axiomatic development Axiom 3—that the disjoint union of two events has a probability equal to the sum—is replaced by

3'. Suppose that $A_1, A_2, \ldots$ are disjoint events. Then

$$P\left(\bigcup_{i=1}^{\infty} A_i\right) = \sum_{i=1}^{\infty} P(A_i)$$

In fact Axiom 3' implies the original Axiom 3 as well as Property 6. See Problems 1.28 and 1.29 for the proofs.

1.6 WHAT ARE ODDS?

Often statements about probabilities are phrased in terms of "odds." "The odds against rain tomorrow are 3:4." "The odds against Clancy of Horsechester in the fifth are 3 to 6." What is the meaning of these "odds"?

Suppose that A is an event and that the odds in favor of A are 3:2. Then if the random experiment is performed $3 + 2 = 5$ times, A can be expected to occur 3 times. That is, the probability of A's occurrence at any one experiment is 3/5. Or, using the examples, above, the probability of no rain tomorrow is 3/7; Clancy will win with probability $6/9 = 2/3$ (however difficult it might be to *compute* these numbers in the first place). Another way of phrasing the idea of odds is this: If I put down $6 for Clancy, then a fair bet would be for you to give me the original $6 plus an additional $3 if Clancy wins; if he loses, you keep my original $6. In this way I will win $3 with probability 2/3 and lose $6 with probability 1/3. On the average, if I bet 30,000 times, I'll win $3 on approximately $(2/3) \cdot 30,000 = 20,000$ bets for a total of $60,000 won; and I'll lose $6 on $(1/3) \cdot 30,000 = 10,000$ bets for a total of $60,000. So I'll come out even in the long run, although on any *one* bet I'll either lose $6 or win $3.

Let A be an event. Then the following four statements are equivalent:

1. The odds in favor of A are r to s.

2. The odds against A are s to r.

3. $P(A) = r/(r + s)$.

4. If I bet $$r$ on A, the bet is fair if I win my original $$r$ plus $$s$ if A occurs (and lose my $$r$ if A does not occur).

PROBLEMS

1.17. Assume that $P(A) = .5$, $P(B^c) = .3$ and $P(A \cup B) = .8$. Find **(a)** $P(A \cap B)$; **(b)** $P(A^c \cup B)$; **(c)** $P(A \cap B^c)$.

1.18. Assume that $P(A) = .6$, $P(A \cap C) = .3$, $P(C) = .4$, $P(B) = .2$, $P(A \cap B \cap C) = .1$, $P(B \cap C) = 1$, and $P(A \cap B) = .1$. Fill in all the probabilities in the Venn diagram for A, B, and C. What are **(a)** $P(A \cap B)$; **(b)** $P(A \cup B \cup C)$; **(c)** $P(A^c \cap (B \cup C))$; **(d)** $P(A - (A \cap C))$?

1.19. Assume that $P(A \cap B) = .3$, $P(A \cap C) = .4$, $P(B \cap C) = .3$, $P(A^c \cap B^c \cap C) = 0$, $P(C) = .6$, $P(A \cup C) = .8$, and $P(B^c \cup C) = .7$. Fill in all the probabilities in the Venn diagram for A, B, and C. What are **(a)** $P(B^c)$; **(b)** $P(A \cap B \cap C^c)$; **(c)** $P(A)$; **(d)** $P(B - (B \cap C))$?

1.20. Assume that $P(A \cup B \cup C) = 1$, $P(A^c) = .5$, $P(B^c) = .6$, $P(C^c) = .4$, $P(A \cup B) = .7$, $P(A \cup C) = .9$, and $P(B \cup C) = .9$. Fill in all the probabilities in the Venn diagram for A, B, and C. What are **(a)** $P(A \cap B \cap C)$; **(b)** $P(A^c \cap B^c)$; **(c)** $P(A \cup B^c \cup C)$; **(d)** $P(A \cap B)$?

1.21. Assume that $\Omega = \{\omega_1, \omega_2, \omega_3\}$ has three sample points and that $P(\{\omega_1, \omega_2\}) = .5$ and $P(\{\omega_1, \omega_3\}) = .6$. Find $P(\omega_i)$ for **(a)** $i = 1$; **(b)** $i = 2$, **(c)** $i = 3$.

1.22. Assume that $\Omega = \{\omega_1, \omega_2, \omega_3, \omega_4\}$ has four sample points and $P(\{\omega_1, \omega_2, \omega_3\}) = .8$, $P(\{\omega_2, \omega_3\}) = .5$, and $P(\{\omega_3, \omega_4\}) = .4$. Find $P(\omega_i)$ for **(a)** $i = 1$; **(b)** $i = 2$; **(c)** $i = 3$; **(d)** $i = 4$.

1.23. Assume that $\Omega = \{\omega_1, \omega_2, \omega_3, \omega_4\}$ has four sample points and $P(\{\omega_1, \omega_2\}) = .6$, $P(\{\omega_2, \omega_3\}) = .4$, and $P(\{\omega_1, \omega_3\}) = .2$. Find $P(\omega_i)$ for **(a)** $i = 1$; **(b)** $i = 2$; **(c)** $i = 3$; **(d)** $i = 4$.

1.24. Suppose that A and B are events in sample space Ω. Show that

$$P(A) = P(A \cap B) + P(A \cap B^c)$$

1.25. Suppose that A, B, and C are events. Show that

$$P(A \cup B \cup C) = P(A) + P(B) + P(C) - P(A \cap B)$$
$$- P(A \cap C) - P(B \cap C) + P(A \cap B \cap C)$$

1.26. Generalize Problem 1.25 to the case of four events, A_1, A_2, A_3, and A_4. Express $P(A_1 \cup A_2 \cup A_3 \cup A_4)$ as a sum and difference of terms of the form $P(A_i)$, $P(A_i \cap A_j)$, $P(A_i \cap A_j \cap A_k)$, and $P(A_1 \cap A_2 \cap A_3 \cap A_4)$.

1.27. Show that Axiom 3 implies $P(\emptyset) = 0$ by applying Axiom 3 to the disjoint union $\Omega \cup \emptyset$.

1.28. Show that Axiom 3' implies Axiom 3.

1.29. Show that Axiom 3' implies Property 6.

The art of conjecturing is defined here as the art
of measuring probabilities . . . in order to be able in our
judgments and actions always to choose or follow the path which is
found to be the best. . . .

James Bernoulli, 1654–1705, The Art of Conjecturing

— Chapter 2 —

Combinatorics

Although isolated problems in probability could be solved before the seventeenth century, a series of letters between the French mathematicians Blaise Pascal (1623–1662) and Pierre de Fermat (1601–1665) first considered general methods and systematic approaches. This correspondence shows both a development of methods of calculation and an emerging insight into the *meanings* of chance and probability. Pascal was a fascinating personality—torn as he was between a very deep religious consciousness and a real brilliance in mathematics. Out of this work emerged *The Art of Conjecturing* by the Swiss mathematician James Bernoulli (1654–1705). Modern treatments of combinatorics—the science of counting the elements in a set—are very much in the spirit of Bernoulli's treatise.

2.1 EQUALLY LIKELY OUTCOMES

Assume that the sample space Ω has a finite number N of outcomes; suppose further that each of these outcomes has the same probability p. Then by Property 9 of Chapter 1,

$$1 = \sum_{\omega \in \Omega} P(\omega) = \sum_{\omega \in \Omega} p = N \cdot p$$

Hence

$$p = P(\omega) = \frac{1}{N}$$

for each outcome $\omega \in \Omega$. The assignment of probabilities to the elements of Ω in such a way that they all have the same probability $1/N$ is specified by saying that Ω has **equally likely outcomes**. When we say that an element of a set is chosen *at random* we mean that all the elements have the same probability of being selected.

Notice that it is impossible to assign equally likely outcomes to a sample space with infinitely many elements. Otherwise, $P(\omega) = 0$ for all ω and

$$P(\Omega) = \sum_{\omega \in \Omega} P(\omega) = \sum_{\omega \in \Omega} 0 = 0$$

which contradicts the fact that $P(\Omega)$ must be 1.

The equally likely outcome assignment of probabilities has a fundamental consequence: Suppose that $A \subseteq \Omega$ is an event. Then*

$$P(A) = \sum_{\omega \in A} \frac{1}{N} = \frac{\#(\text{elements in } A)}{\#(\text{elements in } \Omega)}$$

Hence to compute the probability of any event requires that we know how to compute—to count—the number of outcomes in both the event A and also in the entire sample space Ω.

Example 1

Toss a fair coin once. With H and T representing head and tail, respectively, the sample space is

$$\Omega = \{H, T\}$$

Since the coin is fair, each of the *two* outcomes has probability 1/2. In tossing a coin three times the sample space is

$$\Omega = \{TTT, TTH, THT, HTT, HHT, HTH, THH, HHH\}$$

where, for example, HTT is the elementary outcome

$$HTT = \text{``heads on first, tails on second and third''}$$

Since there is no reason to suppose that any of these *eight* outcomes has a greater chance of occurrence than any of the others, each is assigned the equally likely outcome probability of 1/8. For example,

$$P(1 \text{ head}) = P(\{TTH, THT, HTT\}) = \frac{3}{8}$$

and

$$P(\text{at least 1 head}) = 1 - P(\text{no heads})$$
$$= 1 - P(TTT)$$
$$= \frac{7}{8} \quad \blacksquare$$

*Throughout, we use the notation $\#(\;\cdot\;)$ to stand for the phrase "number of . . . ."

Example 2

Roll a fair die twice and note the two numbers showing uppermost on each die. Then the sample space consists of all ordered pairs of integers from 1 to 6:

$$\Omega = \{ij: 1 \leqslant i, j \leqslant 6\}$$
$$= \{11, 12, 13, 14, 15, 16, 21, 22, 23, 24, 25, 26,$$
$$31, 32, 33, 34, 35, 36, 41, 42, 43, 44, 45, 46,$$
$$51, 52, 53, 54, 55, 56, 61, 62, 63, 64, 65, 66\}$$

where the first integer in each pair indicates the result of the first toss and the second indicates the result of the second toss. There is no reason to suppose that any of these outcomes has more chance than any other; we assign each the probability 1/36 since there are 36 outcomes in Ω. For example,

$$P(\text{sum of the tosses is 5}) = P(\{14, 23, 32, 41\})$$

$$= \frac{4}{36}$$

$$P(\text{first roll result larger than second roll})$$
$$= P(\{21, 31, 32, 41, 42, 43, 51, 52, 53, 54, 61, 62, 63, 64, 65\})$$
$$= \frac{15}{36} \quad \blacksquare$$

Suppose that we formulated the sample space differently. For example, suppose that the results of the two rolls were listed without regard to the actual order in which they occurred. Thus

$$\Omega' = \{11, 12, 13, 14, 15, 16, 22, 23, 24, 25,$$
$$26, 33, 34, 35, 36, 44, 45, 46, 55, 56, 66\}$$

where now outcome ij represents the outcome

$$ij = \text{``}i \text{ was the result of one roll, } j \text{ was}$$
$$\text{the result of the other roll''}$$

without any record of which roll—the first or the second—resulted in which outcome. Then using the equally likely outcome approach, we would have (note there are now 21 outcomes)

$$P(\text{sum of the rolls is 5}) = P(\{14, 23\})$$

$$= \frac{2}{21}$$

different than the result above. The error here is that *even though Ω' is a valid sample space for the random experiment, Ω' does not have equally likely outcomes.*

How do we know ultimately that it is Ω rather than Ω' that has the equally likely outcomes? Because, for example, the two results

"3 on first roll, 2 on second roll"

"2 on first roll, 3 on second roll"

really are distinct and cannot be lumped together as only one outcome.

2.2 THE THREE BASIC RULES OF COMBINATORICS

The counting of the number of outcomes in an event or a sample space can often be classified by the type of reasoning that it uses. We will distinguish three of these—the ones that cover the vast majority of combinatorial situations. It is not that memorization itself of these rules is important; rather, what must be mastered is the intuition lying behind them: One must know *which* one applies in any specific problem and how to apply it. (On the other hand, it is true that one way to develop the intuition is by first memorizing the corresponding rule.) The first rule is common sense. The second and third are obtained more or less readily from the first.

Suppose that a cafeteria has 3 main dishes, 4 different drinks, and 2 desserts. Then the total number of possible dinners is $3 \cdot 4 \cdot 2 = 24$. For *each* of the main courses, there are 4 possible drinks and for *each* combination of main course and drink there are 2 possible desserts. Hence the total number is found by multiplication.

In general, suppose that a certain job requires various subjobs or tasks to be performed; also suppose that the number of ways one of the tasks can be performed does not depend on how the others are performed. Then we have

---

Rule 1: Multiplication Rule

Suppose that

    Task 1 can be performed in n_1 ways.
    Task 2 can be performed in n_2 ways.
        .
        .
        .

Then the total number of ways to complete the job of performing all the tasks is

$$n_1 \cdot n_2 \cdots$$

Example 3

How many different combinations of 2-letter initials are there?

Solution

Task 1. Choose a first initial: 26 possibilities.
Task 2. Choose a second initial: 26 possibilities.

Hence the multiplication rule yields

$$26^2 = 676$$

as the number of 2-letter initial combinations.

$$
\left.
\begin{array}{cccccc}
AA & AB & AC & \cdot \ \cdot \ \cdot & AZ \\
BA & BB & BC & \cdot \ \cdot \ \cdot & BZ \\
\cdot & \cdot & \cdot & \cdot \ \cdot \ \cdot & \cdot \\
ZA & ZB & ZC & \cdot \ \cdot \ \cdot & ZZ
\end{array}
\right\} 26
$$

$$\underbrace{}_{26}$$

■

Example 4

How many outcomes are there in tossing one coin 3 times? *n* times?

Solution

Task 1. Assign H or T to first flip: 2 ways.
Task 2. Assign H or T to second flip: 2 ways.
Task 3. Assign H or T to third flip: 2 ways.

.
.
.

Hence with n flips the total number of ways to do the "job" of assigning H or T to *all* the flips is

$$2 \cdot 2 \cdot 2 \cdots 2 = 2^n$$

For $n = 3$, these are listed in Example 1. ■

A helpful way to picture the multiplication rule is to think of several handles, one for each of the tasks to be performed. Setting each handle corresponds to performing that task in one definite way. Hence the first handle has n_1 possible positions, the second handle has n_2 possible positions, ... Then the total number of ways to complete the entire job of setting all the handles is $n_1 \cdot n_2 \cdots$. For example, in flipping a coin n times we must set n "handles"; handle i is set up if the ith flip results in head; otherwise (tail) handle i is set down as in Fig. 2.1. So

Figure 2.1 Set handle i up if the ith coin lands heads; otherwise, set handle i down.

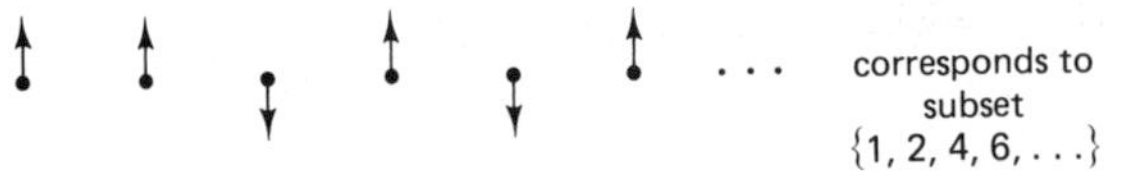

corresponds to
HHTH...

corresponds to
subset
$\{1, 2, 4, 6, \ldots\}$

Figure 2.2 The set consists of the integers 1, 2, 3, . . . Forming a subset is equivalent to setting handles—one handle for each element.

the total number of possible results in flipping n coins is the total number of ways to set the handles—2^n.

2^n is also the **number of subsets** that a set of size n has. In this case label the elements of the set 1, 2, . . . , and n. Set handle i up if the ith element is to be *included* in the subset, while handle i is set *down* if the ith element is *not* included (*see* Fig. 2.2). In this way *each configuration of all n handles corresponds to exactly one subset* of the original set. The configuration in which all handles are up corresponds to the set itself; all handles down corresponds to the empty set $\emptyset$.

Example 5

Hilary, Ralph, and Sam line up for a photograph. How many distinct line-ups *of all 3* are possible? How many are there if Daphne joins the group and all 4 line up?

Solution We can write down all possible line-ups:

$$HSR \quad HRS \quad RSH \quad RHS \quad SHR \quad SRH$$

where, for example, HSR is short hand for

"from left to right it's Hilary, Sam, Ralph"

Hence the answer is 6. Alternatively, the multiplication rule can be applied as follows:

Task 1. Choose one for the left position: 3 ways.
Task 2. Choose one of the *remaining two* for the middle position: 2 ways.
Task 3. Place the *remaining person* on the right: 1 way.

Hence the number of line-ups is

$$3 \cdot 2 \cdot 1 = 6$$

If Daphne joins the group, there are four tasks to perform. Similar reasoning shows that the number of different line-ups is

$$4 \cdot 3 \cdot 2 \cdot 1 = 24$$

Try writing them all down; from our result for line-ups of 3 people, for *each* placement of one of the 4 at the left end of the line, there are 6 ways to line up the remaining three to the right of him/her. ■

Example 6

If the 4 people in Example 5 line up at random, what is the probability that Hilary stands to the immediate right of Ralph? That Hilary stands next to Ralph?

Solution By the words "at random" we mean that all possible line-ups have the same probability; the people are entirely "mixed up" in the lining-up process. By looking at the line-ups in Example 5 we see that with 3 people there are 6 possible line-ups, of which 2 have Hilary standing to the right of Ralph and 4 have Hilary next to Ralph. Hence with 3 people,

$$P(\text{Hilary to the right of Ralph}) = \frac{2}{6}$$

$$P(\text{Hilary next to Ralph}) = \frac{4}{6}$$

For 4 people it is slightly more work to count which of the 24 total line-ups have the required properties.

$$RHSD \quad RHDS \quad SRHD \quad DRHS \quad SDRH \quad DSRH$$

have Hilary to the immediate right of Ralph. Hence

$$P(\text{Hilary to the right of Ralph}) = \frac{6}{24}$$

There are twice as many (12) line-ups that have Hilary next to Ralph. (That is, by symmetry there are also 6 line-ups with Hilary to the immediate *left* of Ralph.) Hence

$$P(\text{Hilary next to Ralph}) = \frac{12}{24}$$

For more people this straightforward counting process becomes tedious, but by more abstract methods, Example 15 shows that for n people,

$$P(\text{Hilary next to Ralph}) = \frac{2}{n} \quad ■$$

In developing the second rule of combinatorics, imagine a set with n objects. We ask for the number of ways to select k of them and line them up.

Definition

A **permutation** of size k from a set of size n is an *ordered subset of size k*.

These are all the permutations of Hilary, Ralph, and Sam:

Size	Permutations of size k
0	
1	*H R S*
2	*HR RH HS SH RS SR*
3	*HRS RHS HSR SHR RSH SRH*

Rule 2: Permutation Rule

The number of different permutations of size k from a set of size n is denoted by $(n)_k$, and is

$$(n)_k = n(n - 1)(n - 2) \cdots (n - k + 1)$$

Thus the number of permutations of size k is the product of all the integers from n down to $n - k + 1$. To see why the permutation rule holds, we use reasoning similar to that used in Example 5. Using the multiplication rule, a line-up of k objects from among n can be performed using these tasks:

Task 1. Choose the first object: n ways.

Task 2. Choose the second object from among the $n - 1$ remaining: $n - 1$ ways.

Task 3. Choose the third object from among the $n - 2$ remaining: $n - 2$ ways.

.
.
.

Task k. Choose the kth object from among the $n - (k - 1) = n - k + 1$ remaining: $n - k + 1$ ways.

Hence the total number of ways to do the entire job of selecting and lining up k objects is, by the multiplication rule,

$$n(n - 1)(n - 2) \cdots (n - k + 1)$$

Note that there are a *total of k terms* in the product—simply start with n, decrement by 1 for each factor, and stop writing terms when the kth term has been multiplied into the product.

Example 7

How many license plates are there in which the first 3 characters are letters, the last 3 are digits, and there are no repetitions?

Solution Imagine a set consisting of the 26 letters. To obtain the letters and their order for the plate, we must select a permutation of size 3 from the set of size 26. Hence the number of different letter permutations is

$$26 \cdot 25 \cdot 24 = 15,600$$

Similarly, starting with 10 possible digits there are

$$10 \cdot 9 \cdot 8 = 720$$

digit permutations. Hence the number of possible plates is

$$26 \cdot 25 \cdot 24 \cdot 10 \cdot 9 \cdot 8 = 11,232,000$$

(see Fig. 2.3). ■

Example 8

How many ways can 5 people occupy 8 telephone booths if no two people are to occupy the same booth?

Solution The problem is this: Is it people or booths that are the objects? Which are being selected? Think of it this way: Each *person* needs a booth, so 5 selections (5 tasks) must be made.

Choose a booth for the first person: 8 ways.

booth for the second person: 7 ways.

.

.

.

booth of the fifth person: $8 - 5 + 1 = 4$ ways.

Thus the answer is

$$(8)_5 = 8 \cdot 7 \cdot 6 \cdot 5 \cdot 4 = 6720$$

Booths are being selected for the *people*, not the reverse. There must be a total of 5 selections. ■

Example 9

In how many ways can 6 dogs be placed in 7 kennels in such a way that each dog has his/her own kennel?

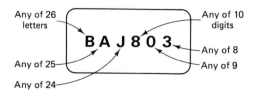

Figure 2.3

Figure 2.4   This is the one way to line up no objects.

Solution   A kennel must be selected for *each* dog: for dog 1, any of 7 kennels; for dog 2, any of 6; . . . .   Thus the total number is

$$(7)_6 = 7 \cdot 6 \cdot 5 \cdot 4 \cdot 3 \cdot 2 = 5040 \quad \blacksquare$$

Definition

n **factorial** is

$$n! = (n)_n = n(n - 1)(n - 2) \cdots 2 \cdot 1$$

and is the number of permutations of size *n* from a set of size *n*—the number of distinct line-ups of *n* objects.

By definition, $0! = 1$.   Although this convention is purely for the sake of simplicity in some algebraic formulas, it can also be interpreted combinatorially. As in Fig. 2.4 there is exactly 1 way to line up 0 objects—don't do it at all!

Example 10

There are

$$10! = 3{,}628{,}800 \text{ permutations of all 10 digits}$$

$$26! \cong 4.0329 \times 10^{26} \text{ permutations of all 26 letters} \quad \blacksquare$$

Notice that

$$
\begin{aligned}
(n)_{n-1} &= n(n - 1)(n - 2) \cdots (n - (n - 1) - 1) \\
&= n(n - 1)(n - 2) \cdots 2 \\
&= n(n - 1)(n - 2) \cdots 2 \cdot 1 \\
&= n!
\end{aligned}
$$

since the number of line-ups of $n - 1$ from among *n* objects is *exactly* equal to the number of line-ups of all *n* objects.   This is so since each line-up of $n - 1$ is equivalent to a line-up of all *n*—simply place the missing object in each line-up of $n - 1$ at the end of the line, as in Fig. 2.5.

Adding last object to line-up of $n - 1$ $\cdots$ to form line-up of all n **Figure 2.5**

Here is a program* to compute $n!$ The value of n is input and then $n!$ is computed *recursively* using the fact that

$$n! = n \cdot (n - 1)!$$

```
var I,N,FACT: integer;
begin
    readln (N);
    FACT: = 1;
    for I: = 2 to N do
        FACT: = I*FACT;
    writeln(FACT);
end.
```

The third rule determines the total number of distinct *unordered* subsets of size k that can be formed from a set of size n.

Definition

A **combination** of size k from a set of size n is an *unordered subset of size k.*

Example 11

From the group consisting of Hilary, Ralph, Sam, and Daphne the combinations of size 2 (the "mobs" consisting of 2 people—*no order*) are

$$\{H, R\} \quad \{H, S\} \quad \{H, D\} \quad \{R, S\} \quad \{R, D\} \quad \{S, D\} \quad \blacksquare$$

To see how to find the number of combinations of size k and thereby to derive Rule 3, we do the following. Suppose that there are n objects and we need to form an *ordered* subset of size k. Rule 2 says that there are $(n)_k$ of these ordered subsets. But suppose that we actually go about the process of forming one of these ordered subsets in the way depicted in Fig. 2.6:

Task 1: Form an *unordered* subset of size k: grab k from among the n.
Task 2: Now *order* the k objects selected in task 1.

Task 2 can be done in $k!$ ways since this is just the number of ways to line up k objects. Hence the multiplication rule implies that

$$(n)_k = \#(\text{ways to do task 1}) \cdot k!$$

or

$$\#(\text{ways to do task 1}) = \frac{(n)_k}{k!}$$

---

*All programs in this text are written in a simplified version of Pascal. Appendix 1 contains a complete description of the syntax.

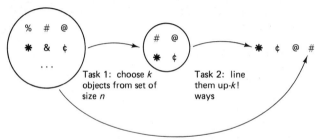

Task 1: choose k
objects from set of
size n

Task 2: line
them up-$k!$
ways

$(n)_k$ = total # (ways to do the job)

Figure 2.6

However,

$$\frac{(n)_k}{k!} = \frac{n(n-1)\cdots(n-k+1)}{k!} \cdot \frac{(n-k)(n-k-1)\cdots 2 \cdot 1}{(n-k)(n-k-1)\cdots 2 \cdot 1}$$

$$= \frac{n!}{k!\,(n-k)!}$$

Summarizing the algebra together with the fact that the number of ways to do task 1 *is exactly* the number of combinations of size k, we conclude:

Rule 3: Combination Rule

The number of different combinations of size k from a set of size n is denoted by $\binom{n}{k}$, and is

$$\binom{n}{k} = \frac{(n)_k}{k!} = \frac{n!}{k!\,(n-k)!}$$

$\binom{n}{k}$ is called a **binomial coefficient**; it is read "n over k binomial" or "n taken k at a time" or "n choose k." [The notation $\binom{n}{k}$ is very similar to one invented by the Swiss mathematician Leonhard Euler (1707–1783).]

Notice the following elementary properties of the binomial coefficients.

---

1. $\binom{n}{0} = 1$

2. $\binom{n}{1} = n$

3. $\binom{n}{k} = \binom{n}{n-k}$

These three follow from the algebraic definition above. But they can also be seen to hold using combinatorial reasoning. Note that there is exactly 1 subset—combination—of size 0, the empty set $\emptyset$; hence $\binom{n}{0} = 1$. There are n subsets of 1 size—the singleton sets; hence $\binom{n}{1} = n$. Finally, to see why Property 3 holds, note that choosing a subset of size k is *equivalent to* choosing a subset of size $n - k$—namely, the $n - k$ *not* chosen. That is, *the number of subsets of size k is the same as the number of subsets of size $n - k$*; hence Property 3.

$$\frac{n - k + 1}{k} \binom{n}{k-1} = \frac{n - k + 1}{k} \frac{n!}{(k - 1)! \, (n - k + 1)!}$$

$$= \frac{n!}{k! \, (n - k)!}$$

$$= \binom{n}{k}$$

> For $1 \leq k \leq n$,
>
> $$\binom{n}{k} = \frac{n - k + 1}{k} \binom{n}{k-1}$$

To compute the binomial coefficients recursively, start with

$$\binom{n}{0} = 1$$

and then

$$\binom{n}{1} = \frac{n - 1 + 1}{1} \binom{n}{0} = n \cdot 1 = n$$

$$\binom{n}{2} = \frac{n - 2 + 1}{2} \binom{n}{1} = \frac{n - 1}{2} \cdot n = \frac{n(n - 1)}{2}$$

$$\cdots \quad \cdots$$

$$\binom{n}{n} = \frac{n - n + 1}{n} \binom{n}{n-1} = \frac{1}{n} \cdot n = 1$$

Example 12

A program for computing the binomial coefficients can be based on this formula. In fact, the following program will input n and will then print the $n + 1$ values

$$\binom{n}{0}, \binom{n}{1}, \binom{n}{2}, \binom{n}{3}, \cdots \binom{n}{n}$$

```
var BIN,K,N:integer;
begin
    readln(N);
    for K:= 0 to N do
        begin
            if K = 0 then BIN:= 1
                    else BIN:= ((N−K+1)∗BIN) div K;
            write(BIN);
        end;
end.
```

The table below, known as **Pascal's triangle**, can be obtained by running the foregoing program repeatedly using $N = 0$, then $N = 1, \ldots$, and finally, $N = 13$. Or better yet, embed the foregoing routine for calculating the Nth row in a larger program for printing many rows (see Problem 2.16).

1   0th row $\binom{0}{0}$
1 1   0th column

1													
1	1												
1	2	1											
1	3	3	1										
1	4	6	4	1									
1	5	10	10	5	1								
1	6	15	20	15	6	1							
1	7	21	35	35	21	7	1						
1	8	28	56	70	56	28	8	1					
1	9	36	84	126	126	84	36	9	1				
1	10	45	120	210	252	210	120	45	10	1			
1	11	55	165	330	462	462	330	165	55	11	1		
1	12	66	220	495	792	924	792	495	220	66	12	1	
1	13	78	286	715	1287	1716	1716	1287	715	286	78	13	1

6th row $\binom{6}{4}$
4th column

13th row $\binom{13}{3}$
3rd column ■

Example 13

How many 2-person groupings can be formed from the total group consisting of the 5 people: Hilary, Ralph, Daphne, Clyde, and Sam?

Solution   Using the table (or directly), the answer is

$$\binom{5}{2} = 10$$

The groupings are

$\{H, R\}$ $\{H, D\}$ $\{H, S\}$ $\{H, C\}$ $\{R, D\}$ $\{R, S\}$ $\{R, C\}$ $\{D, S\}$ $\{D, C\}$ $\{S, C\}$ ■

Example 14

A box contains 4 wooden letter A's and 2 B's.   How many distinct "words" can be formed from the 6 letters?

Solution   There are 6 positions in the word for letters to be placed.   Once the 4 A's have been placed, the 2 B's must occupy the 2 remaining positions. Consequently, the number of distinct "words" is equal to the number of ways to choose 4 positions from 6; that is,

$$\binom{6}{4} = 15$$

These "words" are

```
AAAABB   AAABAB   AABAAB   ABAAAB   BAAAAB
AAABBA   AABABA   ABAABA   BAAABA   AABBAA
ABABAA   BAABAA   ABBAAA   BABAAA   BBAAAA   ■
```

PROBLEMS

2.1. Toss a fair coin and then roll a fair die.   Note the results showing uppermost on each. **(a)** What is the sample space?   Assuming equally likely outcomes what are **(b)** P(head on coin); **(c)** P(an even number on die); **(d)** P(tail on coin and an even number on die)?

2.2. Flip a coin 4 times and note the result of each flip.   **(a)** What is the sample space? **(b)** How many outcomes are in the sample space?   What are **(c)** P(0 heads); **(d)** P(1 head); **(e)** P(2 heads); **(f)** P(3 heads); **(g)** P(4 heads); **(h)** P(an even number of heads); **(i)** P(more than 2 heads)?

2.3. From a group of 5 people—Hilary, Ralph, Daphne, Clyde, and Sam—a committee of size 3 is selected.   **(a)** List all the possible committees.   Assuming equally likely probabilities for all the possible committees, what are **(b)** P(Daphne included); **(c)** P(Daphne included, but not Ralph); **(d)** P(both Daphne and Ralph included)?

2.4. Addresses on mailboxes have 1 letter followed by 3 digits.   **(a)** How many mailboxes are possible (with different addresses)?   **(b)** How many are possible with all digits distinct?   **(c)** How many are possible with no 0 in any of the digit locations?

2.5. In limited versions of BASIC, identifiers can be 1 or 2 characters long, but the first must be a letter and the second a letter or digit. How many identifiers are possible?

2.6. Let $S = \{D, R, H, S, C\}$ be a set with 5 elements. Write out all the subsets of size k for $k = 0, 1, \ldots, 5$ and verify that there are $\binom{n}{k}$ of them. Verify that there are a total of $2^5 = 32$ subsets in all.

2.7. **(a)** From a group of size 6 a committee of size 4 is selected. How many different committees are there? **(b)** If the committee is to have one leader, how many different committees are there?

2.8. Alice, Benjy, Hilary, Daphne, and Clyde line up for a photograph. How many line-ups are there with **(a)** Alice second from the right; **(b)** Benjy at *either* end; **(c)** Alice next to Benjy but to the right of Benjy; **(d)** Alice next to Benjy; **(e)** Daphne in the middle?

2.9. **(a)** How many 3-digit numbers have all 3 digits equal? **(b)** How many with exactly 2 equal and the third different? **(c)** How many with all 3 different? **(d)** How many with all 3 ascending (with third larger than second and second larger than first)? **(e)** With a number consisting of n decimal digits, show that the number of different numbers with the digits ascending is $\binom{10}{n}$.

2.10. A domino is divided into two parts, *each* of which has from 0 to 6 holes. A domino *set* consists of one each of all possible combinations; that is, one domino has no holes on each part, one domino has 1 hole on one part and no holes on the other, . . . , one domino has 3 holes on one part and 5 holes on the other, ... How many dominoes are in a set?

2.11. A classroom has 20 seats and 18 students. **(a)** How many ways are there to select 2 empty seats? **(b)** How many ways are there for the 18 students to occupy the 18 remaining seats? **(c)** How many *total* ways are there for the students to occupy the seats (if each student has a separate seat)?

2.12. A bus starts with 8 people and stops at 12 locations. **(a)** In how many ways can the people get off the bus? (That is, how many total "matchings" of people and stops are there?) **(b)** In how many ways if no 2 people get off at the same stop (that is, if each person gets off at a different stop)?

2.13. A bus has 30 seats arranged in 15 pairs of seats. **(a)** In how many arrangements can 8 people on the bus sit on the 30 seats assuming that no 2 occupy the same seat (no little children)? **(b)** In how many ways can the 8 people occupy the seats if no 2 sit in the same pair?

2.14. Nine children at camp are each assigned to one of two tasks—either serving or cleaning up. There are to be 4 servers and 5 cleaners. **(a)** How many different ways are there to select the servers? (How many groups of 4?) **(b)** If Alice was promised that she could be a server, how many different groups of servers are there? **(c)** If Alice and Benjy are both to be servers, how many ways are there to select 2 more servers? **(d)** If Alice is to be a server and Benjy is to be a cleaner, how many ways are there now to select the remaining 3 servers?

2.15. **(a)** In how many ways can 5 different-colored golf balls be placed into 7 different containers? Assume that any container can contain any number of golf balls (as long as there are a total of 5 golf balls). **(b)** In how many ways if container 1 remains empty? **(c)** In how many ways if no 2 golf balls can go into the same container? **(d)**

What is the probability that no 2 golf balls are in the same container, assuming that the balls are randomly tossed into the containers?

2.16. Write a program that can input a positive integer MAX and then print out MAX + 1 rows of Pascal's triangle row 0 through row number MAX (see Example 12).

2.3 APPLICATIONS OF THE COMBINATORIAL RULES TO PROBABILITY

The most difficult aspect in using the three rules in any particular situation is in seeing how they *apply*. (Which is the *n* and which the *k*? Is it the permutation rule or the multiplication rule?) Unfortunately, there's no rule for how to apply the rules—no metarule, in other words. The only way to understand how to use the rules is to go over so many examples and problems that the process of

> Isolating the important features,
>
> Selecting and applying a combinatorial rule, and
>
> Interpretating the answer

becomes intuitive. Perhaps the single most important aid is

> *Always understand exactly what the sample space is!*

The tendency is to skip this step and jump directly into one or another formula. For the more difficult applications, however, writing down a definition of the sample space usually shows very clearly the most important aspects: Is order important? Are repetitions permitted?

Another useful method is *visualizing how* the random experiment is being performed—the actual mechanics of the process. For example, if a committee of a certain size is to be selected, in just what way is it actually accomplished? Are the individuals selected one by one? Or are they simply chosen as an entire group ("All those in the first row take one step forward.")? Often, pinning the abstraction down to a concrete situation suggests a method for solution.

A picture or doodle symbolizing the random experiment suggests ways of thinking that are not apparent from a description in words. After all, a sentence is a one-dimensional sort of thing; a picture is two-dimensional. A picture has an extra dimension for helping to understand the situation.

Finally, if there are arbitrary *n*'s or *k*'s, try solving the problem for values of *n* or *k* fixed at definite values. The process by which we understand new ideas proceeds from concrete examples to abstract principles or formulas. Sometimes it is possible to infer general answers from examining special cases.

But there is no substitute for spending time thinking through the ideas, examples, and problems. Eventually, the combinatorial ideas become second nature, but this takes effort and the willingness to look at the same examples several times.

Example 15 (*Continuation of Example 6*)

A group of n people, among them Hilary and Ralph, line up for a photograph. What is the probability that Hilary and Ralph are next to each other at the left end of the line? That Hilary and Ralph are next to each other?

Solution Sample space:

$$\Omega = \text{set of permutations of all } n \text{ people}$$

Since there are n people in the group, the number of elements in Ω is $n!$, by the permutation rule. Under the assumption of complete randomness each of these permutations has probability $1/n!$ How many of these $n!$ line-ups have Hilary and Ralph at the left end? To form a line-up with this property do:

> *Task 1.* Place H and R at the left: 2 ways because they could be placed HR or RH.
>
> *Task 2.* Place the *remaining* $n - 2$ people after them: $(n - 2)!$ ways since we are asking for the number of permutations of the remaining $n - 2$.

Hence, by the multiplication rule,

$$\#(\text{ways } H \text{ next to } R \text{ at left}) = 2(n - 2)!$$

$$P(H \text{ and } R \text{ at left}) = \frac{2(n - 2)!}{n!} = \frac{2}{n(n - 1)}$$

Now if we ask for the probability that H and R are next to each other without necessarily being at the left, we still have tasks 1 and 2 to perform—place H before or after R, line up the remaining $n - 2$. But in addition, we have

> *Task 3.* Determine the *starting position* of the pair H and R: $n - 1$ ways. (see Fig. 2.7)

Hence, again by the multiplication rule,

$$P(H \text{ and } R \text{ next to each other}) = \frac{2(n - 2)! \, (n - 1)}{n!} = \frac{2}{n} \quad \blacksquare$$

Example 16

Four digits are selected at random (from among the 10 digits 0, 1, . . ., 9). What is the probability that they are all different?

Solution Sample space Ω accounts for all possible choices of the 4 digits:

$$\Omega = \{ijkl : 0 \leqslant i, j, k, l \leqslant 9\}$$

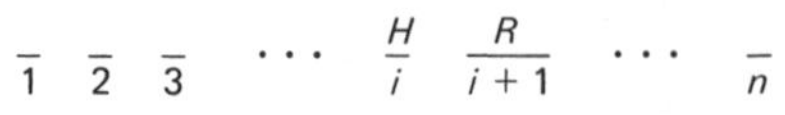

$$\underset{1}{\underline{}} \ \underset{2}{\underline{}} \ \underset{3}{\underline{}} \ \cdots \ \underset{i}{\underset{H}{\underline{}}} \ \underset{i+1}{\underset{R}{\underline{}}} \ \cdots \ \underset{n}{\underline{}}$$

Figure 2.7 The pair {H, R} can start in any of $n - 1$ positions.

For example, 5265 represents the event

"first a 5, then 2, then 6, finally a 5 selected"

By the multiplication rule there are

$$10 \cdot 10 \cdot 10 \cdot 10 = 10^4$$

outcomes. The number of these that have all 4 digits different is the number of permutations of size 4, or $(10)_4$. Hence

$$P(\text{all 4 digits different}) = \frac{(10)_4}{10^4} = .5040$$

If j rather than 4 digits are sampled, then

$$P(\text{all } j \text{ digits are different}) = \frac{(10)_j}{10^j}$$

Number of digits selected	P(all different)
1	1
2	.9
3	.72
4	.504
5	.3024
6	.1512
7	.06048
8	.01814
9	.0036288
10	.0003629

Example 17 *The Birthday Problem*

Assume 365 days in the year and that people's birthdays are randomly distributed throughout the year. (Actually, slightly more babies are born during August–September than at other times of the year.) With k people in a room, what is the probability that *at least* 2 have the same birthday? How many people are required so that this probability is 1/2 or more? (Before looking at the solution, try to guess the answer; the actual number of people required is surprisingly small.)

Solution The words "at least" suggests that we ought to look at the complementary event, which is

"no 2 people have the same birthday"

= "all k people have different birthdays"

But now the problem is very similar to that of Example 16: For k people, birthdays must be selected in such a way that no two are the same. The sample space is

$$\Omega = \{b_1 b_2 \cdots b_k : b_i \text{ is the birth date of person } i\}$$

That is, we label the people from 1 to k; then a sample point is a complete listing $b_1 b_2 \cdots b_k$ of the birthdays of all k people. There are

$$365^k$$

sample points since b_i can take any of 365 values for each i. To have all birthdays different $b_1 b_2 \cdots b_k$ must be a *permutation* (of size k from the set of dates of size 365) since there must be no repetitions—$(365)_k$ ways. Hence

$$P(\text{all } k \text{ birthdays different}) = \frac{(365)_k}{365^k}$$

$$= \frac{365}{365} \cdot \frac{364}{365} \cdots \frac{365 - k + 1}{365}$$

Here is a program to compute these probabilities and part of the output:

```
var PROB: real;
    K: integer;
begin
    PROB:= 1.0;
    for K:= 1 to 50 do
        begin
            PROB:= PROB*(365−K+1)/365;
            writeln (K,1−PROB:10:3);
        end;
end.
```

K	P(≥ 2 among K have same birthday)
.	
.	
.	
15	.253
16	.284
17	.315
18	.347
19	.379
20	.411
21	.443
22	.476
23	.507
24	.538
25	.569
26	.598
27	.627
28	.654
29	.681
30	.706
.	
.	
.	∎

Note that with 23 people, the probability is about 1/2 that at least 2 have the same birthday.

Example 18

A box contains 3 dented and 8 nondented cans. You select 2 cans at random. What is the probability that *at least 1* is dented?

  Solution You select 2 cans. So the sample space is the set of subsets of 2 cans from a total set of all 11 cans. Hence the sample space has

$$\binom{11}{2} = 55$$

possible outcomes. How many of these satisfy the property of at least 1 dented can? To obtain *exactly 1* dented can, 1 can must be selected from the 3 dented and 1 from the 8 nondented. As Fig. 2.8 shows, the number of ways to make these selections is

$$\binom{3}{1}\binom{8}{1} = 24$$

Similarly, there are

$$\binom{3}{2}\binom{8}{0} = 3$$

ways to select 2 dented and 0 nondented cans. Thus

$$P(\text{exactly 1 dented}) = \frac{24}{55}$$

$$P(\text{exactly 2 dented}) = \frac{3}{55}$$

$$P(\text{at least 1 dented}) = \frac{27}{55}$$

Notice that computing the probability of the complementary event results in fewer arithmetic operations:

$$P(\text{at least 1 dented}) = 1 - P(\text{none dented})$$

$$= 1 - \frac{\binom{3}{0}\binom{8}{2}}{\binom{11}{2}}$$

$$= \frac{27}{55} \quad\blacksquare$$

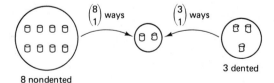

8 nondented   3 dented   **Figure 2.8** Two tasks: Choose one dented and choose one nondented.

Example 19

A poker hand consists of 5 randomly drawn cards from a standard size deck of 52. Find the probabilities of:

  Four of a kind (4 of the same denomination or face value)
  Straight (cards in "order," e.g., a 4, 5, 6, 7, and 8; ace can be high or low)
  Full house (3 of one denomination, 2 of another)
  Two pair (but not four of a kind)
  One pair (but not a full house or two pair)

(See also Problem 2.22.)

  Solution   The sample space consists of all possible hands—all subsets of 5 cards from the set of 52.   Thus there are

$$\binom{52}{5} = 2,598,960$$

different hands.   This is the denominator for all the probabilities.

  Four of a kind. How many of the $\binom{52}{5}$ hands satisfy the property?   Split the selection of a hand that has four of a kind into:

  Task 1. Select the *denomination* for the four: 13 ways
  Task 2. Select the *fifth card*: 48 ways since 4 of the 52 have been used up.

Therefore,

$$P(\text{four of a kind}) = \frac{13 \cdot 48}{\binom{52}{5}} \cong .0002401$$

  Straight.   The idea is the same, but now:

  Task 1.   Choose the *lowest* denomination for the straight; since ace is low or high, the lowest card can be ace, 2, 3, . . . , 10: 10 ways.
  Task 2.   Choose the suit for the lowest card: 4 ways.
  Task 3.   Choose the suit for the next lowest: 4 ways.
  Task 4.   Choose the suit for the next lowest: 4 ways.
  Task 5.   Choose the suit for the next lowest: 4 ways.
  Task 6.   Choose the suit for the highest: 4 ways.

  Hence, by the multiplication rule,

$$P(\text{straight}) = \frac{10 \cdot 4 \cdot 4 \cdot 4 \cdot 4 \cdot 4}{\binom{52}{5}} \cong .003940$$

The other probabilities are also found by splitting the complete "jobs" into subtasks. As before, the notation #(·) denotes "number of . . . ."

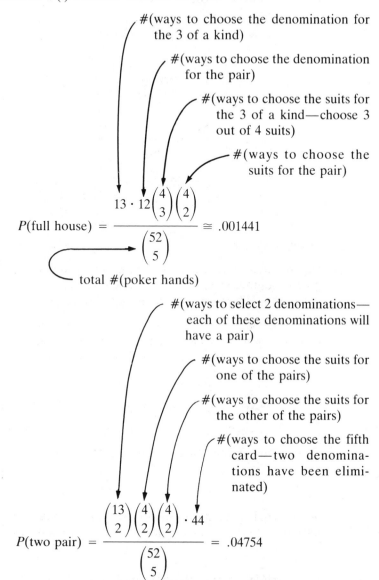

#(ways to choose the denomination for the 3 of a kind)

#(ways to choose the denomination for the pair)

#(ways to choose the suits for the 3 of a kind—choose 3 out of 4 suits)

#(ways to choose the suits for the pair)

$$P(\text{full house}) = \frac{13 \cdot 12\binom{4}{3}\binom{4}{2}}{\binom{52}{5}} \cong .001441$$

total #(poker hands)

#(ways to select 2 denominations—each of these denominations will have a pair)

#(ways to choose the suits for one of the pairs)

#(ways to choose the suits for the other of the pairs)

#(ways to choose the fifth card—two denominations have been eliminated)

$$P(\text{two pair}) = \frac{\binom{13}{2}\binom{4}{2}\binom{4}{2} \cdot 44}{\binom{52}{5}} = .04754$$

[Note that the number of ways to choose the denominations is $13 \cdot 12$ for the full house, but $\binom{13}{2}$ for the two pair *because* the denominations are *distinguishable* for the full house but are *not distinguishable* for the two pair. For example, a hand consisting of 3 sevens and 2 kings is different than a hand consisting of 3 kings and 2 sevens. However, for two pair a hand consisting of 2 kings and 2 sevens is the *same* as a hand consisting of 2 sevens and 2 kings. Order is important for the full house but is not important for two of a kind—a subtle point, but well worth the effort to understand.]

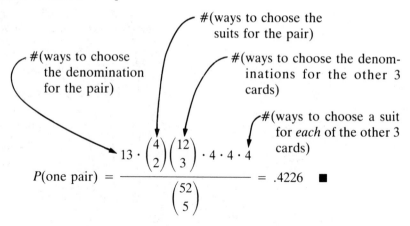

$$P(\text{one pair}) = \frac{13 \cdot \binom{4}{2}\binom{12}{3} \cdot 4 \cdot 4 \cdot 4}{\binom{52}{5}} = .4226 \quad \blacksquare$$

Example 20

Suppose that there are $2n$ people, among whom are Hilary and Ralph. The total group is randomly split into two equal-sized groups of size n. What is the probability that Hilary and Ralph are in the same group?

Solution A convenient way to summarize the result of splitting the group is to specify who is in the first group; then the composition of the second group is known as well. Hence the sample space is

$$\Omega = \{A : A \text{ is a subset of size } n \text{ of the } 2n \text{ people}-$$

$$\text{the set of people in the first group}\}$$

$$= \text{set of all } \textit{unordered} \text{ subsets of size } n$$

By the combination rule, the number of sample points is

$$\binom{2n}{n}$$

Since there is no reason to suppose that any of these are more likely as compositions for the first group, equally likely probabilities are assigned. How many of these have

1. Both Hilary and Ralph as members (both in first group)?

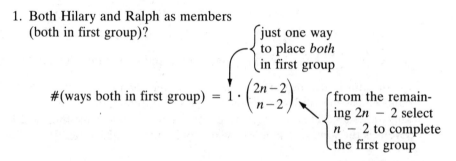

2. Neither Hilary nor Ralph as members (both in second group)?

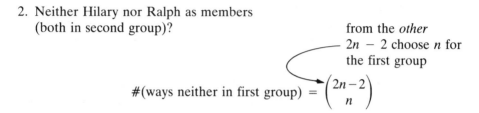

from the *other* 2n − 2 choose n for the first group

$$\#(\text{ways neither in first group}) = \binom{2n-2}{n}$$

Hence

$$P(\text{Ralph and Hilary in same group}) = \frac{\binom{2n-2}{n-2} + \binom{2n-2}{n}}{\binom{2n}{n}} = \frac{n-1}{2n-1}$$

Alternative Solution   Since the answer is a fairly simple expression, this suggests there is a simpler way to obtain it.   Reason this way: Suppose that you are Ralph. If *you* find the probability that Hilary is in your group, then *your answer* is the same as the probability that both Hilary and Ralph are in the same group.   As far as Ralph is concerned, there are $2n - 1$ other people and $n - 1$ chances that Hilary will be chosen as a member of Ralph's group.   Hence

$$P(\text{Hilary in Ralph's group}) = \frac{n-1}{2n-1} \quad \blacksquare$$

PROBLEMS

2.17. Three different-colored ping pong balls are placed randomly into 3 different cans. (More than 1 ball can go into a can.)   Let a typical sample point be (c_1, c_2, c_3), where c_i is equal to the can into which the ith ball is placed.   **(a)** List the sample points in which no can is empty.   How many are there?   **(b)** List the sample points in which can 1 has exactly 1 ball.   How many are there?   **(c)** Obtain these numbers using the combinatorial rules.

2.18. Alice, Benjy, Clyde, and Daphne randomly choose a president and a secretary.   **(a)** What is the sample space?   **(b)** How many sample points have Daphne as either president or secretary?   **(c)** What is the probability that Daphne is an officer?   **(d)** Obtain the same answer using the combinatorial rules.

2.19. You are dealt 4 cards from a standard deck of 52.   What are the probabilities of **(a)** 2 red and 2 black cards; **(b)** no red cards; **(c)** at most 1 red card?

2.20. A box has 10 good and 3 defective light bulbs; 2 are selected at random.   **(a)** What is the sample space?   What are the probabilities that **(b)** 0 are good; **(c)** 1 is good; **(d)** both are good?

2.21. You are dealt 3 cards one after another.   What is the probability that **(a)** the first card is a club; **(b)** the first 2 cards are clubs; **(c)** the first 3 are clubs; **(d)** the second and the third cards are clubs?

2.22. (*Continuation of Example 19*) **(a)** Compute the probability of a flush at poker. (A flush is a hand all of whose cards are of the same suit.) **(b)** Compute the probability of three of a kind [that is, 3 cards of one denomination and 2 cards of different denominations (but not a full house)].

2.23. You are dealt a hand of 13 cards. **(a)** What is the sample space? What are **(b)** P(2 aces); **(c)** P(7 hearts); **(d)** P(7 hearts and 6 clubs); **(e)** P(7 hearts, 4 spades, and 2 clubs); **(f)** P(no hearts); **(g)** P(3 aces and 2 sevens); **(h)** P(2 kings, 3 queens, and 1 jack)?

2.24. Alice and Benjy are in a class of n children. A group of j children is selected at random. What are **(a)** P (both are in the group of j); **(b)** P(neither is in the group); **(c)** P(Alice is in the group, but Benjy is not); **(d)** P(one of them is in the group, but the other is not)?

2.25. A box has 5 different kinds of cookies; there are 10 of each kind. Sam reaches in and grabs 3. What are **(a)** P(all 3 are chocolate chip); **(b)** P(2 are chocolate chip and 1 is vanilla); **(c)** P(1 chocolate chip, 1 vanilla, and 1 oatmeal); **(d)** P(none are chocolate chip); **(e)** P(all 3 are different)?

2.26. Six pool balls are randomly placed into the 6 pockets. **(a)** What is the total number of ways to distribute all the balls in the pockets? What are **(b)** P(northwest corner pocket empty); **(c)** P(each ball in a different pocket); **(d)** P(all balls in 1 pocket); **(e)** P(exactly 1 pocket empty)?

2.27. In bridge each of 4 people is dealt 13 cards. Opposite players are partners. What are **(a)** P(you have 7 spades); **(b)** P(you and your partner together have 10 spades); **(c)** P(you have 7 spades and your partner has 4 spades); **(d)** P(you have 3 aces and your partner has 1 ace)?

2.28. (*Continuation of Problem 2.12*) A bus starts with 8 people and stops at 12 locations; no one else gets on the bus. Assuming that all possible arrangements of people and stops are equally likely, what are the probabilities that **(a)** no one departs at the first stop; **(b)** 1 person departs at the first stop; **(c)** each person gets off at a different stop; **(d)** no one else gets off at the stop at which Daphne gets off?

2.29. A carnival game has 9 holes arranged in a 3 by 3 tic-tac-toe board. Three balls are thrown onto the board; each ball lands in a separate hole. **(a)** How many different arrangements of the 3 balls on the board are there? You win if the balls end up in one row or one column or one of the two diagonals. **(b)** What is the probability that you win, *assuming* that all arrangements are equally likely?

2.30. You are dealt 5 cards one by one from a standard deck. After picking up the first 2 cards you see that one is the ace of hearts and the other is the 7 of hearts. Knowing this, what are the probabilities that after you pick up the remaining 3 cards you will have **(a)** a flush in hearts; **(b)** 3 aces and 2 sevens; **(c)** a full house; **(d)** a pair of aces and a pair of sevens?

2.31. A group of 12 people are randomly split into 3 equal-sized groups of 4 each. What are the probabilities that **(a)** Alice and Benjy both end up in the first group; **(b)** Alice ends up in the first group, but Benjy does not; **(c)** Alice and Benjy end up in the same group (either the first, second, or third)?

2.32. Hilary buys 5 soup cans and Clyde buys 4 soup cans from a shelf with 10 dented and 15 nondented cans. What are the probabilities that **(a)** Hilary gets 1 dented and Clyde gets 2 dented; **(b)** Hilary gets 1 dented; **(c)** Hilary gets 2 dented and Clyde gets at least 2 dented?

2.33. Tickets numbered 1 through 200 were sold in a raffle. As they were sold the numbers were placed into a bin so that the higher numbers were on top. Before selecting four winners, the bin was mixed. The winners were number 163, 195, 188, and 167. Is this sufficient evidence to conclude that the mixing was not complete? Compute P(all 4 numbers were larger than 160).

2.4 THE BINOMIAL FORMULA

The **binomial formula** is perhaps the most frequently occurring context for the binomial coefficients. The formula was known to the fourteenth-century Arab mathematician Al-Kashi. The binomial coefficients themselves were known earlier in twelfth-century China, so perhaps the binomial formula was known there as well.

There are several different proofs for the formula. Maybe you have seen a proof using mathematical induction. Calculus texts usually include a proof using Taylor series. Here a combinatorial proof is given.

Binomial Formula

$$(x + y)^n = \sum_{k=0}^{n} \binom{n}{k} x^{n-k} y^k$$

for positive integer n.

Example 21

Using Pascal's triangle, whose nth row contains the binomial coefficients $\binom{n}{k}$ as k ranges from 0 to n:

$$(x + y)^2 = \binom{2}{0} x^2 + \binom{2}{1} xy + \binom{2}{2} y^2 = x^2 + 2xy + y^2$$

$$(x + y)^3 = x^3 + 3x^2 y + 3xy^2 + y^3$$

$$(x + y)^5 = x^5 + 5x^4 y + 10x^3 y^2 + 10x^2 y^3 + 5xy^4 + y^5 \quad \blacksquare$$

Proof of the Binomial Formula

$$(x + y)^n = (x + y)(x + y) \cdots (x + y)$$

is an n-fold product of binomial terms. A typical term in the product is the result of selecting *either* an x *or* a y from *each* of the n factors $(x + y)$ and multiplying all n terms together. Now ask how many terms in the total product result in $x^{n-k} y^k$. In order that a product of x's and y's result in $x^{n-k} y^k$, $n - k$ selections from the factors $(x + y)$ must result in the selection of x and the other k selections must result in the selection of y rather than x.

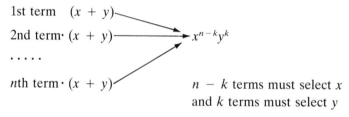

1st term $(x + y)$

2nd term $(x + y)$ $\longrightarrow x^{n-k}y^k$

$\cdots$

nth term $(x + y)$ $n - k$ terms must select x
and k terms must select y

How many ways are there to form the product $x^{n-k}y^k$? As many ways as there are to select $n - k$ terms from among the n terms $(x + y)$; these $n - k$ terms will supply $n - k$ x's; the other k terms will supply k y's to the product $x^{n-k}y^k$. Consequently, the coefficient of $x^{n-k}y^k$ is the number of subsets of size $n - k$ from

a set of size n which is $\binom{n}{n-k} = \binom{n}{k}$. Therefore,

$$(x + y)^n = \binom{n}{0}x^n y^0 + \binom{n}{1}x^{n-1}y^1 + \cdots + \binom{n}{n}x^{n-n}y^n \quad \blacksquare$$

2.5 RANDOM COMMENTS AND PROBLEMS: BINOMIAL COEFFICIENTS (OPTIONAL)

Numerous relations hold among the binomial coefficients, of which Example 12 uses one to construct the nth row of Pascal's triangle. Often, these relations can be proved using combinatorics. It is fascinating that the same statement can have an algebraic proof as well as a proof based solely on a combinatorial interpretation. In this section we show several examples of this.

Example 22

In Pascal's triangle, note that *each entry is the sum of the entry directly above and the entry to the above-left.* Here is a part of the seventh and eight rows:

(35) (35) (21) $\binom{7}{3}\binom{7}{4}\binom{7}{5}$ The sum of
     $+ \quad + $ these two is
    70 56 $\binom{8}{4}\binom{8}{5}$

That is, generally it is true that

$$\binom{n+1}{k} = \binom{n}{k} + \binom{n}{k-1}$$

for all n and $1 \leq k \leq n$. Prove this relation.

Solution 1: *Algebraic Method*   Directly from the definition, we have

$$\binom{n}{k} + \binom{n}{k-1} = \frac{n(n-1)\cdots(n-k+1)}{k!} + \frac{n(n-1)\cdots(n-(k-1)+1)}{(k-1)!}$$

$$= \frac{n(n-1)\cdots(n-k+2)}{(k-1)!}\left[\frac{n-k+1}{k}+1\right]$$

$$= \frac{n+1}{k}\cdot\frac{n(n-1)\cdots(n-k+2)}{(k-1)!}$$

$$= \binom{n+1}{k}$$

Solution 2: *Combinatorial Method* $\binom{n+1}{k}$ is the number of subsets of size

k from a total set of size $n + 1$. Consider choosing a particular subset of size k in the following way. Suppose that one of the $n + 1$ objects is distinguished from the others; for definiteness we will say that that object is red. To form a subset of size k we can *either*

1. *Include* the red object, in which case we have to decide on $k - 1$ objects to include from the *remaining* n nonred objects. There are $\binom{n}{k-1}$ ways to complete the subset.

or

2. *Exclude* the red object, in which case all k objects have to be selected from the n nonred objects.

This is shown schematically in Fig. 2.9. Hence the total number of ways to select a subset of size k is the sum

$$\binom{n+1}{k} = \#(\text{subsets including the red object}) + \#(\text{subsets excluding the red object})$$

$$= \binom{n}{k-1} + \binom{n}{k} \quad\blacksquare$$

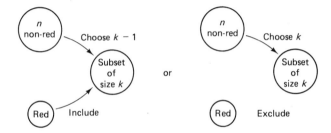

Figure 2.9 A subset of size k can be formed *either* by including the red object *or* by excluding the red object.

Example 23

The recursive relation

$$\binom{n}{k} = \frac{n - k + 1}{k} \binom{n}{k-1}$$

was used in Example 12 to generate Pascal's triangle. Give a combinatorial proof.

Solution The proof consists of a combinatorial interpretation of

$$k\binom{n}{k}$$

From a set of n people how many ways are there to choose a committee of size k with one president? The selection process is divided into tasks in two different ways:

Method A:

    Task 1. Choose a committee of size k: $\binom{n}{k}$ ways.

    Task 2. Choose a president from among the k: k ways.

Hence the total number of such committees is

$$k\binom{n}{k}$$

by the multiplication rule. On the other hand, consider:

Method B:

    Task 1'. Choose a committee of size $k - 1$: $\binom{n}{k-1}$ ways.

    Task 2'. Choose a president from among the $n - (k - 1) = n - k + 1$ folks *not* selected to be the plebians on the committee: $n - k + 1$ ways.

Hence the total number of such committees is

$$(n - k + 1)\binom{n}{k-1}$$

Since this number must agree with the result of Method A, the relationship is proved.

$$k\binom{n}{k} = (n - k + 1)\binom{n}{k-1} \quad \blacksquare$$

PROBLEMS

2.34. Give algebraic and combinatorial proofs that

$$\binom{n}{0} + \binom{n}{1} + \cdots + \binom{n}{n} = \sum_{k=0}^{n} \binom{n}{k} = 2^n$$

2.35. Give a combinatorial proof that

$$\sum_{k=0}^{n} \binom{n}{k}^2 = \sum_{k=0}^{n} \binom{n}{k}\binom{n}{n-k} = \binom{2n}{n}$$

2.36. Give algebraic and combinatorial proofs that

$$\binom{n}{1} + 2\binom{n}{2} + 3\binom{n}{3} + \cdots + n\binom{n}{n} = \sum_{k=0}^{n} k\binom{n}{k} = n \cdot 2^{n-1}$$

2.37. Give algebraic and combinatorial proofs that

$$\binom{n+2}{k} = \binom{n}{k} + 2\binom{n}{k-1} + \binom{n}{k-2}$$

2.38. (*Trinomial Coefficients*) A set of n objects is to be split into 3 groups. The first group is to have n_1 objects, the second is to have n_2 objects, and the third group is to have n_3 objects. Thus

$$n_1 + n_2 + n_3 = n$$

Show that the total number of ways to split the objects into the 3 groups is

$$\binom{n}{n_1}\binom{n-n_1}{n_2}\binom{n-n_1-n_2}{n_3} = \frac{n!}{n_1! \, n_2! \, n_3!}$$

2.39. (*Continuation*) Suppose that there are 5 wooden letter A's, 4 B's, and 3 C's in a box. How many distinct "words" can be formed from all 12 letters?

2.40. (*Multinomial Coefficients: Generalization of Problem 2.38*) A set of n objects is to be split into k groups. n_1 are to go into group 1, n_2 are to go into group 2, . . . , and n_k into group k. Thus

$$n_1 + n_2 + \cdots + n_k = n$$

Show that the total number of ways to split the objects into the k groups is

$$\binom{n}{n_1}\binom{n-n_1}{n_2}\binom{n-n_1-n_2}{n_3} \cdots \binom{n-n_1-\cdots-n_{k-1}}{n_k} = \frac{n!}{n_1! \, n_2! \cdots n_k!}$$

2.41. (*Continuation*) Suppose that there are 5 wooden letter A's, 4 B's, 3 C's, 2 D's, and 1 E in a box. How many distinct "words" can be formed from all 15 letters?

2.42. Fifteen pool balls are randomly distributed into 6 pockets. Find **(a)** P(northwest pocket is empty); **(b)** P(the two side pockets are both empty); **(c)** P(pocket 1 has 5 balls, 2 has 4, 3 has 3, 4 has 2, 5 has 1, and 6 has none); **(d)** P(one pocket has 5 balls, another has 4, another has 3, another has 2, another has 1, and the last has none); **(e)** P(pockets 1, 2, 3, and 4 have 3 balls each, pocket 5 has 2 balls, and pocket 6 has 1 ball); **(f)** P(4 pockets have 3 balls each, another has 2 balls, and the last has 1 ball).

(If you can do Problem 2.42, you have *really* mastered the chapter!)

The theory of probabilities is at bottom nothing
but common sense reduced to calculus.

Pierre Simon de Laplace, 1749–1827,
Analytic Theory of Probabilities

— Chapter 3 —————————————

Conditional Probability
and Independence

In any experiment involving randomness—from playing cards to counting stars—
there lurks in the background a whole set of "givens." There is no such thing as
randomness without a deterministic background; randomness is a counterpoint, a
warp upon the woof of given constraints. For example, in computing card-game
probabilities there is *given* a deck of cards of such and such a composition. The
world cannot possibly be a place of complete randomness precisely because randomness needs a "fixedness" compared to which *it* is the exception. In the examples and techniques of Chapter 2 the fixed background in any specific situation
was obvious; it did not need to be stated explicitly. In this chapter techniques are
considered for dealing with experiments in which the background also has random
features.

3.1 THE DEFINITION OF CONDITIONAL PROBABILITY

Example 1

You have been dealt 1 card from a standard deck of 52. You see that it is an ace.
What is the probability that the next card will be a queen?

Solution After the first card has been dealt, the deck consists of 51 cards,
4 of which are queens. Hence the equally likely outcome approach of Chapter 2

implies that

$$P(\text{next card a Queen}) = \frac{4}{51} \quad \blacksquare$$

In Example 1 we see that partial knowledge has changed the probability. It is not that a new rule is used; rather, the techniques of Chapter 2 are applied to a different sample space.

Suppose that a random experiment is performed and assume further that the event B was known to occur. *Given* this fact, what is the subsequent probability of event A? How does partial knowledge revise the probability of A?

To answer this question, we invoke the *frequency interpretation* of probability. Imagine performing the random experiment a large number N of times. Suppose that of these N repetitions B occurred n_B times and $A \cap B$ occurred $n_{A \cap B}$ times as in Fig. 3.1. Then among the n_B times that the random experiment resulted in B, A occurred $n_{A \cap B}$ times. Consequently, A occurred a fraction equal to

$$\frac{n_{A \cap B}}{n_B}$$

among all the times n_B that B occurred. If N is large, then n_B will be large as well [assuming that $P(B) > 0$]. Intuitively, the ratio will then represent the probability that A occurred *given* knowledge of the fact that B occurred. But

$$\frac{n_{A \cap B}}{n_B} = \frac{n_{A \cap B}/N}{n_B/N} \cong \frac{P(A \cap B)}{P(B)}$$

where the frequency interpretation of probability implies that the approximation will be accurate for large N. Now the intuitive derivation can be cast into the

---

Definition

For any events A and B with $P(B) > 0$, the **conditional probability** *of A given B* is

$$P(A \mid B) = \frac{P(A \cap B)}{P(B)}$$

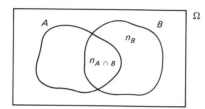

Figure 3.1 The ratio of $n_{A \cap B}$ to n_B is approximately the ratio of $P(A \cap B)$ to $P(B)$.

Example 1′

Solve Example 1 using the definition of conditional probability.

   Solution

$$A = \text{``second card is a queen''}$$

$$B = \text{``first card is an ace''}$$

$$A \cap B = \text{``second card queen and first card ace''}$$

$$P(A \mid B) = \frac{P(A \cap B)}{P(B)} = \frac{4 \cdot 4/52 \cdot 51}{4/52} = \frac{4}{51}$$

as before. ■

Example 2

Roll two dice and observe the numbers showing uppermost on each. Given that the two do *not* show identical results, what is the probability that the sum is 7?

   Solution   Define the events $A = \text{``sum is 7''}$ and $B = \text{``nonidentical results.''}$ The sample space has 36 outcomes, of which $36 - 6 = 30$ are in B and 6 are in $A \cap B$. [Note that $A \cap B = A$. (Why?)] Thus the definition of conditional probability implies that

$$P(\text{sum is 7} \mid \text{nonidentical results})$$

$$= P(A \mid B)$$

$$= \frac{P(A \cap B)}{P(B)}$$

$$= \frac{6/36}{30/36}$$

$$= \frac{1}{5} \quad ■$$

PROBLEMS

3.1. Flip a fair coin three times. What are the probabilities that **(a)** the first flip resulted in heads given a total of 1 head on all three flips; **(b)** there are 2 heads given the first flip resulted in heads; **(c)** the first flip resulted in heads given *at least 1* head on all three flips?

3.2. Roll two dice. What are the probabilities that **(a)** the sum is 7 given that the first die resulted in a 3; **(b)** the sum is 7 given that exactly one of the dice (either the first or the second) resulted in a 3; **(c)** the first die resulted in a 3 given that the sum was 7; **(d)** exactly one of the dice resulted in a 3 given that the sum was 7?

3.3. You have just picked up the first 3 cards of a 5-card hand. Given that you have 2 sevens and 1 jack, what are the probabilities that with the remaining 2 cards you will have (a) 3 sevens; (b) 3 sevens and 2 jacks; (c) 2 sevens and 2 jacks?

3.2 THE THREE BASIC RULES OF CONDITIONAL PROBABILITY

The following rules are straightforward consequences of the definition. However, in the context of a specific application, they seem to have a significance far greater than the simplicity of their proofs.

$$P(A \mid B) = \frac{P(A \cap B)}{P(B)}$$

$$P(A \cap B) = P(A \mid B)P(B)$$

$$P(B \mid A) = \frac{P(A \mid B)P(B)}{P(A)}$$

The first rule is just the definition of conditional probability. The second rule follows by multiplying both sides of the first rule by $P(B)$. The third rule uses the second, but switches the roles of the "conditioning event" and the "conditioned-on event":

$$P(A \mid B)P(B) = P(A \cap B) = P(B \cap A) = P(B \mid A)P(A)$$

where the two outside equalities invoke the second rule. Now erase the two middle terms and divide both sides of the resulting equality by $P(A)$ to obtain the third rule.

Example 3

Using conditional probability ideas, let us compute the probability of 2 clubs when 2 cards are drawn. We know by combinatorial reasoning that the answer is

$$P(2 \text{ clubs}) = \frac{\binom{13}{2}}{\binom{52}{2}} = \frac{1}{17}$$

With conditional probabilities

$$P(2 \text{ clubs}) = P(\text{2nd is club} \mid \text{1st is club})P(\text{1st is club})$$

$$= \frac{12}{51} \cdot \frac{13}{52}$$

$$= \frac{1}{17}$$

Note that the first equality uses the second rule. ∎

In finding $P(A \mid B)$, *usually* the event B occurs prior in time to the event A. That is, *given* that the event B *has already* occurred, we are interested in the *subsequent* chance of A. Usually, finding $P(A \mid B)$ is easier in this case. The third rule is used *mostly in cases where we need to know $P(B \mid A)$ when B occurs before A*.

Example 4

There are two groups of children—5 boys and 10 girls. First, one of the groups—the boys or the girls—is selected. Then one from among that group is selected. What is the chance that Alice will be selected?

Solution Since Alice is a girl,

$$P(\text{Alice selected}) = P(\text{Alice selected} \cap \text{girls' group selected})$$
$$= P(\text{Alice selected} \mid \text{girls' group})P(\text{girls' group})$$
$$= \frac{1}{10} \cdot \frac{1}{2}$$
$$= \frac{1}{20}$$

Note how this probability is *less* than 1/15, which is the chance that Alice is selected from the *entire* group. Why? ∎

Example 5

You are dealt 3 cards. What is the probability that they all have the same suit?

Solution 1: Using combinatorics There are 4 ways to choose the suit; then 3 cards from this suit must be selected.

$$P(\text{all 3 same suit}) = \frac{4\binom{13}{3}}{\binom{52}{3}} = \frac{12 \cdot 11}{51 \cdot 50}$$

Solution 2: Using conditional probability Define the events

$$A_i = \text{``ith card has the same suit as 1st card''}$$

for $i = 2, 3$. Then

$$P(\text{all 3 same suit}) = P(A_3 \cap A_2)$$
$$= P(A_3 \mid A_2) \cdot P(A_2)$$
$$= \frac{11}{50} \cdot \frac{12}{51} \quad ∎$$

The second rule is very useful and can be generalized to more than two events. Let A, B, and C be events. Then using the second rule *twice* yields both these equalities:

$$P(A \cap B \cap C) = P(A \mid B \cap C)P(B \cap C)$$

$$P(A \cap B \cap C) = P(A \mid B \cap C)P(B \mid C)P(C)$$

This *product rule* can be generalized even further:

$$P(A_n \cap \cdots \cap A_1)$$
$$= P(A_n \mid A_{n-1} \cap \cdots \cap A_1)P(A_{n-1} \mid A_{n-2} \cap \cdots \cap A_1)$$
$$\cdots P(A_2 \mid A_1)P(A_1)$$

Example 6

Use conditional probabilities to find the probability of a flush in spades at poker.

Solution Use the rule above with $A_i =$ "*i*th card dealt is a spade."

$$P(5 \text{ spades}) = P(5\text{th is spade} \mid \text{first 4 are spades})$$
$$\cdot P(4\text{th is spade} \mid \text{first 3 are spades})$$
$$\cdot P(3\text{rd is spade} \mid \text{first 2 are spades})$$
$$\cdot P(2\text{nd is spade} \mid \text{first is a spade})$$
$$\cdot P(\text{first is a spade})$$
$$= \frac{9}{48} \cdot \frac{10}{49} \cdot \frac{11}{50} \cdot \frac{12}{51} \cdot \frac{13}{52} \quad \blacksquare$$

PROBLEMS

3.4. A box of 10 cans contains 2 cans that are rusted. You pick out cans one by one. What are the probabilities that **(a)** the first and second cans are both rusted; **(b)** the second can is rusted given that the first is not; **(c)** among the first 4 selected, 2 are rusted; **(d)** the first is rusted given that among the first 4 selected, 2 are rusted?

3.5. You are dealt 4 cards one after another. What are the probabilities that **(a)** the second and first cards are of different suits; **(b)** the third is a different suit from the first 2 given that the first 2 are of the same suit; **(c)** the third is a different suit from the first 2 given that the first 2 are of different suits; **(d)** the fourth is of the last remaining suit given that the first 3 are of three different suits; **(e)** the 4 cards are all of different suits?

3.6. There are N keys on the key ring of which exactly 1 fits the lock. Jessica tries them one by one, carefully placing the ones that do not fit into her pocket until she finds the key that fits. What are the probabilities that **(a)** the first key tried fits; **(b)** the second key does *not* fit given that the first key does not fit; **(c)** the third key does *not* fit given that the first 2 keys tried do not fit; **(d)** the fourth key does *not* fit given that the first 3 keys do not fit; **(e)** the second key fits; **(f)** the third key fits; **(g)** the fourth key fits; **(h)** the jth key fits? $(j \leqslant N)$

3.7. The N numbers $1, 2, 3, \ldots, N$ are lined up at random. What are the probabilities that **(a)** 1 is in the first position in the line-up; **(b)** 2 is in the second position; **(c)** 2 is in the second position given that 1 is in the first position; **(d)** j is in the jth position given that $j - 1, j - 2, \ldots, 1$ are in positions $j - 1, j - 2, \ldots, 1$, respectively; **(e)** j is in the jth position; **(f)** j is in the jth position given that $j - 1$ is in the $(j - 1)$st position?

3.8. Use the three basic rules to show that
(a) $P(A \cap B \mid C)/P(B \mid C) = P(A \mid B \cap C)$
(b) $P(A \mid B \cap C) = P(B \mid A \cap C)P(A \mid C)/P(B \mid C)$
(c) $P(A \cap B \mid C \cap D) = P(B \cap C \mid A \cap D)P(A \mid D)/P(C \mid D)$

3.9. Let B be an event with $P(B) > 0$. Assume that events E and F are disjoint. Use the definition of conditional probability to show that $P(E \cup F \mid B) = P(E \mid B) + P(F \mid B)$. Show that Axioms 1, 2, and 3 for probability in Chapter 1 are satisfied for Q, where $Q(A) = P(A \mid B)$.

3.3 THE LAW OF TOTAL PROBABILITY

There are two coins on the table; one is fair and the other has two heads. You select one at random and flip it. If the result is heads, you win \$1; otherwise, you lose \$1. If the fair coin is selected, you win with probability 1/2; you win with the other coin with probability 1. Intuitively, the probability that you win *if* the coin is selected at random ought to be the average 3/4. This section formalizes the technique of averaging probabilities in this way.

The events $B_1, \ldots, B_n$ form a **partition** of the sample space Ω if every sample point ω is in one and only one B_i. That is,

$$\Omega = \bigcup_{i=1}^{n} B_i$$

and $B_1, \ldots, B_n$ are **pairwise disjoint**.

In the example above, *which* coin is selected partitions the experiment. Thus B_1 = "fair coin selected" and B_2 = "two-headed coin selected."

Now let A be any event in Ω. Often, $P(A)$ is difficult to find directly, but the n numbers $P(A \mid B_i)$ are relatively easy to compute. This was certainly the case with the coin example.

Law of Total Probability

Let $B_1, \ldots, B_n$ form a partition of Ω and suppose that A is any event. Then

$$P(A) = \sum_{i=1}^{n} P(A \mid B_i)P(B_i)$$

Proof of the Law of Total Probability. Since $B_1, \ldots, B_n$ form a partition, each element of A is in one and only one of the sets B_i. (see Fig. 3.2) Thus $\omega \in A$ implies that $\omega \in A \cap B_i$ for *exactly one i*. Therefore,

$$A = (A \cap B_1) \cup (A \cap B_2) \cup \cdots \cup (A \cap B_n)$$

disjointly. Since the union is a *disjoint* union, Property 6 of Chapter 1 implies that

$$P(A) = P(A \cap B_1) + P(A \cap B_2) + \cdots + P(A \cap B_n)$$

$$= P(A \mid B_1)P(B_1) + P(A \mid B_2)P(B_2) + \cdots + P(A \mid B_n)P(B_n)$$

$$= \sum_{i=1}^{n} P(A \mid B_i)P(B_i)$$

where the second equality uses the second basic rule: For each i,

$$P(A \cap B_i) = P(A \mid B_i)P(B_i) \quad \blacksquare$$

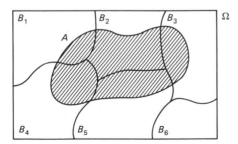

Figure 3.2

Example 7

A factory has 3 machines, labeled A, B, and C.

> A makes 20% of the parts produced by the factory.
> B makes 30% of the parts produced by the factory.
> C makes 50% of the parts produced by the factory.

and

> 6% of the parts made by A are defective.
> 7% of the parts made by B are defective.
> 8% of the parts made by C are defective.

All the parts are tossed into a single box. At the end of the day a part is picked out of the box. What is the probability that it is defective?

Solution The random experiment here is really a *two-stage* affair: *First* the part is made (by either A, B, or C) and *then* it is selected out of the box. Thus we partition on the intermediary possibilities of *which* machine made it. By the law of total probability,

$$P(\text{part defective}) = P(\text{part defective} \mid A \text{ made it})P(A \text{ made it})$$
$$+ P(\text{part defective} \mid B \text{ made it})P(B \text{ made it})$$
$$+ P(\text{part defective} \mid C \text{ made it})P(C \text{ made it})$$
$$= (.06)(.20) + (.07)(.30) + (.08)(.50)$$
$$= .073$$

Note that this probability .073 is an *average* of .06, .07, and .08 of the individual machine-defective probabilities. In fact, the law of total probability says that we must *weight* the numbers .06, .07, and .08 each by the chance that A, B, and C made the part. ■

Example 8 *(Continuation)*

Suppose that a part is selected from the box at day's end and is found to be defective. What is the probability that C made it? That B made it? That A made it?

Solution We are dealing with a situation that is "inverted in time." That is, whether the part was made by C or not occurred *before* it was selected from the box, yet we seek the probability of the *former* event (whether C made it) conditioned on the *latter* event (that it is defective). Thus we use the third basic rule of conditional probability:

$$P(C \text{ made it} \mid \text{part defective})$$
$$= \frac{P(\text{part defective} \mid C \text{ made it})P(C \text{ made it})}{P(\text{part defective})}$$

The denominator was computed in Example 7; thus

$$P(C \text{ made it} \mid \text{part defective}) = \frac{(.08)(.50)}{.073} = \frac{40}{73}$$

Similarly,

$$P(B \text{ made it} \mid \text{part defective}) = \frac{(.07)(.30)}{.073} = \frac{21}{73}$$

$$P(A \text{ made it} \mid \text{part defective}) = \frac{(.06)(.20)}{.073} = \frac{12}{73}$$

Note that the sum of the three probabilities *must add to 1*. (Why?) ■

Summarizing the technique used to obtain the conditional probability of a former event given a latter event yields

---

Bayes' Formula

Suppose that $B_1, \ldots, B_n$ is a partition. To obtain $P(B_i \mid A)$:

1. First obtain

$$P(A) = \sum_{j=1}^{n} P(A \mid B_j)P(B_j)$$

using the law of total probability.
2. Then use the third basic rule:

$$P(B_i \mid A) = \frac{P(A \mid B_i)P(B_i)}{P(A)}$$

Thomas Bayes (1702–1761) was an English Presbyterian minister. Although he wrote on conditional probabilities and how partial knowledge can be used to revise probabilities, Bayes' formula first appears in the writings of Laplace.

Example 9

In the age bracket 25 to 44 in the United States, 1 male in 9000 contracts tuberculosis and 1 female in 15,000 contracts tuberculosis in 1 year. What is the probability that a person in this age category will contract tuberculosis in the next year? *Given a person of this age who has contracted tuberculosis, what is the probability that the person is a man?*

Solution Define the events

A = "person in this age bracket contracts tuberculosis"

B_m = "person is a male"

B_f = "person is a female"

Then under the assumption that there are an equal number of men and women of this age in the United States (certainly valid to a good approximation),

$$P(B_m) = \frac{1}{2} = P(B_f)$$

We are given

$$P(A \mid B_m) = \frac{1}{9000} \qquad P(A \mid B_f) = \frac{1}{15,000}$$

Thus

$$P(\text{person contracts tuberculosis}) = P(A)$$

$$= P(A \mid B_m)P(B_m) + P(A \mid B_f)P(B_f)$$

$$= \frac{1}{9000} \cdot \frac{1}{2} + \frac{1}{15,000} \cdot \frac{1}{2}$$

$$= \frac{12}{135,000}$$

Consequently,

$$P(\text{man} \mid \text{contracted tuberculosis}) = P(B_m \mid A)$$

$$= \frac{P(A \mid B_m)P(B_m)}{P(A)}$$

$$= \frac{(1/9000)(1/2)}{12/135,000}$$

$$= .625$$

Note that this number is slightly over 1/2 since there is a greater chance that a man will contract tuberculosis than that a woman will; at least this qualitative fact could have been predicted before the computations. ■

Example 10

Cards are selected one by one from a standard deck of 52. Find the probabilities that (a) the second card selected is a club, and (b) the third card is a club.

Solution (a) In choosing 2 cards the sample space Ω is the set of ordered pairs of distinct cards.

$$\Omega = \{(C_1, C_2) : C_1 \text{ is 1st and } C_2 \text{ is 2nd card selected}\}$$

Ω is partitioned on whether the *first* card is a club or not:

$$B_1 = \text{``1st card is a club''}$$

$$B_2 = \text{``1st card is not a club''}$$

$$A = \text{``2nd card is a club''}$$

Now

$$P(B_1) = \frac{1}{4} \qquad P(B_2) = \frac{3}{4} \qquad P(A \mid B_1) = \frac{12}{51} \qquad P(A \mid B_2) = \frac{13}{51}$$

Thus the law of total probability implies that

$$P(A) = P(A \mid B_1)P(B_1) + P(A \mid B_2)P(B_2)$$

$$= \frac{12}{51} \cdot \frac{1}{4} + \frac{13}{51} \cdot \frac{3}{4}$$

$$= \frac{51}{51 \cdot 4}$$

$$= 1/4$$

(b) To compute the probability that the third card is a club, partition on the outcome of the first two cards:

$$C = \text{``third card is a club''}$$

$$D_1 = \text{``first and second cards are clubs''}$$

$$D_2 = \text{``first card is a club, but second is not''}$$

$$D_3 = \text{``first card is not a club, but second is''}$$

$$D_4 = \text{``neither the first nor the second is a club''}$$

Consequently, the law of total probability implies that

$$P(C) = P(C \mid D_1)P(D_1) + P(C \mid D_2)P(D_2) + P(C \mid D_3)P(D_3) + P(C \mid D_4)P(D_4)$$

$$= \frac{11}{50} \cdot \frac{13 \cdot 12}{52 \cdot 51} + \frac{12}{50} \cdot \frac{13 \cdot 39}{52 \cdot 51} + \frac{12}{50} \cdot \frac{39 \cdot 13}{52 \cdot 51} + \frac{13}{50} \cdot \frac{39 \cdot 38}{52 \cdot 51}$$

$$= \frac{13(11 \cdot 12 + 12 \cdot 39 + 39 \cdot 12 + 39 \cdot 38)}{52 \cdot 51 \cdot 50}$$

$$= \frac{1}{4}$$

The result is surprising. The probability that the second card is a club is 1/4 and the probability that the third card is a club is also 1/4; this is the *same* as the probability that the first card is a club. ■

Let us generalize Example 10. For a proof, see Problem 3.17.

A container has N objects, G of which are green. Objects are selected one by one without replacing them. The probability that the ith object selected is green is

$$\frac{G}{N}$$

independent of the value of $i = 1, 2, \ldots, N$.

Example 11

A box of 100 parts is known to contain exactly 1 that is faulty. The parts are taken out one by one and tested. What is the probability that the first is the faulty part? The second is the faulty part? The *i*th? How many need to be tested in order to be 80% sure that the faulty part has been found?

Solution There is 1 "green" object (the faulty one) and a total of 100 objects. Thus if the parts are taken out one by one and tested without replacing the tested parts,

$$P(i\text{th part tested is faulty}) = \frac{1}{100}$$

regardless of the value of *i*. Suppose that *k* parts need to be tested before one can be 80% sure of finding the faulty part. Then

$$.80 = P(\text{faulty part found on 1st, 2nd, } \ldots, \text{ or } k\text{th test})$$

$$= \sum_{j=1}^{k} P(j\text{th part tested is faulty})$$

$$= k\,\frac{1}{100}$$

Therefore, $k = 80$ is the number that need to be tested. ■

PROBLEMS

3.10. In the United States, 1 in 60 white babies dies before the age of 1, while 1 in 35 nonwhite babies dies before the age of 1. According to the 1980 census, there are 188 million whites and 38 million nonwhites. Assuming that the probability that a baby is white is 188/(188 + 38), find the probabilities that **(a)** a randomly selected baby will die before the age of 1; **(b)** the baby was nonwhite given that he/she died before the age of 1.

3.11. In the United States, for individuals in the age category 15 to 24 the chance that a male will die from an accident in the next year is 1/845, but the same chance for a female is 1/3664. Given an equal number of males and females in this age category, what are the probabilities that **(a)** a person in this age bracket will die from an accident in the next year; **(b)** the person was a male given that he/she died in an accident?

3.12. Of the light bulbs in the box, 10% are yellow, 30% are green, and 60% are red. Of the yellow bulbs, 1% do not work, while the percentages for green and red are 2% and 8%, respectively. What are the probabilities that **(a)** a randomly chosen bulb *will* work; **(b)** the bulb is yellow given that it did *not* work; **(c)** the bulb is green given that it did *not* work; **(d)** the bulb is red given that it did *not* work? Check that your answers to parts (b), (c), and (d) sum to 1.

3.13. One of the numbers 1, 2, or 3 is selected at random. Then a fair coin is flipped that number of times. What is the probability that the number 3 was selected given **(a)** no heads on the coin flips; **(b)** 1 head; **(c)** 2 heads; **(d)** 3 heads?

3.14. Sheryl has 2 coins. One is fair and the other has two heads. She selects one at random and flips it n times. What are the probabilities that **(a)** all n flips resulted in heads; **(b)** Sheryl selected the two-headed coin given that all n flips resulted in heads?

3.15. There are 3 coins on the table. The first is fair, the second has two heads, and the third has two tails. A coin is selected at random and flipped. It shows tails. **(a)** Before doing any computations, what is your intuitive guess as to the chance that the *other* side shows a head and hence that this is the fair coin? Now compute the probabilities **(b)** that a coin selected at random from the 3 will show a tail when flipped; **(c)** that the coin is the fair coin given that a tail showed.

3.16. Sara has 1 red and N green tags which she can distribute into 2 boxes however she wishes, but at least 1 tag must go into each box. A box is then selected at random and a tag from that box is drawn. If the tag is red, Sara wins. Assume that Sara placed j green tags in the box with the red tag ($0 \le j \le N - 1$). **(a)** In terms of j, what is the probability that Sara wins? **(b)** What value of j maximizes Sara's probability of winning? **(c)** What value of j minimizes Sara's probability of winning? **(d)** Why are these values intuitive?

3.17. Prove the boxed formula following Example 10. Do this in the following way. Imagine that the N objects are lined up at random. The probability that the ith object in the line-up is green is then G/N. (Why?) But why is this the *same* as the probability that the ith object is green if the objects are taken out one by one?

3.18. (*Continuation*) There are G green and R red objects in a box. $G + R = N$. Show directly (without using Problem 3.17) that the probability that the second object selected is green is G/N.

3.19. (*Continuation*) With G green and R red objects in a box, show directly using conditional probabilities that the probability that the third object selected is green is also G/N.

3.4 INDEPENDENCE

When a coin is flipped twice, the result of the first flip—whether a head or a tail—in no way affects the result of the second flip. In choosing a card, whether the card is an ace in no way affects what suit it is. To say that events A and B are independent intuitively means that *regardless* of whether B occurs or not, the probability that A occurs is the same. Thus

$$P(A \mid B) = P(A)$$

But this is an unsymmetric definition in the sense that it *looks* as though A and B are playing different roles: A is the conditioned-on event and B is the conditioning event. On the other hand, the definition of independence ought to be symmetric in A and B. Using the informal version above and the definition of conditional probability, these two equalities hold:

$$P(A) = P(A \mid B) = \frac{P(A \cap B)}{P(B)}$$

Now multiply through by $P(B)$ and delete the middle term in this set of two equalities:

Definition

To say that events A and B are **independent** means that

$$P(A \cap B) = P(A)P(B)$$

Example 12

Whether the 1 card dealt to you is a spade and whether it is an ace ought to be independent events. Verify this.

Solution Four cards are aces, 13 are spades, and 1 is the ace of spades. Let

$$A = \text{"card is a spade"}$$

$$B = \text{"card is an ace"}$$

Then

$$P(A)P(B) = \frac{13}{52} \cdot \frac{4}{52} = \frac{1}{52} = P(A \cap B)$$

Therefore, the definition implies that A and B are independent events. ∎

Example 13

A machine needs two components to be operating. The first will fail during the course of a week with probability .7. The second will fail during a week with probability .2. Assuming that the failures are independent, what is the chance that the machine will still be working at week's end?

Solution Let A and B be the events

$$A = \text{"first component does } not \text{ fail"}$$

$$B = \text{"second component does } not \text{ fail"}$$

Then A and B are independent events and

$$P(\text{machine lasts 1 week}) = P(A \cap B) = .3 \cdot .8 = .24 \quad ∎$$

The idea behind independence is that the two events A and B are unrelated—that the occurrence of one in no way affects whether the other will occur. There is a tendency to confuse this property with the property that A and B are disjoint. In fact, independence and disjointness are distinct and are almost never both true. Suppose that A and B are *both* disjoint *and* independent. Since $A \cap B = \emptyset$,

$$0 = P(A \cap B) = P(A)P(B)$$

Consequently, either $P(A) = 0$ or $P(B) = 0$ or both. *The only way that A and B can be both independent and disjoint is if at least one of them is impossible.*

> **Addition Rule**
>
> A and B disjoint implies that $P(A \cup B) = P(A) + P(B)$.
>
> **Product Rule**
>
> A and B independent implies that $P(A \cap B) = P(A)P(B)$.

Example 14

The chance of a thunderstorm in Tampa on any given day in August is 9/14. Assuming independence, what is the probability that there will be at least 1 thunderstorm on a weekend in August?

Solution   Let

$$A = \text{"storm on Saturday"}$$

$$B = \text{"storm on Sunday"}$$

Then

$$
\begin{aligned}
P(\text{storm sometime on the weekend}) &= P(A \cup B) \\
&= P(A) + P(B) - P(A \cap B) \\
&= P(A) + P(B) - P(A)P(B) \\
&= \frac{9}{14} + \frac{9}{14} - \frac{9}{14} \cdot \frac{9}{14} \\
&= .8724 \quad \blacksquare
\end{aligned}
$$

Intuition claims that if A and B are independent, A^c and B ought to be independent. Thus if the fact that A has occurred in no way affects the chances of whether B will occur, then certainly the fact that A has *not* occurred should also not affect the chance of B occurring.

> If A and B are independent, then so are these pairs:
>
> A^c and B A and B^c A^c and B^c

The proofs for each of the three cases are similar. We will show one. Assume that A and B are independent. Then

$$
\begin{aligned}
P(A^c \cap B) &= P(B - A \cap B) \\
&= P(B) - P(A \cap B) \\
&= P(B) - P(A)P(B) \\
&= (1 - P(A))P(B) \\
&= P(A^c)P(B)
\end{aligned}
$$

Therefore, by definition, A^c and B are independent (see Problem 3.21).

What does it mean for three events A, B, and C to be independent? What we want to say is that all possible pairs as well as the complete group of all three events should obey the product rule.

Definition

Events A, B, and C are *independent* if

$$P(A \cap B) = P(A)P(B)$$

$$P(A \cap C) = P(A)P(C)$$

$$P(B \cap C) = P(B)P(C)$$

$$P(A \cap B \cap C) = P(A)P(B)P(C)$$

One might suppose that it is enough that the product rule be satisfied for all possible *pairs* for the product rule also to hold for the triple A, B, and C. Or that perhaps the last of the foregoing product rules involving all three of the events implies the product rule for each of the pairs. But it turns out that there are examples that contradict the thought that the truth of some of the above implies the truth of any of the others (see Problem 3.28).

Example 15

A window is made with three layers of glass. In a strength test the outside layer cracks with probability .2, the inside layer with probability .3, and the middle layer with probability .15. Assuming that the three layers behave independently, what is the probability that no layer cracks? That at least one layer cracks?

Solution Let A, B, and C be these events:

$$A = \text{"outside layer cracks"}$$

$$B = \text{"middle layer cracks"}$$

$$C = \text{"inside layer cracks"}$$

Then

$$P(\text{no layer cracks}) = P(\text{outside does not crack}$$
$$\cap \text{ middle does not crack} \cap \text{inside does not crack})$$
$$= P(A^c \cap B^c \cap C^s)$$
$$= P(A^c)P(B^c)P(C^c)$$
$$= .8 \cdot .85 \cdot .7$$
$$= .4760$$

$$P(\text{at least one layer cracks}) = 1 - P(\text{no layer cracks})$$
$$= 1 - .4760$$
$$= .5240 \quad \blacksquare$$

With two independent events A and B, we asserted that A^c and B were also independent as well as the other pairs of events formed from A, B, and their complements. In fact, the same is true for three events.

Example 16

Assume that A, B, and C are independent. Prove that A^c, B, and C^c are also independent.

Solution Four equalities must be verified. The product rule holds between A^c and B for this reason: Because A, B, and C are independent, A and B obey the product rule. *Hence A and B are independent.* Therefore, as we showed above, A^c and B are independent. That is,

$$P(A^c \cap B) = P(A^c)P(B)$$

Similarly,

$$P(B \cap C^c) = P(B)P(C^c)$$

Also since A and C are independent, so are A^c and C^c. Thus

$$P(A^c \cap C^c) = P(A^c)P(C^c)$$

Finally, use the Venn diagram shown in Fig. 3.3,

$$P(A^c \cap B \cap C^c) = P(B) - P(A \cap B) - P(B \cap C) + P(A \cap B \cap C)$$
$$= P(B) - P(A)P(B) - P(B)P(C) + P(A)P(B)P(C)$$

On the other hand,

$$P(A^c)P(B)P(C^c) = (1 - P(A))P(B)(1 - P(C))$$
$$= (1 - P(A))(P(B) - P(B)P(C))$$
$$= P(B) - P(B)P(C) - P(A)P(B) + P(A)P(B)P(C)$$

Therefore,

$$P(A^c \cap B \cap C^c) = P(A^c)P(B)P(C^c) \quad \blacksquare$$

If A, B, and C are independent, so is every possible combination of A, B, C, and their complements.

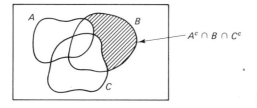

Figure 3.3

Finally, perhaps the simplest way to link the idea of *three* events being independent with the idea of *two* events being independent is this:

> A, B, and C are independent if all the pairs
>
> A and B, A and C, B and C
>
> are independent and in addition
>
> $$P(A \cap B \cap C) = P(A)P(B)P(C)$$

What about for n events? What does it mean to say that $A_1, A_2, \ldots, A_n$ are independent? The difficult step was to generalize from $n = 2$ to $n = 3$.

Definition

$A_1, A_2, \ldots, A_n$ are *independent* means:

The product rule holds for all possible pairs:
$$P(A_i \cap A_j) = P(A_i)P(A_j), \qquad \text{for } i, j \text{ distinct}$$

The product rule holds for all possible triples:
$$P(A_i \cap A_j \cap A_k) = P(A_i)P(A_j)P(A_k) \qquad \text{for } i, j, k \text{ distinct}$$

.
.
.

The product rule holds for the entire family:
$$P(A_1 \cap A_2 \cap \cdots \cap A_n) = P(A_1)P(A_2) \cdots P(A_n)$$

Almost never is the definition used to show that $A_1, \ldots, A_n$ are independent. Usually these events are *assumed* to be independent *from intuition* and then the various product rules are used to compute the required probabilities.

Example 17

Suppose that a coin has probability p of landing heads, where $0 \leq p \leq 1$. What is the probability of n heads in a row?

Solution Let

$$A_i = \text{``}i\text{th flip results in heads''}$$

Then $A_1, A_2, \ldots, A_n$ are independent, so the product rule claims that

$$
\begin{aligned}
P(n \text{ heads in a row}) &= P(A_1 \cap A_2 \cap \cdots \cap A_n) \\
&= P(A_1)P(A_2) \cdots P(A_n) \\
&= p \cdot p \cdots p \\
&= p^n \quad \blacksquare
\end{aligned}
$$

Example 18

A bank of phones consists of 5 phone booths. Each is in working condition with probability .7. What is the probability that at least one is working, assuming independence?

Solution This is similar to flipping coins except that now we say that phone i is working if, so to speak, the ith flip results in heads.

$$P(\text{none working}) = P(\text{1st not working} \cap \cdots \cap \text{5th not working})$$

$$= P(\text{1st not working}) \cdots P(\text{5th not working})$$

$$= (.3)^5$$

$$= .002430$$

Thus

$$P(at\ least\ 1\ \text{working}) = 1 - P(\text{none working})$$

$$= .99757 \quad \blacksquare$$

Just as with two and three events, it also turns out to be true that

---

If $A_1, A_2, \ldots, A_n$ are independent, each possible combination of these sets and their complements is independent as well.

PROBLEMS

3.20. Part 1 is in working order with probability .2; the probabilities that parts 2 and 3 are in working order are .3 and .6, respectively. Assuming that whether they are working are independent events, what are the probabilities that **(a)** all 3 parts are working; **(b)** no parts are working; **(c)** parts 1 and 2 are working, but part 3 is not; **(d)** 2 parts are working, but the third is not; **(e)** at least 2 parts are working?

3.21. In the text we showed that if A and B are independent, so are A^c and B. Assume that A and B are independent; show that A^c and B^c are independent.

3.22. C_1 is a fair coin; C_2 has probability $p > 1/2$ of landing heads. What are the probabilities that **(a)** n flips result in n heads given C_1; **(b)** n flips result in n heads given C_2; **(c)** assuming that one of the coins is selected at random, that n flips result in n heads; **(d)** the coin is C_2 given that n flips result in n heads? **(c)** For $n = 10$, find the probability in part (d) for these values of p: $p = .51, .75, .90, 1.0$.

3.23. A coin is flipped n times, where p = probability of heads at any one flip. **(a)** What is the probability that 1 head will result in all n flips? **(b)** What is the conditional probability that the first flip resulted in heads given that there was 1 head in all n flips? **(c)** That the 1 head occurred at the jth flip?

3.24. In Example 16 we proved that independence of A, B, C implies independence of A^c, B, C^c. Now assume that A, B, C are independent. Prove that A^c, B^c, C^c are independent.

3.25. Assume that A, B, C are independent. Prove that

$$P(A \cup B \cup C) = \frac{1}{2} P(A)(P(B^c) + P(C^c)) + \frac{1}{2} P(B)(P(A^c)$$

$$+ P(C^c)) + \frac{1}{2} P(C)(P(A^c) + P(B^c)) + P(A)P(B)P(C)$$

3.26. Prove that the only events A that are independent of themselves are certain [$P(A) = 1$] or impossible [$P(A) = 0$].

3.27. Assume that A, B, C are independent. Prove that A and $B \cup C$ are independent.

3.28. Flip a fair coin twice. Let the events A, B, and C be defined A = "head on first flip," B = "head on second flip," and C = "exactly 1 head on both flips." **(a)** Show that $P(A \cap B) = P(A)P(B)$, $P(A \cap C) = P(A)P(C)$, and $P(B \cap C) = P(B)P(C)$. Thus each pair of events is independent. **(b)** Show that $P(A \cap B \cap C) \neq P(A)P(B)P(C)$, so that A, B, and C are *not* independent.

3.5 HOW MANY ARE NEEDED FOR "AT LEAST 1"?

In Example 17 we showed that the chance of n heads in a row is p^n, where p is the probability of heads at any one toss. Thus

$$P(\text{at least 1 tail in } n \text{ flips}) = 1 - p^n$$

Example 19

Oysters that produce pearls are not the same variety as those that are eaten. But the chance of finding a pearl in a pearl oyster is 1 in 12,000. What is the chance that in prying open 100 oysters, you *do not* find any pearls?

Solution Analogically, a coin is being flipped $n = 100$ times with $p = 11,999/12,000$ of heads.

$$P(\text{no pearl in 100 oysters}) = P(\text{no pearl in 1 oyster})^{100}$$

$$= \left(\frac{11,999}{12,000}\right)^{100}$$

$$= .9917 \quad \blacksquare$$

Example 20 *(Continuation)*

Through how many oysters must one search in order that the probability of finding at least 1 pearl is 1/2?

Solution The number n must satisfy

$$\frac{1}{2} \leq P(\text{at least 1 pearl in } n \text{ oysters})$$

$$= 1 - \left(\frac{11,999}{12,000}\right)^n$$

$$\left(\frac{11,999}{12,000}\right)^n \leq \frac{1}{2}$$

Thus

$$n \geqslant \frac{\ln 2}{\ln(12{,}000/11{,}999)} \cong 8317 \quad \blacksquare$$

Example 21

The chance that an adult in the United States will be interviewed in a Harris or a Gallup poll during an election year is 1/2000. Find the probability that among 4000 adults at least 1 was interviewed.

Solution

$$P(\text{at least 1 interviewed}) = 1 - P(\text{none interviewed})$$

$$= 1 - \left(\frac{1999}{2000}\right)^{4000}$$

$$= .8647 \quad \blacksquare$$

PROBLEMS

3.29. In the United States, 1 child in 2100 is autistic. What is the probability that in a town of 3000 children at least 1 is autistic?

3.30. In Example 17 of Chapter 2 we saw that 23 people are required so that the probability is about 1/2 that at least 2 have the same birthday. Now fix a specific date, January 1, say. How many people n are required so that $P(\text{at least 1 has January 1 as a birthday}) \geqslant 1/2$?

3.31. A member of the American Bowling Congress bowls a perfect 300 game with probability 1/4000. **(a)** What is the probability of at least 1 perfect game in 5000 games? **(b)** How many are needed to be 25% sure of having a perfect game?

3.32. The chance that a golfer will make a hole-in-one during one round of golf is 1/43,000. What is the probability of *no* hole-in-one if **(a)** 1000 rounds are played; **(b)** 10,000 rounds are played; **(c)** 100,000 rounds are played? **(d)** How many rounds need to be played in order that the probability of at least one hole-in-one is .90? **(e)** How many centuries will this take if one round of golf is played every day?

3.33. What is the probability of n tails in a row with a coin for which the probability of heads is p? Given a fraction α with $0 < \alpha < 1$, show that the number of flips one must perform to be α sure of obtaining at least 1 head is

$$n \cong \frac{\ln(1 - \alpha)}{\ln(1 - p)}$$

Fix p with $0 < p < 1$. Graph n as a function of α for α in the interval $0 < \alpha < 1$.

3.6 RANDOM COMMENTS AND PROBLEMS: SERIES AND PARALLEL SYSTEMS (OPTIONAL)

Consider a system consisting of n components; the ith component is operational with probability p_i and nonworking with probability $q_i = 1 - p_i$. There are two basic ways in which the components can be linked: In *series* all the components must be operational in order that the entire system is operational. In *parallel* at least one component must be operational for the entire system to be operational. Diagrammatically, these can be depicted in Fig. 3.4.

Such a system might be a machine that requires n parts. Or consider a network of roads from city A to city B. In the series system each road must be traversed to get from A to B; in the parallel system each road is a *distinct* route from A to B. By a road being nonoperational, one would mean that the road was impassable due to a flood or a traffic tie-up, for example.

Assume that the n components are independent. This means that if O_i is the event "ith component is operational," then $O_1, \ldots, O_n$ are independent events. Let us compute the probability that the entire system is operational in both series and parallel:

Series link-up:

$$P(\text{series system operational}) = P(\text{all components operational})$$
$$= P(O_1 \cap O_2 \cap \cdots \cap O_n)$$
$$= P(O_1)P(O_2) \cdots P(O_n)$$
$$= p_1 p_2 \cdots p_n$$

Parallel link-up:

$$P(\text{parallel system operational}) = P(\text{at least 1 component operational})$$
$$= 1 - P(\text{no components operational})$$
$$= 1 - P(O_1^c \cap O_2^c \cap \cdots \cap O_n^c)$$
$$= 1 - P(O_1^c P(O_2^c) \cdots P(O_n^c)$$
$$= 1 - q_1 q_2 \cdots q_n$$

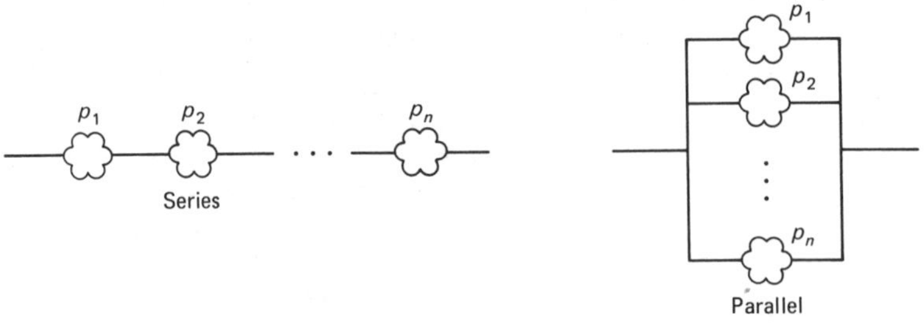

Figure 3.4

Example 22

A radio uses 4 batteries. There is a 3% chance that any 1 battery is discharged. What is the probability that the radio is working?

Solution The radio is a system with four components linked in series since all the batteries must be working. Consequently,

$$P(\text{radio working}) = (.97)^4 = .8853$$

since the probability that each component is working is $p = .97$. ■

Example 23 (*Continuation*)

Two such radios are taken on a picnic. What is the probability that at least 1 will be working?

Solution Now the system consists of two components—the 2 radios—each with $p = .8853$ of being operational. Since the 2 radios are linked in parallel (at least 1 must be working),

$$P(\text{at least 1 working at the picnic}) = 1 - (.1147)^2$$

$$= .9868$$

The system is depicted in Fig. 3.5. ■

As Example 23 shows, a system can be composed of subsystems.

Example 24

A system is configured as in Fig. 3.6 where the numbers denote the probabilities that the individual components are operational. Find the probability that the entire system is operational.

Solution There are two subsystems S_1 and S_2 where S_1 denotes the upper subsystem of two components and S_2 the lower subsystem of two components. Since S_1 consists of components in series,

$$P(S_1 \text{ operational}) = (.7)(.9) = .63$$

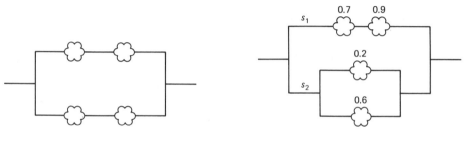

Figure 3.5   **Figure 3.6**

Similarly, since S_2 consists of two components in parallel,

$$P(S_2 \text{ operational}) = 1 - (.8)(.4) = .68$$

Since the entire system consists of the subsystems S_1 and S_2 linked in parallel,

$$P(\text{entire system operational}) = 1 - (.37)(.32) = .8816 \quad \blacksquare$$

PROBLEMS

In each of Problems 3.34 to 3.38, assume that each system is composed of identical components arranged as in the diagrams. Assume that the probability that each component is operational is .4. Find the probability that the entire system is operational.

3.34.

3.35.

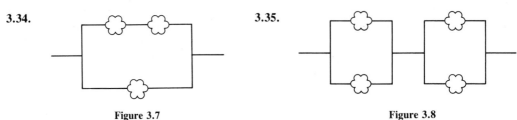

Figure 3.7

Figure 3.8

3.36.

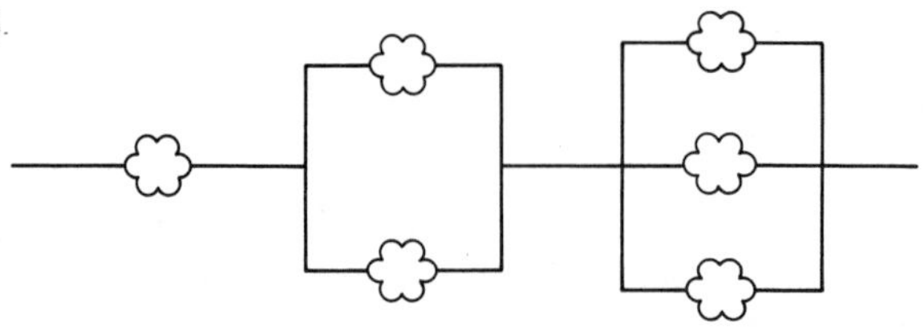

Figure 3.9

3.37.

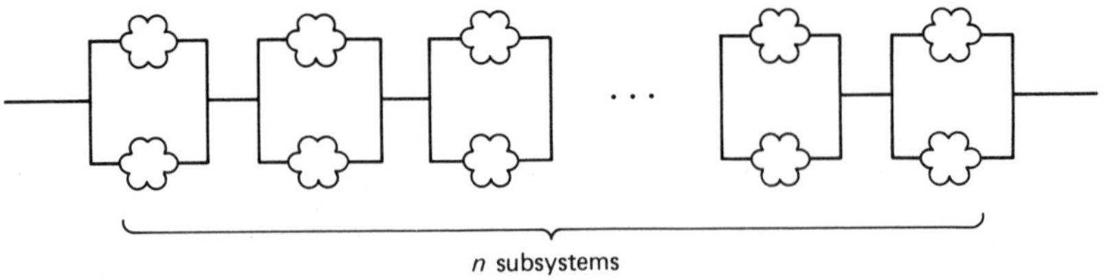

n subsystems

Figure 3.10

Conditional Probability and Independence   Chap. 3

3.38.

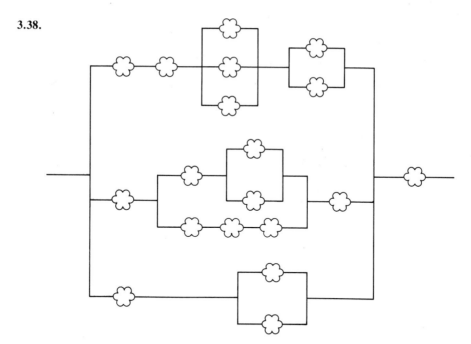

Figure 3.11

> Although men flatter themselves with their great actions,
> they are not so often the result of
> great design as of chance.
>
> *François Duc de la Rochefoucauld, 1613–1680, Reflections*

— Chapter 4

Discrete Random Variables

According to the *New American College Dictionary*, a *variable* is a "symbol which may represent any one of a given set of objects." In applications the set of objects is usually the set of real numbers *R* or some subset of *R*. A **random variable** is a symbol whose value is *a real number determined as the result of a random experiment*. For example, let the random experiment consist of observing the weather at noon. Two random variables are T = the temperature and W = wind speed. Another example: Observe a waiting line at a theater. Three random variables are N = number of people, C = number of children, and L = length of the line in meters. A random variable is *one variable* associated with the outcome of a random experiment. So the *value* of a random variable is random.

4.1 DEFINITION

Let Ω be the sample space associated with a random experiment. Then each $\omega \in \Omega$ specifies *exactly* what happened. That is, ω is an **outcome**. Thus if X is a random variable, each outcome will specify the value of X. This is to say that associated with each $\omega \in \Omega$ there is a number $X(\omega)$. But, in fact, in abstract terms this says no more or no less than the following definition:

> Let Ω be a sample space. A **random variable** X is a *function* with domain Ω and range the real numbers R or a subset of R. In symbols,
>
> $$X: \Omega \to R$$

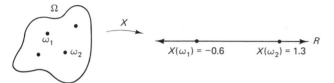

Figure 4.1 X assigns a real number to each $\omega \in \Omega$.

Always when there is a random variable X, there is an associated sample space as in Fig. 4.1. If X is the number of accidents (and hence a real number the result of a random situation), more must be known: On what highway? On what date? The specification of these is tantamount to the specification of the appropriate sample space. Although the explicit description of the sample space is often omitted, the sample space forms the background for a random variable.

Note also that a random variable is a function of the *outcomes*; it is not a function of more complicated events that are composed of more than one outcome.

Example 1

Flip a coin three times. The sample space is

$$\Omega = \{\text{HHH, HHT, HTH, THH, TTH, THT, HTT, TTT}\}$$

Let these be two random variables:

$$X = \text{number of heads} \qquad Y = (\text{number of heads}) \cdot (\text{number of tails})$$

Then

$$
\begin{array}{ll}
X(\text{HHH}) = 3 & Y(\text{HHH}) = 0 \\
X(\text{HHT}) = 2 & Y(\text{HHT}) = 2 \\
X(\text{HTH}) = 2 & Y(\text{HTH}) = 2 \\
X(\text{THH}) = 2 & Y(\text{THH}) = 2 \\
X(\text{TTH}) = 1 & Y(\text{TTH}) = 2 \\
X(\text{THT}) = 1 & Y(\text{THT}) = 2 \\
X(\text{HTT}) = 1 & Y(\text{HTT}) = 2 \\
X(\text{TTT}) = 0 & Y(\text{TTT}) = 0
\end{array}
$$

In fact, there is a relationship between these random variables:

$$Y(\omega) = X(\omega)(3 - X(\omega))$$

Why? ∎

Example 2

Let Z be the number of pairs in a hand of 5 cards. Regardless of how the deck is shuffled and whether complete randomness holds or not, Z takes on the values 0, 1, or 2 depending on the hand. In fact,

$$\Omega = \text{set of 5-card hands}$$

is too large to write down element by element; so a description of Z as in Example 1 is absurd. But *given* a hand, it is clear what the value of Z is: Simply count the number of pairs. Hence $Z: \Omega \rightarrow R$; that is, Z associates a real number with each element of Ω. ∎

Example 3

Let X be a number chosen at random from the unit interval $[0, 1] = \{t : 0 \leqslant t \leqslant 1\}$. Then instead of a finite number of values, X can assume any of an infinite number. In fact,

$$X(t) = t$$

for each t in the unit interval since the random experiment of *selecting* a specific t value means exactly that. In this case it is impossible to list all the values of X as in Example 1. ∎

When the set of values that X can assume (its *range* values, in other words) is finite or "listable" we say that the random variable is **discrete**. If the random variable X is used to *count* the number of times something occurs, the values that X can assume must be finite; even so, the *set* of possible values of X—the range of X—may still be infinite. For example, let X be the number of errors in my next computer program; then there are an *infinite* number of different values that X can take on even though each one is *finite*. The range of X is $\{0, 1, 2, \ldots\}$. Although the range of X is infinite, it is still "listable" or **countable**.* On the other hand, if L is the length of the table in meters, L can take on *any* value between 1 and 10; in this case L is "continuum" valued and its values cannot even be listed in an infinitely long list.

Example 4

Choose a random number in the unit interval $0 \leqslant x \leqslant 1$. Let X be the first digit to the right of the decimal point. Is the range of X finite, countable, or uncountable?

Solution Even though the sample space

$$\Omega = \{x : 0 \leqslant x \leqslant 1\}$$

cannot be listed even in an infinitely long list and is therefore uncountable, the *range* of X is

$$\{0, 1, 2, \ldots, 9\}$$

and so is finite. ∎

A **discrete random variable** is one whose range is finite or countable.

---

*Technically, a countable set is a set that can be placed into one-to-one correspondence with the positive integers 1, 2, 3, ...

This chapter deals with discrete random variables, Chapter 5 with the other type—continuous random variables. *Usually* (but not always), a discrete random variable is used to *count* and a continuous random variable is used to *measure*.

4.2 PROBABILITY DISTRIBUTION OF DISCRETE RANDOM VARIABLES

In dealing with a random variable, we need to know how it is distributed: how the total probability 1 is split up and distributed among all the values that X can assume. In Example 1,

$$P(X = 1) = P(\{TTH, THT, HTT\}) = \frac{3}{8}$$

In Example 2 we know from Chapter 2, Example 19, that

$$P(X = 2) = P(\text{two pair at poker}) = .04754$$

There are three ways to specify the distribution of a discrete random variable X: tables, graphs, and formulas. Which is more convenient depends on the specifics of the random variable. But the idea in all three is to specify just how a specific probability $P(X = x)$ is associated with each range value x.

Example 5

Consider the random variable X of Example 1. Then two tables summarize the distribution.

Outcome	HHH	HHT	HTH	THH	TTH	THT	HTT	TTT
X	3	2	2	2	1	1	1	0
Probability	1/8	1/8	1/8	1/8	1/8	1/8	1/8	1/8

Another table is obtained by using the range values as the labels:

X	0	1	2	3
Probability	1/8	3/8	3/8	1/8

The second table amounts to collapsing those categories in the first table which yield the same value of the random variable. ∎

Example 6

Suppose that there are 100 soup cans on the shelf, among which 6 have missing labels. Grab 10 and let N be the random variable whose value is the number of cans with missing labels. What is the distribution of N? What is $P(N < 2)$?

Solution   The event $\{N = j\}$ is the event that j cans have missing labels and $10 - j$ do not.   Hence

$$P(N = j) = \frac{\binom{6}{j}\binom{94}{10-j}}{\binom{100}{10}}$$

for $j = 0, 1, 2, \ldots , 6$.   This is to express the distribution of N as a *formula*. Computing these binomial coefficients, we can convert the formula to a table as

N	0	1	2	3	4	5	6
Probability	.5223	.3687	.0965	.0118	.0007	.0000	.0000

[Note that the range of N is $\{0, 1, 2, 3, 4, 5, 6\}$.   (Why?)] Hence

$$P(N < 2) = P(N = 0) + P(N = 1)$$
$$= .8910$$

Note also that to four decimal places the last two entries in the table can be deleted from the range of N.   ■

Example 7 *(Continuation)*

Let N be as in Example 6 and assume that random variable M is defined as a function of N by

$$M = 3N^2 + 2$$

That is, for each sample point ω, $M(\omega) = 3N(\omega)^2 + 2$.   Then the probability table for M can be obtained easily from the table for N:

M	2	5	14	29	50
Probability	.5223	.3687	.0965	.0118	.0007

■

Example 8

Suppose that X is the number of heads on 3 flips of a fair coin and W is the waiting time until the first head (or 0 if all 3 flips are tails).   What is the distribution of the sum $Z = X + W$?

Solution   Let us construct a probability table listing all the sample points in Ω and the corresponding values of the two random variables X and W; below these it is easy enough to write their sum $Z = X + W$.

Outcome	HHH	HHT	HTH	THH	TTH	THT	HTT	TTT
X	3	2	2	2	1	1	1	0
W	1	1	1	2	3	2	1	0
$Z = X + W$	4	3	3	4	4	3	2	0
Probability	1/8	1/8	1/8	1/8	1/8	1/8	1/8	1/8

Hence the table for just $Z = X + W$ is

Z	0	2	3	4
Probability	1/8	1/8	3/8	3/8

■

Before leaving this section we emphasize that corresponding to a random variable are *two* probability tables. The *first type* begins with the sample points ω in Ω; these are listed as the first row; in another row are listed the *values* of the random variable corresponding to each sample point; in the last row are the probabilities of the sample points. For the random variable Z in Example 8, here is the first type of probability table:

Outcome	HHH	HHT	HTH	THH	TTH	THT	HTT	TTT
Z	4	3	3	4	4	3	2	0
Probability	1/8	1/8	1/8	1/8	1/8	1/8	1/8	1/8

Usually, the first type of table is easier to construct—the **sample point table**, whose first row consists of the sample points; but for computations the second type of table is usually easier to use—the **range value table**, whose first row consists of the range values.

PROBLEMS

For each of Problems 4.1 to 4.5, what is the sample space and the range of the random variable? Construct two probability tables, one with the sample points as the first row, the values of the random variable as the second row, and the probabilities as the third row. The second table should have the values of the random variable as the first row and the probabilities as the second row.

4.1. Roll a fair die twice. X is the number of 2's.
4.2. Roll a fair die twice. Y is the sum of the two results.

4.3. Roll a fair die twice. Z is 0 if the maximum of the two is larger than 4; otherwise, Z is 2.

4.4. X is the maximum number of consecutive H's in 3 flips of a fair coin. [For example, X(HHT) = 2, X(HTH) = 1.]

4.5. A box contains 3 red and 2 green socks. Choose 2 and set X equal to the number of red socks. Note that there are 10 sample points.

4.6. With X as in Problem 4.1 and Y as in Problem 4.2, construct the probability tables for **(a)** $U = X + Y$; **(b)** $V = X^2 - 3 \cdot Y$.

4.7. Suppose that a box contains 2 blue, 2 red, and 1 yellow light bulb. Select 3 and set X = number of red, Y = number of blue. Construct a probability table with the sample points as the first row, the values of X and Y as the second and third rows, and the probabilities (all equal to 1/10) as the last row. Use this table to construct the table for $Z = X + Y$ in which just the values of Z occur as the first row and the probabilities as the second row.

4.3 THE BERNOULLI, GEOMETRIC, AND BINOMIAL DISTRIBUTIONS

All three of the distributions named in the heading above arise out of similar situations. Consider a sequence of experiments performed one after another; each experiment can have one of two possible outcomes. These are labeled: success or failure, on or off, head or tail, this or that, 0 or 1, and so on, depending on the context—the particular interpretation to be applied to the result. The central features are that

1. Each of the individual experiments or trials is independent of the others in the succession.

2. The probabilities of each possible outcome remain the same from one trial to the next.

For example, in coin flipping, *each* flip is a separate trial which can result in only two possible outcomes, whose probabilities remain constant regardless of the actual results of past flips. Each such trial is called a **Bernoulli trial**. Let

$$p = P(\text{success on one trial})$$

$$q = 1 - p = P(\text{failure on one trial})$$

where p is a constant with

$$0 \leq p \leq 1$$

The simplest random variable associated with such a succession of trials is this one: Perform one trial; let

$$X = \begin{cases} 1 & \text{trial resulted in success} \\ 0 & \text{trial resulted in failure} \end{cases}$$

The random variable X takes on only two values; its distribution is

$$P(X = 1) = p \qquad P(X = 0) = q$$

X	0	1
Probability	q	p

Such a random variable is called a **Bernoulli random variable** and there is not much to say about it that has not already been said, so let's move on.

Consider performing a succession of Bernoulli trials *until the first success*. The sample space is

$$\Omega = \{S,\ FS,\ FFS,\ FFFS,\ \ldots,\ FFFFF\ldots\}$$

where the sample point

$$F \underset{j}{\cdots} FS = \text{``}j \text{ failures before the first success''}$$

Note that the last sample point is

$$FFFFF\cdots = \text{``no success in infinitely many trials''}$$

It will turn out that this possibility has 0 probability of occurring and so can be ignored—dropped from the sample space. If W is the random variable that is equal to the **waiting time until the first success**, then

$$W(F \underset{j-1 \text{ F's}}{\cdots} FS) = j$$

for $j = 1, 2, 3, \ldots$. Since the trials are independent, the product rule can be applied to find the probability that $W = j$:

The Geometric Distribution

If W is the *waiting time for the first success* (the number of the trial on which the first success appeared), then

$$P(W = j) = q^{j-1} \cdot p$$

for $j = 1, 2, 3, \ldots$.

Computing probabilities involving the waiting time W often requires sums of terms $q^{j-1} \cdot p$. For completeness, let us review quickly two useful formulas:

Review of Geometric Series

Let α be a number in the interval

$$-1 < \alpha < +1$$

Then

$$1 + \alpha + \alpha^2 + \cdots = \sum_{i=0}^{\infty} \alpha^i = \frac{1}{1 - \alpha}$$

The series with finitely many terms is also valid for all $\alpha \neq 1$:

$$1 + \alpha + \alpha^2 + \cdots + \alpha^n = \sum_{i=0}^{n} \alpha^i = \frac{1 - \alpha^{n+1}}{1 - \alpha}$$

α is called the **ratio** of the series.

Problem 4.20 asks you to prove these formulas.

Example 9

Compute

(a) $2/25 - 2/125 + 2/625 - \cdots$

(b) $14 - 7 + 3.5 - 1.75 + \cdots$

Solution The trick is to write each of these as a geometric series:

$$(a) \quad \frac{2}{25} - \frac{2}{125} + \frac{2}{625} - \cdots = \frac{2}{25}\left(1 + \frac{1}{-5} + \frac{1}{(-5)^2} - \cdots\right)$$

$$= \frac{2}{25} \cdot \frac{1}{1 - (1/-5)}$$

$$= \frac{1}{15}$$

$$(b) \quad 14 - 7 + 3.5 - 1.75 + \cdots = 14\left(1 - \frac{1}{2} + \frac{1}{4} - \frac{1}{8} + \cdots\right)$$

$$= 14 \cdot \frac{1}{1 - (-1/2)}$$

$$= \frac{28}{3} \quad \blacksquare$$

Sometimes it is important to know the probability with which a geometrically distributed random variable *exceeds* a certain value:

$$P(W > j) = q^j$$

Here are two ways to prove this:

1. *Arguing intuitively*, we note that

$$P(W > j) = P(\text{1st success } after \text{ trial number } j)$$
$$= P(j \text{ failures in succession})$$
$$= q^j$$

where the last line follows from the independence of the j trials.

2. *Arguing from series*, we compute

$$P(W > j) = 1 - P(W \leq j)$$
$$= 1 - [P(W = 1) + P(W = 2) + \cdots + P(W = j)]$$
$$= 1 - [p + qp + q^2 p + \cdots + q^{j-1}p]$$
$$= 1 - p[1 + q + \cdots + q^{j-1}]$$
$$= 1 - p \cdot \frac{1 - q^j}{1 - q}$$
$$= 1 - (1 - q^j)$$
$$= q^j$$

Note also in passing that the chance of infinitely many tails in a row without a head ever appearing is

$$P(W = \infty) = q^\infty = 0$$

for $q < 1$.

Example 10

The probability of a thunderstorm in Tampa, Florida, on any given day in July is .7. Assume that whether there is a storm on one day is independent of the weather on other days. What is the probability that there will be a thunderstorm in the first week of July? That there will be no storm in July? How many days do we have to wait in order to be 95% sure of having at least one storm by that day?

Solution W is the waiting time until a storm.

$$p = .7 \quad q = .3$$
$$P(W = j) = (.3)^{j-1}(.7)$$
$$P(\text{storm during first week}) = P(w \leq 7)$$
$$= 1 - (.3)^7$$
$$= .9997813$$
$$P(\text{no storm in July}) = P(W > 31)$$
$$= (.3)^{31}$$
$$= 6.177 \times 10^{-17}$$

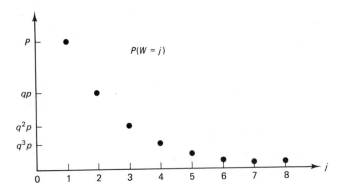

Figure 4.2 The geometric distribution.

To find that day j so that the probability is at least .95 of a storm by that day, solve

$$.95 \leq P(W \leq j)$$

$$.05 \geq P(W > j) = q^j = (.3)^j$$

$$j \cdot \ln (.3) \leq \ln (.05)$$

$$j \geq \ln \frac{(.05)}{\ln (.3)} = 2.488$$

Just 3 days! (Why did the inequality reverse direction between the second-to-last and the last lines?) ∎

Note how the probabilities $P(W = j) = q^{j-1}p$ approach 0 in Fig. 4.2. Each probability is just q times the preceding one:

Example 11

Use series to verify that

$$\sum_{j=1}^{\infty} P(W = j) = 1$$

Solution

$$\sum_{j=1}^{\infty} P(W = j) = p + qp + q^2p + \cdots$$

$$= p(1 + q + q^2 + \cdots)$$

$$= p\frac{1}{1 - q}$$

$$= 1 \quad ∎$$

There is a remarkable property associated with the geometric distribution. It is called the **lack of memory** or **lack of aging property**. *Given* the fact that no head has appeared in the first j flips of a coin, the probability that a head will

Discrete Random Variables   Chap. 4

appear at the next flip is *still p*. As long as p remains constant, independence of the flips implies that in predicting whether the next flip will be a head, the *entire past history* of the coin is irrelevant. This is intuitively clear, but let us see how the formulas also prove it. Suppose that W is geometrically distributed; let j be a positive integer. Then

$$P(\text{success at trial } j + 1 \mid \text{no success on first } j \text{ trials})$$

$$= P(W = j + 1 \mid W > j)$$

$$= \frac{P(W = j + 1 \text{ and } W > j)}{P(W > j)}$$

$$= \frac{P(W = j + 1)}{P(W > j)}$$

$$= \frac{q^j p}{q^j}$$

$$= p$$

where the definition of conditional probability was used to obtain the second equality. The third equality holds since the event $\{W = j + 1 \text{ and } W > j\}$ is the same as the event $\{W = j + 1\}$.

The converse also holds. Suppose that W is a random variable with range $\{1, 2, 3, \ldots\}$. If there is a constant p so that

$$P(W = j + 1 \mid W > j) = p$$

independent of j, Problem 4.18 asks you to show that W is geometrically distributed. Thus W can be interpreted as the waiting time until the first success in a succession of Bernoulli trials. The lack of memory property is the starting point for the development of several models considered in the following chapters.

Example 12

In the past year there were 30 days on which accidents occurred along a certain stretch of highway. Assume that the probability that an accident occurs on any one day is 30/365 and that each day is independent of the others. What is the probability that there will be no accidents during the first 2 weeks of January?

Solution Label the result "accident on jth day" as "success at jth trial." Thus each day corresponds to one Bernoulli trial. The waiting time until an accident is therefore geometrically distributed with $p = 30/365$; thus

$$P(\text{no accident during first 2 weeks of January})$$

$$= P(W > 14)$$

$$= \left(1 - \frac{30}{365}\right)^{14}$$

$$= .3010$$

(Can you think of reasons why p might vary from day to day or why the days might not be independent of each other so that the geometric distribution model is only approximate?) ■

Now consider another random variable defined by a succession of Bernoulli trials. Suppose that a fixed number n of trials is performed. Let X be *the number of successes in all n trials*. Then X has

$$\{0, 1, 2, \ldots, n\}$$

as range. The sample space is

$$\Omega = \text{set of } n\text{-long sequences of } S\text{'s and } F\text{'s}$$

For example, the outcome

$$SSF \cdots F$$

represents the successive results success, success, failure, . . . , failure. Suppose that ω is such an n-long sequence. If there are j S's and therefore $n - j$ F's in ω, then by independence

$$P(\omega) = p^j q^{n-j}$$

Each n-long sequence that satisfies the event

$$\{X = j\} = \text{set of } n\text{-long sequences with exactly } j \text{ } S\text{'s}$$

thus has probability $p^j \cdot q^{n-j}$. How many of these sequences are there? As many as there are ways to distribute j S's among n places—each place corresponding to a success. That is, from the set of n places—each place corresponding to one of the n trials—j must be selected as the places for the successes. Using combinatorial reasoning, the number of ways to select j places from among n is the number of subsets of size j from a set of size n; this is $\binom{n}{j}$. Hence the event $\{X = j\}$ has $\binom{n}{j}$ sample points in it, *each* with probability $p^j q^{n-j}$.

The Binomial Distribution

If X is the number of successes in n Bernoulli trials, then

$$P(X = j) = \binom{n}{j} p^j q^{n-j}$$

for $j = 0, 1, \ldots, n$. The binomial probabilities will be denoted by $B(j, n, p)$ or, more simply, just by $B(j)$.

Example 13

One cookie in 5 is broken. If 20 are grabbed, what are (a) $P(4 \text{ broken})$, (b) $P(\text{at most 2 broken})$, and (c) $P(\text{at least 4 broken})$?

Solution The situation is analogous to a succession of Bernoulli trials, with a broken cookie corresponding to a success. Let X be the number of broken cookies. Hence $p = 1/5$, $q = 1 - p = 4/5$, and $n = 20$. Consequently,

(a) $P(4 \text{ broken}) = P(X = 4) = \binom{20}{4} \cdot .2^4 \cdot .8^{16} = .2182$

(b) $P(\text{at most } 2 \text{ broken}) = P(X = 0 \text{ or } 1 \text{ or } 2)$

$$= \binom{20}{0} \cdot .2^0 \cdot .8^{20} + \binom{20}{1} \cdot .2^1 \cdot .8^{19} + \binom{20}{2} \cdot .2^2 \cdot .8^{18}$$

$$= .8^{18}(.8^2 + 20 \cdot .2 \cdot .8 + 190 \cdot .2^2)$$

$$= .2061$$

(c) $P(\text{at least } 4 \text{ broken}) = 1 - P(X < 4)$

$$= 1 - (P(X = 0) + P(X = 1) + P(X = 2) + P(X = 3))$$

$$= 1 - .8^{17}(.8^3 + 20 \cdot .2 \cdot .8^2 + 190 \cdot .2^2 \cdot .8 + 1140 \cdot .2^3)$$

$$= .5886 \quad \blacksquare$$

Example 14

Of all boards bought at the local lumberyard, 10% are found to be warped, twisted, or otherwise unusable. If 40 boards are bought, what is the chance that at least 38 will be usable?

Solution Each of the 40 boards constitute one Bernoulli trial; each is a success with probability $p = .9$, $q = .1$. With X equal to the number of usable boards,

$$P(X \geqslant 38) = \sum_{j=38}^{40} \binom{40}{j}(.9)^j(.1)^{40-j}$$

$$= (.9)^{38}\left[\binom{40}{38}(.1)^2 + \binom{40}{39}(.9)(.1) + \binom{40}{40}(.9)^2\right]$$

$$= .2228 \quad \blacksquare$$

Example 15

Verify that the sum

$$\sum_{j=0}^{n} P(X = j) = 1$$

for binomially distributed X.

Solution This is by the binomial formula (see Section 2.4):

$$\sum_{j=0}^{n} P(X = j) = \sum_{j=0}^{n} \binom{n}{j}p^j q^{n-j} = (p + q)^n = 1^n = 1 \quad \blacksquare$$

Example 16

A book of 200 pages has 143 typographical errors. Assume that each page has 4000 characters (including blanks). What is the probability that the first page has no typos? Fewer than 3 typos?

Solution Each character is a Bernoulli trial. To examine the first page means that $n = 4000$ trials are performed. With success corresponding to a typo,

$$p = \frac{143}{200 \cdot 4000}$$

which is the chance that *any one character is a typo*. With $X = \#(\text{typos on page } 1)$, X is binomially distributed $n = 4000$, $p = 143/800,000$. Hence

$$P(\text{first page has no typos}) = P(X = 0)$$

$$= \left(1 - \frac{143}{800,000}\right)^{4000}$$

$$= .4892$$

$$P(\text{first page has fewer than 3 typos}) = P(X = 0 \text{ or } 1 \text{ or } 2)$$

$$= \sum_{j=0}^{2} \binom{4000}{j} \left(\frac{143}{800,000}\right)^{j} \left(1 - \frac{143}{800,000}\right)^{4000-j}$$

$$= .9640 \quad \blacksquare$$

Example 17

Write a program that can input n and p; output should be a listing of the binomial probabilities $B(j)$ for $j = 0, 1, \ldots, n$.

Solution The binomial coefficients satisfy this recursion relation derived before Example 12 in Chapter 2:

$$\binom{n}{j} = \frac{n - j + 1}{j} \binom{n}{j-1}$$

Therefore, the binomial probabilities satisfy

$$B(j) = \binom{n}{j} p^j q^{n-j}$$

$$= \frac{n - j + 1}{j} \binom{n}{j-1} pp^{j-1}q^{n-j+1} \frac{1}{q}$$

$$= \frac{n - j + 1}{j} \frac{p}{q} B(j - 1)$$

Consequently, the binomial probabilities can be computed recursively. Start with

$$B(0) = q^n$$

Then use the recursive relation just derived to compute $B(j)$ from the value of $B(j - 1)$ for $j = 1, 2, \ldots, n$. The complete program is

```
var J,N: integer;
    P,B: real;
    begin
        readln(N,P);
        Q: = 1 - P;
        B: = Q**N;
        for J: = 0 to N do
        begin
            if J > 0 then B: = ((N - J + 1)*P)/(J*Q)) * B;
            writeln(J,B:10:4);
        end;
    end.
```

Fig. 4.3 shows several binomial distributions; each has $n = 15$. ■

We see from the graphs that the terms $B(j)$ increase with increasing j and then decrease. In fact, the formula derived in Example 17,

$$B(j) = \frac{n - j + 1}{j} \frac{p}{q} B(j - 1) \qquad \text{for } j = 1, \ldots, n$$

implies that

$$B(j) > B(j - 1)$$

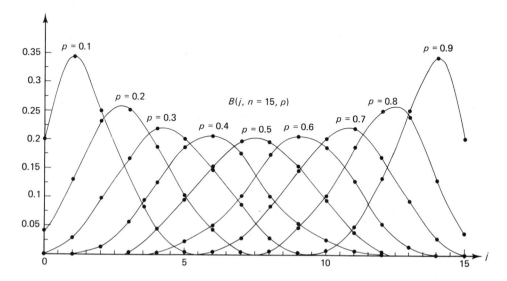

Figure 4.3 The binomial distribution; $n = 15$.

if and only if

$$\frac{n - j + 1}{j} \frac{p}{q} > 1$$

$$(n - j + 1)p > jq$$

$$np - jp + p > jq$$

$$(n + 1)p > j(p + q) = j$$

> The binomial probabilities $B(j)$ increase until
> $$j \cong (n + 1)p$$
> and thereafter decrease.

PROBLEMS

4.8. The probability that Marty will receive mail on a given day is 1/3. What are the probabilities that **(a)** Marty receives mail for the first time in the week on Thursday; **(b)** no mail is received during the week (assume a 6-day week); **(c)** no mail is received on or after Wednesday of this week?

4.9. The old printer in the computer room skips 1 character in 20 (chance of 1/20 of skipping a character). What are
(a) P(a line of 80 characters is printed without a skip);
(b) P(first skipped character is the 20th);
(c) P(at least 1 character skipped in the first 15)?

4.10. In the United States the probability that a prisoner paroled from federal prison will return to prison within 2 years is 1/3. Among 10 prisoners what are **(a)** P(3 return); **(b)** P(at least 4 return); **(c)** P(the number who return is at least 2 but not more than 4)?

4.11. The chance that a professional golfer will break par during a tournament round is 3/7. Of 4 golfers in a foursome, what are **(a)** P(2 break par); **(b)** P(at least 3 break par); **(c)** P(none break par)?

4.12. The probability of rain on any given day during December to March is 14/19 in the Fiji Islands. **(a)** What is the probability of no rain in 3 days? **(b)** How many days n do you have to wait in order to be 99.9% sure of having rain by that day?

4.13. There are 10 terminals in the computer room. At peak hours 85% of them are used; that is, the probability that any one terminal is being used is .85. Find **(a)** P(at least 1 free terminal); **(b)** P(at least 2 free terminals); **(c)** P(all terminals being used).

4.14. In the United States, the probability that a college building will have at least one fire of any kind during the course of 1 year is 2/11. Among 10 dormitories, what are **(a)** P(3 of them have a fire); **(b)** P(no fires in any of them); **(c)** P(at most 2 buildings have a fire)? Use a time span of 1 year.

4.15. Consider a succession of Bernoulli trials with $p = 1/2$. Let W be the waiting time until the first success. **(a)** Show that $P(W = j) = 1/2^j$. **(b)** Intuitively one might guess that $P(W$ is even$) = 1/2$. Show that $P(W$ is even$) = 1/4 + 1/16 + \ldots = 1/3$. **(c)** Find $P(W$ is divisible by 3$)$.

4.16. For every 10,000 miles driven, the probability that a school bus in the United States will be in at least 1 accident is 1/6. For 12 buses in the lot, what are the probabilities that **(a)** none will be in an accident; **(b)** at most 1 of the buses will have at least 1 accident; **(c)** at least 2 buses will have accidents? Assume that *each* is driven 10,000 miles.

4.17. (*Continuation*) Suppose that one bus drives 120,000 miles. Assuming independence (that is, that whether a bus was in an accident during one time period is independent of whether it was in an accident during another time period), what is the probability that it will be involved in an at least 1 accident?

4.18. In the text we showed that a geometrically distributed random variable W has the lack of memory property. Now *assume* that the range of W is $\{1, 2, 3, \ldots\}$ and that

$$P(W = j + 1 \mid W > j) = p$$

for $j = 0, 1, 2, \ldots$, where p is a constant. Show these equalities:

(a) $P(W = j) = pP(W > j - 1)$

(b) $P(W > j) = P(W > j - 1) - P(W = j)$

$\qquad = (1 - p)P(W > j - 1)$

(c) $P(W > j) = (1 - p)^j P(W > 0)$

$\qquad = (1 - p)^j$

(d) $P(W = j) = pP(W > j - 1)$

$\qquad = p(1 - p)^{j-1}$

Consequently, W is geometrically distributed.

4.19. (*Continuation*) Let W be the waiting time until the arrival of a fire alarm in the local fire station. Assume that W is rounded *up* to the correct minute so that the range of W is $\{1, 2, 3, \ldots\}$. Why should W obey the lack of memory property $P(W = j + 1 \mid W > j) = p$ independent of j? If there are an average of 3 alarms reported over a 4-hour stretch (4×60 minutes), what is $p = P($a given minute will have an alarm$)$? What are **(a)** $P($no alarms between 8:00 and 9:00$)$; **(b)** $P($at least 2 alarms between 8:00 and 10:00$)$?

4.20. Here is a proof of the geometric series formulas. Let

$$S = 1 + \alpha + \alpha^2 + \cdots + \alpha^n$$

Show that

(a) $\alpha S = \alpha + \alpha^2 + \cdots + \alpha^{n+1}$

(b) $(1 - \alpha)S = 1 - \alpha^{n+1}$

(c) $S = (1 - \alpha^{n+1})/(1 - \alpha)$ for $\alpha \neq 1$

If $-1 < \alpha < 1$, show that part (c) implies that

$$1 + \alpha + \alpha^2 + \alpha^3 + \cdots = \frac{1}{1 - \alpha}$$

Suppose that a bin contains N blocks, G of which are green and R of which are red. So $G + R = N$. Consider the random experiment of selecting n blocks. There are two procedures for doing this. First, the blocks can be sampled **with replacement**; this means that after a block is selected, its color is noted, the block is replaced into the bin, and the blocks are mixed. Thus the composition of the bin *remains the same* from selection to selection. The second way to choose them is to sample **without replacement**. This means that blocks are *not* replaced after they are selected.

Let the random variable X be *the number of green blocks chosen in n drawings*. In sampling *with* replacement the selections are independent from one to the next and

$$p = P(\text{ green block chosen }) = \frac{G}{N}$$

at any one selection trial. Consequently, X is binomially distributed in sampling with replacement.

In sampling without replacement successive selections are *not* independent; if a green block is chosen at the first draw, the composition of the bin is altered, so the probability of choosing green at the next draw is changed. Using combinatorial ideas the event $\{X = j\}$ means that among n selections, j are green and $n - j$ are red. (see Fig. 4.4) Thus j selections must be made from the G green blocks and $n - j$ must be made from the R red blocks. There are $\binom{N}{n}$ samples of size n from all N blocks. The number of ways to select j green blocks is $\binom{G}{j}$; the number of ways to choose the remaining $n - j$ blocks from the set of

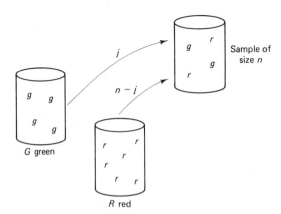

Figure 4.4 Hypergeometric sampling.

R red ones is $\binom{R}{n-j}$. Consequently, the number of ways to choose j green *and* $n - j$ red blocks is the product

$$\binom{G}{j}\binom{R}{n-j}$$

The set of values that j can assume is restricted, however. Not only must $0 \leqslant j \leqslant n$, but the number of green blocks j cannot exceed the total number G of green blocks; similarly, the number of red blocks $n - j$ cannot exceed the total number R of red blocks. Therefore,

$$j \leqslant G \quad \text{and} \quad n - j \leqslant R$$

Summarizing all these observations, we have

The Hypergeometric Distribution

X is the number of green blocks selected without replacement in a sample of size n from a bin with G green and R red blocks ($G + R = N$).

$$P(X = j) = \frac{\binom{G}{j}\binom{R}{n-j}}{\binom{N}{n}}$$

where the nonnegative integer j must satisfy the inequalities

$$j \leqslant G \qquad j \geqslant n - R \qquad j \leqslant n$$

Fortunately applications of the hypergeometric distribution are usually simpler than the boxed formula would suggest. Examples show that it is easier to remember the technique of deriving the distribution than it is to remember the formula.

Sampling without replacement requires the more complicated hypergeometric distribution; sampling with replacement requires the simpler binomial distribution. Thus it is worth noting that the *binomial probabilities approximate the hypergeometric probabilities when* $n \ll N$—that is, when the sample size is small in comparison with the total number of blocks in the bin. This is so since the composition of the bin remains *nearly* the same from one selection to the next if only a small number of blocks is removed.

Example 18

A box of 100 ornamental light bulbs contains 40 green and 60 red bulbs. Four are selected at random. Find the probability that three are red, assuming that the sampling is done (a) with replacement and (b) without replacement.

Solution   We expect both answers to be about the same since the sample size $n = 4 \ll 100 = N$.

(a) Sampling with replacement:

$$P(3 \text{ out of } 4 \text{ are red}) = \binom{4}{3}\left(\frac{60}{100}\right)^3\left(\frac{40}{100}\right)^1 = .3456$$

(b) Sampling without replacement:

$$P(3 \text{ out of } 4 \text{ are red}) = \frac{\binom{60}{3}\binom{40}{1}}{\binom{100}{4}} = .3491 \quad\blacksquare$$

PROBLEMS

4.21. Among 10 boards, 3 have large knots.   Five boards are chosen to build a bookshelf.   (a) Is sampling done with or without replacement?   (b) Let X be the number of boards with large knots.   Construct the probability table for X.

4.22. From a class of 10 boys and 15 girls prizes are randomly awarded to 3 children.   Let N be the number of boys who win prizes.   Construct the probability tables for the random variable N assuming that sampling is done (a) with replacement; (b) without replacement.

4.23. Assume that a bin has 40 green and 60 red blocks.   Four are selected at random.   Let X be the number of green blocks in the sample.   Construct the probability table for X assuming that sampling is (a) with replacement; (b) without replacement.

4.24. Let X have the hypergeometric distribution as in the boxed formula in this section.   Show that

$$P(X = j + 1) = \frac{(G - j)(n - j)}{(j + 1)(R - n + j + 1)}\, P(X = j)$$

Show that this implies that $P(X = j + 1) > P(X = j)$ if and only if

$$j < \frac{(n + 1)(G + 1)}{N + 2} - 1$$

Hence the hypergeometric probabilities first increase, then decrease, just as the binomial probabilities do.

4.25. (*Continuation*) Write a program to input values of R and G as well as the sample size n and output all the hypergeometric probabilities.   (a) After the inputs, determine the smallest value of j so that $P(X = j) > 0$.   This will be the larger of 0 and $n - R$.   (Why?) (b) For this value of j, compute $P(X = j)$.   You will have to compute the binomial coefficients in the boxed formula in this section.   (c) Compute values of $P(X = j)$ for j larger than this minimum value using the recursive formula developed in Problem 4.24.

> Expectation here is not meant in its usual sense in which "to expect" or "to hope" refers to the most favorable outcome. . . . We should understand this word here as the hope of getting the best diminished by the fear of getting the worst.
>
> *James Bernoulli, 1713*

In general, the expectation of a random variable is the single most important number associated with it. Other names for it are the mean and the average.

Let us develop the idea in the language of gambling, although it has a meaning in any context. Suppose that X is a random variable whose value is determined as the result of a random experiment. X is used to define a game as follows. The random experiment is performed, the value of X is determined, and the player receives a number of dollars equal to X. If X is negative, the player loses that number of dollars. The question is: What is a fair entrance fee to play the game? That single value is the expectation of X.

Example 19

Sheryl rolls a die and wins a number of dollars equal to the number of dots showing. What is a fair entrance fee to play the game? A die was tossed 100 times; the total number of dots showing was recorded at the end of each series of 10 tosses.

N = #(flips)	T = total #(dots)	T/N
10	39	3.9
20	67	3.35
30	95	3.167
40	139	3.475
50	178	3.56
60	213	3.55
70	250	3.571
80	280	3.5
90	310	3.444
100	343	3.43

The winnings per game T/N seems to be stabilizing to around $3\frac{1}{2}$. Thus Sheryl ought to pay \$3.50 to play *one* game for the game to be fair ∎

Suppose that x is in the range of X and that the random variable X assumes the value x with probability p_x. If a large number N of games is played, the *frequency interpretation* of probability implies that the fraction of the N games that result in x is approximately p_x. Thus the player wins \x in approximately Np_x games; this results in $x(Np_x)$ dollars won as the result of those games that had outcome x. Consequently, the player's *total* winnings over the course of all N games is approximately

$$\sum_x x(Np_x)$$

Therefore, the winnings *per game* averaged over all N games is approximately

$$\sum_x xp_x$$

Example 20

If X is the number of dots showing on a fair die, the values x can be 1, 2, . . . , or 6, each with probability 1/6.   Thus

$$\sum_x xp_x = 1 \cdot \frac{1}{6} + 2 \cdot \frac{1}{6} + 3 \cdot \frac{1}{6} + 4 \cdot \frac{1}{6} + 5 \cdot \frac{1}{6} + 6 \cdot \frac{1}{6}$$

$$= 3.5$$

in agreement with Example 19.   ■

Definition

Let X be a discrete random variable.   Then the **expectation** or **mean** of X is

$$E(X) = \sum_x xP(X = x)$$

where the sum extends over all values x in the range of X.   Other notations for $E(X)$ are μ and μ_X.

Summarizing the intuitive development, we see that if the random experiment is performed a large number of times, the frequency interpretation of probability implies that the average value of X averaged over all the experiments will be approximately $E(X)$, with the approximation tending to be better the more experiments are performed.   In gambling terminology $E(X)$ is the fair entrance fee.

Note that the number $E(X)$ is not necessarily a value that the random variable X can assume.   The *expected* number of dots showing in one flip of a die is 3.5, but one will never see 3.5 dots showing.   Nor is there necessarily a tendency for values of X close to $E(X)$ to occur with higher probability.   Again, in flipping a die, *all* the values from 1 to 6 are each taken on with equal probability.

The easiest way to remember the formula for $E(X)$ and the key idea of this section is this:

$E(X)$ is the *sum* of the *values* of X times their *probabilities*.

Example 21: *Bernoulli Random Variable*

Let

$$X = \begin{cases} 0 & \text{with probability } q \\ 1 & \text{with probability } p \end{cases}$$

What is $E(X)$?

Solution

$$E(X) = \sum_x xP(X = x) = 0 \cdot P(X = 0) + 1 \cdot P(X = 1) = p$$

That is, if the player flips a coin with probability p of heads and wins \$1 if heads and nothing if tails, the player can expect to win \$$p$. ∎

Obtaining $E(X)$ once a probability table has been constructed is a straight-forward process. One *multiplies the values times the probabilities and adds*.

Example 22

Let X be the number of heads in three flips of a coin with probability p of heads. Find $E(X)$.

Solution Corresponding to the two types of tables considered in Section 4.2, there are two ways to find the expectation.

1. *Sample space approach*. The table with the sample points as first row is

Outcome	TTT	TTH	THT	HTT	HHT	HTH	THH	HHH
X	0	1	1	1	2	2	2	3
Probability	q^3	q^2p	q^2p	q^2p	qp^2	qp^2	qp^2	p^3

The sum of the values times the probabilities is

$$\begin{aligned} E(X) &= 0 \cdot q^3 + 1 \cdot q^2p + 1 \cdot q^2p + 1 \cdot q^2p + 2 \cdot qp^2 + 2 \cdot qp^2 + 2 \cdot qp^2 + 3 \cdot p^3 \\ &= 3 \cdot q^2p + 6 \cdot qp^2 + 3 \cdot p^3 \\ &= 3p(q^2 + 2 \cdot qp + p^2) \\ &= 3p(q + p)^2 \\ &= 3p \end{aligned}$$

2. *Range value approach*. Collapsing the table above yields the other type of table for X (this is tantamount to using the fact that X is in fact binomially distributed).

X	0	1	2	3
Probability	q^3	$3q^2p$	$3qp^2$	p^3

Now the sum of the values times the probabilities is

$$0 \cdot q^3 + 1 \cdot 3q^2 p + 2 \cdot 3qp^2 + 3p^3 = 3q^2 p + 6qp^2 + 3p^3$$

which will simplify to $3p$ in the same way as above. ∎

As Example 22 shows, there are *two ways* to find $E(X)$ for a discrete random variable X. The first is by the definition

$$E(X) = \sum_x xP(X = x)$$

where the sum extends over all x in the range of X. The second uses the fact that X is a function on the sample space Ω. For any given $\omega \in \Omega$, $X(\omega)$ is the value of X; this occurs with probability $P(\omega)$. Summing the values times the probabilities yields this formula:

$$E(X) = \sum_{\omega \in \Omega} X(\omega)P(\omega)$$

We refer to this method for finding $E(X)$ as the *sample point approach* and the definition as the *range value approach*. The fact that they both result in the same number will be proved after the following example.

Example 23

Toss a fair die twice and let W be the *sum* of the two results. Find $E(W)$.

Solution Let us use the sample point approach. Now there are $6 \cdot 6 = 36$ possible outcomes, all of which have the same probability, 1/36. Consider this table, which has the result of the *first* toss along the top, the result of the *second* toss along the left, and the corresponding value of W in the cells of the table:

		First toss				
	1	2	3	4	5	6
1	2	3	4	5	6	7
2	3	4	5	6	7	8
Second toss 3	4	5	6	7	8	9
4	5	6	7	8	9	10
5	6	7	8	9	10	11
6	7	8	9	10	11	12

To compute $E(W)$ by the sample point approach, we take all the values of W in each of the 36 cells of the table, multiply them all by the probability 1/36, and add. That is, take the sum of all 36 cells and divide by 36:

$$E(W) = \frac{2 + 3 + 4 + 5 + 6 + 7 + 3 + 4 + 5 + 6 + \cdots + 7 + 8 + 9 + 10 + 11 + 12}{36}$$

$$= 7 \quad ∎$$

Proof that the Sample Point Approach Yields the Same Result as the Definition of E(X). We need to show that

$$\sum_{\omega \in \Omega} X(\omega)P(\omega) = \sum_{x} xP(X = x)$$

Partition the sample space Ω into various subsets based on the value of the random variable X. This can be done as follows. Let the range of X be $\{x_1, x_2, \ldots, x_n\}$. (A similar proof applies to the case in which the range of X is countably infinite.) The event B_i is defined as

$$B_i = \{\omega \in \Omega : X(\omega) = x_i\}$$

That is, B_i consists exactly of those sample points ω for which $X(\omega) = x_i$. Note that $B_1, \ldots, B_n$ are disjoint (why?) and for *any* ω, $X(\omega) = x_i$ for some i; so every ω is in some B_i. Consequently, $B_1, \ldots, B_n$ form a *partition* of the sample space Ω as in Fig. 4.5. Start with the sample point approach formula:

$$\sum_{\omega \in \Omega} X(\omega)P(\omega) = \sum_{i=1}^{n} \sum_{\omega \in B_i} X(\omega)P(\omega)$$

$$= \sum_{i=1}^{n} \sum_{\omega \in B_i} x_i P(\omega)$$

$$= \sum_{i=1}^{n} x_i \left(\sum_{\omega \in B_i} p(\omega) \right)$$

$$= \sum_{i=1}^{n} x_i P(B_i)$$

$$= \sum_{i=1}^{n} x_i P(X = x_i)$$

$$= \sum_{x} xP(X = x)$$

The first equality uses the fact that each $\omega \in \Omega$ is in exactly one of the partition sets B_i. Thus to sum over all $\omega \in \Omega$ is the same as summing first over all ω in each B_i and then summing these partial sums over all i. The second equality uses the fact that $X(\omega) = x_i$ for $\omega \in B_i$. The third equality interchanges multiplication

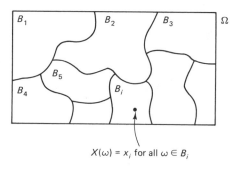

$X(\omega) = x_i$ for all $\omega \in B_i$

Figure 4.5 All ω in each B_i are assigned the same value by X.

by x_i and the sum over all $\omega \in B_i$, using the fact that x_i is constant for all ω in the same B_i. The second-to-last equality uses the definition of the event $B_i = \{\omega \in \Omega : X(\omega) = x_i\} = \{X = x_i\}$. $\blacksquare$

The proof that the sample point and the range value approaches both lead to the same value for $E(X)$ is an abstract version of the types of calculations used in Example 22.

4.6 THE EXPECTATIONS OF GEOMETRIC AND BINOMIAL RANDOM VARIABLES

Suppose that W is *geometrically distributed*. Thus W is the waiting time until the first success in a succession of Bernoulli trials and

$$P(W = j) = q^{j-1}p$$

for $j = 1, 2, \ldots$. Thus

$$E(W) = \text{sum of values times probabilities}$$

$$= \sum_{j=1}^{\infty} jq^{j-1}\, p$$

To compute this sum requires a new technique which is rather startling. Notice that the series is *almost* a geometric series—except for the factor of j in each term. But

$$j \cdot q^{j-1} = \frac{d}{dq}\, q^j$$

Consequently,

$$E(X) = \sum_{j=1}^{\infty} jq^{j-1}p$$

$$= p \sum_{j=1}^{\infty} \frac{d}{dq}\, q^j$$

$$= p \sum_{j=0}^{\infty} \frac{d}{dq}\, q^j$$

$$= p \frac{d}{dq} \left[\sum_{j=0}^{\infty} q^j \right]$$

$$= p \frac{d}{dq} \left(\frac{1}{1 - q} \right)$$

$$= p \frac{1}{(1 - q)^2}$$

$$= \frac{1}{p}$$

The third equality follows from the fact that the term when $j = 0$ is

$$\frac{d}{dq} q^0 = \frac{d}{dq} 1 = 0$$

Hence the $j = 0$ term can be included without changing the sum. The fourth equality follows from the fact that the derivative of a sum is the sum of the derivatives. You know that this is true for the derivative of *finite* number of terms. That it is also true for this series of *infinitely* many terms should be easy to accept, but in fact it is rather difficult to prove and holds only for $|q| < 1$. The fifth equality follows from the formula for the sum of a geometric series. There are two conclusions—one for the sum of a series and the other for the mean of W.

Let $-1 < x < +1$. Then

$$\sum_{j=0}^{\infty} jx^{j-1} = \frac{1}{(1-x)^2}$$

Suppose that W is geometrically distributed. Then

$$E(W) = \frac{1}{p}$$

Intuition helps to see why the waiting time until the first head is $1/p$. Note that $p = $ probability of heads on any one flip. Hence over the course of many flips, p can be interpreted as the *number of heads per flip*. Thus the reciprocal $1/p$ has the interpretation as the *number of flips per head*. That is, one would *expect* to wait a number of flips equal to $1/p$ until the first head, so the expectation of the waiting time is $1/p$. Although this intuitive reasoning is in no way valid as a *proof* that $E(X) = 1/p$, it suggests that the result is very plausible.

Example 24

Alice's third-grade class consists of 23 children. Each day the teacher chooses a child at random to clean the erasers. How long can Alice expect to wait until it is her turn, beginning from the first day of school? How long can Alice expect to wait *between* cleaning erasers? Finally, suppose that a whole month has gone by and Alice has not been selected; now how long can Alice expect to wait?

Solution Each day is represented by one Bernoulli trial. $p = 1/23$ is the probability that Alice will be selected. Since each day one of the children is selected at random, the waiting time W until Alice is selected is geometrically distributed. (W is the *day on which* Alice is first selected.) Thus

$$E(W) = \frac{1}{p} = 23$$

Once Alice is chosen, the distribution of W is also the distribution of the time until the *next* time Alice is selected. Thus

$$E(\text{time between selections}) = E(W) = 23$$

Finally, after a whole month has gone by, p is still 1/23, regardless of whether Alice was chosen or not. Thus the *expected* time until Alice is selected after the first month is still 23 days. (This is a consequence of the lack of memory property in Section 4.3.) ∎

Now consider a binomially distributed random variable X equal to the number of successes in n Bernoulli trials.

$$E(X) = \text{sum of values times probabilities}$$

$$= \sum_{j=0}^{n} jP(X = j)$$

$$= \sum_{j=0}^{n} j\binom{n}{j} p^j q^{n-j}$$

$$= \sum_{j=0}^{n} j \frac{n!}{j!(n-j)!} p^j q^{n-j}$$

$$= \sum_{j=1}^{n} \frac{n!}{(j-1)!\,(n-j)!} p^j q^{n-j}$$

$$= np \sum_{j=1}^{n} \frac{(n-1)!}{(j-1)!((n-1)-(j-1))!} p^{j-1} q^{(n-1)-(j-1)}$$

$$= np \sum_{j=1}^{n} \binom{n-1}{j-1} p^{j-1} q^{(n-1)-(j-1)}$$

$$= np \sum_{k=0}^{n-1} \binom{n-1}{k} p^k q^{(n-1)-k}$$

$$= np(p + q)^{n-1}$$

$$= np$$

The third equality uses the binomial distribution probabilities. The fifth equality is true by canceling j from $j!$, leaving $(j-1)!$, *and also* by the fact that the term for $j = 0$ is itself 0 and can therefore be deleted from the summation. The eighth equality follows by the substitution of k wherever $j - 1$ appears; hence the limits on k are from 0 to $n - 1$. The next-to-last equality uses the binomial formula and the last equality notes that $p + q = 1$.

> If X is binomially distributed n, p, then
>
> $$E(X) = np$$

Here is the intuition: If the chance is p that the coin will land heads in *one* flip, one can expect that n flips will result in n times p many heads.

4.7 INFINITE EXPECTATIONS

The interpretation of the expectation as the fair entrance fee in a gambling game can lead to paradoxes when the expectation turns out to be infinite. The following problem was proposed by John Bernoulli in 1713. Later his younger brother Daniel Bernoulli attempted solutions to the problem during his professorship in St. Petersburg (now Leningrad).

Example 25: *St. Petersburg Paradox*

Peter and Paul play the following game: A fair coin is flipped until the first head appears. If this occurs on the first flip, Paul will pay Peter $2. If the first head appears on the second flip, Paul will pay Peter $4. In general, if there are $n - 1$ tails in a row followed by a head, Paul will pay Peter 2^n. Question: What is the fair entrance fee that Peter should pay Paul to play the game?

   Solution   The fair entrance fee is just the expectation. The first head will occur on the nth flip with probability

$$q^{n-1} \cdot p = \left(\frac{1}{2}\right)^{n-1} \cdot \frac{1}{2} = \left(\frac{1}{2}\right)^n$$

Thus

$$E(\text{winnings}) = \sum_{n=1}^{\infty} 2^n \left(\frac{1}{2}\right)^n = \sum_{n=1}^{\infty} 1 = \infty$$

To be fair, Peter should pay Paul ∞ to play the game. That is, for *any* finite entrance fee Peter can expect to leave the game *ahead*. But on *any one* game Peter will win some finite number of dollars; in fact, he will win 2^n with probability $1/2^n$. The two alternatives: Peter pays Paul some finite entrance fee; then Peter can expect to win more than this. Or Peter pays Paul ∞ (if that were possible); then Peter can expect to lose since he will win some finite amount in one game.

∎

   What, finally, is the resolution of the St. Petersburg paradox? This depends on what *interpretation* is given to the entire axiomatic structure of probability theory. Mathematical models are *models* of reality; in any theory there are points of contact with the real world at which theory and reality do not quite mesh. It is precisely at these places where a deeper understanding of reality and a more sophisticated model are developed.
   Let us return to the initial intuition that led to the definition of the expectation. Consider Peter and Paul playing N games. Each time the coin is flipped until the

first head; then Paul pays Peter 2^n if the first head occurred at flip number n. Let X_i be equal to Peter's winnings at the ith game. Thus

$$A_N = \frac{X_1 + \cdots + X_N}{N}$$

is the *average* of Peter's winnings over the first N games. Now each X_i is finite and so each A_N is finite, being the average of a finite number of finite numbers. What will happen in reality is this: The sequence $A_1, A_2, A_3, \ldots$ of averages will tend to get larger and larger.Not uniformly, though. There may be many places in the sequence where $A_{N+1} < A_N$, but over the long run the terms A_N will tend to become larger and in fact in the limit

$$\lim_{N \to \infty} A_N = \infty$$

even though, to repeat, the winnings on any one game are finite.

Intuition into the paradox is perhaps lacking since N must be very large in order that A_N is large. In fact (see the book by Feller listed in the Bibliography), it can be shown that $A_N/\ln N$ tends to 1 as $N \to \infty$. But $\ln N$ is a very slowly increasing function. With $N = 100$ (100 games), $\ln N$ (and therefore A_N) will be approximately 4.6; for $N = 10,000$, $\ln N \cong 9.2$. In order that $\ln N$ (and therefore A_N) be 100, N must be $e^{100} \cong 2.7 \times 10^{43}$.

PROBLEMS

4.26. A shelf has 2 math books and 3 physics books. Two of the books are selected at random. Let X be the number of math books in the sample. Construct a probability table for X. Find $E(X)$ using the table.

4.27. (*Continuation*) Assume that 3 books are selected rather than 2. Now construct a probability table for X and find $E(X)$.

4.28. (*Continuation*) (a) Assume that 4 books are selected; what is $E(X)$? (b) What is $E(X)$ assuming that all 5 are selected?

4.29. Find the expectations of the random variables X, Y, and $Z = X + Y$ defined in Problem 4.7.

4.30. Roll a fair die twice. Let X be the result of the first flip and Y the result of the second flip. Construct a probability table for the random variable $X - Y$ and compute its expectation.

4.31. Flip 2 coins; the first has probability p_1 of heads and the second p_2 of heads. (That is, *each* coin is flipped once.) Let X be the total number of heads; thus X is 0, 1, or 2. (a) What is the sample space? Construct a probability table for X using the four sample points as first row. Show that $E(X) = p_1 + p_2$ using the sample point approach. (b) Construct a probability table for X in which the first row has the range values 0, 1, and 2 as the first row. Now compute $E(X)$ using the range value approach.

4.32. (*Continuation*) Flip 3 coins each once. Let p_i be the probability of heads for the ith coin. With X equal to the total number of heads on the three flips, show that $E(X) = p_1 + p_2 + p_3$.

4.33. In Problem 4.8, how many days can Marty expect to wait before receiving mail?

4.34. From the beginning of a new line, how many characters can the old printer in Problem 4.9 be expected to print correctly before the first character is skipped? Assuming that half a line (40 characters) has been printed correctly, from this point how many correct characters can be expected before the first character is skipped?

4.35. Among 30 prisoners in Problem 4.10, how many can be expected to return to prison within 2 years?

4.36. How many golfers in Problem 4.11 can expect to break par during one round?

4.37. A shipment consists of 100 bags of bolts; each bag has 5 bolts. The probability that *any 1 bolt* is defective is 1/13. **(a)** What is the probability that any one bag will have at least 1 defective? **(b)** How many bolts among the total of 500 bolts can be expected to be nondefective? **(c)** How many of the 100 bags can be expected to be without any defective bolts?

4.38. Suppose that a coin with probability p of heads is flipped until the first head or until there are N tails in a row, whichever occurs first. Let X be the number of the flip on which the first head occurs; if there is no head on all N flips, then set $X = N + 1$. Show that

$$X = \begin{cases} j & \text{with probability } q^{j-1}p \text{ for } j = 1, 2, \ldots, N \\ N + 1 & \text{with probability } q^N \end{cases}$$

Show that

$$E(X) = \frac{1 - q^{N+1}}{p}$$

Verify that $E(X) \to 1/p$ as $N \to \infty$ for $0 < p \leq 1$. Why is this intuitively reasonable? For fixed finite N use L'Hopital's Rule to verify that

$$E(X) = \frac{1 - q^{N+1}}{1 - q}$$

$$\to N + 1$$

as $q \to 1$. Why is this also reasonable?

4.8 THE DISTRIBUTION FUNCTION OF A DISCRETE RANDOM VARIABLE

Let X be a discrete random variable. For each real number x, $P(X \leq x)$ is a real number in the interval $[0, 1]$. Thus

$$F(x) = P(X \leq x)$$

is a *function* of the real variable x with values in $[0, 1]$. It is the *cumulative distribution function* of the random variable X because it indicates how the distribution of X "accumulates" probability as the value x of X increases. We will usually simply refer to F as the distribution function, however.

Example 26

What is the distribution function for a Bernoulli random variable?

Solution X equals 0, 1 with respective probabilities q, p. Thus $P(X \leqslant x)$ = 0 if $x < 0$; for $x \geqslant 1$, $P(X \leqslant x) = 1$; for $0 \leqslant x < 1$ $P(X \leqslant x) = P(X = 0) = q$. Thus

$$F(x) = \begin{cases} 0 & x < 0 \\ q & 0 \leqslant x < 1 \\ 1 & 1 \leqslant x \end{cases}$$

The graph of F is shown in Fig. 4.6. ■

In fact, the distribution function for a discrete random variable is always a **step function**. Suppose that the range of X is $\{x_1, \ldots, x_N\}$, where $x_1 < x_2 < \cdots < x_N$, and let $p_i = P(X = x_i)$. For any x the distribution function at x is

$$F(x) = P(X \leqslant x) = \sum P(X = x_i) = \sum p_i$$

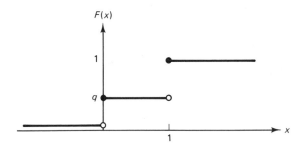

Figure 4.6 Distribution function for a Bernoulli random variable.

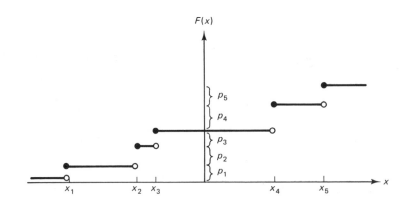

Figure 4.7 $N = 5$. The distribution function has jumps of height p_i at x_i.

Discrete Random Variables   Chap. 4

where the sum extends over all i so that $x_i \leqslant x$. F therefore has discontinuities at the points $x = x_i$ of height p_i. For $\varepsilon > 0$ so small that $x_{i-1} < x_i - \varepsilon$,

$$F(x_i - \varepsilon) = p_1 + \cdots + p_{i-1}$$

$$F(x_i) = p_1 + \cdots + p_i$$

In words, the function F is constant between x_{i-1} and x_i; F is **right continuous**, which is to say that $F(x_i)$ is the limit of $F(x)$ as x decreases to x_i. These features are reflected in Fig. 4.7.

Example 27

Graph the distribution function for the geometric distribution.

    Solution The graph is shown in Fig. 4.8. $X = j$ with probability $q^{j-1}p$ for $j = 1, 2, \ldots$ Thus the distribution function F has a jump of height $q^{j-1}p$ at j for $j = 1, 2, \ldots$. In fact, given $x \geqslant 1$, there is a unique j with $j \leqslant x < j + 1$, in which case

$$F(x) = P(X \leqslant x) = P(X \leqslant j) = 1 - P(X > j) = 1 - q^j$$

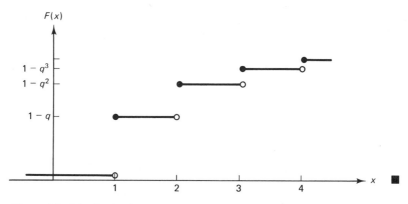

Figure 4.8 Distribution function for a geometrically distributed variable.

    The distribution function of a discrete random variable will be used in Chapter 7.

4.9 RANDOM COMMENTS AND PROBLEMS: OTHER DISCRETE DISTRIBUTIONS (OPTIONAL)

There are two other types of discrete random variables that have wide applicability but are not quite as central as the geometric, binomial, and hypergeometric. These are the multinomial and the negative binomial. We develop these through a series of problems.

    Trinomial Distribution: Consider performing a succession of independent trials each of which can have any of *three* possible outcomes. Suppose that the *i*th trial results in success (S) with probability p, failure (F) with probability q, and neither (N) with probability r, where

$$p + q + r = 1$$

The following three problems derive the probability that among n trials there will be i S's, j F's, and k N's, where $i + j + k = n$ since there are a total of n results among all n trials.

4.39. A typical sample point is an n-long sequence of S's, F's, and N's: *SSFNFN* $\cdots$ *S*. If there are i S's, j F's, and k N's in an n-long sequence ω, show that $P(\omega) = p^i q^j r^k$.

4.40. How many n-long sequences are there that have i S's, j F's, and k N's? Consider n places. How many ways are there to choose i places for the S's? From the *remaining* $n - i$ places, how many ways are there to choose j places for the F's? Use combinatorial reasoning to show that the total number of n-long sequences with i S's, j F's, and $k = n - i - j$ N's is

$$\binom{n}{i}\binom{n-i}{j} = \frac{n!}{i!j!k!}$$

(See also Problem 2.38.)

4.41. Conclude that the probability that n trials will result in i S's, j F's, and $k = n - i - j$ N's is

$$\frac{n!}{i!j!k!} p^i q^j r^k$$

4.42. Show that if $r = 0$, the result of Problem 4.41 is the binomial probability of i S's in n trials.

Multinomial Distribution: Consider performing a succession of independent trials each of which can have any of N outcomes. Each trial results in outcome j with probability p_j. Note that

$$p_1 + \cdots + p_N = 1$$

4.43. Using steps analogous to those leading to the trinomial distribution, show that in a succession of n trials

$$P(i_1 \text{ trials result in outcome 1,}$$

$$i_2 \text{ trials result in outcome 2,}$$

$$\cdots \cdots$$

$$i_N \text{ trials result in outcome } N) = \frac{n!}{i_1! \cdots i_N!} p_1^{i_1} \cdots p_N^{i_N}$$

(See also Problem 2.40.) Note that $i_1 + \cdots + i_N = n$.

Negative Binomial Distribution: The geometric distribution governs the waiting time until the *first* success in a succession of Bernoulli trials. Fix a positive integer r and let W be the waiting time until the rth success. Thus the range for W is $\{r, r + 1, r + 2, \ldots\}$. That is, $W = j$ if the rth S occurred on the jth trial; consequently, $j \geq r$. W is said to have the negative binomial distribution.

4.44. Suppose that $W = j$. Then there were $r - 1$ successes on the first $j - 1$ trials *and* the jth trial resulted in a success. Show that

$$P(W = j) = P(r - 1 \text{ S's on } j - 1 \text{ trials followed by an } S)$$

$$= P(r - 1 \text{ S's on } j - 1 \text{ trials})p$$

$$= \binom{j-1}{r-1} p^{r-1} q^{j-1-(r-1)} p$$

$$= \binom{j-1}{r-1} p^{r} q^{j-r}$$

for $j = r, r + 1, r + 2, \ldots$.

4.45. Show that W has the geometric distribution when $r = 1$.

— Chapter 5 —————————

Continuous Random Variables

This chapter is devoted to random variables whose ranges are not discrete, but are intervals of the real numbers R. Such random variables are called *continuous random variables*. Widely applicable distributions are developed, although one of the most useful—the normal distribution and the "bell-shaped curve"—is deferred to Chapter 10.

5.1 FROM DISCRETE TO CONTINUOUS: TWO MOTIVATING EXAMPLES

Example A

Each week the remote jungle station receives a shipment of supplies by parachute. Because of slight differences in how the shipment is thrown out of the plane as well as changes in the wind, the distance X from the station to the actual landing spot will vary from week to week. Suppose that records have been kept over the course of 2 years so that now the station has 104 different values of the distance X—one for each landing. A graphical method for depicting the data uses two dimensions. Count the number of X values in each tenth of a mile. Suppose that there were 17 landings within .1 mile from the station, 15 between .1 and .2 miles from the station, and so on as in Fig. 5.1. Now place bars over each interval

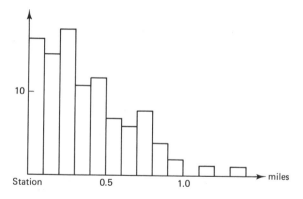

Figure 5.1

whose *height* equals the number of landings in that interval. Such a bar graph is called a **histogram**.

It is not altogether clear how many intervals should be used. We would want enough bars in the graph to reveal basic features of the data, but not so many that the graph becomes too jagged. Perhaps after another 2 years (104 more landing observations) there would be enough data to use twice as many intervals, each 1/20 of a mile wide.

Let us compute the total area of all the bars. For the 104 landings during the first 2 years, each landing resulted in a bar (or a vertical length of bar) that was 1 unit high and .1 unit wide. Thus the total area is $104 \times 1 \times .1 = 10.4$.

Suppose we are asked to find the probability that tomorrow's landing spot will be within .5 mile of the station. Examining the data, we count 45 of the 104 past landings within .5 mile; so we would estimate the probability to be $45/104 = .4327$, slightly under 1/2. We could also obtain the same answer using *areas* in the historgram. The total area to the left of .5 is $45 \times 1 \times .1 = 4.5$; the ratio of this area to the total area is $4.5/10.4 = .4327$.

In this way probabilities can be found by computing areas. To make this task easier, let us scale the heights of all the bars so that the *total area* is 1. This implies that each landing should add a height equal to h, where

$$104 \times h \times .1 = 1$$

$$h = \frac{1}{10.4}$$

If the histogram is scaled down by a factor of 1/10.4, then to find the probability that tomorrow's landing will be within m miles of the station, we would find m on the horizontal axis and compute the *area* of that part of the histogram to the *left* of m as in Fig. 5.2.

As the years go by, more landing data are added to the histograms. If there are n landings, we would decide on an interval width Δx by compromise: the histogram should reveal basic features of the distribution of landing distances, but

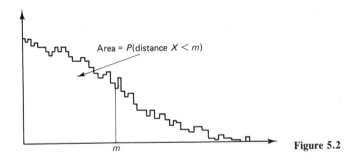

Area = P(distance $X < m$)

Figure 5.2

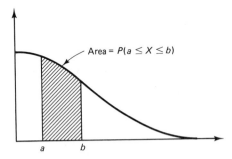

Area = $P(a \leq X \leq b)$

Figure 5.3 The limit distribution curve.

not be too jagged. To normalize the histogram so that the total area is 1, we would use a height h for each data point that satisfied

$$\text{total area} = n(\Delta x)h = 1$$

As n becomes larger and Δx smaller, it is not difficult to imagine that the tops of the bars in the histogram smooth out into a continuous curve. This limit curve would represent the ideal or theoretical distribution of the landing distance. Let X be tomorrow's unknown landing distance from the station. From the curve we could find $P(X \leq m)$ as the area to the left of m. In fact, for any two numbers $a < b$, $P(a \leq X \leq b)$ is the area under the curve between a and b as in Fig. 5.3.

Of course, it is impossible to have infinitely many landing data points, and consequently we could never completely know the exact shape of the limit curve, but as more and more data points are gathered, the limit curve would begin to emerge from the empirical data. ■

Example B

In Example A we saw how real data lead to a "distribution curve" and that areas under the curve can be interpreted as probabilities. Let us see how a theoretical model can be used to create such a curve. Consider the random experiment of looking at the clock on the wall and noting the position T of the second hand. T could be any number in the interval $(0, 60]$. Although we might be able to measure T to the closest tenth of a second, a continuously moving pointer will be at *each* value t in the interval $(0, 60]$.

Let us see how to compute $P(a < T \le b)$ for two times $a < b$ in the interval $(0, 60]$. Since we glance at the second hand at a time that is completely random during its 1-minute cycle time, we have no way to single out some times as being more likely than others. It is just as likely that T will be in the second half of the minute ($30 < T \le 60$) as in the first half of the minute ($0 < T \le 30$). If the time interval $b - a$ is 5 seconds, we can find $P(a < T \le b)$ by reasoning in this way: There are a total of twelve 5-second intervals in the minute starting at a; since there is no reason to suspect that any of these is more likely than any other, the equally likely outcome approach implies that

$$P(a < T \le b) = \frac{1}{12}$$

Similarly, if $b - a = 10$ seconds, $P(a < T \le b) = 1/6$. In general, the time interval $(a, b]$ occupies a fraction $(b - a)/60$ of the entire minute. This is the fraction of the minute that T actually points to a time in $(a, b]$. Thus we assign

$$P(a < T \le b) = \frac{b - a}{60}$$

To find a way to depict this in terms of areas as we did in Example A, consider the curve of constant height over the interval $(0, 60]$. In order that the total area be 1, the height must be 1/60. (See Fig. 5.4) Then, as in Example A,

$$P(a < T \le b) = \text{area under curve between } a \text{ and } b$$

Notice that for any particular time t_0,

$$P(T = t_0) \le P(t_0 - \varepsilon \; T \le t_0) = \frac{\varepsilon}{60}$$

for any $\varepsilon > 0$. By letting $\varepsilon \to 0$, we see that

$$P(T = t_0) = 0$$

That is, even though *some number* is chosen ($P(T \in (0, 60]) = 1$), the probability that the number is *any particular* number t_0 is 0. This may seem to be a paradox, but it can be understood by dwelling on what we can *know* about the actual time T. We might be able to measure T to the closest second, or perhaps to the closest hundredth of a second, but however we try, the actual value of T can only be measured (and hence known) to within a certain accuracy. For example, if the actual value of T is 42.60291 . . . , there is a point beyond which one can only say ". . ." The time may be there, but we can't know it exactly. The probability that the time starts with these digits is

$$P(\,42.60291 \le T < 42.60292) = \frac{.00001}{60}$$

$T = 42.60291\ldots$

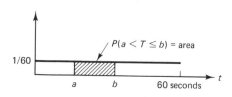

$P(a < T \le b) = $ area

$1/60$

a b 60 seconds   **Figure 5.4**

which is small, but nonzero. The fact that any particular time has zero probability of occurring really does not conflict with anything we can actually *know* about the result of the random experiment. ■

5.2 DEFINITIONS OF THE DISTRIBUTION AND DENSITY FUNCTIONS

Suppose that X is a continuous random variable. Let the function F be defined by

$$F(x) = P(X \leqslant x)$$

Since as x varies, $P(X \leqslant x)$ in general also varies, F actually is a function of the real variable x. F is called the **cummulative distribution function** (or just the **distribution function**). Notice that regardless of the particular way in which X is distributed, F must obey certain properties. First note that set inclusion holds between these events:

$$\{X \leqslant x\} \subseteq \{X \leqslant x'\}$$

whenever $x \leqslant x'$. Therefore,

$$F(x) = P(X \leqslant x) \leqslant P(X \leqslant x') = F(x')$$

Also, as $x \to \infty$, the event $\{X \leqslant x\}$ approaches the sure event since the random variable X must take on *some* finite value. Thus

$$\lim_{x \to \infty} F(x) = \lim_{x \to \infty} P(X \leqslant x) = 1$$

Finally, as $x \to -\infty$, the event $\{X \leqslant x\}$ approaches the empty set $\emptyset$ since, again, X must take on some finite value. Therefore,

$$\lim_{x \to -\infty} F(x) = 0$$

To summarize:

Definition

Given a random variable X the *distribution function* is

$$F(x) = P(X \leqslant x)$$

and satisfies:

1. As x increases, so does $F(x)$.
2. $F(x) \to 1$ as $x \to \infty$.
3. $F(x) \to 0$ as $x \to -\infty$.

The three basic properties of the distribution function F are most easily remembered graphically as in Fig. 5.5.

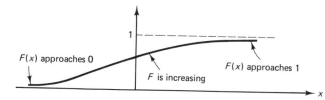

$F(x)$ approaches 0

F is increasing

$F(x)$ approaches 1

Figure 5.5 The distribution function for random variable X.

We make the assumption that F is continuous and has *a derivative except possibly at a finite number of points.* Examples of distribution functions not having a derivative at an infinite number of points are rather bizarre. Virtually all real applications of continuous random variables obey this restriction.

Definition

Let X have distribution function F; the *density function* is defined by

$$f(x) = F'(x)$$

at points where F is differentiable.

Example 1

The uniform distribution on the interval $(0, 60]$ is developed in Example B. For time t, the distribution function for T is

$$F(t) = P(T \leq t) = \begin{cases} 0 & t \leq 0 \\ \dfrac{t}{60} & 0 \leq t \leq 60 \\ 1 & 60 \leq t \end{cases}$$

Hence the density function is

$$f(t) = \begin{cases} 0 & t < 0 \\ \dfrac{1}{60} & 0 < t < 60 \\ 0 & 60 < t \end{cases}$$

except at points where F is not differentiable—namely, 0 and 1. Note how f has discontinuities at these points. ∎

Example 2

Suppose that X has the distribution function

$$F(x) = \begin{cases} 0 & x \leq 0 \\ \dfrac{x}{x + 1} & 0 \leq x \end{cases}$$

Find the density function and these probabilities: $P(X \leqslant 1)$, $P(X > 2)$, and $P(3 < x \leqslant 4)$.

Solution By differentiation the density function is

$$f(x) = F'(x) = \begin{cases} 0 & x < 0 \\ \dfrac{1}{(x + 1)^2} & 0 < x \end{cases}$$

Using the definition of the distribution function, we see that

$$P(X \leqslant 1) = F(1) = \frac{1}{1 + 1} = \frac{1}{2}$$

$$P(X > 2) = 1 - P(X \leqslant 2) = 1 - \frac{2}{1 + 2} = \frac{1}{3}$$

Note that the event $\{X \leqslant 4\}$ is the disjoint union

$$\{X \leqslant 4\} = \{X \leqslant 3\} \cup \{3 < X \leqslant 4\}$$

Therefore,

$$P(X \leqslant 4) = P(X \leqslant 3) + P(3 < X \leqslant 4)$$

or

$$\frac{4}{4 + 1} = \frac{3}{3 + 1} + P(3 < X \leqslant 4)$$

$$P(3 < X \leqslant 4) = \frac{4}{5} - \frac{3}{4} = \frac{1}{20}$$

Note again how the discontinuity of the density function at 0 is reflected in the abrupt change in the slope of the distribution function. (see Fig. 5.6) In fact, by definition, the slope of the distribution *is* the density. ∎

The *derivative equation* $F' = f$ can be turned into an *integration equation*:

$$F'(u) = f(u)$$

$$\int_{-\infty}^{x} F'(u)\, du = \int_{-\infty}^{x} f(u)\, du$$

$$F(x) = F(x) - F(-\infty) = \int_{-\infty}^{x} f(u)\, du$$

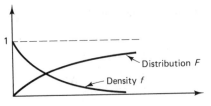

Figure 5.6

where the last equation follows since $F(-\infty) = P(X \leq -\infty) = 0$. To summarize the relationship between the distribution and density:

> 1. $F'(x) = f(x)$ except at the points where F is not differentiable.
>
> 2. $\int_{-\infty}^{x} f(u)\, du = F(x)$.

The reason the density function is important is that the distribution function only tells us probabilities of the form $P(X \leq x)$, whereas other probabilities have formulas in terms of integrals of the density. Suppose that $a < b$ are fixed real numbers.

$$P(a < X \leq b) = P(X \leq b) - P(X \leq a)$$

$$= F(b) - F(a)$$

$$= \int_{-\infty}^{b} f(u)\, du - \int_{-\infty}^{a} f(u)\, du$$

$$= \int_{a}^{b} f(u)\, du \qquad *$$

Note also that the probability that X is *any one* particular point x_0 is 0:

$$P(X = x_0) \leq P(x_0 - \varepsilon < X \leq x_0)$$

$$= \int_{x_0 - \varepsilon}^{x_0} f(u)\, du$$

$$\cong f(x_0)\varepsilon$$

$$\to 0$$

as $\varepsilon \to 0$. This implies *two facts true of all continuous random variables*:

1. All continuous models share the paradox of Example B: The chance that a *particular point* is assumed by X is 0.
2. In the formula ($*$) the two inequalities *each* can be $\leq$ or $<$ without changing the probability. For example,

$$P(a \leq X \leq b) = P(X = a) + P(a < X \leq b) = P(a < X \leq b)$$

Consequently, *we can be rather careless when dealing with the difference between $\leq$ and $<$* without changing the values of computed probabilities.

Notice also that at points where F is *not* differentiable, f cannot be assigned a value by the equation

$$f(x) = F'(x)$$

On the other hand, we *are* free to assign $f(x)$ *any value* at such a point. This is so because all meaningful probabilities or quantities that can be measured are all formulas involving *integrals* of f; and we know from calculus that the value of an integral is independent of the value of the integrand at a finite number of points. We simply assume that $f(x) = F'(x)$ at points where F' exists; at those finite number of points where F' does not exist, we assume that f is not defined.

If the probability that X resides in a union of several intervals needs to be found, it can be done in this way: Suppose that I is a finite (or even a countable) union of *disjoint* intervals

$$I = \bigcup_j I_j = \bigcup_j (a_j, b_j]$$

where by the Remark 2 above, it is immaterial whether any, some, or all of these intervals are closed or open at either boundary. Since the intervals are disjoint,

$$P(X \in I) = \sum_j P(X \in I_j) = \sum_j \int_{a_j}^{b_j} f(u)\, du$$

Since probabilities can always be found as integrals of the density function, why is the distribution function used at all? The reason is that in applications it is usually easier to find the distribution function first.

Useful Rule (But not always applicable)

To find the density function of a random variable X, first find the distribution function F and then set

$$f(x) = F'(x)$$

Example 3

A dart is thrown at a target of radius 1. The dart lands at random somewhere on the target. Find the density function of the *distance from the center X*. Also find $P(X \leqslant 1/2)$.

Solution The total area of the target is $\pi r^2 = \pi$. The location of the dart is random; so if A is an area inside the target, we assign

$$P(\text{dart in } A) = \text{proportion of the total area occupied by } A$$

$$= \frac{A}{\pi}$$

$P(\text{dart in } A)$
$= A/\pi$

Fraction area
A takes up
is $\pi x^2/\pi$

Figure 5.7 Probabilities are proportional to areas.

Let A be the circle of radius x with the same center. To say that the dart lands in A is to say that $X \leqslant x$. (see Fig. 5.7) Hence

$$F(x) = P(X \leqslant x)$$
$$= P(\text{dart in } A)$$
$$= \frac{\pi x^2}{\pi}$$
$$= x^2$$

Therefore, the density function is

$$f(x) = 2x$$

for $0 < x < 1$. And $f(x) = 0$ for x *not* between 0 and 1.

$$P\left(X \leqslant \frac{1}{2}\right) = F\left(\frac{1}{2}\right) = \left(\frac{1}{2}\right)^2 = \frac{1}{4} \quad \blacksquare$$

Finally, we summarize some of the basic facts that are obvious from the development but have yet to be made explicit:

For a continuous random variable X:

$P(X \in I) = $ area under f over the set I.

$F(b)$ is the area under the graph of f from $-\infty$ to b.

$0 \leqslant f(x) = F'(x)$ at points where F' exists.

$\displaystyle\int_{-\infty}^{\infty} f(u)\, du = 1.$

(see Fig. 5.8) The last property is true since the integral is $P(-\infty < X < \infty) = 1$; the next-to-last property is true since F is a *non-decreasing* function.

Example 4

Suppose that the density function for a random variable is

$$f(x) = \begin{cases} 0 & x < 1 \\ \dfrac{c}{x^3} & 1 < x \end{cases}$$

where c is some constant. Find c. Find $P(X \geqslant 3)$.

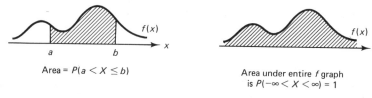

Area = $P(a < X \leqslant b)$

Area under entire f graph
is $P(-\infty < X < \infty) = 1$

Figure 5.8 Areas under the density function are probabilities.

Solution   Using the *normalization* condition that the total area under f is 1,

$$1 = \int_{-\infty}^{\infty} f(u) \, du = \int_{1}^{\infty} \frac{c}{u^3} \, du = \frac{-c}{2u^2}\Big|_{1}^{\infty} = \frac{c}{2}$$

Hence $c = 2$ and

$$P(X \geqslant 3) = \int_{3}^{\infty} \frac{2}{u^3} \, du = \frac{-1}{u^2}\Big|_{3}^{\infty} = \frac{1}{9} \quad \blacksquare$$

Note that

$$P(x < X \leqslant x + \Delta x) = \int_{x}^{x+\Delta x} f(u) \, du \cong f(x) \, \Delta x$$

Taking the limit as Δx approaches the infinitesimal dx:

$$\boxed{P(x < X \leqslant x + dx) = f(x) \, dx}$$

Geometrically, this can be seen by asking for the probability that X is between x and $x + dx$ in terms of the *area under the f curve from x to x + dx*; this is the infinitesimally thin spike of height $f(x)$ and infinitesimal width dx.   (see Fig. 5.9)

The fact that the area under the density f from a to b is $P(a < X \leqslant b)$ combined with the relation $F' = f$ implies that *the slope f of F measures the rate of increase of probability*.   (see Fig. 5.10)

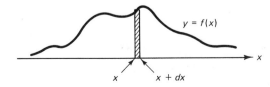

y = f(x)

Figure 5.9 $P(x < X \leq x + dx) = f(x) \, dx$.

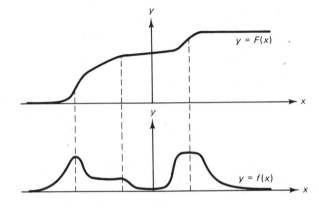

y = F(x)

y = f(x)

Figure 5.10   The density f is the rate of increase of the distribution F.

PROBLEMS

In Problem 5.1 to 5.3, the density function for a random variable X is given in terms of a constant c. Find the value of c. What is the corresponding distribution function? Sketch both the density and the distribution functions. Finally, find the probabilities.

5.1. $f(x) = \begin{cases} 0 & x < 0 \\ \dfrac{c}{(x+1)^4} & 0 < x \end{cases}$ $\longrightarrow$ to find c,

$\int_0^\infty \dfrac{c}{(x+1)^4} = 1$ Solve for c.

and $\int_0^x \dfrac{3}{(1+u)^4} du$

$F(x) = \int_0^x \dfrac{3}{(1+u)^4} du$

$3 \int_0^x \dfrac{1}{(1+u)^3} \left(\dfrac{-1}{3}\right) = -\left(\dfrac{1}{(1+x^3)} - \dfrac{1}{(1+0)^3}\right)$

$= -\left(\dfrac{1}{(1+x^3)}\right) = \dfrac{-1}{1+x^3} + 1$

$P(X > 4), \quad P(X < 2), \quad P(1 \le X < 3)$

5.2. $f(x) = \begin{cases} ce^x & x < 0 \\ ce^{-x} & 0 > x \end{cases}$

$P(X > 1), P(-3 < X \le 4), \quad P(X < -2)$

5.3. $f(x) = \begin{cases} 0 & x < -1 \quad \text{or} \quad x > 2 \\ cx^2 & -1 < x < 2 \end{cases}$

$P(X > 0), \quad P(X < 1), \quad P(0 \le X < 1)$

5.4. For each of the density functions in Fig. 5.11 sketch the distribution function.

5.5. For each of the distribution functions in Fig. 5.12 sketch the density function.

5.6. Let S be a sphere of radius R together with its interior (volume $4\pi R^3/3$). What fraction of the total volume is within distance x of the center of the sphere? Let a point be chosen at random in S and let the random variable X be the distance from the point to the center of the sphere. What is $P(X \le x)$? Find the distribution and density functions for X and graph them. Find $P(X > R/2)$ and $P(X < .8 \cdot R)$.

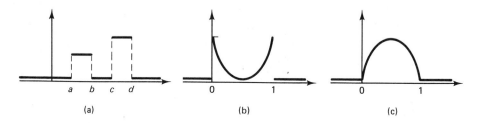

| | | |
| (a) | (b) | (c) |

Figure 5.11

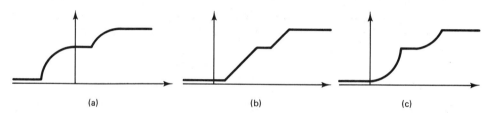

| | | |
| (a) | (b) | (c) |

Figure 5.12

5.3 THE EXPECTATION OF A CONTINUOUS RANDOM VARIABLE

In Section 4.5 the expectation of a discrete random variable was defined as the sum of the values times the probabilities. We use this *heuristic* idea to develop a formula for the expectation of a continuous random variable X with density function f. For small Δx the probability that X resides in the interval $(x, x + \Delta x]$ is

$$P(x < X \leq x + \Delta x) \cong f(x)\, \Delta x$$

since the right-hand side is the approximate area under the density curve between x and $x + \Delta x$. Now imagine the whole real line $(-\infty, \infty)$ split into intervals each of length Δx as in Fig. 5.13. If Δx is small, the value of any number in $(x, x + \Delta x]$ will be approximately x. Thus the sum of the values of X times the probabilities is approximately

$$\sum_i x_i P(x_i < X \leq x_i + \Delta x) \cong \sum_i x_i f(x_i)\, \Delta x$$

As $\Delta x \to 0$ the summation on the right should tend to an integral over all x from $-\infty$ to ∞. Thus the following definition is justified and follows from extending the idea of the expectation from the discrete to the continuous case.

Definition

Let X be a continuous random variable with density function f. Then the **expectation** of X is

$$E(X) = \int_{-\infty}^{\infty} xf(x)\, dx$$

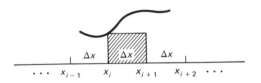

Δx Δx Δx

$\cdots\quad x_{i-1}\qquad x_i\qquad x_{i+1}\qquad x_{i+2}\quad\cdots$ **Figure 5.13**

(There are examples where the integral defining $E(X)$ is infinite. In fact, it may turn out in special cases that the integral from 0 to ∞ is $+\infty$ and the integral from $-\infty$ to 0 is $-\infty$. In this case $E(X)$ has the indeterminate form $\infty + (-\infty)$. Technically, to avoid such problems $E(X)$ is defined as in the boxed formula only under the condition that the integral converges absolutely, that is,

$$\int_{-\infty}^{\infty} |x|\, f(x)\, dx < \infty)$$

Example 5

Find the expectation of the random variable whose density is given in Example 4.

Continuous Random Variables   Chap. 5

Solution   Note that $f(x) = 0$ for $1 > x$.

$$E(X) = \int_{-\infty}^{\infty} xf(x)\,dx = \int_{1}^{\infty} x\frac{2}{x^3}\,dx = -\left.\frac{2}{x}\right|_{1}^{\infty} = 2 \quad \blacksquare$$

Example 6

Find the expected distance of the dart from the center of the target in Example 3.

Solution   Note that $f(x) \neq 0$ for $0 < x < 1$.

$$E(X) = \int_{-\infty}^{\infty} xf(x)\,dx = \int_{0}^{1} x \cdot 2x\,dx = \left.\frac{2}{3}x^3\right|_{0}^{1} = \frac{2}{3} \quad \blacksquare$$

PROBLEMS

In Problems 5.7 to 5.11, find the expectations of the random variables with the given densities.

5.7. Problem 5.3.

5.8. Problem 5.2.

5.9. $f(x) = \begin{cases} 0, & x < 0 \text{ or } \pi/2 < x \\ \cos(x), & 0 < x < \pi/2 \end{cases}$

5.10. $f(x) = \begin{cases} (n+1)x^n, & 0 < x < 1 \\ 0, & x < 0 \text{ or } 1 < x \end{cases}$

5.11. Problem 5.1.

5.12. Suppose that X is a continuous random variable concentrated on the interval $(0, \infty)$. (That is, $f(x) = 0$ for $x \leqslant 0$.) Let $G(x) = P(X > x) = 1 - F(x)$. Assume that $xG(x) \to 0$ as $x \to \infty$. Use integration by parts with $u' = 1$ and $v = G(x)$ to show that

$$E(X) = \int_{0}^{\infty} G(x)\,dx$$

Use the result of Problem 5.12 to compute the expectation in

5.13. Problem 5.9.

5.14. Problem 5.10.

5.15. Problem 5.1.

5.4 THE UNIFORM DISTRIBUTION

Let $a < b$ be two fixed real numbers.   Choose a number X at *random* from the interval $[a, b]$.   This means that each interval of length s should have the same probability of containing X.   Thus if f is the density function for X, then for $a \leqslant y \leqslant z \leqslant b$,

$$P(y < X \leqslant z) = \int_{y}^{z} f(u)\,du$$

depends only on the length $z - y$ *of the interval.* Arguing infinitesimally yields

$$P(x < X \leqslant x + dx) = f(x)\ dx$$

depends only on the length dx. Thus $f(x)$ is a constant c independent of $x \in [a, b]$. But

$$1 = \int_{-\infty}^{\infty} f(u)\ du = \int_{a}^{b} c\ du = c(b - a)$$

Hence $c = 1/(b - a)$ and

> The *uniform density function* on the interval $[a, b]$ is
>
> $$f(u) = \begin{cases} 0 & u < a \\ \dfrac{1}{b - a} & a < u < b \\ 0 & b < u \end{cases}$$
>
> The *uniform distribution function* on $[a, b]$ is
>
> $$F(x) = \begin{cases} 0 & u \leqslant a \\ \dfrac{x - a}{b - a} & a \leqslant u \leqslant b \\ & b \leqslant u \\ 1 \end{cases}$$

where the middle formula for the distribution function is obtained by straightforward integration of f from a to x for x in $[a, b]$. These functions are graphed in Fig. 5.14.

Fig. 5.15 shows a sample of 20 random numbers selected from the unit interval $[0, 1]$. (Chapter 7 considers methods for obtaining such samples by computer.) Notice that purely by randomness there tend to be clumps of more densely populated intervals. Even though each number is uniformly selected, it would be very unusual for the numbers to fill in the interval uniformly as equally spaced points.

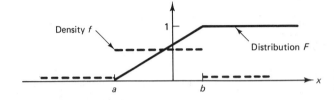

Figure 5.14 The uniform distribution and density functions.

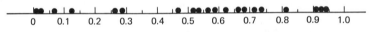

Figure 5.15

Example 7

Choose a number X at random from the interval $[0, 2]$. What is the probability that the first digit to the right of the decimal point is a 3? That the second digit is a 7?

Solution $a = 0; b = 2$. Thus the density function is $f(u) = 1/2$ for $0 < u < 2$. The events are unions.

$$\{\text{1st digit of } X \text{ to right of decimal point is 3}\}$$
$$= \{.3 \leqslant X < .4\} \cup \{1.3 \leqslant X < 1.4\}$$

This union of two intervals has probability

$$P(\text{1st digit is 3}) = \int_{.3}^{.4} \frac{1}{2} \, du + \int_{1.3}^{1.4} \frac{1}{2} \, du = .1$$

Also,

$$\{\text{2nd digit of } X \text{ to right of decimal point is 7}\}$$
$$= \{.07 \leqslant X < .08\} \cup \{.17 \leqslant X < .18\} \cup \cdots \cup \{1.97 \leqslant X < 1.98\}$$

This is a union of 20 (count 'em!) intervals *each* of length .01. The probability that X is in any one of these intervals of length .01 is the same as

$$P(.07 \leqslant X < .08) = \int_{.07}^{.08} \frac{1}{2} \, du = \frac{.01}{2} = .005$$

Hence adding 20 of these probabilities implies that

$$P(\text{2nd digit is a 7}) = 20 \cdot .005 = .1 \quad \blacksquare$$

Let X be uniformly distributed on the interval $[a, b]$. The mean of X ought to be at the midpoint $(a + b)/2$. To show this, use the definition of expectation:

$$E(X) = \int_{-\infty}^{\infty} x f(x) \, dx$$

$$= \int_{a}^{b} x \frac{1}{b - a} \, dx$$

$$= \frac{1}{b - a} \cdot \frac{1}{2} x^2 \Big|_{a}^{b}$$

$$= \frac{1}{2} \cdot \frac{b^2 - a^2}{b - a}$$

$$= \frac{b + a}{2}$$

If X is uniformly distributed on $[a, b]$, then $E(X) = \dfrac{a + b}{2}$.

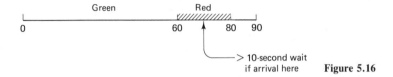

Green | Red

0   60   80   90

> 10-second wait
if arrival here   **Figure 5.16**

Example 8

The traffic light is green for 1 minute and red for 1/2 minute. What is the probability that you will arrive during a red-light phase? What is the probability that *given* that you have arrived at a red light, you will have to wait more than 10 seconds?

Solution During a complete cycle of 90 seconds, your arrival time U can be assumed to be *uniformly distributed* on $[0, 90]$. Hence the density is $f(u) = 1/90$ for $0 < u < 90$.

$$P(\text{arrival during red light}) = P(U > 60 \text{ seconds})$$

$$= \int_{60}^{90} \frac{1}{90} \, du$$

$$= \frac{1}{3}$$

which is certainly what one would expect.

$$P(\text{wait more than 10 seconds} \mid \text{arrival during red})$$

$$= P(U < 80 \text{ seconds} \mid U > 60 \text{ seconds})$$

$$= \frac{P(60 < U < 80)}{P(U > 60)}$$

$$= \frac{20/90}{30/90}$$

$$= \frac{2}{3}$$

which is also intuitive. (see Fig. 5.16)   ■

PROBLEMS

5.16. Let X be uniformly distributed on the interval $[0, 1]$. What is the density function for X? Find **(a)** $P(\text{1st digit to the right of the decimal point is a 6})$; **(b)** $P(\text{2nd digit is a 3})$; **(c)** $P(\text{2nd digit is 7} \mid \text{1st digit is 2})$; **(d)** $P(n\text{th digit is } d)$ for d a fixed digit.

5.17. Jimmy is to arrive at 7:00. Because of random traffic patterns the actual arrival time is uniformly distributed between 7:00 and 7:30. Jessica arrives to meet Jimmy at 7:15. Find **(a)** $P(\text{Jessica arrives before Jimmy})$; **(b)** $P(\text{Jessica waits less than 5 minutes})$; **(c)** $P(\text{Jessica waits less than 10 minutes} \mid \text{Jessica arrives before Jimmy})$.

5.18. Suppose that X is uniformly distributed on the interval $[0, b]$. Assume that d is a fixed number with $0 < d \leqslant b$. Let A be the event $A = \{X \leqslant d\}$. Show that X, given A, is uniformly distributed on $[0, d]$. That is, show that $P(X \leqslant t \mid X \leqslant d) = t/d$ for $0 \leqslant t \leqslant d$.

5.19. Ten customers, among whom are Stan and Marty, arrive at a store between 8:00 A.M. and noon. Each arrives according to a uniform distribution over the entire 4-hour interval. Assuming independence of arrivals of each of the customers, find **(a)** P(Stan arrives before 11:00); **(b)** P(Stan and Marty both arrive after 11:00). **(c)** Let X be the *number* of customers (among the 10) who arrive after 11:00. What is the distribution of X? Find **(d)** $P(X = 4)$; **(e)** $P(X < 3)$.

5.20. Use the result of Problem 5.12 to find $E(U)$ for U uniformly distributed on $[0, b]$.

5.5 THE EXPONENTIAL DISTRIBUTION

Let T denote the lifetime of some type of apparatus—a light bulb, perhaps, or other electrical or mechanical device. This *component* is assumed to be operational for some positive time (the random time T) after which it is burned out. We say that

> T has the **lack of memory** or **aging property** if no matter how long the component has been operational, the probability that it will last an additional time s is independent of the time it has already been burning.

To translate the lack of memory property to a mathematical statement and start the derivation of the distribution and density, let $s, t \geqslant 0$ be times. Then lack of memory implies that

$$P(T > t + s \mid T > t) = P(T > s)$$

in terms of conditional probabilities.

The lack of memory property is equivalent to the assumption that the component undergoes no aging. Given that it has lasted until time t, it behaves as though it were brand new. At first glance it would seem obvious that any real component would *not* obey the lack of aging property since there is always aging with time and greater likelihood of failure. (For many devices one would actually expect a higher likelihood of failure when it is first plugged in as it is subjected to the first surge of current; if it survives an initial period, it will probably last a long time.) On the other hand, suppose that the component fails only due to some *external* circumstance—a power surge caused by an electrical storm, for example. Then no matter how old the component is, its age has no bearing on its subsequent functioning. By "component" we mean to include more general kinds of things (or even events) than electrical devices: any object, phenomenon, or piece of equipment that has two states—on–off, alive–dead, functioning–nonfunctioning, up–down. For example, each dish in a set will break when dropped—each dish eventually "burns out," but its breakage is completely independent of its present condition. (Not totally so—very new and very old dishes will be treated with more care.) Thus we have the phenomenon of one or two dishes in a set continuing to last long after the rest have broken; each time a dish is used it is brand new as far as its breakage because of age is concerned. The lack of memory property actually does apply to any "component" whose failure is due to circumstances that cannot be determined by knowing only its internal state—its age. Thus the property is widely applicable after all.

A radioactive atom *must* have a lifetime that obeys the lack of aging property precisely because all atoms of a certain type are essentially identical; they do not encode the length of time they have existed. Atoms are too simple to age!

Nor is it only lifetimes—things "extended in time"—that can have lack of memory. For example, the distances between flaws in a length of sheet metal may have the property. Or the distances between wildflowers along a highway; or the distances between raindrops on a sidewalk square; or. . . .

Let us now derive the distribution and density of the random variable T using the Useful Rule in Section 5.2. Let

$$G(t) = P(T > t)$$

for $t \geq 0$. Then for $h \geq 0$

$$
\begin{aligned}
G(t + h) &= P(T > t + h) \\
&= P(T > t + h \quad \text{and} \quad T > t) \\
&= P(T > t + h \mid T > t)P(T > t) \\
&= P(T > h)P(T > t) \\
&= G(h)G(t)
\end{aligned}
$$

The second equality follows by the *equality* of the events

$$\{T > t + h\} = \{T > t + h \quad \text{and} \quad T > t\}$$

The third equality invokes the definition of conditional probability. The next-to-last equality *is* the lack of memory property.

Subtracting $G(t)$ from both sides, dividing by h, and letting h approach 0 yields $G'(t)$ on the left side. On the right we obtain

$$G'(t) = \lim_{h \to 0} G(t) \frac{G(h) - 1}{h}$$

$$= G(t) \lim_{h \to 0} \frac{G(h) - 1}{h}$$

Assuming that the component is not originally defective, $G(0) = P(T > 0) = 1$. (It must last for *some* positive time.) Thus

$$G'(t) = G(t) \lim_{h \to 0} \frac{G(h) - G(0)}{h}$$

$$= G(t) \cdot G'(0)$$

by definition of the derivative of $G(t)$ at $t = 0$. Thus

$$G'(t) = -\lambda G(t)$$

where we have set the constant λ equal to $-G'(0)$. [Note that $G(t) = P(T > t)$ is a *decreasing* function of $t \geqslant 0$; thus $G'(0) < 0$, so $\lambda > 0$.] The solution to this *differential equation* with initial condition $G(0) = 1$ is (see Problem 5.27)

$$G(t) = e^{-\lambda t}$$

Since $G(t) = P(X > t) = 1 - F(t)$ and since $F(t) = 0$ for $t < 0$ (why?), we know a formula for the distribution F and by differentiation a formula also for the density f. To summarize:

The *exponential density function* with parameter λ is

$$f(u) = \begin{cases} 0 & u < 0 \\ \lambda e^{-\lambda u} & 0 < u \end{cases}$$

The *exponential distribution function* is

$$F(x) = \begin{cases} 0 & x \leqslant 0 \\ 1 - e^{-\lambda x} & 0 \leqslant x \end{cases}$$

These functions are graphed in Fig. 5.17.

One final question about the model remains to be answered: What is the parameter λ? There are two useful interpretations: Let us first compute the half-life $t_{1/2}$ of the component. If there were a large number N of components, then at time $t_{1/2}$ half of them would still be operating (and the other half would have burned out). In terms of *one* component with lifetime the random variable T:

$$\frac{1}{2} = P(T > t_{1/2}) = G(t_{1/2}) = \exp\left(-\lambda t_{1/2}\right)$$

where exp is used to denote the exponential function. Take logs and solve:

$$-\lambda t_{1/2} = \ln \frac{1}{2} = -\ln 2$$

$$\lambda = \frac{\ln 2}{t_{1/2}}$$

The second interpretation for the parameter λ is also intuitive. λ is the reciprocal

Distribution F

Density f

Figure 5.17 The exponential distribution and density functions.

of the expectation. To see this, suppose that T is exponentially distributed with parameter λ. Use the definition of expectation developed in Section 5.3:

$$E(T) = \int_{-\infty}^{\infty} tf(t)\, dt$$

$$= \int_{0}^{\infty} t\lambda e^{-\lambda t}\, dt$$

$$= \frac{1}{\lambda} \int_{0}^{\infty} ue^{-u}\, du$$

$$= \frac{1}{\lambda} [-ue^{-u} - e^{-u}]_{0}^{\infty}$$

$$= \frac{1}{\lambda}$$

where the next-to-last equality follows by an integration by parts.

In evaluating the indefinite integral at the limit ∞, we used the fact that the exponential function e^u tends to ∞ faster than the function u. In general, recall the following result which follows directly from L'Hôpital's rule:

Let $P(x)$ be a polynomial. Then

$$\lim_{x \to \infty} \frac{P(x)}{e^x} = 0$$

Let T be exponentially distributed with parameter λ. Then λ has two interpretations:

1. $\lambda = \ln(2)/t_{1/2}$, where $t_{1/2}$ is the half-life.
2. $E(T) = 1/\lambda$.

Example 9

A book on reserve at the library has a checkout time that is exponentially distributed with *average* 30 minutes. If you arrive at noon and find the book checked out, what is the chance that you will have to wait less than 15 minutes?

Solution Let T denote your waiting time.

$$\lambda = \frac{1}{\text{average}} = \frac{1}{30}$$

$$P(T < 15) = 1 - e^{-15(1/30)} = 1 - e^{-1/2} \doteq .3935 \quad \blacksquare$$

Example 10

The half-life of uranium 238 is 4.5×10^9 years. Given one atom, what is the probability that it will decay within 2×10^9 years?

Solution As we saw, the lifetime is exponentially distributed.

$$\lambda = \frac{\ln 2}{4.5 \times 10^9} = 1.540 \times 10^{-10}$$

$$\begin{aligned}
P(\text{lifetime} < 2 \times 10^9) &= 1 - e^{-\lambda t} \\
&= 1 - \exp(-1.540 \times 10^{-10} \cdot 2 \times 10^9) \\
&= 1 - e^{-.3080} \\
&= .2651 \quad \blacksquare
\end{aligned}$$

Let us conclude this section by emphasizing the close connections among the various ways of thinking about the exponential distribution. As before, let T denote the lifetime and $G(t)$ the probability that the component lasts until *after* time t. Then the following are *logically equivalent*:

1. T is exponentially distributed.
2. T has the lack of memory property.
3. $G(t) = e^{-\lambda t}$.
4. $G'(t) = -\lambda G(t)$.
5. *Constant failure rate property*: $G'(t)/G(t) =$ (negative) constant.

Property 5 is certainly equivalent to Property 4. On the other hand, it has an interesting probabilistic interpretation: Note that

$$P(T > t) = P(T > t + \Delta t) + P(t < T \leq t + \Delta t)$$

$$\begin{aligned}
P(t < T \leq t + \Delta t) &= P(T > t) - P(T > t + \Delta t) \\
&= G(t) - G(t + \Delta t) \\
&\cong -G'(t)\,\Delta t
\end{aligned}$$

Therefore,

$$\begin{aligned}
P(t < T \leq t + \Delta t \mid T > t) &= \frac{P(t < T \leq t + \Delta t \ \text{ and } \ T > t)}{P(T > t)} \\
&= \frac{P(t < T \leq t + \Delta t)}{P(T > t)} \\
&\cong -\frac{G'(t)}{G(t)}\,\Delta t
\end{aligned}$$

Definition

The *failure rate* is $-G'(t)/G(t)$.   Given that the component has survived until time t, the failure rate times Δt is the approximate probability that the component will fail in the next Δt time units for small Δt.

If the failure rate decreases with time, the component becomes more reliable as it ages.   Stating that the failure rate is constant is equivalent to the lack of memory property.

For another interpretation, suppose that a large number of components are all installed at time 0.   Then the fraction of these components still operating at time t that will fail in the next Δt time units is approximately $-(G'(t)/G(t))\,\Delta t$.

PROBLEMS

5.21. Why might the distance between wildflowers along a forest path be exponentially distributed?   Assume an average of three clumps per 100 feet.   Let T be the distance from the start of the path to the first clump.   Take $E(T) = 100/3$.   Why is $\lambda = .03$? Find **(a)** $P(T \le 20)$; **(b)** $P(T > 15)$; **(c)** $P(20 \le T \le 40)$.

5.22. Why should the time T until the next accident along a highway be exponentially distributed?   Assume an average of 2 accidents every 4 weeks.   Take $E(T) = 4/2 = 2$.   Why is $\lambda = 1/2$?   Find **(a)** $P(T < 3$ weeks$)$; **(b)** $P(T \ge 2$ weeks$)$; **(c)** $P(1$ week $< T < 2$ weeks, 1 day$)$.

5.23. The half-life of oxygen 19 is 29 seconds.   **(a)** Find the parameter λ for the lifetime distribution of one atom.   Find **(b)** $P($atom lasts less than 15 seconds$)$; **(c)** $P($atom lasts at least 33 seconds$)$.   **(d)** Find a constant k so that with 95% probability the atom will decay at some time in the interval $[0, k]$.

5.24. Assume the amount of rainfall in a shower is exponentially distributed with average 1/2 inch per shower.   Find **(a)** λ; **(b)** $P(T > 3/4)$; **(c)** $P(T < 1/2 \mid T > 1/4)$; **(d)** $P(T > d \mid T > c)$ for $d > c$, where T is the amount of rain in a shower.   Show that the answer to part (d) follows from the lack of memory property also.

5.25. Let T be the amount of time a toy remains on a store shelf before being sold.   Why might T be exponentially distributed?   Assuming that it is, suppose that after a new shipment of toys, half of them are sold in 4 weeks.   **(a)** What is the parameter for T?   Find **(b)** $P(T < 6$ weeks$)$; **(c)** $P(T > 2$ months$)$; **(d)** $P(1$ month $< T \le 2$ months$)$. (Assume that a month has 30 days.)

5.26. The 3/4-life of a radioactive element is the time required for 3/4 of a sample of it to decay.   More generally, the α-life is the time for fraction α to decay for $0 < \alpha < 1$. Let t_α denote the α-life.   Find t_α as a function of α and the parameter λ.   Graph t_α as a function of α for fixed λ.

5.27. Solve this differential equation used in the derivation of the exponential distribution:

$$G'(t) = -\lambda G(t)$$

$$G(0) = 1$$

by rewriting the differential equation as

$$\frac{dG}{G} = -\lambda\, dt$$

and integrating. Use the initial condition to evaluate the constant of integration.

5.28. Use the result of Problem 5.12 to compute the expectation of an exponentially distributed random variable.

5.6 MODELS WITH AGING (OPTIONAL)

Let T denote the time of failure of a component. In Section 5.5 we showed that a useful definition of failure rate is

$$\phi/(t) = \frac{-G'(t)}{G(t)}$$

where $G(t) = P(T > t)$. The main conclusion of that section was that *T has a constant failure rate if and only if T is exponentially distributed.* In this section more general models are developed.

Rewrite the equation above and integrate to obtain

$$\frac{dG}{dt} = -\phi(t)G(t)$$

$$\frac{dG}{G} = -\phi/(t)\, dt$$

$$\ln\,(G(s)) - \ln\,(G(0)) = -\int_0^s \phi/(t)\, dt$$

But $G(0) = P(T > 0) = 1$. Hence

$$\ln G(s) = -\int_0^s \phi(t)\, dt$$

Take the exponential of both sides to obtain:

> If the failure rate is the function $\phi(t)$, then
>
> $$P(T > t) = G(t) = \exp\left[-\int_0^t \phi(u)\, du\right]$$

Example 11

Suppose that the failure rate increases at a rate proportional to the age. Find and graph $P(T > t) = G(t)$.

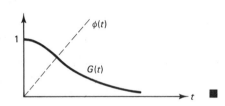

Figure 5.18

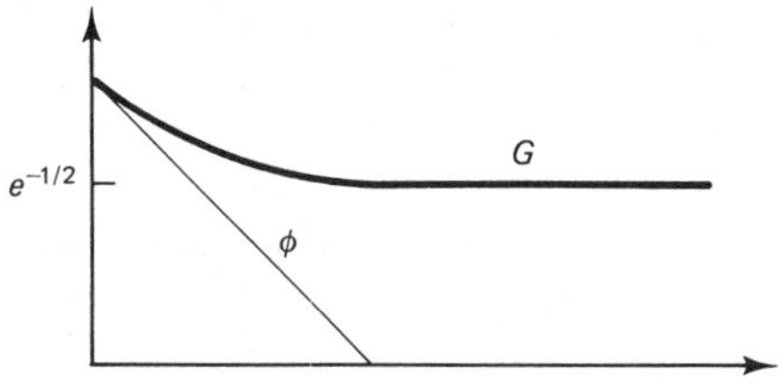

Figure 5.19

Solution By assumption

$$\phi(t) = kt$$

for some constant k. Hence

$$G(t) = \exp\left(-\int_0^t ku\ du\right) = e^{-kt^2/2}$$

(see Fig. 5.18)

Example 12

Suppose that the failure rate decreases to 0 at some finite time. In fact, assume that

$$\phi(t) = \begin{cases} 1 - t & 0 < t < 1 \\ 0 & 1 < t \end{cases}$$

Then

$$P(T > t) = G(t) = \exp\left(\int_0^t \phi(u)\ du\right) = \begin{cases} \exp\left(-t + \dfrac{t^2}{2}\right) & 0 \leq t \leq 1 \\ e^{-1/2} & 1 \leq t \end{cases}$$

The interpretation is that with probability $e^{-1/2} = .6065$ the component lasts until time 1 and thereafter is immune from breakdown. (See Fig. 5.19)

PROBLEMS

5.29. Let T denote the lifetime of a component and $G(t) = P(T > t)$. Find $G(t)$ if the failure rate is **(a)** $\phi(t) = 1/(t + 1)$; **(b)** $\phi(t) = 1/(t + 1)^2$. **(c)** Note that $\lim_{t \to \infty} G(t) = P(T = \infty) > 0$ in part (b). What is the interpretation of this?

5.30. (*The Weibull Distribution*) Let $k > 0$ and $\gamma > -1$ be constants. Suppose that $\phi(t) = kt^\gamma$. **(a)** Find $G(t)$. Graph ϕ and G for the two cases **(b)** $\gamma < 0$ (failure rate decreases) and **(c)** $\gamma > 0$ (failure rate increases).

5.31. For each of the failure rates in Fig. 5.20, sketch the corresponding function $G(t) = P(T > t)$.

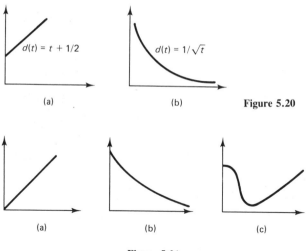

(a)   (b)   Figure 5.20

(a)   (b)   (c)

Figure 5.21

5.32. What kinds of "components" might have failure rate functions whose qualitative shapes are as in Fig. 5.21?

5.7 FUNCTIONS OF CONTINUOUS RANDOM VARIABLES

Suppose that X is the temperature measured in degrees Celsius. X has a density f_X. Suppose also that Y is the same temperature measured in degrees Fahrenheit. Then Y also has a density f_Y. Since there is a direct relationship between X and Y, there ought to be some way of determining the density f_Y in terms of the density f_X.

More generally, assume that X is a random variable with density f_X and that Y is obtained by a formula $Y = g(X)$, where g is some function. Often, g is a *change in scale*,

$$g(x) = ax + b$$

for some constants a and b; this was the case in the conversion of Celsius to Fahrenheit above. The question is: How is the density f_Y obtained from f_X?

Example 13

Suppose that U is uniformly distributed on $[0, 2]$. Find the density for $Z = U^2$.

Solution Since the value of U must be in the interval $[0, 2]$, the random variable $Z = U^2$ must have a value in the interval $[0, 4]$. For $z \in [0, 4]$ we compute the distribution function of Z:

$$F_Z(z) = P(Z \leqslant z) = P(U^2 \leqslant z) = P(U \leqslant \sqrt{z}) = \int_0^{\sqrt{z}} \frac{1}{2} \, du = \frac{\sqrt{z}}{2}$$

Now differentiate to obtain the density

$$
f_Z(z) = \begin{cases} 0 & z < 0 \\ \dfrac{1}{4\sqrt{z}} & 0 < z \le 4 \\ 0 & 4 < z \quad \blacksquare \end{cases}
$$

Example 14

Suppose that U is uniformly distributed on $[0, 1]$. Find the density of $Z = 3U + 5$.

Solution The intuition is that since U is uniformly distributed and since Z is U after a *change of scale*, then Z ought to be uniformly distributed as well. To check this, note first that Z must have a value in the interval $[5, 8]$ since U has a value in $[0, 1]$ and $Z = 3U + 5$. For $z \in [5, 8]$,

$$
\begin{aligned}
F_Z(z) &= P(Z \le z) \\
&= P(3U + 5 \le z) \\
&= P(U \le (z - 5)/3) \\
&= \frac{z - 5}{3}
\end{aligned}
$$

Differentiate to obtain the density:

$$
f_Z(z) = \begin{cases} 0 & z < 5 \\ \dfrac{1}{3} & 5 < z < 8 \\ 0 & 8 < z \end{cases}
$$

which implies that Z is uniform on the interval $[5, 8]$ of length 3. $\blacksquare$

Generalizing from these two examples, here is a

Rule to Find the Density of $Y = g(X)$

1. Determine the set I of values on which $f_Y \ne 0$ (the values on which Y is *concentrated*).
2. For $y \in I$, compute the distribution function of Y,

$$
F_Y(y) = P(Y \le y) = P(g(X) \le y)
$$

in terms of the distribution function of X.
3. Differentiate to find the density function of Y.

Continuous Random Variables   Chap. 5

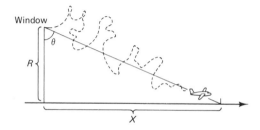

Window

θ

R

X

Figure 5.22

PROBLEMS

5.33. Suppose that U is uniformly distributed on $[0, 1]$. Find the density functions of these random variables:

$$X = \ln U \qquad Y = U^3 + 2 \qquad Z = \frac{1}{U}$$

5.34. Suppose that T is exponentially distributed with parameter λ. Find the density functions of these random variables:

$$X = T^2 \qquad Y = \frac{1}{T} \qquad Z = \ln T$$

5.35. Suppose that the lifetime until breakdown of a machine is exponentially distributed with average lifetime 200 hours. Suppose also that the cost of operation decreases with time; more specifically, if the machine is operating at time t, the cost per unit time $= 3/(t + 1)$. That is, when brand new the machine costs \$3 per hour; after 2 hours the cost is $3/(2 + 1)$ per hour. Let Y denote the *total cost* of the machine until break down. Show that *if* the machine breaks down at time t, then

$$Y = \int_0^t \frac{3}{u + 1} \, du$$

Show that $Y = 3 \ln (T + 1)$ in terms of the random variable T. Now find the density function of Y.

5.36. (a) Find the density of a random variable X whose square X^2 is uniformly distributed on $[0, 1]$. **(b)** Fix n. Find the density of a random variable Y whose nth power Y^n is uniformly distributed on $[0, 1]$.

5.37. A child throws a toy glider from a second-story window R feet off the ground. Because of variation of air currents, assume that the distance X that the glider travels horizontally before landing is exponentially distributed with average distance 50 feet. Let the angle θ be as in Fig. 5.22. Show that $\theta = \tan^{-1} (X/R)$. On what interval is the random angle θ concentrated? Find the density for θ.

5.8 CONTINUOUS RANDOM VARIABLES AND CONDITIONAL PROBABILITIES (OPTIONAL)

Suppose that A is an event whose probability depends on the value of a random variable X. In fact, assume that it is easier to find the probabilities $P(A \mid X = x)$ than it is to find $P(A)$ directly. If X is discrete, the Law of Total Probability implies that

$$P(A) = \sum_x P(A \mid X = x)P(X = x)$$

where the summation extends over all values x in the range of X. To find the analogous expression when X is continuous, use reasoning similar to that used in extending the definition of the expectation from the discrete to the continuous cases: The summation Σ turns into the integral sign $\int$ and the nonzero probability $P(X = x)$ turns into the infinitesimally small chance that X is infinitesimally close to x. That is,

$$P(X = x) \text{ is replaced by } P(x < X \leq x + dx) = f(x)\ dx$$

where f is the density function of X. Thus:

The Law of Total Probability When Conditioning on a Continuous Random Variable X

Let A be an event and let f be the density of X. Then

$$P(A) = \int_{-\infty}^{\infty} P(A \mid X = x)f(x)\ dx$$

Example 15

Assume that a coin is flipped twice, but the probability p of heads *is itself* a random number uniformly chosen from the interval $[0, 1]$. What are the chances of (a) 0 heads? (b) 1 head? (c) 2 heads?

    Solution   Let the random variable X be the probability of heads. Then X is uniformly distributed on $[0, 1]$; thus the density $f(x)$ of X is 1 for $0 < x < 1$. In two flips

$$P(0 \text{ heads} \mid X = x) = (1 - x)^2$$
$$P(1 \text{ head} \mid X = x) = 2 \cdot x(1 - x)$$
$$P(2 \text{ heads} \mid X = x) = x^2$$

in terms of the probability x of heads on one flip. Therefore

$$P(0 \text{ heads}) = \int_0^1 (1 - x)^2 \cdot 1\ dx = \frac{1}{3}$$

$$P(1 \text{ head}) = 2 \cdot \int_0^1 x(1 - x)dx = \frac{1}{3}$$

$$P(2 \text{ heads}) = \int_0^1 x^2\ dx = \frac{1}{3} \quad \blacksquare$$

Example 16

To generalize the last example, let us ask for the probability of j heads in n flips of a p-coin where p is *uniformly distributed* on $[0, 1]$. Since *given* that $p = x$, the number of heads has the binomial distribution and since the uniform density on $[0, 1]$ is the constant function 1

$$P(j \text{ heads on } n \text{ flips}) = \int_0^1 \binom{n}{j} x^j (1 - x)^{n-j} \cdot 1 \, dx$$

$$= \binom{n}{j} \int_0^1 x^j (1 - x)^{n-j} \, dx$$

$$= 1/(n + 1)$$

(See Problem 5.41 for the computation of this integral.) Hence we have the interesting conclusion that *if the probability p is selected completely at random, then the chance of j heads in n flips is $1(n + 1)$ independent of j; the events {0 heads}, {1 head}, . . . , {n heads} all have the same probability!* ∎

Example 17: *Buffon Needle Experiment*

A grid consists of parallel lines 1 unit apart. Drop a needle exactly 1 unit in length onto the grid. What is the chance that the needle comes to rest on top of one of the lines?

Solution   Let X be the distance from the foot of the needle to the line to the *left*; as in Fig. 5.23 let Φ be the angle that the needle subtends with the positive horizontal. X and Φ are both random variables with

$$0 \leqslant X < 1, \qquad 0 \leqslant \Phi < \pi$$

Since the needle is dropped at random onto the grid, we *assume* that X is uniformly distributed on $[0, 1)$ and that Φ is uniformly distributed on $[0, \pi)$. Thus the densities f_X for X and f_Φ for Φ are

$$f_X(x) = 1 \qquad 0 < x < 1$$

$$f_\Phi(s) = \frac{1}{\pi} \qquad 0 < s < \pi$$

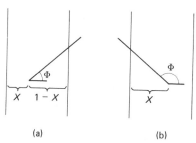

(a)

(b)

Figure 5.23   (a) Needle leans to right; (b) needle leans to left.

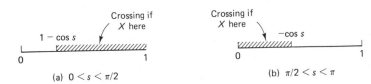

Crossing if
X here

Crossing if
X here

$1 - \cos s$

$-\cos s$

0   1

0   1

(a) $0 < s < \pi/2$

(b) $\pi/2 < s < \pi$

Figure 5.24

The law of total probability is used with conditioning on the values of the angle Φ: Given that $\Phi = s$, what is the probability that the needle crosses a grid line? Examining the diagrams above, we see that there will be a crossing if

$$0 < s < \frac{\pi}{2} \quad \text{and} \quad \cos s > 1 - x$$

or

$$\frac{\pi}{2} < s < \pi \quad \text{and} \quad -\cos s > x$$

[Note that $\cos s$ is negative in this case.] *Given that* $\Phi = s$, the needle will cross a line if the value x of X is in the marked intervals in Fig. 5.24. Thus

$$P(\text{crossing} \mid \Phi = s) = \begin{cases} \cos s & 0 < s < \dfrac{\pi}{2} \\ -\cos s & \dfrac{\pi}{2} < s < \pi \end{cases}$$

Therefore

$$P(\text{crossing}) = \int_0^\pi P(\text{crossing} \mid \Phi = s) f_\Phi(s) \, ds$$

$$= \int_0^{\pi/2} \cos s \, \frac{1}{\pi} \, ds + \int_{\pi/2}^\pi (-\cos s) \, \frac{1}{\pi} \, ds$$

$$= \frac{1}{\pi} [\sin s \mid_0^{\pi/2} - \sin s \mid_{\pi/2}^\pi]$$

$$= \frac{2}{\pi} \quad \blacksquare$$

Notice that this provides an experimental way to find π! Simply construct the grid, tabulate the number of crossings n in a total of N trials; by the frequency interpretation of probability, $n/N \cong 2/\pi$ for N large. Unfortunately, N must be very large to obtain accuracy to even two or three decimal places (see Chapter 7, Example 16).

G. L. Buffon (1707–1788), who first considered this example, wrote a 44-volume treatise on natural history. He applied probability to many areas, using it to justify, for example, that the planets resulted from a collision of the sun and a comet. He also contributed to population studies and interpretations of mortality tables.

PROBLEMS

5.38. Perform a succession of Bernoulli trials until the first success. Assume that p is uniformly distributed on $[0, 1]$. Show that

$$P(\text{1st } F \text{ on } n\text{th trial}) = \int_0^1 x^{n-1}(1 - x)\, dx = \frac{1}{n(n + 1)}$$

5.39. (*Continuation*) Let T be the number of the trial on which the first F occurs in Problem 5.38. Show that $E(T) = \infty$. [Note that $\Sigma\, 1/(n + 1) = \infty$.]

5.40. The time it takes to serve a customer at a grocery checkout counter is exponentially distributed with parameter λ. But because people at various times during the day have more or fewer groceries and people are working at different speeds, the average length of time $1/\lambda$ *is itself* a random variable. Assume that λ is *uniformly distributed* on $[.1, 1]$ (so that the average checkout time is concentrated on $[1, 10]$ minutes). Find $P(\text{checkout time for a customer} \leqslant 5 \text{ minutes})$.

5.41. Compute the integral in Example 16. Let

$$I_j = \int_0^1 x^j(1 - x)^{n-j}\, dx$$

Use an integration by parts with $v = x^j$ and $du = (1 - x)^{n-j}\, dx$ to show that

$$I_j = \frac{j}{n - j + 1}\, I_{j-1}$$

for $1 \leqslant j \leqslant n$. Show that

$$I_0 = \frac{1}{n + 1}$$

directly and hence that

$$I_1 = \frac{1}{n}\, I_0 = \frac{1}{n + 1}\binom{n}{1}^{-1}$$

$$I_2 = \frac{2}{(n - 1)n}\, I_0 = \frac{1}{n + 1}\binom{n}{2}^{-1}$$

$$\cdots$$

$$I_j = \frac{1}{n + 1}\binom{n}{j}^{-1}$$

5.42. (*The Janitor Problem*) A janitor unlocks an auditorium at some time uniformly distributed between 8:00 and 9:00. Call this time T. Then between T and 9:00, another janitor turns on the lights. Let this second time be S and assume that S is uniformly distributed between T and 9:00. The problem is to find the density for the time that the lights are on. Assume that T is uniformly distributed on $[0, 1]$ and S is uniformly distributed on $[T, 1]$. Show that

$$P(\text{lights on at least time } u \mid T = t) = \begin{cases} 0 & 1 - t < u \\ \dfrac{1 - t - u}{1 - t} & 1 - t > u \end{cases}$$

$$= \begin{cases} 0 & 1 - u < t \\ \dfrac{1 - t - u}{1 - t} & t < 1 - u \end{cases}$$

Show that

$$P(\text{lights on at least time } u) = \int_{1-u}^{1} 0 \, dt + \int_{0}^{1-u} \frac{1 - t - u}{1 - t} \, dt$$

$$= 1 - u + u \, \ln u$$

Conclude that the density of the time the lights are on is

$$f(u) = \begin{cases} 0 & u < 0 \quad \text{or} \quad 1 < u \\ -\ln u & 0 < u < 1 \end{cases}$$

5.43. (*Continuation*) Find the probabilities that the lights are on at least (a) 15 minutes; (b) 1/2 hour.

5.9 RANDOM COMMENTS AND PROBLEMS: OTHER CONTINUOUS DISTRIBUTIONS (OPTIONAL)

We have developed both discrete and continuous random variables. The first problem is an example of a *mixed* type.

5.44. Suppose that a machine part lasts a time that is exponentially distributed with parameter λ. The replacement policy is to replace the part when it burns out *or* at time T_0, whichever occurs first. Show that $P(\text{replaced at time } T_0) = e^{-\lambda T_0}$. Sketch the distribution function $F(t) = P(T \leq t)$. How is the fact that T is a mixed discrete and continuous random variable revealed in the graph? Show that the definition of expectation as "sum of the values times probabilities" yields

$$E(T) = \int_{0}^{T_0} t\lambda e^{-\lambda t} \, dt + T_0 e^{-\lambda T_0}$$

Compute $E(T)$ and show that $E(T) \to 1/\lambda$ as $T_0 \to \infty$.

5.45. (*The Cauchy Distribution*) A fireworks display is spinning around in a circle. As it does so, sparks fly off; ignoring the curved arc due to gravity and also ignoring the sparks that fly up rather than down toward the ground, a spark will travel along a straight line at a random angle θ till it hits the ground as in Fig. 5.25. The distribution of the random position X from the point of impact to the point on the ground directly below the sparkler is the **Cauchy distribution**. Compute the

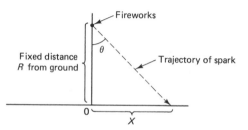
Figure 5.25

density and distribution functions for X: Note that the random angle θ is uniformly distributed on $(-\pi/2, \pi/2)$. Assume that angles are measured counterclockwise from the negative y axis so that $\theta = 0$ corresponds to the spark flying straight down. Show that $X/R = \tan\theta$. Show that the density and distribution for X are

$$f(u) = \frac{1}{\pi}\frac{R}{R^2 + u^2} \qquad -\infty < u < \infty$$

$$F(x) = \frac{1}{\pi}\left[\tan^{-1}\frac{x}{R} + \frac{\pi}{2}\right] \qquad -\infty < x < \infty$$

These functions are graphed in Fig. 5.26.

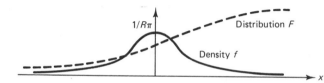

Figure 5.26 The Cauchy distribution and density functions.

5.46. (*The Arcsine Distribution*) A projectile launched at angle θ to the horizontal with initial speed v will land at position $X = (v^2/g) \cdot \sin 2\theta$, where $g = 9.8$ meters per second per second. (see Fig. 5.27) Assume that θ is uniformly distributed on $(0, \pi)$. Find the distribution and density functions for X.

Figure 5.27

— Chapter 6

The Poisson Distribution and the Poisson Process

Imagine performing 10 Bernoulli trials each lasting .1 minute and each with probability $p = .2$ of success. The number of S's recorded at the end of the minute is random, but the expected number is $np = 10 \cdot .2 = 2$. Next, perform 100 Bernoulli trials each lasting .01 minute and each with probability $p = .02$ of success. At the end of the minute the expected number of S's is also $np = 2$. In this way more Bernoulli trials can be performed, each lasting less time, but if $np = 2$, then the expected number is 2 S's regardless of the value of n.

In the limit a Bernoulli trial would be performed each instant of time. The probability of success p would have approached 0 in such a way that $np = 2$. The distribution obtained in the limit is the **Poisson distribution**—named after Simeon Denis Poisson (1781–1840), who named his model the "law of small numbers." One of its first applications was to the number of deaths by kicking horses in the Prussian army.

So far we have considered static models with just one or a few random variables. However, if X_t denotes the number of disintegrations of a radioactive substance between time 0 and time t, then the infinite set of random variables $\{x_t\}_{t=0}^{\infty}$ is required to model the system's evolution in time.

A random process $\{X_t\}$ consisting of an entire "list" of random variables X_t is called a **stochastic process**. The index t can be either discrete or continuum valued.

The Poisson distribution leads naturally to such a process.

6.1 DEFINITION OF THE POISSON DISTRIBUTION

The Poisson distribution is an approximation to the binomial distribution when the number n of trials is large and the probability of success p is small. Before considering this limit law, let us first define the distribution and derive its basic properties.

A Poisson-distributed random variable X has as range the nonnegative integers $\{0, 1, 2, \ldots\}$. Let $\lambda > 0$ be a fixed constant.

The Poisson Distribution with Parameter λ

$$P(X = j) = \frac{\lambda^j}{j!} e^{-\lambda}$$

for $j = 0, 1, 2, \ldots$ The Possion probabilities will be denoted by $P(j, \lambda)$ or simply by $P(j)$.

Of use in dealing with sums of Poisson probabilities will be the **Taylor series** representation for the exponential function expanded about 0:

$$e^x = \sum_{j=0}^{\infty} \frac{x^j}{j!} = 1 + x + \frac{x^2}{2!} + \frac{x^3}{3!} + \cdots$$

valid for all $-\infty < x < \infty$.

Example 1

Suppose that the number of acorns that dropped onto the porch during the night is Poisson distributed with parameter $\lambda = 2$. Find (a) $P(X = 0)$, (b) $P(X \leq 3)$, (c) $P(X \geq 2)$, and (d) $P(X = 0 \mid X < 2)$.

Solution

(a) $P(X = 0) = \dfrac{2^0}{0!} e^{-2} = e^{-2} = .1353$

(b) $P(X \leq 3) = P(X = 0) + P(X = 1) + P(X = 2) + P(X = 3)$

$$= \frac{2^0}{0!} e^{-2} + \frac{2^1}{1!} e^{-2} + \frac{2^2}{2!} e^{-2} + \frac{2^3}{3!} e^{-2}$$

$$= e^{-2}\left(1 + 2 + 2 + \frac{8}{6}\right)$$

$$= .8571$$

(c) $P(X \geq 2) = 1 - P(X \leq 1)$

$$= 1 - [P(X = 0) + P(X = 1)]$$

$$= 1 - e^{-2}(1 + 2)$$

$$= .5940$$

(d) $P(X = 0 \mid X < 2) = \dfrac{P(X = 0 \text{ and } X < 2)}{P(X < 2)}$

$$= \frac{P(X = 0)}{P(X < 2)}$$

$$= \frac{e^{-2}}{e^{-2}(1 + 2)}$$

$$= \frac{1}{3} \quad \blacksquare$$

Example 2

Show that the Poisson probabilities add to 1.

Solution

$$\sum_{j=0}^{\infty} P(X = j) = \sum_{j=0}^{\infty} \frac{\lambda^j}{j!} e^{-\lambda} = e^{-\lambda} \sum_{j=0}^{\infty} \frac{\lambda^j}{j!} = e^{-\lambda} e^{\lambda} = 1$$

where the second-to-last equality uses the Taylor series representation for e^λ. $\quad \blacksquare$

For the Poisson distribution to be applicable, λ must have an intuitive interpretation:

> Suppose that X is Poisson distributed with parameter λ. Then
> $$\lambda = E(X)$$

Proof. The expectation is the sum of the values times the probabilities:

$$E(X) = \sum_{j=0}^{\infty} j \frac{\lambda^j}{j!} e^{-\lambda}$$

$$= \sum_{j=1}^{\infty} j \frac{\lambda^j}{j!} e^{-\lambda}$$

$$= \sum_{j=1}^{\infty} \frac{\lambda \lambda^{j-1}}{(j-1)!} e^{-\lambda}$$

$$= \lambda e^{-\lambda} \sum_{j-1=0}^{\infty} \frac{\lambda^{j-1}}{(j-1)!}$$

$$= \lambda e^{-\lambda} \sum_{k=0}^{\infty} \frac{\lambda^k}{k!}$$

$$= \lambda e^{-\lambda} e^{\lambda}$$

$$= \lambda$$

The second equality follows since the term corresponding to $j = 0$ in the infinite series is 0; thus the index j can start at 1 rather than at 0. The third-from-last equality follows by a *change of index* by setting $k = j - 1$. The second-to-last equality uses the Taylor series expansion of e^{λ}. ■

Thus in Example 1 the average number of acorns or the expected number is 2; if one performs an acorn count each morning in October, the average at the end of the month should be 2—more or less.

Note that the Poisson probabilities can be obtained recursively. Since

$$\frac{\lambda^j}{j!} = \frac{\lambda \lambda^{j-1}}{j(j-1)!}$$

multiplying both sides by $e^{-\lambda}$ implies that

$$\boxed{\begin{array}{c} P(j) = \dfrac{\lambda}{j} P(j-1) \\[2mm] \text{for } j = 1, 2, 3, \ldots . \end{array}}$$

Example 3

Write a program that will input L (for λ) and positive integer N; output should be a listing of the Poisson probabilities $P(j, \lambda)$ for $j = 0, 1, 2, \ldots, N$—the first $N + 1$ of the infinitely many.

Solution   Use the recursion relation just derived with recursion starting with

$$P(0) = \frac{\lambda^0}{0!} e^{-\lambda} = e^{-\lambda}$$

Thus

```
var J,N: integer;
    L,P: real;
```

```
begin
    readln(L,N);
    P: = exp(−L);

    for J: = 0 to N do
        begin
            if J > 0 then P: = (L/J) * P;
            writeln(J,P:10:4);
        end;
end.
```

Fig. 6.1 shows several Poisson distributions for various values of λ. ■

As with the binomial probabilities $B(j)$, the graphs of the Poisson probabilities also show first an increase and then a decrease.   In fact, the recursion relation implies that

$$P(j) > P(j − 1)$$

if and only if

$$\frac{\lambda}{j} > 1$$

$$\lambda > j$$

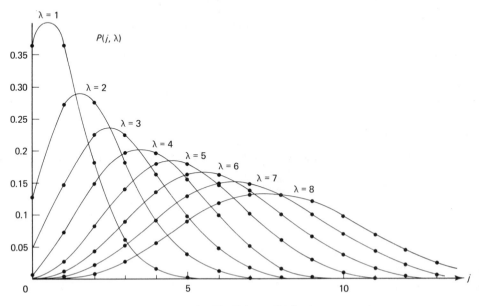

Figure 6.1   The Poisson distribution.

Hence

> the Poisson probabilities $P(j)$ increase until
>
> $$j \cong \lambda$$
>
> and then decrease.

Since our interpretation of λ is as the average, we can also say that the *maximum of the values of the Poisson probabilities occurs at approximately the expected or average value.* Note that if $\lambda < 1$, then $P(j)$ does not exhibit any increase at all; in this case

$$P(0) > P(1) > P(2) > \cdots$$

Example 4

Suppose that the number of stray dogs X picked up per day is Poisson distributed with average 3.2 per day. Find

$$P(\text{fewer than 5 picked up in 2 days})$$

Also find a number N so that on 90% of the days N or fewer dogs are picked up.

Solution Since the parameter λ is the average, for 2 days the parameter $\lambda = 2 \cdot 3.2 = 6.4$. Hence

$$P(\text{fewer than 5 picked up in 2 days}) = \sum_{j=0}^{4} \frac{6.4^j}{j!} e^{-6.4}$$

$$= .2351$$

To solve for N in the second part, note that

$$.90 = P(N \text{ or fewer dogs picked up})$$

$$= \sum_{j=0}^{N} \frac{3.2^j}{j!} e^{-3.2}$$

$$= e^{-3.2}\left(1 + 3.2 + \frac{3.2^2}{2} + \cdots + \frac{3.2^N}{N!}\right)$$

Computing these values successively, we find that

$$P(5 \text{ or fewer}) = .8946 < .90 < .9554 = P(6 \text{ or fewer})$$

Hence we take $N = 6$. ∎

Example 5

Suppose that the number of saplings encountered along a forest path is Poisson distributed. In distance s feet one can expect an average $.03s$ saplings. Find the probability that no sapling is found in 100 feet.

Solution If X_s is the number of saplings in s feet, then X_s is Poisson distributed with parameter $.03s$.   Hence

$$P(X_{100} = 0) = \frac{(.03 \cdot 100)^0}{0!} \, e^{-.03 \cdot 100} = e^{-3} = .04979 \quad \blacksquare$$

Example 6 (*Continuation*)

Find the distance s so that we can be 95% sure of finding *at least one* sapling in distance s.

Solution s must satisfy

$$.95 = P(X_s \geqslant 1)$$

$$= 1 - P(X_s = 0)$$

$$= 1 - e^{-.03s}$$

$$e^{-.03s} = .05$$

$$s = - \frac{\ln (.05)}{.03} = 99.86 \quad \blacksquare$$

PROBLEMS

6.1. Assume that the number of customers in a store at any given time is Poisson distributed with average 3.5.   What are **(a)** P(no customers at 3:15); **(b)** P(2 customers at 3:15); **(c)** P(at least 3 customers at 3:15)?

6.2. Assume that the number of uninspected cars caught at a state police checkpoint is Poisson distributed with average 2.1 per hour.   Find **(a)** P(no cars caught in a 1-hour stretch); **(b)** P(at least 2 cars caught in 1 hour); **(c)** P(more than 5 caught in 1 hour).

6.3. (*Continuation*) **(a)** What is the average number of cars caught in t hours?   What are **(b)** P(no cars caught in 1/4 hour); **(c)** P(at least 3 in $1\frac{1}{2}$ hours); **(d)** P(at least 1 car caught within 10 minutes of setting up the checkpoint)?

6.4. (*Continuation*) Let t_0 be that time so that there is a probability of .95 that at least 10 cars will be caught between time 0 and time t_0.   Show that t_0 must satisfy

$$.05 = e^{-2.1t_0} \left[1 + 2.1t_0 + \cdots + \frac{(2.1t_0)^9}{9!} \right]$$

Write a program to compute t_0.   (You might do this by first *guessing* what t_0 is.   Then have your program print out values of the right-hand side for t_0 ranging about your guess in increments of 1 minute $= 1/60$ hour.   Are any of the computed values close to .05?)

6.2 THE POISSON APPROXIMATION TO THE BINOMIAL DISTRIBUTION

In this section we show that the Poisson probabilities $P(j, \lambda)$ approximate the binomial probabilities $B(j, n, p)$ under certain conditions. This is useful because for n large,

$$B(j, n, p) = \binom{n}{j} p^j q^{n-j}$$

requires far more operations to compute than does

$$P(j, \lambda) = \frac{\lambda^j}{j!} e^{-\lambda}$$

(See Problem 6.8.)

The Poisson Approximation to the Binomial Distribution

Suppose that n is "large," p is "small," and

$$\lambda = np$$

is "reasonable" (of order of magnitude 1). Then

$$B(j, n, p) = \binom{n}{j} p^j q^{-j} \cong \frac{\lambda^j}{j!} e^{-\lambda} = P(j, \lambda)$$

Example 7

One in 50 fiction books published in the United States becomes a best-seller. Suppose that a company publishes 100 books. With X equal to the number of best-sellers among the 100, find the exact value of $P(X = 3)$ and $P(X \leqslant 4)$; compare these with the Poisson approximations.

Solution X is binomially distributed with $n = 100$, $p = 1/50$. Hence

$$P(X = 3) = \binom{100}{3} (.02)^3 (.98)^{97} = .1823$$

$$P(X \leqslant 4) = \sum_{j=0}^{4} \binom{100}{j} (.02)^j (.98)^{100-j} = .9492$$

Using the Poisson approximation, we see that $n = 100$ is "large," $p = .02$ is "small," and

$$\lambda = np = 100 \cdot .02 = 2$$

is of order of magnitude 1. Hence

$$P(X = 3) \cong \frac{2^3}{3!} e^{-2} = .1804$$

$$P(X \le 4) \cong \sum_{j=0}^{4} \frac{2^j}{j!} e^{-2} = e^{-2}\left(1 + 2 + 2 + \frac{8}{6} + \frac{16}{24}\right)$$

$$= .9473 \quad \blacksquare$$

Here is a table showing how the Poisson probabilities approximate the binomial probabilities as $n \to \infty$, $p \to 0$ in such a way that $\lambda = np$ remains constant at 2.

	Binomial			Poisson
j	$n = 10$ $p = .2$	$n = 20$ $p = .1$	$n = 40$ $p = .05$	$\lambda = 2$
0	.1074	.1216	.1285	.1353
1	.2684	.2702	.2706	.2707
2	.3020	.2852	.2777	.2707
3	.2013	.1901	.1851	.1804
4	.0881	.0898	.0901	.0902
5	.0264	.0319	.0342	.0361
6	.0055	.0089	.0105	.0120
7	.0008	.0020	.0027	.0034
8	.0001	.0004	.0006	.0009
9	.0000	.0001	.0001	.0002

Proof of the Poisson Approximation. We will show the following fact:

> Assume that $n \to \infty$ and $p \to 0$ in such a way that
> $$\lambda = np$$
> remains fixed. Then
> $$\lim \binom{n}{j} p^j (1 - p)^{n-j} = \frac{\lambda^j}{j!} e^{-\lambda}$$
> for each *fixed j*.

The following limit theorem from calculus is required:

$$\lim_{n \to \infty} \left(1 + \frac{c}{n}\right)^n = e^c \qquad (*)$$

for a fixed constant c. This is proved using L'Hôpital's rule. For completeness we prove it here. We will show that the *natural log* of the left-hand side approaches c as $n \to \infty$.

$$\lim_{n \to \infty} \ln \left(1 + \frac{c}{n} \right)^n = \lim_{n \to \infty} n \ln \left(1 + \frac{c}{n} \right)$$

$$= \lim_{n \to \infty} \frac{\ln (1 + c/n)}{1/n}$$

$$= \lim_{x \to 0} \frac{\ln (1 + cx)}{x}$$

$$= \lim_{x \to 0} \frac{c/(1 + cx)}{1}$$

$$= c$$

where the next-to-last equality uses L'Hôpital's rule.

Here is the proof of the Poisson approximation. Let j be a *fixed* nonnegative integer:

$$\binom{n}{j} p^j q^{n-j} = \frac{n!}{j!(n-j)!} p^j(1 - p)^{n-j}$$

$$= \frac{n(n-1) \cdots (n - j + 1)}{j!} p^j(1 - p)^{-j}(1 - p)^n$$

$$= \frac{1}{j!} \underbrace{np(n-1)p \cdots (n - j + 1)p}_{j \text{ terms}} (1 - p)^{-j}\left(1 - \frac{\lambda}{n}\right)^n \qquad (1)$$

But

$$np(n-1)p \cdots (n - j + 1)p \to \lambda^j \qquad (2)$$

as $n \to \infty$, $p \to 0$ in such a way that $\lambda = np$ remains fixed. This is so since $n - i \cong n$ for $n \gg i$, and therefore $(n - i)p \to \lambda$ for each fixed i. Also,

$$(1 - p)^{-j} \to 1 \qquad (3)$$

as $p \to 0$ since j is a fixed integer. Finally,

$$\left(1 - \frac{\lambda}{n}\right)^n \to e^{-\lambda} \qquad (4)$$

as $n \to \infty$ by the limit theorem (*) above. Combining equations (1) to (4) yields

$$\binom{n}{j} p^j q^{n-j} \to \frac{1}{j!} \lambda^j \cdot 1 \cdot e^{-\lambda}$$

$$= \frac{\lambda^j}{j!} e^{-\lambda} \qquad \blacksquare$$

Example 8

In the United States, approximately 1 infant in 54 dies before the age of 1. Among 213 babies born in half a year at a certain hospital, what is the probability that fewer than 3 babies will die before their first birthdays?

Solution There are $n = 213$ Bernoulli trials. $p = 1/54$ is the probability that any one child will die. Hence

$$P(0, 1, \text{ or } 2 \text{ will die}) = \sum_{j=0}^{2} \binom{213}{j} \left(\frac{1}{54}\right)^j \left(\frac{53}{54}\right)^{213-j}$$

$$= .2436$$

is the exact probability. Using the Poisson approximation,

$$\lambda = np = \frac{213}{54} = 3.944$$

Hence

$$P(0, 1, \text{ or } 2 \text{ will die}) \cong e^{-3.944} \left(1 + 3.944 + \frac{3.944^2}{2}\right)$$

$$= .2464 \quad \blacksquare$$

Example 9 (*Continuation of Example 16 in Chapter 4*)

A book of 200 pages has 143 typographical errors. Assuming that each page has 4000 characters, what is the probability that page 1 has no typos? Fewer than 3 typos?

Solution With X equal to the number of typos,

$$P(X = j) = \binom{4000}{j} p^j q^{4000-j}$$

where

$$p = \frac{143}{200 \cdot 4000} \qquad n = 4000$$

n is large, p is small, and

$$\lambda = np = 4000 \cdot \frac{143}{200 \cdot 4000} = .715$$

is of order of magnitude 1. Hence the Poisson approximation implies that

$$P(X = j) \cong \frac{\lambda^j}{j!} e^{-\lambda}$$

and consequently,

$$P(X = 0) \cong e^{-.715} = .4892$$

$$P(X < 3) \cong e^{-.715}\left(1 + .715 + \frac{.715^2}{2}\right) = .9640 \quad \blacksquare$$

Example 10

The probability that there will be a fire in any particular house during the course of a year is 1/150 in the United States. In a town of 500 houses, what is the probability of more than 4 fires in the next year?

Solution $n = 500$ Bernoulli trials are performed with $p = 1/150$. With X equal to the number of fires, X is binomially distributed.

$$P(X = j) = \binom{500}{j}\left(\frac{1}{150}\right)^j\left(1 - \frac{1}{150}\right)^{500-j}$$

$$\cong \frac{\lambda^j}{j!}e^{-\lambda}$$

where

$$\lambda = np = \frac{500}{150} = 3.333$$

Thus

$$P(X > 4) = 1 - P(X \le 4)$$

$$\cong 1 - e^{-3.333}\left(1 + 3.333 + \frac{3.333^2}{2} + \frac{3.333^3}{6} + \frac{3.333^4}{24}\right)$$

$$= .2435 \quad \blacksquare$$

PROBLEMS

6.5. One in 3000 persons in the age group 20 to 44 is blind in the United States. In a town in which 10,000 are in this age group, what are **(a)** P(no one is blind); **(b)** P(at least 2 are blind); **(c)** the average or expected number of blind people in this age bracket?

6.6. In Philadelphia, 1 person in 3930 is murdered during the course of a year. In a section of the city in which 5000 people reside, what are **(a)** the expected number of murders; **(b)** P(1 murder); **(c)** P(fewer than 3 murders); **(d)** P(fewer than 6, but more than 2 murders)?

6.7. The probability that a major league baseball game in California being postponed due to bad weather is 1/160. Of 200 games, what are **(a)** the expected number of postponements; **(b)** P(2 postponements); **(c)** P(more than 3 postponements); **(d)** a number k so that the probability is at least .99 that there will be fewer than k postponements?

6.8. How many arithmetic operations are required to find **(a)** $B(j, n, p)$; **(b)** $P(j, \lambda)$?

6.3 THE POISSON PROCESS

Calls arrive at a sales order department. The arrival of each call marks a "happening" that occurs at a definite time. Let N_t denote the number of arrivals in the interval $[0, t]$. For each fixed t, N_t is a random variable with range $\{0, 1, 2, \ldots\}$ (There could be 0 calls or 1 call or $\ldots$ between time 0 and time t.) N_t is a nondecreasing function of t: An arrival of a call increases N_t by 1; during those intervals in which no call arrives, N_t remains constant.

We make several assumptions about the **stochastic process** $\{N_t\}_{t=0}^{\infty}$:

The Poisson Postulates:

1. Nonoverlapping intervals are independent. Suppose that $I_1, \ldots, I_n$ are disjoint intervals. Then events defined in terms of these intervals are independent. Thus for any nonnegative integers $j_1, \ldots, j_n$,

$$P(j_1 \text{ calls in } I_1, \ldots, j_n \text{ calls in } I_n) = P(j_1 \text{ calls in } I_1) \cdots P(j_n \text{ calls in } I_n)$$

2. Fix a time t with $0 \leq t < \infty$. For a small interval Δt the chance of a call arriving in the interval $[t, t + \Delta t)$ is approximately proportional to the length of the interval Δt: There is a constant $\lambda > 0$ so that

$$\frac{P(\text{exactly 1 call in } [t, t + \Delta t))}{\Delta t} \to \lambda$$

as $\Delta t \to 0$. (For small time intervals, doubling the length of the interval doubles the probability that a call will arrive.)

3. Fix a time t with $0 \leq t < \infty$. For a small interval Δt the chance of *more than 1* call arriving in the interval $[t, t + \Delta t)$ is negligible for small Δt. That is,

$$\frac{P(\text{more than 1 call in } [t, t + \Delta t))}{\Delta t} \to 0$$

as $\Delta t \to 0$.

Are these postulates reasonable? The intuition is that there is some "average rate" λ at which calls arrive at the sales order department. Even though the number that arrive in *this* half-hour is random, over the course of the day the total number of calls divided by the length of the time will be approximately λ—about constant from day to day (ignoring seasonal changes due to holiday shopping, and so on). Are disjoint time intervals independent? This should be the case since, for example, whether one person calls before noon should have no effect on the number of calls after noon; also, the arrival of a call does not produce a "downtime" during which other calls are rejected. (We assume that there are enough lines so that no one receives a busy signal.) Postulate 2 states that the arrival rate is roughly constant: There is no tendency for calls to clump around certain times of the day. The calls arrive randomly, but at a more or less uniform rate. Postulate

3 states that an incoming call does not trigger more calls; there is no "avalanche effect" to the calls; the arriving calls are independent of one another.

In Fig. 6.2 "x" marks the time of an incoming call.

We seek to find the distribution of the random variable $N_t = \#$(calls arriving in the interval $[0, t]$). It is clear that N_t can only take on nonnegative integer values, but it remains to show that $N_t = \infty$ is *not* a real possibility. This would mean a jam-up at the sales order department.

Split the interval $[0, t]$ into a large number n of subintervals. If each of the subintervals has length Δt, then

$$n \, \Delta t = t$$

so

$$n = \frac{t}{\Delta t}$$

The number of incoming calls received in *each of these subintervals is independent of the number arriving in the other subintervals* by Postulate 1. Let

$$p_{\Delta t} = P(\text{exactly 1 call received in an interval of length } \Delta t)$$

For small Δt Postulate 3 states that the probability that more than 1 call arriving in any one subinterval is negligible. Thus the n subintervals constitute n Bernoulli trials with a success meaning that a call arrived; $p = p_{\Delta t}$. (see Fig. 6.3) The three postulates lead directly to the conclusion that the number of calls arriving in $[0, t]$ (the value of N_t) is the number of successes in n Bernoulli trials (neglecting the possibility of more than 1 call in a subinterval). Consequently, for small Δt, the number of arrivals N_t in $[0, t]$ has approximately the same distribution as the number of successes in n Bernoulli trials with $p = p_{\Delta t}$. Therefore,

$$P(j \text{ calls in } [0, t]) \cong \binom{n}{j} p_{\Delta t}^{j} (1 - p_{\Delta t})^{n-j}$$

where the approximation will be better the larger the value of n and consequently the finer the subdivision of $[0, t]$ into subintervals. We apply the Poisson approximation formula of the preceding section to this binomial probability. Let $\Delta t \to 0$. Then

$$n = \frac{t}{\Delta t} \to \infty$$

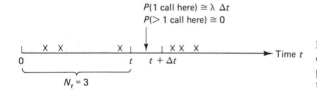

$P(1 \text{ call here}) \cong \lambda \, \Delta t$
$P(> 1 \text{ call here}) \cong 0$

Figure 6.2 N_t counts the number of calls in $[0, t]$; Δt is so small that the probability of more than 1 call in an interval Δt is negligible.

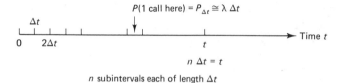

Figure 6.3 Approximate the Poisson process by a succession of Bernoulli trials; $p_{\Delta t}$ = probability of success.

and

$$np_{\Delta t} = t \frac{p_{\Delta t}}{\Delta t}$$

$$= t \frac{P(\text{exactly one call in interval of length } \Delta t)}{\Delta t}$$

$$\rightarrow \lambda t$$

as $\Delta t \rightarrow 0$ by Postulate 2.   Hence the Poisson approximation formula implies

$$P(j \text{ calls in } [0, t]) \rightarrow \frac{(\lambda t)^j}{j!} e^{-\lambda t}$$

as $\Delta t \rightarrow 0$.

The Poisson Process

Suppose that the three Poisson postulates are satisfied.   Then the number of events N_t in the interval $[0, t]$ is Poisson distributed with parameter λt.

$$P(N_t = j) = \frac{(\lambda t)^j}{j!} e^{-\lambda t}$$

In particular,

$$E(N_t) = \lambda t$$

Sometimes a Poisson process is called a Poisson stream, emphasizing the model in which N_t counts the number of arrivals.

Note that the interval $[0, t]$ can be replaced by half-open intervals $(0, t]$ or $[0, t)$ or by the open interval $(0, t)$.   This is so since the probability that a call arrives at *exactly* time t is 0.   (see Problem 6.13).

Note also that the interval $[0, t]$ can be replaced by any interval of length t. If s, t are nonnegative times, then

$$N_{s+t} - N_s = \#(\text{calls in } [0, s + t]) - \#(\text{calls in } [0, s])$$

$$= \#(\text{calls in } (s, s + t])$$

has the same distribution as the number of calls in $(0, t)$.   Consequently, $N_{s+t} - N_s$ Poisson distributed with parameter λt.

Example 11

Three calls arrive every half-hour, on the average. What are (a) P(no calls in an hour), (b) P(2 calls in 15 minutes), and (c) P(more than 2 calls between 11:00 and 11:45)?

Solution $\lambda = 6$/hour. Thus

(a) P(no calls in 1 hour) $= \dfrac{(6t)^0}{0!} e^{-6t} = e^{-6} = .002479$

(b) P(2 calls in 15 minutes) $= \dfrac{(6t)^2}{2!} e^{-6t}$

$$= \frac{(6/4)^2}{2} e^{-6/4}$$

$$= .2510$$

(c) In a 45-minute interval

$$\lambda t = 6 \cdot \frac{3}{4} = 4.5$$

Thus

$$P(\text{more than 2 calls in 45 minutes}) = 1 - \left(\frac{4.5^0}{0!} + \frac{4.5^1}{1!} + \frac{4.5^2}{2!} \right) e^{-4.5}$$

$$= .8264 \quad \blacksquare$$

Disintegrations of atoms in a radioactive source ought to obey the Poisson postulates. First, however many atoms have decayed in one interval of time should be independent of how many decay in other nonoverlapping intervals. (Actually, this is not altogether accurate since the source consists of a *finite number* of atoms; consequently, the number that disintegrate in one interval *reduces* the number available during subsequent time intervals; but this number is such a small fraction of the total number of atoms for time intervals small compared to the half-life that it can be ignored.) Second, the chance that an atom will decay is not a function of the time of day or other variables: The chance of observing a disintegration is proportional to the interval of time for small intervals. Third, we assume that decays do not occur in bunches—no chain reactions.

Example 12

Suppose that 1000 disintegrations from a sample were registered over the course of an hour. What is the probability that in 5 seconds (a) no disintegrations and (b) more than 2 disintegrations will be observed?

Solution

$$\lambda = \frac{1000}{\text{hour}} = \frac{1000}{3600 \text{ seconds}} = \frac{5}{18 \text{ seconds}}$$

Thus

$$\lambda t = \frac{5}{18} \cdot 5 = \frac{25}{18}$$

(a) $P(\text{none in 5 seconds}) = \frac{(\lambda t)^0}{0!} e^{-\lambda t} = e^{-25/18} = .2494$

(b) $P(\text{more than 2 in 5 seconds}) = 1 - P(0, 1, \text{or } 2 \text{ in 5 seconds})$

$$= 1 - \sum_{j=0}^{2} \frac{(\lambda t)^j}{j!} e^{-\lambda t}$$

$$= 1 - e^{-25/18}\left(1 + \frac{25}{18} + \frac{(25/18)^2}{2}\right)$$

$$= .1638 \quad\blacksquare$$

Note: Here is a way to remember how to find λ. The value of λt must be dimensionless in order to exponentiate it. If t has dimensions of time, then λ must have dimensions of 1/time. For example, one call per 5 minutes implies that $\lambda = 1/5$ minutes.

The parameter t need not be time. The next two examples show how t might be distance, area, or even volume. $\blacksquare$

Example 13

Suppose that weak spots along a length of cable follow a Poisson stream model with an average of 1 weak point per 20 feet. What is the probability that a 100-foot length has fewer than 3 weak spots?

Solution Here t is distance in feet. $\lambda = 1/20$ feet.

$$\lambda t = \frac{100}{20} = 5$$

Thus

$$P(\text{fewer than 3 spots}) = e^{-5} \cdot \left(1 + 5 + \frac{5^2}{2}\right)$$

$$= .1247 \quad\blacksquare$$

Example 14

A bag of 200 chocolate chips is dumped into a batch of cookie dough; 40 cookies are made. Why is the number of chips in a given cookie Poisson distributed? What is the probability that a randomly selected cookie has at least 4 chips?

Solution The parameter t is now volume of cookie dough. The three postulates translate here to: The chance that a chip is found in a *volume* of size t is proportional to the size t for t small; chips cannot occupy the same space, so the chance of finding more than 1 in a small volume t is negligible; finally, under the assumption that the chips have been thoroughly mixed into the dough, whether one volume has a certain number of chips should be independent of whether another volume has some number of chips. (Can you see why these postulates hold only approximately?) Consequently, the number of chips in a volume of dough should be Poisson distributed with parameter λt, where λ is the average number per cookie. For one cookie,

$$\lambda t = \frac{200}{40} = 5$$

since one cookie occupies 1/40 of the entire volume. That is, the expected number of chips in 1 cookie is 5. Thus

$$P(\text{cookie has at least 4 chips}) = 1 - \sum_{j=0}^{3} \frac{5^j}{j!} e^{-5}$$

$$= 1 - \left(1 + 5 + \frac{25}{2} + \frac{125}{6}\right) e^{-5}$$

$$= .7350 \quad \blacksquare$$

PROBLEMS

6.9. Assume that calls for help at a volunteer call-in hotline occur at the rate of $\lambda = 3$ calls/half-hour on the average. Assume each call lasts *exactly* 5 minutes. Find **(a)** $P(\text{no calls arrived between 7:00 and 7:15})$; **(b)** $P(\text{no calls arriving or continuing between 7:00 and 7:15})$; **(c)** $P(\text{no calls until at least 7:15} \mid \text{no calls at 7:00})$.

6.10. Flaws in sheet metal occur at the average rate of .7 flaws per foot. You buy a length of 2 feet. Find **(a)** $P(\text{no flaws in your sample})$; **(b)** $P(\text{at least 2 flaws})$.

6.11. Suppose that picnic spots in a park occur at locations that are randomly, but Poisson distributed with average 1.5 spots per 10,000 square feet. Find **(a)** $P(\text{no picnic spots in a certain 5000-square-foot area})$; **(b)** $P(\text{distance to closest spot to ours is at least 50 feet})$.

6.12. Orders for hot dogs come into Benjy's bar and grill at a rate that is Poisson distributed with an average of 1.8 orders per 5 minutes. How many hot dog orders can be expected **(a)** per hour; **(b)** per 8-hour day? **(c)** How many hot dogs should Benjy have on hand to be 50% sure that the supply will last 15 minutes?

6.13. Consider a Poisson stream with parameter λ. Let t be a fixed time. **(a)** Compute $P(j \text{ calls in } [t, t + \varepsilon])$ where $\varepsilon > 0$. **(b)** Show that $P(> 0 \text{ calls at a time } t) \leq P(> 0 \text{ calls in } [t, t + \varepsilon]) \to 0$ as $\varepsilon \to 0$.

6.4 CONNECTIONS AMONG THE POISSON, EXPONENTIAL, AND UNIFORM DISTRIBUTIONS

These three distributions were derived from distinct models; therefore, it is surprising that they can each be seen as different aspects of the *same* model. Each represents a particular perspective on the same random phenomenon. Consider a Poisson stream as in the preceding section. Suppose that calls come into a central exchange at the rate λ per minute. Then $N_t = \#$(calls in the interval $[0, t]$) is Poisson distributed with parameter λt. The **interarrival times** are the times *between* calls.

The *interarrival times* in a Poisson stream are *exponentially distributed* with the same parameter λ. In particular, the time until the first call is *exponentially distributed* with parameter λ.

The interarrival times $T_1, T_2, \ldots$ are depicted in Fig. 6.4.

To see why the exponential distribution holds, let T_1 be the *time until the first call*. Then

$$P(T_1 > t) = P(\textit{no arrivals in } [0, t])$$

$$= P(N_t = 0)$$

$$= \frac{(\lambda t)^0}{0!} e^{-\lambda t}$$

$$= e^{-\lambda t}$$

implies that T_1 is exponentially distributed with parameter λ (see Section 5.5).

Suppose that a call arrives at time t_0. Since nonoverlapping intervals are independent in a Poisson stream, it is as though the process starts from scratch as far as additional calls at later times are concerned. Hence the time until the *next* call—the interarrival time—is, as we have just shown, exponentially distributed with parameter λ. Hence the interarrival times $T_1, T_2, \ldots$ in Fig. 6.4 are each exponentially distributed with parameter λ.

Next assume a Poisson stream with parameter λ. *Assume that 1 call arrived* in the interval $[0, t_0]$. When did it arrive? If U denotes the arrival time, then U is concentrated on $[0, t_0]$. For $t \in [0, t_0]$,

$$P(U \leq t) = P(1 \text{ call in } [0, t] \mid 1 \text{ call in } [0, t_0])$$

$$= \frac{P(1 \text{ call in } [0, t] \text{ and } 1 \text{ call in } [0, t_0])}{P(1 \text{ call in } [0, t_0])}$$

$$= \frac{P(1 \text{ call in } [0, t] \text{ and none in } (t, t_0])}{P(1 \text{ call in } [0, t_0])}$$

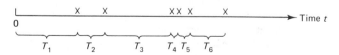

Figure 6.4 The interarrival times T_1, T_2, T_3, . . . in a Poisson stream are exponentially distributed with the *same* parameter.

$$= \frac{P(1 \text{ call in } [0, t]) P(\text{none in } (t, t_0])}{P(1 \text{ call in } [0, t_0])}$$

$$= \frac{\lambda t e^{-\lambda t} e^{-\lambda(t_0 - t)}}{\lambda t_0 e^{-\lambda t_0}}$$

$$= \frac{t}{t_0}$$

The second equality uses the definition of conditional probability; the fourth equality follows by Postulate 1 that events relating to disjoint time intervals are independent; the fifth equality notes that the number of calls in a time interval s is Poisson distributed with parameter λs regardless of when that time interval begins.

Differentiation of the extreme members of this equality with respect to t shows that U has constant density $1/t_0$ on $[0, t_0]$.

If one call arrived in a certain interval in a Poisson stream, *when* it arrived is uniformly distributed on that interval.

6.5 THE POISSON RENEWAL PROCESS

Consider a system that needs a particular type of component to be operational. The system comes with a number of spare components and as soon as one component wears out, another is installed immediately. In this way the entire system is "renewed" after each burn out. Some examples:

System	Component lifetime
Light fixture	Lifetime of each light bulb
Radio	Lifetime of each battery
Day's amount of work	Time to do each task
Computer	Time to run each program
Accidents on a high-way	Time between accidents

You can see that the applicablity of such systems is vast. We assume that *each component lifetime is exponentially distributed with parameter* λ and hence average component lifetime $1/\lambda$; also assume an independence condition—that events relating to the lifetime of one component are independent of events relating to lifetimes of other components.

Let S_n be the *total lifetime of the first n components*. Thus S_n is both the sum of the first n component lifetimes as well as the time of the nth component burnout. The renewal process defines an "event counting process" $\{N_t\}_{t=0}^{\infty}$ by setting

$$N_t = \#(\text{burnouts in } [0, t])$$

as in Fig. 6.5. That is, associated with a renewal process is a *stochastic process* $\{N_t\}_{t=0}^{\infty}$. N_t is simply the number of component renewals in $[0, t]$.

We now show a remarkable fact: If the component lifetimes in a renewal process are each exponentially distributed with parameter λ, then the event counting process $\{N_t\}_{t=0}^{\infty}$ is a Poisson process with parameter λ. That is, the number of renewals N_t in $[0, t]$ is Poisson distributed with parameter λt. We prove this by showing that the three Poisson postulates of Section 6.3 are satisfied by a renewal process in which each component lifetime is exponentially distributed with parameter λ. This depends on the fact that the component lifetimes, being exponentially distributed, obey the lack of memory property.

1. The number of burnouts in nonoverlapping time intervals I_1, I_2 are independent. This is so since regardless of the number of burnouts in the first interval I_1, the lack of memory property *applied to each component* ensures that the component in operation at the end of I_1 continues operating as though it were brand new—just plugged in. Thus the numbers of burnouts in I_1 and I_2 are independent. Similarly, events relating to any number of disjoint time intervals are independent.

2. The component in operation at time t will burn out in $[t, t + \Delta t]$ with probability

$$1 - e^{-\lambda \Delta t}$$

since component lifetimes are exponentially distributed. (Note that the lack of memory property has been used: regardless of how long the component in operation at time t has been operating, its lifetime beginning at time t has the same exponential distribution.) (see Fig. 6.6)

$$\frac{P(\geqslant 1 \text{ burnout in } [t, t + \Delta t])}{\Delta t} = \frac{1 - e^{-\lambda \Delta t}}{\Delta t} \to \lambda \qquad (*)$$

using L'Hôpital's rule to obtain the limit. *If two components burn out in* $[t, t + \Delta t]$, *then* certainly the lifetimes of each must be no greater than Δt. Thus

$$P(\geqslant 2 \text{ burnouts in } [t, t + \Delta t]) \leqslant P(1 \text{ burnout in } [t, t + \Delta t])^2$$

     The Poisson Distribution and the Poisson Process   Chap. 6

Figure 6.5 Each burnout corresponds to the arrival of a call (at time of burnout, the maintenance person *calls* in the news).

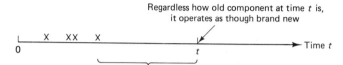

Regardless how old component at time t is, it operates as though brand new

Time t

Figure 6.6

Thus as $\Delta t \to 0$,

$$\frac{P(\geqslant 2 \text{ burnouts in } [t, t + \Delta t])}{\Delta t} \leqslant \frac{(1 - e^{-\lambda \Delta t})^2}{\Delta t} \to 0 \qquad (**)$$

again by L'Hôpital's rule. Since the event {1 burnout} is the set difference {$\geqslant 1$ burnout} − {$\geqslant 2$ burnouts}, equation (**) subtracted from equation (*) implies that as $\Delta t \to 0$,

$$\frac{P(\text{exactly 1 burnout in } [t, t + \Delta t])}{\Delta t} \to \lambda$$

which is Postulate 2.

3. Postulate 3 states that the probability of more than 1 burnout in a time interval of length Δt is negligible compared to Δt. Actually, this is equation (**).

Assume that the component lifetimes in a renewal process are exponentially distributed with parameter λ. Then the *counting process* $\{N_t\}_{t=0}^{\infty}$, where

$$N_t = \#(\text{burnouts in the time interval } [0, t])$$

is a Poisson stream with parameter λ. (In particular, we can expect λ renewals per unit time.)

Example 15

Assume that light bulbs have exponentially distributed lifetimes with an average life of 2 months. What is the probability that fewer than 5 bulbs burn out in 3 months?

Solution   Recall from Section 5.5 that the parameter λ for the exponential distribution is the *reciprocal* of the average or expectation. Thus

$$\lambda = \frac{1}{2}$$

With $N_t = \#(\text{burnouts in } [0, t])$,

$$P(< 5 \text{ burnouts in 3 months}) = P(N_3 < 5)$$

$$= \sum_{j=0}^{4} \frac{(\lambda t)^j}{j!} e^{-\lambda t} \Bigg|_{\lambda t = 3\left(\frac{1}{2}\right)}$$

$$= e^{-3/2} \left[1 + \frac{3}{2} + \frac{(3/2)^2}{2} + \frac{(3/2)^3}{3!} + \frac{(3/2)^4}{4!} \right]$$

$$= .9814 \quad \blacksquare$$

The renewal process with exponentially distributed component lifetimes and the Poisson process are actually the *same* model! Using the renewal process language, if I keep track of the number of *renewals* N_t in the time interval $[0, t]$, then N_t is Poisson distributed with parameter λ. On the other hand, in the Poisson process the time *between* calls is exponentially distributed with parameter λ.

To be even more specific, let

$$S_n = \text{lifetime of the first } n \text{ components}$$

in the renewal process. (Thus if the lifetimes of the first four components are 13, 4, 8, and 3 days, respectively, then $S_1 = 13$, $S_2 = 17$, $S_3 = 25$, and $S_4 = 28$. That is, S_n is the *cumulative* lifetime.) And S_0 is *defined* to be 0. The event

$$\{S_n \leq t\}$$

is the event that by time t, n components have burned out; in the language of the Poisson process, this is the event $\{N_t \geq n\}$.

$$\boxed{\begin{array}{l} \text{For } t \geq 0 \text{ and } n \geq 0, \\[4pt] \{S_n \leq t\} = \{N_t \geq n\} \end{array}}$$

Fig. 6.7 shows the equality of these events explicitly.

Example 16

Books are returned to the library at *intervals* which are exponentially distributed with average 5 minutes. What is the probability that the third book will be returned within 19 minutes after the library opens?

Solution Note that the parameter is the *reciprocal*

$$\lambda = \frac{1}{5} = .2 \qquad \lambda t = .2 \cdot 19 = 3.8$$

S_3 is the time that the third book is returned.

$$P(S_3 \leq 19) = P(N_{19} \geq 3)$$

$$= 1 - P(N_{19} = 0, 1, \text{ or } 2)$$

$$= 1 - e^{-3.8} \left[1 + 3.8 + \frac{(3.8)^2}{2!} \right]$$

$$= .7311 \quad \blacksquare$$

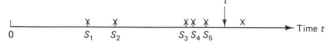

$\{S_5 \le t\}$ is the same event as $\{N_t \ge 5\}$ **Figure 6.7**

Example 17

Assume that light bulbs have an exponentially distributed lifetime with an average life span of 3 months. How many are required so that we can be 90% sure that the lamp into which they are installed will still be working 1 year from now?

Solution

$$\lambda = \frac{1}{3} \qquad \lambda t = \frac{1}{3} \cdot 12 = 4$$

n must satisfy

$$.90 \le P(S_n > 12)$$

$$= P(N_{12} < n)$$

$$= e^{-4} \left[1 + 4 + \frac{4^2}{2} + \cdots + \frac{4^{n-1}}{(n-1)!} \right]$$

The smallest value of n is

$$n = 8 \quad \blacksquare$$

Note that $\{S_n \le t\} = \{N_t \ge n\}$ implies that $\{S_n > t\} = \{N_t < n\}$ by taking complements (see Problem 6.22).

PROBLEMS

6.14. Why is the exponential distribution a good model for the interarrival times for customers at a souvenir stand? Assume an average of 10 customers per hour. **(a)** What is λ? Find **(b)** P(fewer than 4 customers in half an hour); **(c)** P(at least 1 customer in the next 5 minutes).

6.15. Assume that a computer runs programs sequentially (one after another) and that the time required for each is exponentially distributed with average time .1 second. Let X be the number of programs run in .5 second. **(a)** What is the distribution of X? Find **(b)** $P(X \le 2)$; **(c)** $P(3 \le X < 5)$.

6.16. The number of leaves falling off the big oak tree in the front yard averages 100 per hour in mid-October. Why should the Poisson distribution be a good model for the number during the course of a minute? Find **(a)** P(no leaves during the next minute); **(b)** P(more than 4 in the next minute).

6.17. Assume that batteries last for a time that is exponentially distributed with average 2 months. If a transmitter needs one battery at a time and 4 (including the original) are taken on an expedition, what are **(a)** P(transmitter lasts at least 11 months); **(b)** P(transmitter inoperative after only 6 months)?

6.18. (*Continuation*) How many batteries are required to be 70% sure that the transmitter will still be operational after 8 months?

6.19. Hilary's work consists of a number of tasks performed one after another. Each takes a random length of time exponentially distributed with average length of time until completion 3/4 hour. (What might be Hilary's work?) What is the maximum number n of tasks that Hilary can be assigned so that the time S_n until completion of all n is less than or equal to 4 hours with probability exceeding 70%.

6.20. Why might the distance between litter along a highway be exponentially distributed? If the average distance between litter patches is 75 feet, find the probability that the next 500-foot stretch will contain at least 6 litter patches.

6.21. For the renewal process, write a program that can input a time T, the parameter L (for λ), and a fraction A. Output should be the *smallest* number M of components so that the system consisting of M components used sequentially will last until at least time T with probability at least A. Test your program on Problem 6.18.

6.22. Although $\{S_n \leqslant t\}$ is the same event as $\{N_t \geqslant n\}$, show by a diagram that it is *not* true that $\{S_n < t\}$ is the same event as $\{N_t > n\}$, in general.

6.6 THE GAMMA DISTRIBUTION

In the renewal process the random variable S_n is the burnout time of the nth component; it is the sum of the lifetimes of the first n components. Thus S_n is a continuous random variable. In this section the distribution and density functions for S_n are computed.

Example 18

Buses arrive at the depot with exponentially distributed interarrival times with average time μ between buses. Thus the bus arrivals constitute a Poisson stream with parameter $\lambda = 1/\mu$. (Why?) Therefore, the waiting time until the first bus after *you* arrive is exponentially distributed with parameter λ. Find the density for the time S_2 of the second bus's arrival.

Solution As usual, first find the distribution function and then differentiate to find the density.

$$P(S_2 \leqslant t) = P(N_t \geqslant 2)$$

$$= 1 - P(N_t = 0 \text{ or } 1)$$

$$= 1 - e^{-\lambda t}(1 + \lambda t)$$

Differentiating to find the density f for S_2 yields

$$f(t) = \lambda e^{-\lambda t}(1 + \lambda t) - \lambda e^{-\lambda t}$$

$$= \lambda^2 t e^{-\lambda t} \quad \blacksquare$$

Example 19 (*Depends on Optional Section 5.6*)

A radio comes with an original and one spare battery. Each lasts an exponentially distributed lifetime average μ months. Find the failure rate function for the radio.

Solution Note that S_2 is the total lifetime of the radio; the parameter is

$$\lambda = \frac{1}{\mu}$$

Recall that the failure rate is $-G'(t)/G(t)$, where

$$G(t) = P(S_2 > t) = P(N_t < 2) = e^{-\lambda t}(1 + \lambda t)$$

Thus the failure rate is

$$\phi(t) = -\frac{G'(t)}{G(t)} = -\frac{-\lambda e^{-\lambda t}(1 + \lambda t) + \lambda e^{-\lambda t}}{e^{-\lambda t}(1 + \lambda t)} = \frac{\lambda^2 t}{1 + \lambda t}$$

(see Fig. 6.8). Note that the failure rate increases from 0 to the asymptotic value of λ. This is intuitive since starting with *two* batteries one expects a low failure rate for times close to 0. For large times, it is more and more certain that the second battery has been installed; if so, the failure rate is the *constant* failure rate λ for the exponentially distributed lifetime of the second battery. ∎

Notice that in general the time S_n of the nth component burnout is a continuous random variable concentrated on $(0, \infty)$. (Negative lifetimes cannot occur.) The density of S_2 was found in Example 18. The general case uses the same technique: The distribution function for S_n is

$$F_n(t) = P(S_n \leq t)$$

$$= P(N_t \geq n)$$

$$= 1 - P(N_t = 0, 1, \ldots, \text{ or } n - 1)$$

$$= 1 - e^{-\lambda t}\left[1 + \lambda t + \frac{(\lambda t)^2}{2!} + \cdots + \frac{(\lambda t)^{n-1}}{(n - 1)!}\right]$$

Differentiate to find the density:

$$f_n(t) = \frac{d}{dt} P(S_n \leq t)$$

→ Sum of the first n waiting times

$$= \lambda e^{-\lambda t}\left[1 + \lambda t + \frac{(\lambda t)^2}{2!} + \cdots + \frac{(\lambda t)^{n-1}}{(n - 1)!}\right]$$

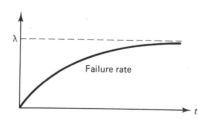

Failure rate

Figure 6.8 The failure rate function for two components used sequentially.

$$- e^{-\lambda t} \left[\lambda + \lambda(\lambda t) + \cdots + \frac{\lambda(\lambda t)^{n-2}}{(n-2)!} \right]$$

$$= \lambda e^{-\lambda t} \frac{(\lambda t)^{n-1}}{(n-1)!}$$

The distribution of the time S_n until the nth renewal in a Poisson process is called the **gamma distribution**. The density function for S_n is

$$f_n(t) = \begin{cases} 0 & t < 0 \\ \dfrac{\lambda^n t^{n-1}}{(n-1)!} e^{-\lambda t} & 0 < t \end{cases}$$

The formula for the gamma distribution function is unwieldy. It is most easily remembered through the relationship between S_n and N_t:

$$P(S_n \le t) = P(N_t \ge n)$$

Then use the Poisson distribution to write the right-hand side as a sum as we did in the derivation of the density above.

When $n = 1$, S_1 is the lifetime of one component. This *must* turn out to be exponentially distributed. In fact, setting $n = 1$ in the formula for the density implies that

$$f_1(t) = \frac{\lambda^1 t^{1-1}}{(1-1)!} e^{-\lambda t} = \lambda e^{-\lambda t}$$

for $t > 0$—the exponential density. ■

Example 20

Sketch the gamma density function $f_n(t)$ for $t > 0$.

Solution Using the expression above, we have

$$f_n'(t) = \frac{\lambda^n}{(n-1)!} [(n-1)t^{n-2}e^{-\lambda t} - \lambda t^{n-1}e^{-\lambda t}]$$

$$= \frac{\lambda^n}{(n-1)!} t^{n-2}e^{-\lambda t}[(n-1) - \lambda t]$$

for $n \ge 2$. Thus

$$f_n'(t) = 0$$

implies that

$$t = \begin{cases} \dfrac{n-1}{\lambda} & \text{for } n \ge 2 \\ \dfrac{n-1}{\lambda} & \text{or } \quad t = 0 \quad \text{for } n \ge 3 \end{cases}$$

At these points f_n has a horizontal tangent. The second derivative could be computed to see whether these points are maxima or minima; on the other hand, since f_n is a density, it is nonnegative and has total area 1. Hence the graph must be asymptotic to 0 at $t = \infty$. All these facts are summarized in Fig. 6.9. ■

The expectation $E(S_n)$ of S_n can be found by integration. Note that it can also be derived intuitively: Since the lifetime of each component is exponentially distributed with parameter λ, the expected lifetime of each component is $1/\lambda$. S_n is the waiting time until the nth burnout; so $E(S_n)$ should be n times the expected lifetime of each: $E(S_n)$ should be $n(1/\lambda) = n/\lambda$.

By integration,

$$E(S_n) = \int_{-\infty}^{\infty} tf_n(t)\, dt$$

$$= \int_0^{\infty} t\, \frac{\lambda^n t^{n-1}}{(n-1)!}\, e^{-\lambda t}\, dt$$

$$= \frac{1}{(n-1)!} \int_0^{\infty} (\lambda t)^n e^{-\lambda t}\, dt$$

$$= \frac{1}{\lambda}\, \frac{1}{(n-1)!} \int_0^{\infty} x^n e^{-x}\, dx$$

$$= \frac{1}{\lambda}\, \frac{1}{(n-1)!} \left[-x^n e^{-x} \Big|_0^{\infty} + n \int_0^{\infty} x^{n-1} e^{-x}\, dx \right]$$

$$= 0 + \frac{1}{\lambda}\, \frac{n}{(n-1)!} \int_0^{\infty} x^{n-1} e^{-x}\, dx$$

$$= \frac{n}{n-1} \left[\frac{1}{\lambda}\, \frac{1}{(n-2)!} \int_0^{\infty} x^{n-1} e^{-x}\, dx \right]$$

The fourth equality uses the change of variable $x = \lambda t$. The next equality uses integration by parts with $u' = e^{-x}$ and $v = x^n$. Notice that the expression in brackets in the last line is the same formula for $E(S_n)$ except that n is replaced by $n - 1$. (Compare the expression in brackets in the last line with the right-hand side of the fourth equality.) Thus the following recurrence relation has been derived:

$$E(S_n) = \frac{n}{n-1}\, E(S_{n-1})$$

But S_1 has mean $1/\lambda$. Thus

$$E(S_2) = \frac{2}{1} E(S_1) = \frac{2}{\lambda}$$

$$E(S_3) = \frac{3}{2} E(S_2) = \frac{3}{\lambda}$$

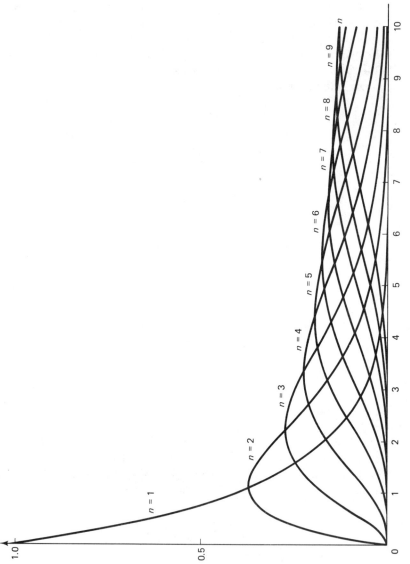

Figure 6.9 The gamma density functions; $\lambda = 1$.

and by induction:

> If S_n is gamma distributed with parameters n, λ, then
>
> $$E(S_n) = \frac{n}{\lambda}$$

Example 21

Write a program that can input the number of components N, the parameter L (for λ), and a time T. Output should be

$$P(S_N \leq T) = P(N_T \geq N) = 1 - e^{-LT} \sum_{j=0}^{N-1} \frac{(LT)^j}{j!}$$

Solution Let TERM be the general term in the sum

$$\text{TERM:} = \frac{(LT)^j}{j!}$$

A recursive formula for the next TERM as a function of the preceding one is

$$\text{TERM:} = \frac{LT}{j} \cdot \text{TERM}$$

The TERMs must be added, multiplied by e^{-LT}, and subtracted from 1. The complete program:

```
var N,J: integer;
    SUM,TERM,L,T,PROB: real;
begin
    readln(N,L,T);
    SUM: = 0.0;
    for J: = 0 to N-1 do
        begin
            if J = 0 then TERM: = 1.0
                    else TERM: = L*T*TERM/J;
            SUM: = SUM + TERM;
        end;
    PROB: = 1 - exp(-L*T)*SUM;
    writeln(PROB:10:4);
end.  ■
```

In summarizing these ideas a useful analog is the correspondence between discrete and continuous processes. For discrete processes a succession of Bernoulli trials is performed; here an event (failure or success) can occur only at discrete times. For continuous processes we use calls arriving at an exchange (or light bulb changing or . . .). But the lack of memory property is the same: The next Bernoulli trial has a result that does not "remember" previous outcomes; whether a call arrives in the next interval of time is independent of the number that have arrived so far.

	Discrete	Continuous
Probability	$P(S$ on one trial$) = p$	$P($event in $(t, t + dt]) = \lambda\, dt$
Interarrival times	Geometric $P($1st S on trial $n)$ $= q^{n-1}p$	Exponential $P(t <$ time until 1st event $\leq t + dt)$ $= \lambda e^{-\lambda t}\, dt$
Counting process	Binomial $P(j$ S's on n trials$)$ $= \binom{n}{j} p^j q^{n-j}$	Poisson $P(j$ events in $[0, t])$ $= \dfrac{(\lambda t)^j}{j!}\, e^{-\lambda t}$
Renewal	Each occurrence of an S counts as a renewal	Each occurrence of a call counts as a renewal

PROBLEMS

6.23. Louise sells encyclopedias door to door. She stops for the day after 4 sales. Assume that the time between sales is exponentially distributed. **(a)** If she can expect to work for 7 hours to make the 4 sales, what is the parameter λ? What is the probability that she will stop **(b)** before 6 hours; **(c)** after 9 hours?

6.24. Assume that cars arrive at a toll booth with exponentially distributed interarrival times. **(a)** If the tenth car can be expected to arrive at 25 minutes after the booth is opened, what is the parameter λ for the renewal process? What are **(b)** $P($no cars in 5 minutes$)$; **(c)** $P(20$ cars in half an hour$)$; **(d)** $P($at least 5 cars in 10 minutes$)$?

6.25. (*Continuation of Example 19*) Find the failure rate functions for S_3 and S_4.

6.26. (*Continuation*) Graph the failure rate functions for S_2, S_3 and S_4 on the same graph.

6.27. For $n \geq 1$ show that

$$P(S_n > t + s \mid S_n > t) \to e^{-\lambda s} \qquad \text{as } t \to \infty$$

by using the definition of conditional probability and the distribution function for S_n. What is an intuitive interpretation of this result?

6.28. Show that the gamma densities are *normalized*: For each $n \geq 1$,

$$\int_0^\infty f_n(t)\, dt = 1$$

6.29. (*The Generalized Gamma Distribution*) The gamma distribution can be generalized to the case in which n is not necessarily a positive integer: Define the *function*

$$\Gamma(\alpha) = \int_0^\infty t^{\alpha-1} e^{-t}\, dt$$

This is the *gamma function*. Show by an integration by parts that

$$\Gamma(\alpha) = (\alpha - 1)\Gamma(\alpha - 1)$$

for $\alpha > 0$. Show that $\Gamma(n) = (n - 1)!$ for n a positive integer. For λ, $\alpha > 0$, let

$$f(t) = \begin{cases} 0 & t < 0 \\ \dfrac{\lambda^\alpha t^{\alpha-1} e^{-\lambda t}}{\Gamma(\alpha)} & t > 0 \end{cases}$$

Show that f is normalized—the integral of f from $-\infty$ to ∞ is 1.

6.30. (*The Waiting-Time Paradox*) Buses arrive at the street corner according to a Poisson stream with parameter $\lambda = .1$. Thus in time t an average of λt buses arrive. The interarrival time between buses is exponentially distributed with average time $1/\lambda$ between buses. Benjy ran to the corner just as a bus was leaving. So Benjy *knows* that he can expect to wait $1/\lambda = 10$ minutes in the freezing cold. After 9 minutes, still no bus. But Alice has just arrived. Benjy says, "Just 1 more minute to wait."

Alice replies: "But because of the lack of memory property and the fact that I have just arrived, my waiting time is exponentially distributed with parameter 1/10 from *right now*. So *I* can expect to wait 10 minutes; and *you* can expect to wait 10 + 9 = 19 minutes."

How do you resolve this paradox? Who's right, Benjy or Alice?

6.31. (*Continuation*) Consider this discrete analog. Benjy has flipped a coin 9 times; p = probability of heads = 1/10. The waiting time until a head is $1/p = 10$. After 9 flips, all of which resulted in a tail, can Benjy expect to wait one more flip for the head? Or is Alice right in saying that the expected waiting time from this time is still 10 flips?

6.7 RANDOM COMMENTS AND PROBLEMS: CONDITIONING ON THE POISSON DISTRIBUTION (OPTIONAL)

Here are several examples of conditioning on Poisson and exponentially distributed random variables:

Example 22

Assume that the number of seeds N dropped by a plant is Poisson distributed with parameter λ. Suppose that each seed germinates with probability p independently of the other seeds dropped. Show that the total number of seeds germinated is Poisson distributed with parameter λp.

Solution Condition on the prior event of the number of seeds dropped N. *Given* the event $\{N = n\}$, each of the n seeds represents one Bernoulli trial. Consequently, the number of seeds germinating is binomially distributed with n trials and p = probability of success. Thus

$$P(j \text{ seeds germinate}) = \sum_{n=j}^{\infty} P(j \text{ seeds germinate} \mid N = n)P(N = n)$$

$$= \sum_{n=j}^{\infty} \binom{n}{j} p^j q^{n-j} \frac{\lambda^n}{n!} e^{-\lambda}$$

$$= p^j \cdot e^{-\lambda} \sum_{n=j}^{\infty} \frac{q^{n-j}\lambda^n}{j!(n-j)!}$$

$$= \frac{(\lambda p)^j}{j!} e^{-\lambda} \sum_{n=j}^{\infty} \frac{(q\lambda)^{n-j}}{(n-j)!}$$

$$= \frac{(\lambda p)^j}{j!} e^{-\lambda} \sum_{k=0}^{\infty} \frac{(q\lambda)^k}{k!}$$

$$= \frac{(\lambda p)^j}{j!} e^{-\lambda} e^{q\lambda}$$

$$= \frac{(\lambda p)^j}{j!} e^{-\lambda p}$$

Note that the sum extends from $n = j$ to ∞ since the number n of seeds dropped must be at least as large as the number of germinating seeds. ∎

PROBLEMS

6.32. Assume that the number of persons checking into the hospital emergency room is Poisson distributed with average 23.1 per evening. Assume that 1 in 40 registrants ends in death. What is the probability that there will be **(a)** at least 1 death during the course of the evening; **(b)** at most 2 deaths? (Use the Example 22 with seeds = registrants and germination = death.)

6.33. Suppose that customers enter a store according to a Poisson stream with average 40.7 for a whole day. Suppose that 2 out of 5 customers result in a sale. What is the distribution for the number of sales in half a day?

6.34. The local fire station receives alarms at the rate of .6 per hour. But 2 out of 7 turn out to be false alarms. **(a)** Why should the incoming calls be a Poisson stream? **(b)** What is the average number of real fires per 8-hour shift? Find **(c)** P(fewer than 4 fires in one shift); **(d)** P(3 false alarms in one shift); **(e)** P(at most 5 calls (real or false alarms) during half a shift).

6.35. People arrive at a bus stop according to a Poisson stream with parameter λ. The bus arrives sometime uniformly distributed in the interval $[0, b]$. Show that

$$P(n \text{ people waiting when the bus arrives})$$

$$= \frac{1}{b} \int_0^b \frac{(\lambda t)^n}{n!} e^{-\lambda t} \, dt$$

$$= \frac{1}{\lambda b \cdot n!} \int_0^{\lambda b} s^n e^{-s} \, ds$$

Compute this integral.

6.36. (*Continuation*) Suppose that the time of arrival of the bus has an exponential distribution with parameter ρ. Show that

$$P(n \text{ people waiting when the bus arrives})$$

$$= \int_0^{\infty} \frac{(\lambda t)^n}{n!} \rho e^{-(\lambda + \rho) t} \, dt$$

$$= \frac{\lambda^n \rho}{(\lambda + \rho)^{n+1}}$$

What is $E(\#(\text{people when bus arrives}))$?

All nature is but art unknown to thee,
All chance, direction which thou canst not see;

Alexander Pope, 1688–1744, An Essay on Man

— Chapter 7 —————————

Interlude: Modeling Randomness

This chapter develops methods for computer simulations of random models. Simulations can build intuition into the "workings" of randomness and develop insight into how random processes differ from deterministic ones; the algorithmic approach one must take to write a program leads to a different understanding of the model complementary to theoretical derivations. In addition, computer simulations are sometimes the *only* method for grinding out numbers from equations that are difficult to solve.

A generalized algorithmic language is used; it is in fact a subset of Pascal, since Pascal is an excellent language in which to express the flow of logic in an algorithm. The terminology is explained in Appendix 1; you should be able to understand it readily if you know any computer language—not necessarily Pascal.

7.1 RANDOM NUMBER GENERATORS

At the heart of simulations of random models is a method for producing random numbers—a procedure or function that will churn out number after number uniformly distributed in the interval [0, 1]. The method explained in this section is the method used by most programming languages which have built in random number generators.

Actually, the random number generator will be a specific formula that produces random numbers in a completely deterministic way. This is a contradiction to the very idea of randomness. Consequently, the numbers produced by the random number generator are often called pseudorandom because, although they have a very definite pattern, they appear to have no *discernible* pattern detectable without knowing the exact formula used. The fact that the *same* sequence of pseudorandom numbers is generated each time the generator is used is even useful in helping debug programs and understanding the results of the simulation. Randomness means "no pattern"; pseudorandomness means "no apparent pattern."

Start with positive integers MULT (for multiplier), ADDR (for adder), and NORM (for normalizer). SEED is to be a pseudorandom number satisfying

$$0 \leqslant SEED < NORM$$

Each time a new random number is needed, it is produced from the previous value of SEED by the formula

$$SEED := (MULT*SEED + ADDR) \bmod NORM$$

That is, first SEED gets multiplied by MULT, then ADDR is added on, and finally the *remainder upon division* by NORM is the new value of SEED.

Example 1

Use these values

$$MULT := 6 \quad ADDR := 5 \quad NORM := 11$$

What values of SEED will be produced if the initial value of SEED is 0? If the initial value is 4?

Solution Each time the new value of SEED is

$$SEED := (6*SEED + 5) \bmod 11$$

With SEED initially 0 this sequence is generated:

$$0 \quad 5 \quad 2 \quad 6 \quad 8 \quad 9 \quad 4 \quad 7 \quad 3 \quad 1 \quad 0 \quad 5 \quad 2 \quad 6 \quad 8 \quad \dots$$

With SEED initially 4 this sequence is generated:

$$4 \quad 7 \quad 3 \quad 1 \quad 0 \quad 5 \quad 2 \quad 6 \quad 8 \quad 9 \quad 4 \quad 7 \quad 3 \quad 1 \quad 0 \quad 5 \quad 2 \quad \dots \quad \blacksquare$$

From Example 1 two facts are apparent: First, since the next number in the sequence is generated from *only* the value of the previous number, *if any number is generated again, the entire list is a repetition from that point on.* Second, *the "cycle length"*—the number of distinct numbers before repetition occurs—*can be at most of length equal to the value of NORM.* This is so since the *mod* function produces the remainder upon division by NORM, which necessarily is a number between 0 and NORM-1; thus there are NORM many possible remainders—NORM many possible values of the random number SEED, that is; and as soon as one is repeated, repetition of the entire list occurs. A good random number generator would use values of MULT, ADDR, and NORM so that the cycle length is large.

Example 2

Consider the generator

$$\text{SEED} := (6*\text{SEED} + 3) \bmod 7$$

Then with different initial values of SEED, these sequences are generated:

```
0 3 0 3 0 3 0 3 0 3 ...
1 2 1 2 1 2 1 2 1 2 ...
4 6 4 6 4 6 4 6 4 6 ...
5 5 5 5 5 5 5 5 5 5 ...
```

Although the value of NORM = 7 suggests that the cycle length might be the maximum value of 7, the actual cycle lengths are small; if SEED is initially 5, then the random number generator is quite useless. ■

The theory of what values of the parameters result in good random number generators is complicated and more a subject of abstract algebra than of probability. Our interest here is in *using* a random number generator and the following theorem is stated without proof.*

Theorem

The random number generator will produce the maximum cycle length NORM of pseudorandom numbers with any initial value of SEED under *either* of these conditions:

1. NORM is a power of 10.
   ADDR ends in (units digit) 1, 3, 7, or 9.
   MULT-1 is a multiple of 20.
2. NORM is a power of 2.
   ADDR is odd.
   MULT-1 is a multiple of 4.

Example 3

With NORM = 10, ADDR = 27, and MULT = 21, the maximum cycle length of NORM = 10 is obtained. To check this, we use

$$\text{SEED} := (21*\text{SEED} + 27) \bmod 10$$

*See Donald E. Knuth, *The Art of Computer Programming*, Vol. 2 (Reading, Mass.: Addison-Wesley Publishing Co. Inc., 1971), Chapter 3.

to produce each successive value of SEED. With SEED initially 0 this sequence is obtained:

$$0 \quad 7 \quad 4 \quad 1 \quad 8 \quad 5 \quad 2 \quad 9 \quad 6 \quad 3 \quad 0 \quad \cdots$$

which has cycle length 10.

With NORM = 16, ADDR = 7, and MULT = 21, the maximum cycle length of NORM = 16 is obtained. Here

SEED := (21*SEED + 7) mod 16

yields this sequence with SEED initially 0:

$$0 \quad 7 \quad 10 \quad 9 \quad 4 \quad 11 \quad 14 \quad 13 \quad 8 \quad 15 \quad 2 \quad 1 \quad 12 \quad 3 \quad 6 \quad 5 \quad 0 \quad \cdots$$

which does in fact have cycle length 16. ■

Finding remainders when dividing by powers of 10 can be done quickly by human beings. For example, 237 mod 100 = 37; 3451 mod 10 = 1; 9087 mod 1000 = 87. But computers (using binary arithmetic) can find remainders more quickly when dividing by powers of 2. Programs will run faster, therefore, if NORM is a power of 2.

Besides long cycle lengths, a random number generator must satisfy this condition: The result of any arithmetic computation in calculating SEED from the previous value of SEED must not exceed the maximum integer that can be stored on the computer; otherwise, an overflow condition will result. For computers that store integers in 32 bits, for example, this maximum integer is $2,147,483,647 = 2^{31} - 1$. The maximum value used in computing the *next* value of SEED is

MULT*(maximum value of SEED) + ADDR

But the maximum value of SEED is NORM − 1. Consequently, MULT, ADDR, and NORM should be chosen so that

MULT*(NORM-1) + ADDR

does not exceed the maximum integer size.

Example 4

Using the theorem, the following would produce random number generators with maximum cycle length NORM:

NORM	ADDR	MULT	MULT*(NORM-1) + ADDR = maximum integer produced
100	41	641	63,500
10,000	4,857	2,601	26,012,256
1024	57	981	1,003,620
32,768	8,485	22,073	723,274,476

■

Interlude: Modeling Randomness   Chap. 7

In summary, since large cycle lengths are desirable, MULT, ADDR, and NORM should be chosen satisfying the conditions of the theorem in such a way that (NORM-1)*MULT + ADDR is close to the maximum integer size. Then *any* initial value of SEED will produce NORM many pseudorandom numbers without repetition. Note that there is no point in using an initial value of SEED > NORM − 1 since each succeeding value of SEED will be less than NORM. Why?

So far, the random number generator produces integers SEED with $0 \leq$ SEED < NORM. To obtain a number in the unit interval, simply divide SEED by NORM.

With an initial value of SEED and constants MULT, ADDR, and NORM, pseudorandom numbers in the unit interval [0, 1) are obtained by these two instructions:

```
SEED := (MULT*SEED + ADDR) mod NORM;
RND := SEED/NORM
```

Example 5

Write a program to generate 100 random numbers in [0, 1].

Solution
```
const NORM = 10000;
      ADDR =  4857;
      MULT =  8601;
var I, SEED: integer;
    RND: real;
begin
   SEED:= 0;
   for I:= 1 to 100 do
      begin
         SEED:= (MULT*SEED + ADDR) mod NORM;
         RND:= SEED/NORM;
         write(RND:8:3);
      end;
end.
```

Pseudorandom numbers produced in this way have a good chance of passing various tests for randomness. For example, the mean of the numbers is approximately 1/2; approximately one-tenth of them will fall into each of the intervals [0, .1), [.1, .2), . . ., [.9, 1). With any *finite* sequence, however, there can be no complete test of randomness. In addition, since the pseudorandom numbers are obtained by a deterministic formula, if the random model that is being simulated incorporates a "pattern" that coincides with the "pattern" of the random number generator formula, then the generator may prove to be a bad one for that model. Before using a particular random number generator (choice of NORM, ADDR, and MULT), one should perform a few simple checks. Have a listing of several hundred of them and visually inspect the list; do they *appear* to be random? Have the average printed out. Is it close to 1/2? And so on. (See Problems 7.6 to 7.10.)

Also note that a random number generator is only capable of producing NORM many distinct values of RND. If more are required for a simulation, the values of NORM, ADDR, and MULT should be changed.

Example 6: *Simulating Bernoulli Trials*

Input a probability p of success for each Bernoulli trial and an integer MAX; output MAX many Bernoulli trial simulations (MAX many letters "S" or "F").

Solution After generating each value of RND as in Example 5, a decision has to be made whether the value of RND is to correspond to an S or to an F. But the probability that RND is less than p is exactly p, since the interval $[0, p)$ occupies a fraction p of the entire unit interval $[0, 1]$. Thus RND simulates a success if RND $< p$; otherwise, RND simulates a failure.

```
const NORM = 10000;
      ADDR =  4857;
      MULT =  8601;
var I,SEED,MAX: integer;
    RND,P:real;
begin
    SEED: = 0;
    readln(P,MAX);
    for I: = 1 to MAX do
        begin
            SEED: = (MULT*SEED + ADDR) mod NORM;
            RND: = SEED/NORM;
            if RND < P then write ('S')
                         else write ('F');
        end;
end.   ■
```

PROBLEMS

7.1. With the following values of NORM, ADDR, MULT, and initial value of SEED, write out the sequence of successive values of SEED generated from SEED := (MULT*SEED + ADDR) mod NORM. Start with SEED=0.

	MULT	ADDR	NORM
(a)	4	3	7
(b)	5	3	16
(c)	2	3	16
(d)	5	7	10
(e)	1	9	10
(f)	7	4	9

For which of these is the cycle length equal to NORM? Which of them satisfy the conditions of the theorem?

7.2. If NORM = 1035, ADDR = 6355, and MULT = 2309, what is the maximum value of MULT*SEED + ADDR obtained with an initial value of SEED less than NORM?

7.3. Show that M mod NORM = M_1 mod NORM if and only if M − M_1 is a multiple of NORM. Show that, consequently, if MULT − $MULT_1$ is a multiple of NORM, then

$$(MULT*SEED + ADDR) \bmod NORM = (MULT_1*SEED + ADDR) \bmod NORM$$

Hence MULT, ADDR, NORM produce the same random number generator as $MULT_1$, ADDR, NORM.

7.4. Show that MULT, ADDR, NORM produce the same random number generator as MULT, $ADDR_1$, NORM if ADDR − $ADDR_1$ is a multiple of NORM.

Note that Problem 7.3 implies that there is no point in taking MULT larger than NORM. This is so since if MULT > NORM, then the *same* random number generator is obtained by subtracting NORM from MULT enough times so that the new value of MULT < NORM. Similarly, Problem 7.4 shows that ADDR can be taken to be less than NORM without eliminating any generators.

7.5. What will happen if MULT = 1? Plot 10 successive values of SEED if the initial value of SEED is 0 and SEED: = (1*SEED + 17) mod 400. What is wrong with this generator?

In the following program problems use the same values of NORM, ADDR, and MULT.

7.6. Find out what the maximum integer is on your computer. Then choose NORM, ADDR, and MULT satisfying the theorem, but so that (NORM-1)*MULT + ADDR does not exceed this maximum.

7.7. With your choice of NORM, ADDR, and MULT, write a program that uses the initial value of SEED equal to 0. Loop through until SEED returns to 0. Print out the number of cycles of the loop performed. This number should be NORM (if you have chosen your random number generator in accordance with the theorem). Also print out the *average* of all the RND values.

7.8. Write a program that will input MAX equal to the number of random numbers RND : = SEED/NORM to be generated. Output all these numbers (make sure that MAX is not *too* large!) and check that they appear to be randomly distributed on [0, 1] without any obvious pattern.

7.9. With the same random number generator, write a program to input MAX. Compute MAX many values of RND starting with the initial value of SEED equal to 0. Print out the number of values of RND in each of the intervals [0, .1), [.1, .2), . . ., [.9, 1]. These should each be close to MAX/10. Run the program with several inputs of MAX.

7.10. With the same random number generator, write a program to loop through MAX distinct values of RND (starting with initial value of SEED equal to 0) and compute the number of times the current value of RND is larger than the preceding value of RND. This number should be approximately MAX/2.

Recall that the frequency interpretation of probability claims that if a random experiment is performed a large number MAX of times and the event A occurs n times, then $P(A) \cong n/\text{MAX}$.

> To simulate $P(A)$, input a large value MAX, simulate the random experiment MAX times, add 1 to SUM each time the simulation results in event A, and output SUM/MAX.

Recall also that if X is a random variable, then $E(X)$ is approximately the average of the X values over a large number of repetitions of the random experiment.

> To simulate $E(X)$, input a large value MAX, simulate the random experiment MAX times, add the value of X on each to SUM, and output SUM/MAX.

How large should MAX be so that the approximations are accurate? The answer requires the central limit theorem and the law of large numbers (Chapter 10). But consider this: If MAX = 1000 and SUM is an integer, then SUM/MAX can only have at most *three* nonzero digits to the right of the decimal point. For accuracy to this many places, MAX has to be taken considerably larger than 1000.

Example 7

Three balls are tossed randomly into 5 cans. What is the probability that they all land in different cans?

Solution There are 5^3 ways to distribute all the balls into the cans, 5_3 of which have the balls in different cans. Hence the exact probability is

$$\frac{5_3}{5^3} = \frac{5 \cdot 4 \cdot 3}{5 \cdot 5 \cdot 5} = .48$$

To simulate the probabilities, input an integer MAX, then MAX many times simulate three container numbers CAN[1], CAN[2], CAN[3]; these are integers from 1 to 5 representing the cans. If CAN[1], CAN[2], and CAN[3] are distinct, add 1 to SUM.

```
const NORM = 10000;
      ADDR =  4857;
      MULT =  8601;
var I,SEED,MAX,SUM,J: integer;
    RND: real;
    CAN: array [1..3] of integer;
```

```
begin
    SEED: = 0; SUM: = 0;
    readln(MAX);

    for I: = 1 to MAX do
        begin
            for J: = 1 to 3 do
                begin
                    SEED: = (MULT*SEED + ADDR) mod NORM;
                    RND: = SEED/NORM;
                    CAN[J]: = trunc(5*RND + 1);
                end;
            if (CAN[1] <> CAN[2]) and
                (CAN[1] <> CAN[3]) and
                (CAN[2] <> CAN[3]) then SUM: = SUM + 1;
        end;
    writeln(SUM/MAX:10:4);
end.  ■
```

7.3 SIMULATING DISCRETE DISTRIBUTIONS WITH A FINITE NUMBER OF OUTCOMES

Example 6 simulated Bernoulli trials in which there were two possible outcomes, success or failure. Generalizing, suppose that a random experiment can have $N + 1$ possible outcomes; outcome i occurs with probability p_i. Thus

$$p_0 + \cdots + p_N = 1$$

If RND is uniformly distributed in the unit interval [0, 1), then fraction p_0 of the RND values will be in the interval $[0, p_0)$, fraction p_1 of the RND values will be in the interval $[p_0, p_0 + p_1)$, ... Thus to simulate an outcome i, use this procedure: Generate RND, and determine which interval contains RND. More specifically, if RND $< p_0$, set $i = 0$; if not, but RND $< p_0 + p_1$, set $i = 1$; if not, but RND $< p_0 + p_1 + p_2$, set $i = 2$; .... That is, the simulation results in outcome i if i is the *smallest integer* so that RND $< p_0 + \cdots + p_i$. Note that such an i exists since $p_0 + \cdots + p_N = 1$ and RND $\in$ [0, 1). Henceforth we will denote these probabilities using array notation. In the variable declarations part of the programs, P will be array [0..100] of real. (N is assumed to be $\leq$ 100.) Thus in particular, P[I] denotes p_i. (See Fig. 7.1.)

Simulation with a Finite Number of Outcomes

Determine N and the probabilities P[0], . . . , P[N]. Form the sums

$$SUM[I] := P[0] + \cdots + P[I]$$

for I := 0 to N. Generate RND and find the smallest value of I so that RND < SUM[I].

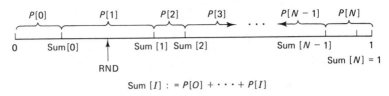

$$\text{Sum}[I] : = P[O] + \cdots + P[I]$$

Figure 7.1

Example 8

A random experiment can have outcome 0, 1, . . . , or N. Write a program that can input MAX (the number of simulations to perform), N, and the N + 1 probabilities P[0], . . ., P[N]. Output all MAX many simulations of the experiment.

Solution Both P and SUM are arrays. A while loop is used to find the smallest I so that RND < SUM[I].

```
const NORM = 10000;
      ADDR =  4857;
      MULT =  8601;
var I,SEED,MAX,J,N: integer;
    RND, SUM: real;
    P,SUM: array [0..100] of real;

begin
    readln (MAX,N);
    for J: = 0 to N do read(P[J]);

    SUM[0] : = P[0];
    for J: = 1 to N do SUM[J]: = SUM[J – 1] + P[J];

    SEED: = 0;
    for J: = 1 to MAX do
        begin
            SEED: = (MULT*SEED + ADDR) mod NORM;
            RND: = SEED/NORM;

            I: = 0;

            while RND >=SUM[I] do I: = I+1;

            write(I);
        end;
end.  ∎
```

Example 9

Use the method above to simulate 100 rolls of a fair die.

Solution   Each outcome has equal probability 1/6.   Hence they do not have to be input into the program.   Neither does SUM[I] have to be stored since SUM[I] = 1/6.   Why?

```
const NORM =  10000;
      ADDR =   4857;
      MULT =   8601;
 var I,SEED,J: integer;
      RND: real;

begin
    SEED: = 0;

    for J: = 1 to 100 do
        begin
            SEED: = (MULT*SEED + ADDR) mod NORM;
            RND: = SEED/NORM;

            I: = 1;

            while RND > = 1/6 do I: = I+1;

            write(I);
        end;
end.
```

Note that I is initialized to 1 before the while loop rather than 0 as in Example 8. Why?   ■

Example 10: *Simulating a Binomial Random Variable*

Input MAX,N,P and simulate MAX many experiments; *each* consists of performing N Bernoulli trials with probability P of success and determining the *number* of successes on all N trials.

Solution   There are two methods.   The first is to simulate a total of MAX · N many Bernoulli trials, split them into groups of N each; for each group of N, count the total number of successes.   (Problem 7.13 asks that you do this.)   The second method is to compute the binomial probabilities

$$P[I] := \binom{N}{I} P^I \cdot Q^{N-I}$$

and the cumulative sums as in the boxed method above.   The probabilities P[I] will be computed recursively using

$$P[I] := \frac{N - I + 1}{I} \frac{P}{Q} \cdot P[I - 1]$$

as in Chapter 4, Example 17.   The body of the program is

```
begin
    readln(MAX,N,P);

    Q: = 1 − P;
    P[0]: = Q**N;

    for J: = 1 to N do P[J]: = ((N − J + 1)/J)*(P/Q)*P[J − 1];

    SUM[0] := P[0];

    for J: = 1 to N do SUM[J]: = SUM[J − 1] + P[J];

    SEED: = 0;
    for J: = 1 to MAX do
        begin
            SEED: = (MULT*SEED + ADDR) mod NORM;
            RND: = SEED/NORM;

            I: = 0;

            while RND > = SUM[I] do I: = I + 1;

            write(I);
        end;
end.    ■
```

Let X be a random variable with range $\{0, 1, \ldots, N\}$ and $P(X = i) = p_i$. Let us see how the foregoing method for simulating a value of X appears graphically. The *distribution function* for X is $F(t) = P(X \leq t)$ as a function of t.   Since X is discrete, F is a *step function* with jumps at the integer points $i = 0, 1, \ldots, N$.

To simulate a value of X, the method is to compute RND and find the smallest i so that RND $< p_0 + \cdots + p_i$.   Graphically, the value RND is plotted on the y axis; a horizontal line is drawn from RND; where it intersects the steps determines the simulated value i.   (See Fig. 7.2.)

More generally, if the discrete random variable X has range $\{x_0, x_1, \ldots, x_N\}$ with the values increasing ($x_i < x_{i+1}$), then the distribution function of X is a step function; if $p_i = P(X = x_i)$, then

$$F(x) = P(X \leq x) = \Sigma P(X = x_i) = \Sigma p_i$$

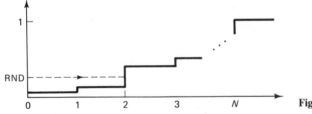

Figure 7.2

Interlude: Modeling Randomness   Chap. 7

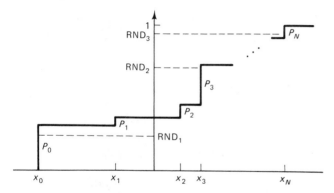

Figure 7.3 RND_1 simulates x_0; RND_2 simulates x_3; RND_3 simulates x_N.

where the sums extend over all indices i with $x_i \leqslant x$. Graphically, the distribution function appears as in Fig. 7.3. Then the graphical method for simulating a value of X is this: First generate RND, locate RND on the y axis, and find the x value exactly below the intersection point of the horizontal line through RND and the graph of F.

PROBLEMS

7.11. A box contains 4 red and 3 blue pencils. Three are selected at random without replacing any of them. Let X be the number of red pencils in the sample. What is $P(X = i)$ for $i = 0, 1, 2, 3$? Write a program to simulate and print 100 samples. That is, output should appear as a list of integers

$$2 \quad 3 \quad 0 \quad 2 \quad 0 \quad 1 \quad 1 \quad \ldots$$

indicating "2 red in first sample, 3 red in second sample, 0 in third sample, ..." Input should be P[I] for $i = 0, 1, 2, 3$.

7.12. Input MAX and P and simulate MAX many experiments. *Each* consists of flipping a coin twice with probability P of heads. Outcome 0 corresponds to 0 heads (TT) with probability $Q^2 = (1 - P)^2$; outcome 1 corresponds to HT with probability P·Q; outcome 2 corresponds to TH; and outcome 3 corresponds to HH.

7.13. Input MAX, N, and P and simulate MAX many experiments; each consists in performing N Bernoulli trials as in Example 10. Do this by performing MAX·N many simulations of Bernoulli trials. An outline of the program is

```
SEED: = 0;
for J: = 1 to MAX do
    begin
        SUM: = 0;
        for K: = 1 to N do
            begin
                generate RND and increment SUM if RND < P
            end;
        write(SUM);
    end;
```

7.14. (*Continuation*) Have your program print the average number of successes for the MAX many simulations. This should be close to the expectation N·P.

7.4 SIMULATING DISCRETE DISTRIBUTIONS WITH A COUNTABLY INFINITE NUMBER OF OUTCOMES

Assume throughout this section that random variable X has range {0, 1, 2, . . .}. Let P[I] = $P(X = I)$. To simulate a value for X requires splitting the unit interval [0, 1] into countably many subintervals, then selecting uniformly distributed RND, and finally determining in which subinterval RND is located.

Using the techniques of the preceding section would require first finding the *infinitely* many sums

$$\text{SUM[I]} := \text{P[0]} + \cdots + \text{P[I]}$$

for I := 0 to ∞ as in Fig. 7.4. Since these infinitely many operations are impossible on a computer, we need an alternative. One possibility is to find a value M so that SUM[M] is *nearly* 1. If the value of RND is less than this value, the simulation should produce the smallest I so that RND < SUM[I] as before; if, however, RND ⩾ SUM[M], the simulation will produce outcome M + 1.

An alternative and the one used here is to compute successively values of SUM[I], stopping when RND < SUM[I] for the first time. This method is less efficient than the first method since with many simulations the value SUM[0], SUM[1], . . . must be calculated many times. On the other hand, there is no top cutoff value as the upper bound for the simulated value of X. One can improve the method by storing SUM[0], SUM[1], . . . as they are computed. Then when the next RND is generated, one checks to see if RND is less than any of sums SUM[I] computed so far; if not, more values of SUM[I] are computed (and stored) until a value of I is found with RND < SUM[I]. This improvement is worthwhile, but for the sake of clarity will not be incorporated in the examples (see Problem 7.18).

Example 11: *Simulating a Geometric Random Variable*

Recall that if *W* is the waiting time until the first success in a succession of Bernoulli trials, then

$$P(X = j) = q^{j-1}p$$

for $j = 1, 2, 3, . . .$ Write a program to input MAX (number of simulations) and P and output the MAX many waiting times *j* simulated.

Solution The recursive formula

$$P(X = j) = q^{j-1}p = qq^{j-2}p = qP(X = j - 1)$$

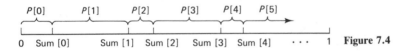

P[0] P[1] P[2] P[3] P[4] P[5]

0 Sum [0] Sum [1] Sum [2] Sum [3] Sum [4] · · · 1 **Figure 7.4**

0   1   **Figure 7.5**

is used (but see Problem 7.17 for an alternative method).   These probabilities split
the interval [0, 1] as in Fig. 7.5.

```
const NORM =  10000;
      ADDR  =   4857;
      MULT  =   8601;
var I,SEED,J,MAX: integer;
    RND,SUM,PROB,P,Q: real;

begin
    readln(MAX,P);
    Q: = 1-P;

    SEED: = 0;
    for J: = 1 to MAX do
        begin
            SEED: = (MULT*SEED + ADDR) mod NORM;
            RND: = SEED/NORM;

            PROB: = P; SUM: = P; I: = 1;

            while RND>=SUM do
                begin
                    PROB: = Q*PROB;
                    SUM: = SUM + PROB;
                    I: = I+1;
                end;
            write(I);
        end;
end.   ■
```

Example 12: *Simulating a Poisson Random Variable*

Input should be MAX for the number of simulations and L for the parameter λ.
Output should be MAX many simulations of a Poisson distributed random variable
X with parameter L.

   Solution   Recall (Section 6.1) that the Poisson probabilities satisfy this recursive formula:

$$P(X = i) = \frac{L}{i} P(X = i - 1)$$

for $i = 1, 2, \ldots$, where L is the parameter.   The program is similar to that of
Example 11.   There are only two differences: the *initialization*

$$\text{PROB} := P(X = 0) = e^{-L}$$

and the *modification*

```
        PROB := L*PROB/I
```

using the recursive formula. The body of the program is

```
        begin
            readln(MAX,L);

            SEED:= 0;
            for J:= 1 to MAX do
                begin
                    generate RND;

                    PROB:= exp(-L); SUM:= PROB; I:= 0;

                    while RND>=SUM do
                        begin
                            I:= I+1;
                            PROB:= L*PROB/I;
                            SUM:= SUM + PROB;
                        end;

                    write(I);

                end;
        end.    ■
```

PROBLEMS

7.15. Let X be Poisson distributed. $E(X) = \lambda$. Write a program that will input L (for λ) and simulate 1000 values of X. After each series of 100 simulations, print out the sum of all the simulations of X so far generated and the ratio of this number to the number of simulations. This number should be close to the expectation λ. Run the program for several values of L.

7.16. Let X be geometrically distributed. What is $E(X)$? Write a program that will input P and simulate 1000 values of X. Print out the average of all 1000 X values. Run the program for several values of P.

7.17. X is geometrically distributed. Recall (Section 4.3) that $P(X \leq j) = 1 - q^j$. Use this method (rather than the one in Example 11) to write a program that will input P and positive integer K. Perform 1000 simulations and print the number of times X exceeds K. (This should be approximately $1000P(X > K) = 1000q^K$.)

7.18. Incorporate the improvement discussed before Example 11 into that example. Declare another variable TOP (integer) whose value is the *largest I* so that SUM[I] has been computed. After RND is generated, check to see whether RND < SUM[TOP]. If not, compute SUM[I] for I > TOP until RND < SUM[I]; then set TOP equal to I.

Interlude: Modeling Randomness   Chap. 7

7.5 SIMULATING CONTINUOUS DISTRIBUTIONS

The methods developed so far are useless for simulating a continuous random variable X. To see how to do this, we approximate X by a discrete random variable Y_ε which is defined to be within ε of X *regardless* of the actual value of X. More specifically, let $\varepsilon > 0$ be given. Given the value x of the random variable X, there is a *unique integer j* so that

$$(j - 1) \, \varepsilon < x \le j\varepsilon$$

For example, if $\varepsilon = .1$ and $x = 4.57$, then $45(.1) < x \le 46(.1)$ implies that $j = 46$; with $\varepsilon = .1$ and $x = -37.208$, then $-373(.1) < x \le -372(.1)$ implies that $j = -372$.

Given $X = x$, the random variable Y_ε is *defined* to be the unique value of $j\varepsilon$ so that $(j - 1) \, \varepsilon < x \le j\varepsilon$. More simply stated, given a value x of the random variable X, Y_ε is defined to be x rounded up to the nearest multiple of ε. Note these properties of the *discrete approximation* Y_ε to X:

1. $Y_\varepsilon - \varepsilon < X \le Y_\varepsilon$.
2. $Y_\varepsilon = X$ if X is an integer multiple of ε.
3. The range of $Y_\varepsilon = \{\ldots, -3\varepsilon, -2\varepsilon, -\varepsilon, 0, \varepsilon, 2\varepsilon, 3\varepsilon, \ldots\}$.

Let F and F_ε be the distribution functions for X and Y_ε, respectively. At multiples of ε, F and F_ε are equal:

$$F_\varepsilon(j\varepsilon) = P(Y_\varepsilon \le j\varepsilon) = P(X \le j\varepsilon) = F(j\varepsilon)$$

since $Y_\varepsilon \le j\varepsilon$ if and only if $X \le j\varepsilon$. Also since $X \le Y_\varepsilon$, if $Y_\varepsilon \le t$, then $X \le t$. Thus set inclusion holds between these events:

$$\{Y_\varepsilon \le t\} \subseteq \{X \le t\}$$

Thus for *any* value of t,

$$F_\varepsilon(t) = P(Y_\varepsilon \le t) \le P(X \le t) = F(t)$$

Since Y_ε is discrete, its distribution function is a step function with jumps at points in its range. Fig 7.6 summarizes these facts in graphs of the distribution functions: Note that as $\varepsilon \to 0$, the distribution function F_ε will approximate F more and more closely.

To simulate a value of X, do this: Choose a value $\varepsilon > 0$, simulate a value t of Y_ε; this can be done using the methods of the preceding sections because Y_ε is *discrete*. Then an approximation to a simulated value of X will be t. Although this appears complicated, in the limit as $\varepsilon \to 0$, the method turns out to be very straightforward.

How is a value simulated for Y_ε? Since Y_ε is discrete the method before Fig. 7.3 can be used. First generate RND, find RND on the y axis, then draw a horizontal line through RND; the point on the x axis below the intersection point of the horizontal line and the distribution function for Y_ε is the simulated value of

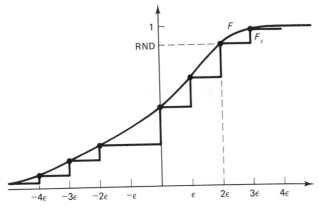

Figure 7.6 To approximate a simulation for random variable X with distribution F, simulate Y_ε with distribution F_ε.

Y_ε. Notice what happens in the limit as $\varepsilon \to 0$: *The distribution function for Y_ε approaches the distribution function for X.*

Consequently, we can dispense with the discrete random variable Y_ε and summarize the technique so far: To simulate a value of X, graph its distribution function F, generate RND, find RND on the y axis, and find the point just below the intersection of the horizontal line through RND and the graph of F as in Fig. 7.7.

In fact, the graphical device can be simplified further. If RND produces simulated value x as in the diagram, then x must be that point which satisfies $F(x) = $ RND. That is, once RND is generated, the simulated value of X is F^{-1} (RND).

Recall from Chapter 5 that X is *concentrated* on the set I if I is the interval on which $F' = $ density f is nonzero. I is the set on which F is *increasing*. (The slope of F is 0 on I^c.) Thus the inverse F^{-1} of F is a function from $(0, 1)$ to I.

The following method summarizes the theory developed in this section:

Simulating a Continuous Random Variable

Let X have distribution function F. Let F^{-1} be the inverse of F on the interval of concentration I. To simulate a value of X:

1. First generate RND.

2. F^{-1} (RND) is the simulated value.

Example 13: *Simulating a Uniform Random Variable on* $[a, b]$

Let U be uniformly distributed on $[a, b]$. The distribution function is

$$F(x) = \begin{cases} 0 & x \leq a \\ \dfrac{x - a}{b - a} & a \leq x \leq b \\ 0 & b \leq x \end{cases}$$

Interlude: Modeling Randomness   Chap. 7

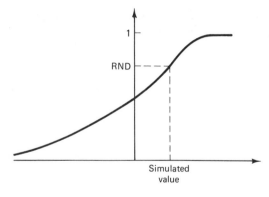

RND

Simulated
value

Figure 7.7 In the limit as $\varepsilon \to 0$, simulated values of Y_ε approach a simulated value of X.

Thus the interval of concentration is the interval on which F is increasing, this is $[a, b]$. Written in terms of the dependent variable y, the expression for $F(x)$ is

$$y = \frac{x - a}{b - a}$$

To find the inverse, find x in terms of y:

$$x - a = (b - a)y$$

$$x = (b - a)y + a$$

This function is an expression for F^{-1}. Thus to simulate a value for X first generate RND, then set $X = (b - a) \cdot \text{RND} + a$.

Note that if X is uniformly distributed on the unit interval $[0, 1]$, then $a = 0$ and $b = 1$. Thus the simulated value of X is $(1 - 0) \text{RND} + 0 = \text{RND}$, which certainly is intuitive since RND itself is assumed to be uniformly distributed on the unit interval. ∎

Review: Finding F^{-1}

1. First write $y = F(x)$ as an expression in x.

2. Solve for x in terms of y.

3. This new expression is the formula for F^{-1}.

Example 14

Write a program to simulate 100 values of X, where X has density

$$f(x) = \begin{cases} 0 & x < 1 \\ \dfrac{2}{x^3} & 1 < x \end{cases}$$

Also, simulate $E(X)$.

Solution The interval of concentration is the interval on which f is nonzero. This is $(1, \infty)$. For $x \in (1, \infty)$ the distribution function is

$$y = F(x) = \int_1^x \frac{2}{t^3} \, dt = -\frac{1}{t^2}\Big|_1^x = 1 - \frac{1}{x^2}$$

Inverting, we have

$$\frac{1}{x^2} = 1 - y$$

$$x = \frac{1}{\sqrt{1 - y}}$$

Thus

$$F^{-1}(x) = \frac{1}{\sqrt{1 - x}}$$

The body of the program is

```
begin
    SEED: = 0; SUM: = 0;
    for I: = 1 to 100 do
        begin
            SEED: = (MULT*SEED + ADDR) mod NORM;
            RND: = SEED/NORM;

            X: = 1/((1 − RND)**(1/2));
            write(X:10:4)

            SUM: = SUM + X;
        end;

    writeln;
    writeln('EXPECTED VALUE ', SUM/100:12:4);
end.
```  ■

Example 15: *Simulating an Exponentially Distributed Random Variable*

Let X have exponential density with parameter λ:

$$f(x) = \begin{cases} 0 & x < \hat{0} \\ \lambda e^{-\lambda x} & 0 < x \end{cases}$$

Then the interval on which the density is nonzero is $(0, \infty)$. For $x > 0$,

$$y = \int_0^x \lambda e^{-\lambda t} \, dt = 1 - e^{-\lambda x}$$

$$e^{-\lambda x} = 1 - y$$

$$x = \frac{-\ln(1 - y)}{\lambda}$$

Hence the transformation from uniformly selected RND to X is

$$X := \frac{-\ln(1 - \text{RND})}{\lambda}$$

Otherwise, the program is identical to that of Example 14. Note that $1 - \text{RND}$ is also a random number in $[0, 1]$. Thus to simplify the calculations, one might simply set

$$X := \frac{-\ln(\text{RND})}{\lambda}$$

There is one small technical point, though. Since one of the values of SEED is 0, RND = SEED/NORM will also be 0. $\ln(\text{RND})$ would then result in a program interrupt since $\ln(0)$ must be computed. This does not happen with $\ln(1 - \text{RND})$ since RND $\in [0, 1)$. ∎

Example 16: *Buffon Needle Experiment*

Recall Example 17 of Chapter 5, in which a needle 1 unit long is dropped onto a grid of parallel lines 1 unit apart. We saw that

$$P(\text{needle crosses line}) = \frac{2}{\pi}$$

Write a program using this result to determine experimentally the value of π.

Solution These two random variables were defined in that example:

$$X = \text{distance of foot of needle to line to left}$$

$$\Phi = \text{angle needle subtends with positive horizontal axis}$$

Then X is uniformly distributed on $[0, 1)$ and Φ is uniformly distributed on $[0, \pi)$. A crossing occurs if and only if

$$0 \leqslant s \leqslant \frac{\pi}{2} \qquad \text{and} \qquad \cos s > 1 - x$$

or

$$\frac{\pi}{2} < s < \pi \qquad \text{and} \qquad -\cos s > x$$

where x is the value of X and s is the value of Φ. RND simulates X, but $\pi \cdot$ RND simulates Φ since Φ is uniformly distributed on $[0, \pi)$. (Use Example 13 with $a = 0$, $b = \pi$.) With MAX equal to the total number of needle tosses, SUM is initialized to 0. SUM is incremented by 1 each time values of X and Φ are simulated which satisfy the conditions for a crossing. The body of the program is

```
begin
    SEED: = 0; SUM: = 0; PI: = 3.1415927;
    readln(MAX);
```

```
for I: = 1 to MAX do
    begin
        SEED: = (MULT*SEED + ADDR) mod NORM;
        X: = SEED/NORM;

        SEED: = (MULT*SEED + ADDR) mod NORM;
        S: = PI*SEED/NORM;

        if S <= PI/2 then if cos(S) > 1−X then SUM: = SUM+1;

        if S > PI/2 then if −cos(S) > X then SUM: = SUM+1;
    end;

    writeln(SUM/MAX:10:4);
end.
```

The simulated value of $2/\pi$ is SUM/MAX; therefore, for large values of MAX, $\pi \cong 2*\text{MAX/SUM}$. Here are the results for several runs:

MAX	2*MAX/SUM
100	3.9216
500	3.3223
1,000	3.2949
5,000	3.1250
10,000	3.1358

PROBLEMS

7.19. Let X have density function

$$f(x) = \begin{cases} 0 & x < 0 \quad \text{or} \quad 1 < x \\ 3x^2 & 0 < x < 1 \end{cases}$$

What is the distribution function F? On what interval is it concentrated? What is F^{-1}? Write a program to simulate 500 values of X and print the number that fall into each of the intervals $[0, .1), [.1, .2), \ldots [.9, 1]$. Campare these with the probabilities calculated using the density function.

7.20. Let X have density function

$$f(x) = \begin{cases} 0 & x < 0 \\ \dfrac{2}{(x + 1)^3} & 0 < x \end{cases}$$

What are the distribution function F, the interval of concentration, and F^{-1}? Determine constants x_1, x_2, x_3 so that X falls into each of the intervals

$$(0, x_1) \qquad (x_1, x_2) \qquad (x_2, x_3) \qquad (x_3, \infty)$$

with probability 1/4. Simulate 200 values of X and print out the number that fall into each of these four categories.

7.21. Let X be exponentially distributed with parameter $L = \lambda$. $E(X) = 1/L$. Write a program to input MAX, simulate MAX many values of X, and print their average. Is it close to $1/L$? Run the program for several values of L.

7.22. (*The Cauchy Distribution*) Write a program to simulate the Cauchy distribution of Problem 5.45. Inputs should be MAX (number of simulations) and R.

7.23. Simulate the janitor problem (Problems 5.42 and 5.43). Input MAX (number of simulations) and a time U. Output should be the fraction of the number of simulations in which the lights were on at least time U. Run the program for $U = 1/4$, $1/2$ and compare each with the answer to Problem 5.43.

7.24. (*Continuation*) Let V be the time that the lights are on. Compute $E(V)$ from the results of Problem 5.42. Run 1000 simulations of V and output the average.

7.25. Assume that the number of accidents along a certain stretch of highway is Poisson distributed with parameter (average) λ. λ depends, however, on the visibility; assume that the visibility V ranges from 1 (clear daylight) to a minimum of .2 (foggy night). Assume that the relation between the average number of accidents λ and V is

$$\lambda = 2V^{-1}$$

where V itself is uniformly distributed on the interval [.2, 1]. Write a program to input MAX = number of simulations and output MAX many simulations of the number of accidents. For *each* simulation the value of V must be simulated and then using $\lambda = 2/V$ the number of accidents is simulated and output. Also have the *average number* of accidents output.

— Chapter 8 —————————

Joint Probability Distributions

In most of the models developed so far the main interest was in how *one* random variable was distributed. The object of this chapter is to present methods for dealing with random experiments in which more than one quantity is random. For example, three random variables associated with the weather are the temperature, humidity, and wind speed. There are certainly relations among them; thus very cold temperatures are often accompanied by high winds. But the relation is not completely deterministic; there is only a *tendency* for high winds and low temperatures to be related. The exact relationship itself incorporates random features that may be more complex than are the individual distributions of the random variables.

The clue to understanding such situations in which more than one random variable is involved takes us to the very definitions of sample space and random variable. Suppose that X and Y are both random variables on the sample space Ω. This means that X and Y are both functions

$$X, Y: \Omega \to R$$

from Ω to the real numbers R. To find how X and Y are related, look at how the values $X(\omega)$ and $Y(\omega)$ are related for each sample point ω. First discrete random variables are considered, then continuous ones.

8.1 JOINT DISTRIBUTIONS OF DISCRETE RANDOM VARIABLES

We saw in Chapter 4 how tables are useful in understanding the distribution of a discrete random variable. They are equally useful in dealing with joint distributions.

Example 1

Flip a fair coin three times. Let X equal the number of heads and Y equal the number of the flip on which the first head occurred (or 0 if no head occurs). Then here is a probability table with the sample points as first row:

Outcome	HHH	HHT	HTH	THH	TTH	THT	HTT	TTT
X	3	2	2	2	1	1	1	0
Y	1	1	1	2	3	2	1	0
Probability	1/8	1/8	1/8	1/8	1/8	1/8	1/8	1/8

From this table we can construct a table with values of X along the top, values of Y along the left, and the probabilities as entries:

		X			
		0	1	2	3
	0	1/8	0	0	0
	1	0	1/8	1/4	1/8
Y	2	0	1/8	1/8	0
	3	0	1/8	0	0

This table is a complete summary of all the probabilities

$$P(X = x \quad \text{and} \quad Y = y)$$

over all the values x in the range of X and the values y in the range of Y. For example, $P(X = 2 \text{ and } Y = 1) = 1/4$. ■

Example 2

From the table in Example 1, find

$$P(X \leqslant 2 \quad \text{and} \quad Y = 1)$$
$$P(X \leqslant 2 \quad \text{and} \quad Y \leqslant 1)$$
$$P(X \leqslant 2 \quad \text{or} \quad Y \leqslant 1)$$

Solution We simply consult the table:

$$P(X \leqslant 2 \quad \text{and} \quad Y = 1) = P(X = 0, 1, \text{ or } 2 \quad \text{and} \quad Y = 1)$$

$$= 0 + \frac{1}{8} + \frac{1}{4}$$

$$= \frac{3}{8}$$

$$P(X \leqslant 2 \text{ and } Y \leqslant 1) = \sum_{i,j} P(X = i \text{ and } Y = j)$$

where the sum extends over all i from 0 to 2 and j from 0 to 1. Hence

$$P(X \leqslant 2 \quad \text{and} \quad Y \leqslant 1) = \frac{1}{2}$$

Finally,

$$P(X \leqslant 2 \quad \text{or} \quad Y \leqslant 1) = P(X \leqslant 2) + P(Y \leqslant 1) - P(X \leqslant 2 \quad \text{and} \quad Y \leqslant 1)$$

$$= \frac{7}{8} + \frac{5}{8} - \frac{1}{2}$$

$$= 1$$

Note that this last probability can also be computed using the complementary event:

$$P(X \leqslant 2 \quad \text{or} \quad Y \leqslant 1) = 1 - P(X > 2 \quad \text{and} \quad Y > 1) = 1 - 0 \quad \blacksquare$$

> For two discrete random variables the probability table for the joint proba-
> bility distribution has the values of one along the top and the values of the
> other along the left.

There is straightforward procedure for obtaining the distribution of *one* of the random variables from the table. Suppose that the values along the top correspond to random variable X and those along the left to random variable Y. Then

$$p_{xy} = P(X = x \quad \text{and} \quad Y = y)$$

is the entry in *column x* and *row y*. To obtain

$$P(X = x) = \sum_{y} P(X = x \quad \text{and} \quad Y = y) = \sum_{y} p_{xy}$$

all the entries in *column x* are added. Similarly, to obtain

$$P(Y = y) = \sum_{x} P(X = x \quad \text{and} \quad Y = y) = \sum_{x} p_{xy}$$

all the entries in *row y* are added.

Example 3

Using the table of Example 1 with an extra row and column equal to the sum, we obtain

		X			
		0	1	2	3	
	0	1/8	0	0	0	1/8
	1	0	1/8	1/4	1/8	1/2
Y	2	0	1/8	1/8	0	1/4
	3	0	1/8	0	0	1/8
		1/8	3/8	3/8	1/8	

Thus we see at a glance, for example, that

$$P(X = 2) = \frac{3}{8}$$

$$P(Y = 2) = \frac{1}{4} \quad \blacksquare$$

Note that the probabilities of the individual distributions for X and Y are written in the *margins of the table*.

Given the joint probabilities

$$p_{xy} = P(X = x \quad \text{and} \quad Y = y)$$

the **marginal distributions** for X and Y are their individual distributions. These are obtained by

$$P(X = x) = \sum_y P(X = x \quad \text{and} \quad Y = y)$$

$$P(Y = y) = \sum_x P(X = x \quad \text{and} \quad Y = y)$$

Example 4

A bin contains 3 bolts, 4 washers, and 2 screws. Grab 3; let B be the number of bolts and W be the number of washers. What is the probability table for B and W, and what are the marginal distributions?

Solution The joint probabilities are computed using combinatorics. Thus there are a total of $3 + 4 + 2 = 9$ items.

$$P(B = 0 \quad \text{and} \quad W = 1) = \frac{\binom{3}{0}\binom{4}{1}\binom{2}{2}}{\binom{9}{3}}$$

More generally,

$$P(B = b \text{ and } W = w) = \frac{\binom{3}{b}\binom{4}{w}\binom{2}{3-b-w}}{\binom{9}{3}}$$

The probability table with marginals is therefore

		B				
		0	1	2	3	
	0	0	3/84	6/84	1/84	10/84
	1	4/84	24/84	12/84	0	40/84
W	2	12/84	18/84	0	0	30/84
	3	4/84	0	0	0	4/84
		20/84	45/84	18/84	1/84	

For example, the marginal probabilities imply that

$$P(B = 2) = \frac{18}{84}$$

$$P(W \leqslant 1) = \frac{50}{84} \quad \blacksquare$$

8.2 INDEPENDENT DISCRETE RANDOM VARIABLES

In Chapter 3 the *events* A and B were defined to be independent if

$$P(A \cap B) = P(A)P(B)$$

The definition for independence of random variables is similar. The idea is that X and Y are independent if *any* event defined in terms of X is *independent* of *any* event defined in terms of Y. But events defined by discrete random variables can be decomposed into sums of probabilities of the form $P(X = x)$ and $P(Y = y)$.

Definition

Discrete random variables X and Y are independent if

$$P(X = x \text{ and } Y = y) = P(X = x)P(Y = y)$$

for all values x in the range of X and y in the range of Y.

Note: For X and Y to be independent, the product rule above must be satisfied for *all* values x and y in the ranges of X and Y. If for *just one pair* x and y the equality fails, then X and Y are *not* independent.

Example 5

From a bin with 3 red and 6 nonred light bulbs, sample 2. Let X equal 1 if the first bulb is red; otherwise, X is 0. Similarly, Y is 1 if the second bulb is red; otherwise, Y is 0. Are X and Y independent?

   Solution The question cannot be answered until we know whether the sampling is *with* or *without* replacement. *With* replacement implies that the bin has the same composition from selection to selection and so X and Y will be independent. Sampling *without* replacement suggests that X and Y are not independent. Quite arbitrarily, we choose values 1 for both X and Y and compute

$$P(X = 1 \quad \text{and} \quad Y = 1) = P(\text{first and second are red})$$

$$= \frac{\binom{3}{2}}{\binom{9}{2}}$$

$$= \frac{3}{36}$$

On the other hand,

$$P(X = 1) = \frac{3}{9}$$

and

$$P(Y = 1) = P(Y = 1 \mid X = 0)P(X = 0) + P(Y = 1 \mid X = 1)P(X = 1)$$

$$= \frac{3}{8} \cdot \frac{6}{9} + \frac{2}{8} \cdot \frac{3}{9}$$

$$= \frac{1}{3}$$

Thus

$$P(X = 1)P(Y = 1) = \frac{1}{9} \neq \frac{1}{12} = P(X = 1 \text{ and } Y = 1)$$

so X and Y are *not* independent. ∎

   Suppose that we have the joint probability table for X and Y. Since the marginals are the values of $P(X = x)$ and $P(Y = y)$, and since the entries in the table are $P(X = x \text{ and } Y = y)$, there is a very straightforward way to check whether X and Y are independent once the table has been constructed:

> Discrete random variables X and Y are independent if and only if each entry in the probability table is the product of the corresponding row and column marginals.

Example 6

Suppose that the range of X is {0, 1, 2} and the range of Y is {4, 5, 6}. With these probabilities in the table given, fill in the rest of the table under the assumption of independence.

		X = 0	X = 1	X = 2	
Y	4	1/6	a	b	c
	5	d	e	f	g
	6	1/6	k	h	i
		j	1/3	1/3	

Solution $j = 1 - (1/3 + 1/3) = 1/3$ since the marginal probabilities for X must add to 1. Hence $d = 0$ since the column under $X = 0$ must add to $P(X = 0) = j = 1/3$. Since $d = 0$, independence implies that $g = 0$ and consequently that $e = 0$ and $f = 0$. Now $ij = 1/6$, so $i = 1/2$. Thus $k = h = 1/6$. Finally, $a = b = 1/6$ since each of the column sums must be 1/3; this in turn implies that $c = 1/2$.

		X = 0	X = 1	X = 2	
Y	4	1/6	1/6	1/6	1/2
	5	0	0	0	0
	6	1/6	1/6	1/6	1/2
		1/3	1/3	1/3	

■

Example 7 (*Continuation*)

Construct a probability table for $Z = X + Y$.

Solution The range of Z is {4, 5, 6, 7, 8}. Collapsing those entries in the table above which yield the same value for $Z = X + Y$ implies that

Z	4	5	6	7	8
Probability	1/6	1/6	1/3	1/6	1/6

■

Suppose that X and Y are independent, that X is Poisson distributed with parameter (mean) α, and that Y is Poisson distributed with parameter β. Consider the random variable $Z = X + Y$. To find the distribution of Z, note first that X, Y, and consequently Z have range $\{0, 1, 2, \ldots\}$. For Z to equal k, X must have some value j where $j \leq k$; Y must then have value $k - j$. Hence

$$P(Z = k) = \sum_{j=0}^{k} P(X = j \text{ and } Y = k - j)$$

$$= \sum_{j=0}^{k} \frac{\alpha^j}{j!} e^{-\alpha} \frac{\beta^{k-j}}{(k-j)!} e^{-\beta}$$

$$= e^{-\alpha-\beta} \frac{1}{k!} \sum_{j=0}^{k} \frac{k!}{j!\,(k-j)!} \alpha^j \beta^{k-j}$$

$$= e^{-(\alpha+\beta)} \frac{1}{k!} (\alpha + \beta)^k$$

where the last equality follows from the binomial formula. But this is precisely the Poisson distribution with parameter equal to $\alpha + \beta$.

If X and Y are independent, each Poisson distributed one with parameter α and the other with parameter β, then

$$Z = X + Y$$

is Poisson distributed with parameter equal to the sum of the parameters $\alpha + \beta$.

Example 8

Let X and Y be the number of requests to the Pascal and FORTRAN compilers, respectively, during 10 minutes at the school computer. Assume that X and Y are independent, each Poisson distributed. Suppose that the average number of Pascal requests is 2.3 and the average number of FORTRAN requests is 1.8 in 10 minutes. Find the probability that there were fewer than 4 requests of either type between 10:00 and 10:10. Find the probability of more than 7 requests between 10:00 and 10:20.

Solution Since the parameter for the Poisson distribution *is* the average, the result above says that the total number of requests in 10 minutes is Poisson distributed with parameter

$$2.3 + 1.8 = 4.1$$

Hence

$$P(\text{fewer than 4 in 10 minutes}) = e^{-4.1}\left(1 + 4.1 + \frac{4.1^2}{2} + \frac{4.1^3}{6}\right)$$

$$= .4142$$

The number of requests in 20 minutes is Poisson distributed with parameter

$$4.1 + 4.1 = 8.2$$

Hence

$$P(\text{more than 7 in 20 minutes}) = 1 - e^{-8.2} \sum_{j=0}^{7} \frac{8.2^j}{j!}$$

$$= .5746 \quad \blacksquare$$

PROBLEMS

8.1. Suppose that this is the joint probability table for X and Y:

		\(X\)			
		1	2	3	4
	1	.07	.02	.05	.09
Y	3	.12	.21	.03	0
	5	.33	.05	.01	.02

(a) Find $P(X \leqslant 3$ and $Y > 4)$; (b) $P(X \leqslant 3$ or $Y > 4)$. (c) What are the marginal distributions for X and Y? Find (d) $P(X \leqslant 3)$; (e) $P(Y > 4)$.

8.2. Suppose that this is the joint probability table for U and V:

		\(V\)			
		1	2	3	4
	0	.1	0	0	0
	−1	.1	.1	0	0
U	−2	.1	.1	.1	0
	−3	.1	.1	.1	.1

Find (a) $P(U \geqslant -2$ and $V \geqslant 2)$; (b) $P(U \geqslant -2$ or $V \geqslant 2)$. (c) What are the marginal distributions for U and V? Find (d) $P(U \geqslant -2)$; (e) $P(V \geqslant 2)$. (f) What is the distribution of $U + V$?

8.3. A drawer contains 5 white, 4 black, and 3 striped socks. Grab 4; let X be the number of striped and Y be the number of black socks. Construct the joint probability table for X and Y; include the marginal probabilities.

8.4. If X and Y have this as their joint probability table, fill in the missing entries:

			X		
		4	5	6	
	0	.1			.3
Y	1		.1		.2
	2			.3	
		.1		.4	

8.5. Suppose that X and Y are independent and that this is their joint probability table. Fill in the missing entries:

			X		
		4	5	6	
	0	.2			.6
Y	1		.1		
	2				
			.4		

8.6. Suppose that X and Y are independent and that these are the distribution tables for X and Y:

X	0	1	2	3	4
Probability	.1	.1	.3	.2	.3

Y	5	6	7	8	9
Probability	.2	.3	.2	.1	.2

What is the joint probability table? Find $P(X \cdot Y < 14)$ and $P(Y - X < 4)$.

8.7. Suppose that the number of pine saplings in a 100-square-foot area is Poisson distributed with an average of 3.5; and assume that the number of maple saplings in the same area is also Poisson distributed but with an average of 2.8. Find **(a)** P(a 100-square-foot area contains at least 5 saplings); **(b)** P(a 200-square-foot area contains fewer than 4 saplings).

8.8. The number of junk mail letters received per day is Poisson distributed with an average of 4; the number of *real* letters is Poisson distributed with an average of 2. Assuming independence between the two types; find **(a)** P(no letters received on Monday); **(b)** P(at least 5 letters on Monday and/or Tuesday); **(c)** P(3 junk letters on Friday | total of 5 letters on Friday).

8.9. Cars enter a toll booth at the rate of 1.4 per minute and buses at the rate of .2 per minute. Assume that each is Poisson distributed. Find (a) P(at least 2 vehicles in 1 minute); (b) P(at least 3 vehicles in 2 minutes); (c) P(at least 3 cars | 5 vehicles in 3 minutes).

8.10. A total of $n + m$ Bernoulli trials are performed with p = probability of success. Let X be the number of successes in the first n trials and Y be the number of successes in the last m trials. What are the distributions of X and Y? Are they independent? Show that $X + Y$ is binomially distributed, $n + m$ trials.

8.3 JOINT DISTRIBUTIONS OF CONTINUOUS RANDOM VARIABLES

For one continuous random variable X the distribution is determined by the density function f. In terms of infinitesimals

$$P(x < X \leqslant x + dx) = f(x) \, dx$$

This is the concept that is generalized to obtain the joint distribution of more than one continuous random variable.

> Let X and Y be continuous random variables. The joint density function $h(x, y)$ is a function of two variables that is defined by
>
> $$P(x < X \leqslant x + dx \quad \text{and} \quad y < Y \leqslant y + dy) = h(x, y) \, dx \, dy$$

Thus $h(x, y) \, dx \, dy$ is the *infinitesimal probability* that (X, Y) falls in the infinitesimal rectangle of the xy plane in Fig. 8.1.

In a real situation we need to calculate probabilities of the form

$$P(a < X \leqslant b \quad \text{and} \quad c < Y \leqslant d)$$

that is, the probability that X resides in the interval $(a, b]$ and Y falls in the interval $(c, d]$. Geometrically, this is the probability that the ordered pair (X, Y) falls in the rectangle with corners (a, c), (a, d), (b, c), and (b, d). To obtain this, we add infinitesimal probabilities and since there are "continuum many" of them, an integral sign is used:

$$P(a < X \leqslant b \quad \text{and} \quad c < Y \leqslant d) = \int_a^b \int_c^d h(x, y) \, dy \, dx$$

Note that regions of the xy plane where $h(x, y)$ is zero must be regions in which the ordered pair (X, Y) *cannot* occur. Only where the density function is positive can the actual values of (X, Y) be found.

Example 9

Suppose that the joint density function of X and Y is

$$h(x, y) = \begin{cases} 6xy^2 & 0 < x < 1 \quad \text{and} \quad 0 < y < 1 \\ 0 & (x, y) \text{ not in the unit square} \end{cases}$$

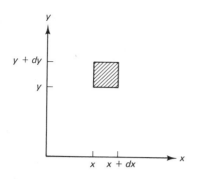

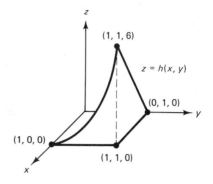

Figure 8.1

Figure 8.2 The joint density h is nonzero only in the unit space.

The graph of h is sketched in Fig. 8.2; note that it is a *surface* in 3 dimensions since h is a function of the two variables x and y. Thus the actual values of (X, Y) must reside in the square with sides $(0, 0)$, $(0, 1)$, $(1, 0)$, and $(1, 1)$. Find (a) $P(1/2 < X \leq 3/4$ and $0 < Y \leq 1/3)$; (b) $P(1/2 < X$ and $1/3 < Y)$; (c) $P(1/2 < X \leq 3/4)$.

Solution Each of these can be found by integration.

(a) $P\left(\dfrac{1}{2} < X \leq \dfrac{3}{4} \quad \text{and} \quad 0 < Y \leq \dfrac{1}{3}\right) = \displaystyle\int_{1/2}^{3/4} \int_{0}^{1/3} 6xy^2 \; dy \; dx$

$$= \int_{1/2}^{3/4} 2xy^3 \;\big|_{y=0}^{y=1/3} \; dx$$

$$= \int_{1/2}^{3/4} \frac{2x}{27} \; dx$$

$$= \frac{5}{16 \cdot 27}$$

(b) $P\left(\dfrac{1}{2} < X \quad \text{and} \quad \dfrac{1}{3} < Y\right) = P\left(\dfrac{1}{2} < X \leq 1 \quad \text{and} \quad \dfrac{1}{3} < Y \leq 1\right)$

$$= \int_{1/2}^{1} \int_{1/3}^{1} 6xy^2 \; dy \; dx$$

$$= \int_{1/2}^{1} 2xy^3 \big|_{y=1/3}^{y=1} \; dx$$

$$= \int_{1/2}^{1} \frac{52x}{27} \; dx$$

$$= \frac{26 \cdot 3}{27 \cdot 4}$$

(c) $P\left(\dfrac{1}{2} < X \le \dfrac{3}{4}\right) = P\left(\dfrac{1}{2} < X \le \dfrac{3}{4} \quad \text{and} \quad 0 < Y \le 1\right)$

$$= \int_{1/2}^{3/4} \int_0^1 6xy^2 \, dy \, dx$$

$$= \dfrac{9}{16} - \dfrac{1}{4} \quad \blacksquare$$

Recall from Chapter 5 that the density function of a single random variable X must satisfy two properties: Since X must have *some* value, the integral of the density function from $-\infty$ to $+\infty$ must be 1. Since *all* probabilities are nonnegative, the density function must be itself nonnegative. For exactly these reasons:

The joint density function of two random variables X and Y must satisfy

1. $\displaystyle\int_{-\infty}^{\infty} \int_{-\infty}^{\infty} h(x, y) \, dx \, dy = P(-\infty < X < \infty \quad \text{and} \quad -\infty < Y < \infty) = 1$

2. $h(x, y) \geq 0 \quad$ for all x, y

Example 10

Verify that

$$h(x, y) = \begin{cases} \dfrac{4x}{y^3} & 0 < x < 1 \quad \text{and} \quad 1 < y \\ 0 & \text{otherwise} \end{cases}$$

is a joint density function. What is $P(Y > 5)$?

Solution Since exponentials are positive, $h(x, y)$ is certainly nonnegative, and

$$\int_{-\infty}^{\infty} \int_{-\infty}^{\infty} h(x, y) \, dx \, dy = \int_1^{\infty} \int_0^1 4\,\frac{x}{y^3} \, dx \, dy$$

$$= \int_1^{\infty} \frac{4}{y^3} \frac{x^2}{2}\bigg|_{x=0}^{x=1} \, dy$$

$$= \int_1^{\infty} \frac{2}{y^3} \, dy$$

$$= 1$$

Hence $h(x, y)$ *is* a joint density function.

$$P(Y > 5) = P(0 < X < 1 \quad \text{and} \quad 5 < Y < \infty)$$

$$= \int_5^\infty \int_0^1 4 \frac{x}{y^3} \, dx \, dy$$

$$= \frac{1}{25} \quad \blacksquare$$

In Chapter 5 we found the geometric approach of value in dealing with one continuous random variable. Thus the probability that X has a value in the interval $(a, b]$ is the *area* underneath the graph of the density function between a and b. A similar interpretation has already been indicated for the joint density of X and Y: Given a region $\mathbf{A}$ in the xy plane, the probability that (X, Y) is in $\mathbf{A}$ is the integral of $h(x, y)$ over $\mathbf{A}$; that is, the probability is the *volume* under the graph of $h(x, y)$ over the region $\mathbf{A}$ in the xy plane as depicted in Fig. 8.3.

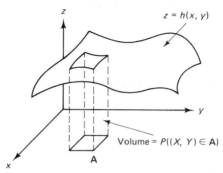

Figure 8.3

Because of the difficulty of graphing functions of two variables, however, the geometric interpretation is of limited use here. But it *does* at least show this: The probability is zero that the ordered pair (X, Y) assumes any one particular value. This is so since this probability is the *volume* under $h(x, y)$ over just one point; but the *volume* of this *line segment* is 0. In terms of integrals,

$$P(X = a \quad \text{and} \quad Y = b) = \int_b^b \int_a^a h(x, y) \, dx \, dy = 0$$

Thus, just as in the single-random-variable case, *we can be rather careless in distinguishing between inequalities and* **strict** *inequalities.*

$$\left.\begin{matrix} < \\ > \end{matrix}\right\} \text{ are equivalent to } \left\{\begin{matrix} \le \\ \ge \end{matrix}\right.$$

Although this is *not* true for discrete random variables, it *is* true for continuous random variables.

The joint density function $h(x, y)$ encodes all information about the distribution of X and Y. Thus it should be possible to obtain the individual densities of X and Y from h. In the discrete case in the preceding section, the individual distributions—the marginal distributions—were found by summing along rows or columns. Analogously, in the continuous case the individual densities are obtained by the continuous analog of summation—integration. Let us compute the distribution function F of X:

$$F(t) = P(X \leq t)$$

$$= P(-\infty < X \leq t \quad \text{and} \quad -\infty < Y < \infty)$$

$$= \int_{-\infty}^{t} \int_{-\infty}^{\infty} h(x, y) \, dy \, dx$$

$$= \int_{-\infty}^{t} \left[\int_{-\infty}^{\infty} h(x, y) \, dy \right] dx$$

The density function is obtained by differentiating the distribution function. But the derivative of an integral (no matter how complicated the integrand) is the integrand. Therefore, the density function for X is

$$f(t) = \int_{-\infty}^{\infty} h(t, y) \, dy$$

A similar integration yields the density function for Y.

Let $h(x, y)$ be the joint density function for X, Y. Then the individual or *marginal* density functions f for X and g for Y are obtained by integrating $h(x, y)$ out with respect to one variable:

$$f(x) = \int_{-\infty}^{\infty} h(x, y) \, dy$$

$$g(y) = \int_{-\infty}^{\infty} h(x, y) \, dx$$

Example 11

For the joint density function of Example 10, find the distributions of X and of Y separately. Also find

$$P\left(X < \frac{1}{2} \,\middle|\, Y > 6\right)$$

Solution With f the density for X and g the density for Y,

$$f(x) = \int_{1}^{\infty} 4 \frac{x}{y^3} \, dy = -2 \frac{x}{y^2} \Big|_{y=1}^{y=\infty} = 2x$$

for $0 < x < 1$; $f(x) = 0$ for $x < 0$ or $x > 1$. Why? Similarly, $g(y) = 0$ for $y <$

1 and for $y > 1$,

$$g(y) = \int_0^1 4\frac{x}{y^3} dx = 2\frac{x^2}{y^2}\Big|_{x=0}^{x=1} = \frac{2}{y^3}$$

$$P\left(X < \frac{1}{2}\Big| Y > 6\right) = \frac{P(X < 1/2 \text{ and } Y > 6)}{P(Y > 6)}$$

But

$$P\left(X < \frac{1}{2} \text{ and } Y > 6\right) = \int_0^{1/2} \int_6^\infty 4\frac{x}{y^3} dy\, dx = \frac{1}{144}$$

$$P(Y > 6) = \int_6^\infty g(y)\, dy = \int_6^\infty \frac{2}{y^3} dy = \frac{1}{36}$$

Hence division yields

$$P\left(X < \frac{1}{2}\Big| Y > 6\right) = \frac{36}{144} = \frac{1}{4} \quad \blacksquare$$

Example 12

Suppose that X, Y have joint density function

$$h(x, y) = \begin{cases} c \sin (x + y) & 0 < x, y < \frac{\pi}{2} \\ \\ 0 & \text{either } x \text{ or } y \text{ not in } \left[0, \frac{\pi}{2}\right] \end{cases}$$

Find the value of the constant c. Find the individual densities of X and Y.

Solution Since $h(x, y)$ is nonzero *only in the square* $0 < x, y < \pi/2$,

$$1 = \int_0^{\pi/2} \int_0^{\pi/2} c \sin (x + y)\, dx\, dy$$

$$= \int_0^{\pi/2} [-c \cos (x + y)]_{x=0}^{x=\pi/2}\, dy$$

$$= \int_0^{\pi/2} \left(c \cos y - c \cos \left(\frac{\pi}{2} + y\right)\right) dy$$

$$= 2c$$

Therefore,

$$c = \frac{1}{2}$$

But $f(x)$ must be 0 for $x < 0$ or $x > \pi/2$. For $0 < x < \pi/2$

$$f(x) = \int_0^{\pi/2} \frac{1}{2} \sin(x + y) \, dy$$

$$= \frac{1}{2}\left(\cos x - \cos\left(\frac{\pi}{2} + x\right)\right)$$

$$= \frac{1}{2}(\cos x + \sin x)$$

In similar fashion the density function for Y could be computed. But here is a shortcut: Since the joint density function $h(x, y)$ is *symmetric* in the variables x and y, the density function for Y has the same form as the density function for X with the roles of x and y reversed:

$$g(y) = \begin{cases} 0 & y < 0 \quad \text{or} \quad \frac{\pi}{2} < y \\ \frac{1}{2}(\cos y + \sin y) & 0 < y < \frac{\pi}{2} \end{cases} \quad \blacksquare$$

8.4 INDEPENDENT CONTINUOUS RANDOM VARIABLES

Suppose that X and Y are continuous random variables with joint density function $h(x, y)$; let f be the density function of X and g the density function of Y. Intuitively, X and Y are *independent if any event defined by X is independent of any event defined by Y.* To see what this means in terms of the density functions, consider the event that X is in the interval $[x_0, x_0 + \Delta x]$ *and* Y is in the interval $[y_0, y_0 + \Delta y]$. Using the joint density, we obtain

$$P(x_0 \leq X \leq x_0 + \Delta x \quad \text{and} \quad y_0 \leq Y \leq y_0 + \Delta y) = \int_{x_0}^{x_0 + \Delta x} \int_{y_0}^{y_0 + \Delta y} h(x, y) \, dy \, dx$$

$$\cong h(x_0, y_0) \, \Delta y \, \Delta x$$

for small Δx and Δy. On the other hand, assuming that the events $x_0 \leq X \leq x_0 + \Delta x$ and $y_0 \leq Y \leq y_0 + \Delta y$ are independent,

$$P(x_0 \leq X \leq x_0 + \Delta x \quad \text{and} \quad y_0 \leq Y \leq y_0 + \Delta y)$$

$$= P(x_0 \leq X \leq x_0 + \Delta x) P(y_0 \leq Y \leq y_0 + \Delta y)$$

$$= \int_{x_0}^{x_0 + \Delta x} f(x) \, dx \int_{y_0}^{y_0 + \Delta y} g(y) \, dy$$

$$\cong f(x_0) \, \Delta x \, g(y_0) \, \Delta y$$

for small values of Δx and Δy. By equating these two expressions and canceling $\Delta x \, \Delta y$, we motivate this

---

Definition

Continuous random variables X and Y are independent if their joint density function is the *product* of the individual density functions:

$$h(x, y) = f(x)g(y)$$

Example 13 (*Continuation of Examples 10 and 11*)

X and Y are independent random variables because their joint density is the product of the individual densities: For $0 < x < 1$ and $1 < y$

$$h(x, y) = 4\frac{x}{y^3} = 2x\frac{2}{y^3} = f(x)g(y) \quad \blacksquare$$

There is a converse to the boxed formula above: *If* the joint density function can be factored

$$h(x, y) = f(x)g(y)$$

then X and Y are independent (although f and g are not necessarily the densities for X and Y). (See Problem 8.13 for the proof.)

Example 14

Let T_1 and T_2 be the lifetimes of two components used sequentially. That is, assume that component 1 operates for time T_1, after which component 2 is plugged in. Assume that the two lifetimes T_1, T_2 are independent. Also assume that T_1 has the *uniform distribution* on $[0, 2]$ while T_2 has the *exponential distribution* with parameter 3. Find the probability that the *second* component will last at least 2.5 time units *after* the first component is plugged in. That is, find

$$P(T_1 + T_2 \geqslant 2.5)$$

Solution The densities f_1 for T_1 and f_2 for T_2 are

$$f_1(x) = \begin{cases} \dfrac{1}{2} & 0 < x < 2 \\ 0 & \text{otherwise} \end{cases} \qquad f_2(x) = \begin{cases} 3e^{-3x} & 0 < x \\ 0 & x < 0 \end{cases}$$

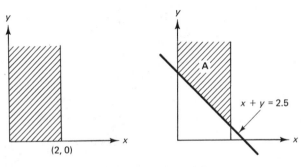

Figure 8.4   **Figure 8.5**

Since T_1 and T_2 are independent, their joint density function is the product of the individual densities:

$$h(x, y) = \begin{cases} \dfrac{1}{2} \cdot 3e^{-3y} & 0 < x < 2 \quad \text{and} \quad y > 0 \\ 0 & \text{otherwise} \end{cases}$$

The joint density is nonzero in the region of the xy plane shown in Fig. 8.4. The set of points (x, y) (where x represents the value of T_1 and y represents the value of T_2) satisfying $x + y \geq 2.5$ is the region **A** in Fig. 8.5. Hence

$$P(T_1 + T_2 \geq 2.5) = \iint_A h(x, y) \, dy \, dx$$

$$= \int_0^2 \int_{2.5-x}^\infty \frac{1}{2} \cdot 3e^{-3y} \, dy \, dx$$

$$= \int_0^2 \frac{1}{2} [-e^{-3y}]_{2.5-x}^\infty \, dx$$

$$= \int_0^2 \frac{1}{2} e^{-7.5+3x} \, dx$$

$$= \frac{1}{2} e^{-7.5} \cdot \frac{1}{3} e^{3x} \big|_0^2$$

$$= \frac{1}{6} e^{-7.5}(e^6 - 1) \quad \blacksquare$$

Example 15

Suppose that X and Y are independent and have densities f and g, respectively,

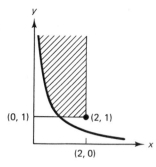

(0, 1) (2, 1)

(2, 0)

Figure 8.6 The joint density is concentrated in the infinite strip.

where

$$f(x) = \begin{cases} \dfrac{3x^2}{8} & 0 < x < 2 \\ 0 & x < 0 \end{cases}$$

$$g(y) = \begin{cases} y^{-2} & 1 < y \\ 0 & y < 1 \end{cases}$$

Find $P(XY > 1)$.

Solution The joint density is concentrated in a strip.

$$h(x, y) = \begin{cases} \dfrac{3x^2}{8y^2} & 0 < x < 2 \quad \text{and} \quad 1 < y \\ 0 & \text{otherwise} \end{cases}$$

Since x represents the value of the random variable X and y represents the value of Y, $P(XY > 1)$ is the integral of h over the region in the xy plane where $xy > 1$ (see Fig. 8.6). Hence

$$P(XY > 1) = \int_1^\infty \int_{1/y}^2 \frac{3x^2}{8} \frac{1}{y^2} \, dx \, dy$$

$$= \int_1^\infty \frac{1}{y^2} \frac{x^3}{8} \Big|_{x=1/y}^{x=2} \, dy$$

$$= \int_1^\infty \left(\frac{1}{y^2} - \frac{1}{8y^5} \right) dy$$

$$= -\frac{1}{y} + \frac{1}{32y^4} \Big|_1^\infty$$

$$= \frac{31}{32} \quad \blacksquare$$

Let **A** be a region of the plane. To find $P((X, Y) \in \mathbf{A})$, first sketch the region **A** and use it to find the limits of integration in the formula

$$P((X, Y) \in \mathbf{A}) = \iint_{\mathbf{A}} h(x, y) \, dx \, dy$$

PROBLEMS

8.11. Suppose that X and Y have joint density function

$$h(x, y) = \begin{cases} c(x + y) & 0 < x < 1 \quad \text{and} \quad 0 < y < 1 \\ 0 & \text{otherwise} \end{cases}$$

(a) Find c. (b) Find the marginal densities. (c) Are X and Y independent? Find (d) $P(X \leqslant 1/3)$; (e) $P(Y \geqslant 1/2)$.

8.12. Suppose that X and Y have joint density function

$$h(x, y) = \begin{cases} \dfrac{c}{(x + 1)^2 (y + 1)^3} & 0 < x \quad \text{and} \quad 0 < y \\ 0 & \text{otherwise} \end{cases}$$

(a) Find c. (b) Find the marginal densities. (c) Are X and Y independent? Find (d) $P(X > 2)$; (e) $P(Y \leqslant 3)$

8.13. Suppose that X and Y have joint density function

$$h(x, y) = f(x)g(y)$$

which can be written as a function of x times a function of y. Show that the densities of X and Y are, respectively,

$$cf(x) \quad \text{and} \quad dg(y)$$

where the *constants* c and d are

$$c = \int_{-\infty}^{\infty} g(y) \, dy \qquad d = \int_{-\infty}^{\infty} f(x) \, dx$$

and cd $= 1$. Conclude that X and Y are independent.

8.14. Use the result of Problem 8.13 to check whether X and Y are independent if their joint density function is

(a) $\begin{cases} \dfrac{2}{x^2 y^3} & 1 < x \quad \text{and} \quad 1 < y \\ 0 & \text{otherwise} \end{cases}$

(b) $\begin{cases} \dfrac{2x}{y} & 0 < x < 1 \quad \text{and} \quad 1 < y < e \\ 0 & \text{otherwise} \end{cases}$

$$\text{(c)} \quad \begin{cases} c\left(\dfrac{1}{x} + \dfrac{1}{y}\right) & 1 < x < 2 \quad \text{and} \quad 1 < y < 2 \qquad \text{where } c \text{ is a constant} \\ 0 & \text{otherwise} \end{cases}$$

$$\text{(d)} \quad \begin{cases} 2x & 0 < x < 1 \quad \text{and} \quad 0 < y < 1 \\ 0 & \text{otherwise} \end{cases}$$

For each part, also find the individual densities of X and Y.

8.15. Suppose that X and Y are independent each with exponential distribution with parameter $\lambda = 3$. **(a)** What is the joint density function? Sketch the regions in the xy plane where **(b)** $x + 2y \leqslant 2$; **(c)** $x + y \leqslant 2$; **(d)** $x - y \leqslant 2$. Find **(e)** $P(X + 2Y \leqslant 2)$; **(f)** $P(X + Y \leqslant 2)$; **(g)** $P(X - Y \leqslant 2)$.

8.16. Suppose that X and Y are independent; X is uniformly distributed on $[0, 1]$ and Y is uniformly distributed on $[0, 2]$. **(a)** What is the joint density function? Find **(b)** $P(X + Y \leqslant 2)$; **(c)** $P(X - Y > 0.5)$; **(d)** $P(XY < 1)$ by computing areas.

8.17. Suppose that X and Y are independent. X is exponentially distributed with parameter 5 and Y has density

$$g(y) = \begin{cases} \dfrac{1}{y^2} & 1 < y \\ 0 & y < 1 \end{cases}$$

Find **(a)** $P(XY > 1)$; **(b)** $P(\text{Max } \{X, Y\} < 2)$. **(c)** Sketch each region in the xy plane.

8.5 THE SUM OF CONTINUOUS INDEPENDENT RANDOM VARIABLES (OPTIONAL)

Let X and Y be the lifetimes of two components used sequentially: as soon as the first component fails, the second is installed. Under the assumption that X and Y are independent, what is the distribution of the lifetime of the system consisting of the two components? In this section a formula for the density function of $Z = X + Y$ is derived.

As before, let f and g denote the density functions of X and Y, respectively. By independence the joint density is

$$h(x, y) = f(x)g(y)$$

To find the density for Z, first the distribution function is found and then differentiated.

Given a fixed value z, to find $P(Z \leqslant z) = P(X + Y \leqslant z)$ requires that the joint density function be integrated over the set $\mathbf{A}$ in the xy plane depicted in Fig. 8.7 where

$$\mathbf{A} = \{(x, y) : x + y \leqslant z\}$$

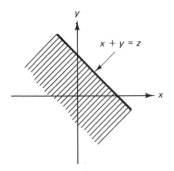

Figure 8.7 The shaded region is $\{(x, y) : x + y \leq z\}$.

Thus the distribution function for Z is

$$F_Z(z) = P(X + Y \leq z)$$

$$= \int_{-\infty}^{\infty} \int_{-\infty}^{z-x} h(x, y) \, dy \, dx$$

$$= \int_{-\infty}^{\infty} \int_{-\infty}^{z-x} f(x)g(y) \, dy \, dx$$

$$= \int_{-\infty}^{\infty} f(x)G(y)\big|_{-\infty}^{z-x} \, dx$$

$$= \int_{-\infty}^{\infty} f(x)G(z - x) \, dx$$

where G is the *distribution function* of Y; the second-to-last equality follows by the fact that the distribution function G is the *integral of the density function g*. To obtain the density function for $X + Y$, differentiate this last expression with respect to z. Interchanging the derivative and the integral and noting that the derivative of distribution function G is density function g implies this result:

Let X and Y be independent with density functions f and g. Then the density function for the sum $Z = X + Y$ is given by the **convolution** of f and g:

$$f_Z(z) = \int_{-\infty}^{\infty} f(x)g(z - x) \, dx$$

Example 16

Suppose that a radio uses one battery. The original battery will last a random length of time X that is exponentially distributed with average lifetime 1 week. A spare is bought of higher quality; once installed, the spare will last time Y that is exponentially distributed with average life 2 weeks. If the radio together with the original and the spare batteries are taken on a trip, what is the distribution of the total time $X + Y$ until both batteries have died? Find P(radio lasts at least 4 weeks).

Joint Probability Distributions   Chap. 8

Solution Since the *parameter for the exponential distribution is the reciprocal of the average*, the density functions f for X and g for Y are

$$f(x) = \begin{cases} 0 & x < 0 \\ e^{-x} & 0 < x \end{cases} \qquad g(y) = \begin{cases} 0 & y < 0 \\ .5e^{-.5y} & 0 < y \end{cases}$$

Hence the density function of the *total lifetime* $X + Y$ of both batteries is

$$h(z) = \int_{-\infty}^{\infty} f(x)g(z - x)\, dx$$

Note that $f(x) = 0$ for $x < 0$ and $g(z - x) = 0$ for $z - x < 0$. Thus the integrand

$$f(x)g(z - x) = 0$$

for

$$x < 0 \quad \text{or} \quad z - x < 0$$

That is,

$$x < 0 \quad \text{or} \quad x > z$$

Thus the limits in the integral defining h can be taken from $x = 0$ to $x = z$:

$$h(z) = \int_0^z e^{-x} \cdot .5e^{-.5(z-x)}\, dx$$

$$= .5e^{-.5z} \int_0^z e^{-.5x}\, dx$$

$$= e^{-.5z}(1 - e^{-.5z})$$

$$= e^{-.5z} - e^{-z}$$

This is the density for $Z = X + Y$.

$$P(\text{radio lasts at least 4 weeks}) = P(X + Y \geqslant 4)$$

$$= \int_4^{\infty} h(z)\, dz$$

$$= \int_4^{\infty} (e^{-.5z} - e^{-z})\, dz$$

$$= 2e^{-.5 \cdot 4} - e^{-4}$$

$$= .2524 \quad \blacksquare$$

If X and Y are independent and both concentrated on $(0, \infty)$, the convolution formula for the density of $Z = X + Y$ is

$$f_Z(z) = \int_0^z f(x)g(z - x)\, dx$$

In Example 16 the case when the spare and the original both have the *same* distribution is of particular interest. In this case the lifetime of the radio is the sum of two independent, exponentially distributed random variables with the same parameter. But in Section 6.6 we showed by another approach that this sum is gamma distributed. Let us see how the convolution formula also leads to the gamma distribution.

Example 17

Suppose that

$$f(x) = g(x) = \begin{cases} 0 & x < 0 \\ \lambda e^{-\lambda x} & x > 0 \end{cases}$$

and that X and Y have densities f and g. Show that the density of $S = X + Y$ is the gamma density with $n = 2$.

Solution

$$h(z) = \int_{-\infty}^{\infty} f(x)g(z - x) \, dx$$

$$= \int_{0}^{z} \lambda e^{-\lambda x} \lambda e^{-\lambda(z-x)} \, dx$$

$$= \lambda^2 \int_{0}^{z} e^{-\lambda z} \, dx$$

$$= \lambda^2 z e^{-\lambda z} \quad \blacksquare$$

PROBLEMS

8.18. Suppose that X and Y are independent; X is exponentially distributed with parameter α and Y is exponentially distributed with parameter β. Assume that $\alpha \neq \beta$. Find the density for $X + Y$.

8.19. (*Continuation*) Assume that the length of time until the light burns out is exponentially distributed with parameter $\alpha = 2$ (average life 1/2 unit of time.) Assume that the fix-it time is also exponentially distributed with parameter $\beta = 3$ (1/3 unit of time until it is fixed, on the average). Find the probability that the light burns out *and* is fixed before time 1.

8.20. Show that the density for $X + Y$ derived in Problem 8.18 approaches

$$\begin{cases} \alpha^2 x e^{-\alpha x} & x > 0 \\ 0 & 0 > x \end{cases}$$

as $\beta \to \alpha$. (*Hint:* Use L'Hôpital's rule.) Show that this confirms the formula for the sum of two independent exponentially distributed random variables with the *same* parameter derived in Example 17.

8.21. Suppose that U and V are independent and each is uniformly distributed on $[0, 1]$.

Let $W = U + V$. With f and g both equal to the uniform density on $[0, 1]$, show that the density for W is

$$h(z) = \int_{-\infty}^{\infty} f(x)g(z - x)\, dx = \begin{cases} \displaystyle\int_{0}^{z} 1\, dx & \text{for } 0 < z < 1 \\[2ex] \displaystyle\int_{z-1}^{1} 1\, dx & \text{for } 1 < z < 2 \end{cases}$$

by considering the intervals on which $f(x)$ and $g(z - x)$ are both nonzero. Compute the integrals and sketch the density h.

8.22. (*Continuation*) Suppose that X and Y are independent each uniformly distributed on $[0, 1]$. Use the density computed in Problem 8.21 to find $P(X + Y < 1)$, $P(X + Y \geq 1.5)$, and check your answers by computing areas.

8.23. Suppose that X is exponentially distributed with parameter $\lambda = 2$ and Y is uniformly distributed on $[0, 1]$. What is the joint density of X and Y? Show that the density for $X + Y$ is

$$\int_{0}^{z} 2e^{-2x}\, dx \qquad \text{for } 0 < z < 1$$

$$\int_{z-1}^{z} 2e^{-2x}\, dx \qquad \text{for } 1 < z$$

Compute these integrals.

8.6 *n* INDEPENDENT RANDOM VARIABLES

Let $X_1, \ldots, X_n$ be n random variables. Generalizing the definition for two random variables, we say that they are independent if all possible *events* defined by them are independent:

Definition

$X_1, \ldots, X_n$ are (mutually) *independent* if for all sets $A_1, \ldots, A_n$ of real numbers

$$P(X_1 \in A_1, \ldots, X_n \in A_n) = P(X_1 \in A_1) \cdots P(X_n \in A_n)$$

For discrete random variables a simpler characterization is possible: The sets A_i can be restricted to the particular singleton sets consisting of points in the range of X_i:

If $X_1, \ldots, X_n$ are *discrete*, then independence means that

$$P(X = x_1, \ldots, X_n = x_n) = P(X_1 = x_1) \cdots P(X_n = x_n)$$

for all possible values $x_1, \ldots, x_n$ in the ranges of $X_1, \ldots, X_n$.

Example 18

Perform n Bernoulli trials. Define the n random variables $X_1, \ldots, X_n$ by

$$X_i = \begin{cases} 1 & i\text{th trial results in success} \\ 0 & i\text{th trial results in failure} \end{cases}$$

Then $X_1, \ldots, X_n$ are independent. This is intuitively obvious, but let's see how the definition above can be verified: Let j of the *values* x_i be 1 and the other $n - j$ values be 0. Then the *event*

$$\{X_1 = x_1, \ldots, X_n = x_n\}$$

corresponds to a particular n-long sequence of S's and F's in which there are j successes and $n - j$ failures. Hence the probability of this event is $p^j q^{n-j}$. On the other hand, $P(X_i = x_i)$ is either p or q depending on whether x_i is 1 or 0, respectively. Hence

$$P(X_1 = x_1) \cdots P(X_n = x_n) = p^j q^{n-j}$$

since j factors are p and the other $n - j$ factors are q. Note that each X_i is a Bernoulli random variable and the sum

$$S = X_1 + \cdots + X_n$$

is *exactly* the number of successes on all n trials; this is so because a success at trial i implies that X_i is 1 and hence 1 is added to S. In this way S literally *counts the number of successes* on all n trials. Thus S is *binomially distributed*. ∎

But note this: One rarely verifies directly that random variables are independent. Usually, they are known to be independent by intuition. It is the consequence—the product rule—that is used.

There is one property of independent random variables that has vast consequences. It is that separate "groupings" of independent random variables are also independent. For example, if $X_1, \ldots, X_5$ are independent, then

$$X_1(X_2^4 + \cos(X_5)) \quad \text{and} \quad \tan(X_3 - e^{X_4})$$

are also independent, however complicated their distributions.

Here is a *special case* of the general proof: Suppose that X_1, X_2, X_3 are independent and each is discrete. Let us show that

$$X_1 + X_2 \quad \text{and} \quad X_3^2$$

are independent using the characterization of independence for discrete random variables:

$$P(X_1 + X_2 = z \quad \text{and} \quad X_3^2 = w) = \sum_x P(X_1 = x, X_2 = z - x, X_3 = \pm\sqrt{w})$$

$$= \sum_x P(X_1 = x) P(X_2 = z - x) P(X_3 = \pm\sqrt{w})$$

$$= \left[\sum_x P(X_1 = x) P(X_2 = z - x) \right] P(X_3 = \pm\sqrt{w})$$

$$= P(X_1 + X_2 = z) P(X_3^2 = w)$$

where the sum after the first equality is over all values x that X_1 can take on; the second equality follows the definition of independence for X_1, X_2 and X_3.

Assume that $X_1, \ldots, X_n$ are independent. Let h_1 be a real-valued function of j variables and h_2 be a real-valued function of k variables. Then the two random variables

$$Z_1 = h_1(X_1, \ldots, X_j)$$

$$Z_2 = h_2(X_{j+1}, \ldots, X_{j+k})$$

are independent.

(Only for notational convenience are the two groups the first j and the last k; the same result holds for any two or more groupings of distinct independent random variables.)

Example 19

Let

$$h_1(x, y, z) = xy + z \qquad h_2(x, y) = \sin xe^y$$

Then the result above implies that if $X_1, \ldots, X_5$ are independent, so are

$$Z_1 = X_1X_2 + X_3 \qquad \text{and} \qquad Z_2 = \sin X_4 e^{X_5} \quad \blacksquare$$

Of particular interest are independent random variables *each* of which has the same distribution. For example, in flipping a coin n times, if X_i is 1 or 0 depending on whether the ith flip results in heads or tails (as in Example 18), not only are $X_1, \ldots, X_n$ independent, but they are all distributed in the same way.

Definition

$X_1, \ldots, X_n$ are said to be **independent, identically distributed random variables** (IIDRVs) if they are independent and each has the same distribution.

Example 20

A sign consists of 10 light bulbs. Their lifetimes are independent, each with density (in terms of months)

$$f(x) = \begin{cases} \dfrac{1}{x^2} & x > 1 \\ 0 & x < 1 \end{cases}$$

Find (a) P(no bulb burns out before 2 months) and (b) P(only 2 bulbs left at 3 months).

Solution (a) If T_i is the lifetime of the ith bulb, then $T_1, \ldots, T_{10}$ are IIDRVs.

$$P(T_i > 2 \text{ months}) = \int_2^\infty \frac{1}{x^2} \, dx = \frac{1}{2}$$

Thus, by independence,

$$P(\text{no bulb burns out before 2 months}) = P(T_i > 2)^{10}$$

$$= \left(\frac{1}{2}\right)^{10}$$

(b) $$P(T_i < 3) = \int_1^3 \frac{1}{x^2} \, dx = \frac{2}{3}$$

The number of bulbs burning at 3 months is binomially distributed with $p = 1/3$. (Each bulb is a Bernoulli trial.) Thus

$$P(\text{2 bulbs burning at 3 months}) = \binom{10}{2}\left(\frac{1}{3}\right)^2\left(\frac{2}{3}\right)^8$$

$$= .1951 \quad \blacksquare$$

In Section 8.2 we showed that the sum of two independent Poisson random variables is again Poisson distributed with parameter equal to the sum of the individual parameters. Not surprisingly, this result generalizes:

Suppose that $X_1, \ldots, X_n$ are independent each Poisson distributed with parameters $\alpha_1, \ldots, \alpha_n$. Then

$$S = X_1 + \cdots + X_n$$

is Poisson distributed with parameter

$$\lambda = \alpha_1 + \cdots + \alpha_n$$

If the random variables are IIDRV, the parameter is

$$\lambda = n\alpha$$

Proof. From Section 8.2 we know that $X_1 + X_2$ is Poisson distributed with parameter the sum $\alpha_1 + \alpha_2$. Since X_1, X_2, and X_3 are independent, so are the two random variables $X_1 + X_2$ and X_3. But each is Poisson distributed. Hence by the *same* result in Section 8.2,

$$X_1 + X_2 + X_3 = (X_1 + X_2) + X_3$$

is Poisson distributed with parameter

$$\alpha_1 + \alpha_2 + \alpha_3 = (\alpha_1 + \alpha_2) + \alpha_3$$

Continue in this way (by induction in other words) until you obtain the sum of all n of the random variables. $\blacksquare$

Example 21

Assume that the number of shoplifters caught at a large department store is Poisson distributed with an average of .7 per day. Find P(none caught in a 6-day week) and P(at least 3 caught in 2 days).

    Solution   Since the average *is* the parameter for the Poisson distribution, the parameter for each day is $\alpha = .7$. Since the number caught on each of the 6 days constitute IIDRVs, the number caught in 6 days is Poisson distributed with parameter $6 \cdot .7 = 4.2$. Hence

$$P(\textit{none} \text{ caught in 6 days}) = e^{-4.2}\frac{4.2^0}{0!} = e^{-4.2} = .0150$$

Similarly,

$$P(\textit{at least } 3 \text{ in 2 days}) = 1 - P(0, 1, \text{ or 2 in 2 days})$$

$$= 1 - e^{-1.4}\left(1 + 1.4 + \frac{1.4^2}{2}\right)$$

$$= .1665 \quad \blacksquare$$

PROBLEMS

8.24. A store sells glazed doughnuts at the average rate of 1.3 per hour, chocolate at the rate of .6 per hour, and jelly filled at the rate of 2.8 per hour. Assume that the numbers of each sold are independent and each is Poisson distributed. What is the distribution of the total number of doughnuts sold **(a)** in 1 hour; **(b)** in n hours? **(c)** Find P(at least 2 sold in 15 minutes).

8.25. (*Continuation*) **(a)** How many of *each* kind should the store stock if it wants to be 90% certain that it will have enough of *each* kind to meet the demand for 1 hour? **(b)** If it doesn't care what kind it has as long as there are enough doughnuts of any kind to meet demand, how many need to be stocked to be 90% certain to have enough for one hour?

8.26. In Chapter 6 we derived the gamma density. Do this with the techniques of the present chapter. Let

$$S_n = T_1 + \cdots + T_n$$

be the sum of n IIDRVs each exponentially distributed with parameter λ. Show that S_n has the gamma density by mathematical induction: S_1 in fact is exponentially distributed and so is gamma distributed. Assume that the density of S_n is

$$f_n(x) = \begin{cases} 0 & x < 0 \\ \dfrac{\lambda^n x^{n-1}}{(n-1)!}e^{-\lambda x} & 0 < x \end{cases}$$

Show that $S_{n+1} = S_n + T_{n+1}$ has density (for $z > 0$)

$$f_{n+1}(z) = \int_0^z \frac{\lambda^n x^{n-1}}{(n-1)!} e^{-\lambda x} \lambda e^{-\lambda(z-x)} \, dx$$

$$= \lambda^{n+1} z^n \frac{e^{-\lambda z}}{n!}$$

Conclude by induction that S_{n+1} is gamma distributed.

8.27. Two percent of the cereal boxes are crushed. A carton has 24 boxes. There are 5 cartons in the back room. **(a)** What is the probability that a carton has no crushed boxes? Let X_i = number of crushed boxes in carton i for $i = 1, \ldots, 5$. **(b)** What is the distribution of X_i? Let S be the total number of crushed boxes in all the cartons; let T be the number of cartons that have at least 1 crushed box. Find **(c)** $P(S = 2)$; **(d)** $P(T < 2)$.

8.28. The office has 3 phones. The first rings at the rate of 1.2 times per 5 minutes, the second at the rate of .8 times per 5 minutes, and the third at the rate of 2.4 times in the same interval. Find **(a)** P(no calls in 2 minutes); **(b)** P(at least 3 calls in 4 minutes); **(c)** P(it was the first phone | exactly 1 call in 3 minutes).

8.7 THE NONHOMOGENEOUS POISSON PROCESS

Recall that the parameter λ in the Poisson process of Chapter 6 is the average number of calls per unit time. λ was assumed to be constant. With the mathematical tools developed in this chapter, this assumption can be generalized. $\lambda = \lambda(t)$ will here be a function of t. For example, if $\lambda(7.1) = 2$, the average number of calls per unit time *at* time 7.1 is 2. We will call the function $\lambda = \lambda(t)$ the *intensity function*.

Suppose that calls arrive at the sales order department in such a way that these postulates are satisfied:

1′. Nonoverlapping intervals are independent; same as Postulate 1 in Section 6.3.

2′. Fix a time t with $0 \leq t < \infty$. For a small interval Δt the chance of a call arriving in the interval $(t, t + \Delta t]$ is approximately proportional to the length Δt:

$$\frac{P(\text{exactly 1 call in } (t, t + \Delta t])}{\Delta t} \to \lambda(t)$$

as $\Delta t \to 0$. The difference between this postulate and Postulate 2 in Section 6.3 is that the average rate λ is a *function* of the time t.

3′. The chance of more than 1 call in an interval of length Δt is negligible for $\Delta t \cong 0$, same Postulate 3 in Chapter 6.

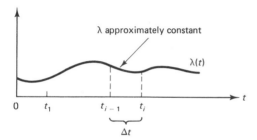

Figure 8.8 The number of arrivals in the ith interval is approximately Poisson distributed with parameter $\lambda(t_i)\, \Delta t$.

For example, the rate of incoming calls may taper off during the noon hour; it may rise to a peak at about 10:00 in the morning and around 2:00 in the afternoon. Or as another example, accidents along a highway ought to obey Postulates 1' to 3'. But the accident rate $\lambda(t)$ surely is a function of t: More accidents are likely during rush hours; fewer on the weekends.

Another name for the nonhomogeneous Poisson process is the *Poisson process in a varying environment* since the entire environment determines the actual value of the intensity function $\lambda(t)$.

As in Chapter 6, let

$$N_t = \#(\text{calls arriving in the interval } [0, t])$$

We know from that chapter that if λ is constant, then N_t is Poisson distributed with parameter λt. We now want to derive the distribution of N_t with λ a function of t. To do this, split the entire interval $[0, t]$ into subintervals each of size Δt. Let Δt be so small that the "intensity function" $\lambda(t)$ is approximately a constant on each of the subintervals as in Fig. 8.8. Since $\lambda(t) \cong \lambda(t_i)$ on the ith subinterval, the number of calls arriving during this interval is approximately *Poisson distributed* with parameters $\lambda(t_i)\, \Delta t$. Let the actual number of calls be N_i.

The total number of calls in $[0, t]$ is

$$N_t = N_1 + \cdots + N_n$$

which is a *sum of n independent Poisson random variables.* Consequently, by the result of the preceding section, N_t is also Poisson distributed with parameter equal to the *sum of the parameters*:

$$\lambda(t_1)\, \Delta t + \lambda(t_2)\, \Delta t + \cdots + \lambda(t_n)\, \Delta t = \sum_{j=1}^{n} \lambda(t_j)\, \Delta t$$

As the number of subintervals $n \to \infty$ and the size of each subinterval $\Delta t \to 0$, the sum approximates more and more closely the integral

$$\int_0^t \lambda(u)\, du$$

The Nonhomogeneous Poisson Process

Suppose that the intensity function $\lambda = \lambda(t)$ is a function of time. Let $N_t = \#(\text{arrivals in } [0, t])$. Set

$$\Lambda(t) = \int_0^t \lambda(u) \, du$$

Then N_t is Poisson distributed with parameter (and hence mean) $\Lambda(t)$: For $j \geq 0$,

$$P(N_t = j) = \frac{\Lambda(t)^j}{j!} e^{-\Lambda(t)}$$

Example 22

Assume that the intensity function $\lambda(t) = \lambda$ is a constant. Show that the result above says that N_t is Poisson distributed with parameter λt.

Solution With $\lambda(t) = \lambda$ a constant, the parameter for N_t is

$$\Lambda(t) = \int_0^t \lambda(u) \, du = \lambda t \quad \blacksquare$$

Example 23

Suppose that the intensity function is linear.

$$\lambda(t) = \begin{cases} 1 - t & 0 < t < 1 \\ 0 & 1 < t \end{cases}$$

(Thus calls can *only* arrive during the interval $[0, 1]$ since $\lambda(t)$ is 0 thereafter.) Find the probability of (a) $P(\text{no calls in } [0, .5])$; (b) $P(\text{at least 1 call in } [0, \infty))$; (c) $P(\text{call in } [0, .5] \mid \text{exactly 1 call in } [0, \infty))$.

Solution (a) For the interval $[0, .5]$, the parameter is

$$\int_0^{.5} (1 - u) \, du = u - \frac{u^2}{2} \Big|_0^{.5} = \frac{3}{8}$$

Thus

$$P(\text{no call in } [0, .5]) = \frac{(3/8)^0}{0!} e^{-3/8} = .6873$$

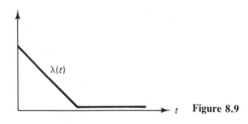

Figure 8.9

Joint Probability Distributions   Chap. 8

(b) For the interval $[0, \infty)$, the parameter is

$$\int_0^\infty \lambda(u)\, du = \int_0^1 (1 - u)\, du = u - \frac{u^2}{2}\Big|_0^1 = \frac{1}{2}$$

Thus

$$P(\text{at least 1 call in } [0, \infty)) = 1 - P(\text{no call})$$
$$= 1 - e^{-1/2}$$
$$= .3935$$

(c) Finally,

$$P(\text{call in } [0, .5] \,|\, \text{exactly 1 call in } [0, \infty))$$

$$= \frac{P(\text{call in } [0, .5] \text{ and no call in } (.5, 1])}{P(\text{exactly 1 call in } [0, 1])}$$

$$= \frac{\dfrac{(3/8)^1}{1!} e^{-3/8} \cdot \dfrac{(1/8)^0}{0!} e^{-1/8}}{\dfrac{(1/2)^1}{1!} e^{-1/2}}$$

$$= \frac{3/8}{1/2}$$

$$= \frac{3}{4}$$

Notice that the parameter for the interval $(.5, \infty)$ is the same as the parameter for the interval $[.5, 1]$, which is $1/8$. Why? ∎

PROBLEMS

8.29. Suppose that N_t is the number of calls for a Poisson process in an environment in which the intensity function is

$$\lambda(t) = \begin{cases} \sin(t) & 0 < t < \pi \\ 0 & \pi < t \end{cases}$$

Find **(a)** $P(N_{\pi/2} = 1)$; **(b)** $P(N_\pi < 3)$; **(c)** $P(\text{more than 2 calls in } [0, \infty))$.

8.30. N_t is the number of calls for a Poisson process in an environment in which the intensity function is

$$\lambda(t) = \frac{1}{t + 1}$$

for $t > 0$. Find $P(N_t = j)$ for $j = 0, 1, 2, \ldots$ What is $E(N_t)$?

Time t

Figure 8.10 x's mark failure times.
$B_{4,2} = s/(s + u)$.

8.8 THE BETA DISTRIBUTION (OPTIONAL)

Consider a renewal process as defined in Sections 6.5 and 6.6: Components are installed successively; the successive lifetimes $T_1, T_2, \ldots$ form a sequence of IIDRVs each exponentially distributed with parameter λ(mean life $1/\lambda$). In Chapter 6 we showed that the total lifetime of the first n components

$$S_n = T_1 + \cdots + T_n$$

is *gamma distributed* with parameters n, λ. The density function of S_n is

$$f_n(u) = \begin{cases} 0 & u < 0 \\ \dfrac{\lambda^n u^{n-1}}{(n-1)!} e^{-\lambda u} & u > 0 \end{cases}$$

Let n, m be fixed positive integers. Consider the random variable

$$B = B_{n,m} = \frac{S_n}{S_{n+m}}$$

Thus B is the fraction of *the time that the first n components were operational over the total amount of time that the first $n + m$ were operational.* B is concentrated on the unit interval $[0, 1]$ since $0 < S_n < S_{n+m}$. The distribution of $B = B_{n,m}$ is called the **beta distribution** with parameters n and m. (see Fig. 8.10) It turns out that the distribution does not depend on the parameter λ. (Can you see an intuitive reason why this is so?)

Let us derive the density function $f_{n,m}$ for $B_{n,m}$. Let n and m be positive integers. Let

$$S_n = T_1 + \cdots + T_n$$

$$R_m = T_{n+1} + \cdots + T_{n+m}$$

be, respectively, the lifetime of the first n and the lifetime of the last m components in a succession of $n + m$ component installations. Since $\{T_i\}_{i=1}^{n+m}$ are IIDRVs, S_n and R_m are independent. Also, S_n is gamma distributed with parameters n and λ, while R_m is gamma distributed with parameters m and λ. Note also that

$$S_{n+m} = S_n + R_m$$

Let $0 < t < 1$; the distribution function for $B = B_{n,m}$ is

$$F(t) = P(B_{n,m} \leqslant t)$$

$$= P\left(\frac{S_n}{S_n + R_m} \leqslant t\right)$$

Joint Probability Distributions   Chap. 8

$$= P(S_n \leq t(S_n + R_m))$$

$$= P((1 - t)S_n \leq tR_m)$$

Since S_n and R_m are independent, their joint density function is

$$h(x, y) = \begin{cases} \dfrac{\lambda^n x^{n-1}}{(n-1)!} e^{-\lambda x} \dfrac{\lambda^m y^{m-1}}{(m-1)!} e^{-\lambda y} & 0 < x \quad \text{and} \quad 0 < y \\ 0 & \text{otherwise} \end{cases}$$

With x corresponding to S_n and y to R_m, $F(t)$ is the integral of h over the region depicted in Fig. 8.11.

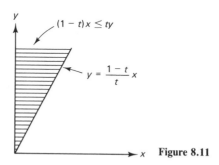

Figure 8.11

Consequently,

$$F(t) = \int_0^\infty \int_0^{ty/(1-t)} h(x, y) \, dx \, dy$$

$$= \frac{\lambda^{n+m}}{(n-1)!(m-1)!} \int_0^\infty \int_0^{ty/(1-t)} x^{n-1} y^{m-1} e^{-\lambda x} e^{-\lambda y} \, dx \, dy$$

To obtain the density function f for B, differentiate this double integral with respect to t. Since the only part that is a function of t is the upper limit on x,

$$F'(t) = \frac{\lambda^{n+m}}{(n-1)!(m-1)!} \int_0^\infty \left[\frac{d}{dt} \int_0^{ty/(1-t)} x^{n-1} e^{-\lambda x} \, dx \right] y^{m-1} e^{-\lambda y} \, dy$$

$$= \frac{\lambda^{n+m}}{(n-1)!(m-1)!} \int_0^\infty \frac{y}{(1-t)^2} \left(\frac{ty}{1-t} \right)^{n-1} e^{-\lambda ty/(1-t)} y^{m-1} e^{-\lambda y} \, dy$$

$$= \frac{\lambda^{n+m}}{(n-1)!(m-1)!} \frac{t^{n-1}}{(1-t)^{n+1}} \int_0^\infty y^{n+m-1} e^{-\lambda y/(1-t)} \, dy$$

Note how the chain rule was used to obtain the second equality:

$$\frac{d}{dt} \int_0^{g(t)} f(x) \, dx = g'(t)f(g(t))$$

when the upper limit of integration is itself a function of t. Returning to the computation of $F'(t)$, substitute $u = \lambda y/(1 - t)$. Then $y = (1 - t)u/\lambda$, $dy = (1 - t)/\lambda\ du$, so

$$F'(t) = \frac{\lambda^{n+m}}{(n - 1)!\,(m - 1)!} \cdot \frac{t^{n-1}}{(1 - t)^{n+1}} \int_0^\infty \left(\frac{(1 - t)u}{\lambda}\right)^{n+m-1} e^{-u} \frac{1 - t}{\lambda}\,du$$

$$= \frac{1}{(n - 1)!\,(m - 1)!} t^{n-1}\,(1 - t)^{m-1} \int_0^\infty u^{n+m-1}\,e^{-u}\,du$$

The value of the last integral can be found using integration by parts. In fact $\int_0^\infty u^j e^{-u}\,du = j \int_0^\infty u^{j-1} e^{-u}\,du$ for $j \geqslant 1$. This implies that the above integral is $(n + m - 1)!$

The beta density function with parameters $n \geqslant 1$ and $m \geqslant 1$ is

$$f_{n,m}(t) = \begin{cases} \dfrac{(n + m - 1)!}{(n - 1)!\,(m - 1)!} t^{n-1}(1 - t)^{m-1} & 0 < t < 1 \\ 0 & t < 0 \quad\text{or}\quad 1 < t \end{cases}$$

Fig. 8.12 depicts graphs of the beta density functions for various values of n and m.

Example 24

Find $P(B_{3,1} \leqslant 1/2)$ and $P(B_{6,2} \geqslant 4/5)$. For the first, we are asking for the probability that the *first three* components last less than half the time of *four* $(3 + 1)$ components used sequentially. For the second, we are asking for the probability that the *first six* last at least four-fifths the total time of *eight* $(6 + 2)$.

Solution $B_{3,1}$ has density

$$f(t) = \frac{3!}{2!0!} t^2(1 - t)^0 = 3t^2$$

for $0 < t < 1$. Therefore,

$$P\left(B_{3,1} \leqslant \frac{1}{2}\right) = \int_0^{1/2} f(t)\,dt = t^3 \Big|_0^{1/2} = \frac{1}{8}$$

$B_{6,2}$ has density

$$f(t) = \frac{7!}{5!1!} t^5(1 - t)^1 = 42(t^5 - t^6)$$

for $0 < t < 1$. Therefore,

$$P\left(B_{6,2} \geqslant \frac{4}{5}\right) = \int_{4/5}^1 f(t)\,dt = 42\left[\frac{t^6}{6} - \frac{t^7}{7}\right]_{4/5}^1 = .4233 \quad \blacksquare$$

Note that when $n = 1$ and $m = 1$, then B is the fraction of the time until

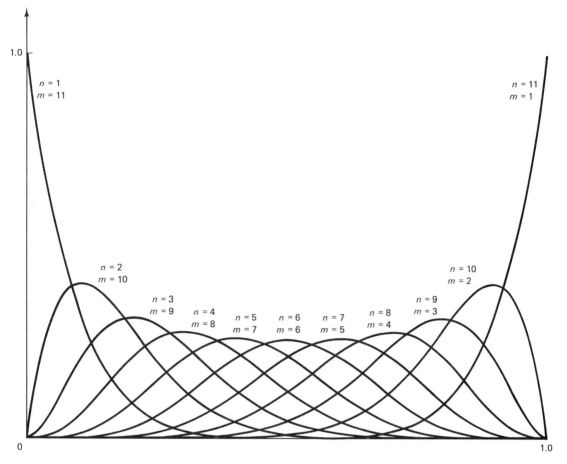

Figure 8.12 The beta density functions.

the second burnout that the first component lasts. The density of $B = B_{1,1}$ from above is

$$f(t) = \frac{1!}{0!0!} t^0(1 - t)^0 = 1$$

Thus $B_{1,1}$ is *uniformly distributed* on the interval $(0, 1)$. Note how this also follows from Section 6.4: Between time 0 and the time of the second component burnout, there was exactly one component (the first) burnout. *When* this occurred is uniformly distributed by the results of Chapter 6.

PROBLEMS

8.31. Five components are used successively. The lifetimes are exponentially distributed and independent each with parameter λ. Find $P(B_{3,2} \leq t)$ for $t =$ **(a)** 1/4; **(b)** 1/2; **(c)** 3/4.

8.32. Show that $f_{n,m}(t) = f_{m,n}(1 - t)$ and interpret this fact intuitively.

8.33. Let $n + m = 5$; plot $f_{1,4}, f_{2,3}, f_{3,2}$, and $f_{4,1}$.

8.34. Show that the beta densities are normalized: Let

$$I_{n,m} = \int_0^1 f_{n,m}(t) \, dt$$

Use an integration by parts to show that $I_{n,m} = I_{n+1,m-1}$. Find $I_{n+m-1,1}$ directly and conclude that $I_{n,m} = 1$ for all n, m.

8.35. Find $E(B_{n,m})$: First show that $E(B_{n,1}) = n/(n + 1)$. (Does this make intuitive sense?) Use an integration by parts to show that

$$E(B_{n,m}) = \frac{n}{n + 1} E(B_{n+1,m-1})$$

Use this *recursive formula* to conclude that

$$E(B_{n,m}) = \frac{n}{n + 1} \frac{n + 1}{n + 2} \frac{n + 2}{n + 3} \cdots \frac{n + m - 2}{n + m - 1} E(B_{n+m-1,1})$$

$$= \frac{n}{n + m}$$

8.9 RANDOM COMMENTS AND PROBLEMS: CONDITIONAL DENSITIES (OPTIONAL)

Suppose that X and Y are continuous random variables, but not necessarily independent. Then the specific value of Y, once known, helps to predict the value of X. That is, the density function of X can be revised *given* that Y is known to have a definite value y.

Throughout, assume that X and Y have joint density function $h(x, y)$ and that $f(x)$ and $g(y)$ are the marginal densities for X and Y, respectively. To find the *conditional density function* for X given $Y = y$, compute

$$P(x < X \leq x + \Delta x \mid y < Y \leq y + \Delta y)$$

$$= \frac{P(x < X \leq x + \Delta x \quad \text{and} \quad y < Y \leq y + \Delta y)}{P(y < Y \leq y + \Delta y)}$$

$$= \frac{\int_y^{y+\Delta y} \int_x^{x+\Delta x} h(s, t) \, ds \, dt}{\int_y^{y+\Delta y} g(t) \, dt}$$

$$\cong \frac{h(x, y) \, \Delta x \, \Delta y}{g(y)}$$

$$= \frac{h(x, y)}{g(y)} \Delta x$$

where the approximation is valid for small Δx and Δy. As Δy tends to zero, we can define the probability that $X \in (x, x + \Delta x]$ given $Y = y$ approximately as

$$P(x < X \leqslant x + \Delta x \mid Y = y) \cong \frac{h(x, y)}{g(y)} \Delta x$$

As $\Delta x \to$ the infinitesimal dx, we obtain motivation for the following

---

Definition

The *conditional density for X given* $Y = y$ is

$$f(x|y) = \frac{h(x, y)}{g(y)}$$

defined at points y with $g(y) \neq 0$. Similarly, the *conditional density for Y given* $X = x$ is

$$g(y|x) = \frac{h(x, y)}{f(x)}$$

defined at points x where $f(x) \neq 0$.

Example 25

Suppose that the joint density function for X and Y is

$$h(x, y) = \begin{cases} \frac{3}{8}(x + y^2) & 0 < x < 2 \text{ and } 0 < y < 1 \\ 0 & \text{otherwise} \end{cases}$$

Find the conditional density of X given $Y = y$ for $0 < y < 1$.

Solution First find the marginal density for Y; for $0 < y < 1$,

$$g(y) = \int_0^2 h(x, y) \, dx = \frac{3}{8} \int_0^2 (x + y^2) \, dx = \frac{3}{4}(1 + y^2)$$

Therefore, for $0 < y < 1$,

$$f(x|y) = \frac{h(x, y)}{g(y)} = \frac{1}{2} \frac{x + y^2}{1 + y^2}$$

for values of x such that $0 < x < 2$. For x outside this interval, $f(x|y) = 0$. $f(x|y)$ is *only* defined for $0 < y < 1$. (It makes sense to seek $P(\text{event } A|Y = y)$ only if y is actually a value in the range of Y.) ∎

Note that if X and Y are independent, then $h(x, y) = f(x)g(y)$, and conse-quently,

---

X and Y *independent* implies that

$$f(x|y) = f(x) \qquad g(y|x) = g(y)$$

Given a value of Y, the *conditional expectation* of X can be defined using the conditional density of X given $Y = y$. In fact, by *definition*,

$$E(X \mid Y = y) = \int_{-\infty}^{\infty} xf(x|y) \, dx$$

Similarly,

$$E(Y \mid X = x) = \int_{-\infty}^{\infty} yg(y|x) \, dy$$

Example 26

For $0 < y < 1$ compute the conditional expectation of X given $Y = y$ in Example 25.

Solution

$$E(X \mid Y = y) = \int_{0}^{2} x \cdot \frac{1}{2} \frac{x + y^2}{1 + y^2} \, dx$$

$$= \frac{1}{2(1 + y^2)} \int_{0}^{2} x(x + y^2) \, dx$$

$$= \frac{4 + 3y^2}{3(1 + y^2)} \quad \blacksquare$$

PROBLEMS

Find the conditional densities of X given $Y = y$ and Y given $X = x$ for the joint densities of the following. Also find $E(X \mid Y = y)$ and $E(Y \mid X = x)$.

8.36. Problem 8.11.

8.37. Problem 8.14(c) and (d).

8.38. In Problem 8.36 use the expression for $f(x \mid y)$ to find $P(X < 1/2 \mid Y = 1/3)$.

I shall never believe that God plays dice with the world.

Albert Einstein, 1879–1955,
Einstein: His Life and Times by Philipp Frank*

— Chapter 9 ——————————

Variances, Covariances, Correlation Coefficients, and More on Expectations

The expectation of a random variable is a number that summarizes its distribution. In gambling language the expectation is the fair entrance fee. But two games with the same expectation can be vastly different; in the first the stakes are high; thus the player can expect either to win much *or* lose much even though the expected winnings are the same as in the second game, where the stakes are low. The *variance* is a number that summarizes this variation.

Two random variables may be independent. Or they may be very highly associated; that is, the actual value of one may allow one to be fairly sure of the value of the other. The *correlation coefficient* between two random variables is a single number that summarizes their degree of association.

The key mnemonic tool for remembering (and helping to derive) the formulas to be developed is this: The expectation of a random variable is the sum of its values times the probabilities. As we saw in Chapter 5, even continuous random variables obey this rule of thumb if one replaces sums by integrals and probabilities by "infinitesimal probabilities" $f(x)\ dx$, where f is the density function.

*From P. Frank, *Einstein: His Life and Times*. Translated by George Rosen. Copyright © Alfred A. Knopf, Inc. Reprinted by permission of the publisher.

9.1 EXPECTATIONS OF FUNCTIONS OF RANDOM VARIABLES

How is the expectation of a function of X computed? For examples, the expectations of $\sin X$ or e^x or $(9/5)X + 32$? Suppose for definiteness that X is discrete; let h be a function and define the random variable Z by $Z = h(X)$. Consider this gambling game: If the random experiment results in $X = x$, Martha wins \$$x$ and Ronnie wins \$$h(x)$. The fair entrance fee for Martha is $E(X)$, but what is the fair entrance fee for Ronnie? He will win \$$h(x)$ with probability $P(X = x)$. Thus the "sum of the values time the probabilities" implies that he should pay $\Sigma\, h(x)P(X = x)$, where the sum extends over the values x in the range of X.

Similarly, if a continuous random variable X assumes the value x with infinitesimal probability $f(x)\, dx$, the random variable $h(X)$ will assume the value $h(x)$. Thus the "integral of the values times the infinitesimal probabilities" leads to the second formula:

Definition

Let h be a real-valued function of a real variable.

1. If X is discrete,

$$E(h(X)) = \sum_x h(x)P(X = x)$$

where the sum extends over all x in the range of X.

2. If X is continuous with density f,

$$E(h(X)) = \int_{-\infty}^{\infty} h(x)f(x)\, dx$$

Example 1

Suppose that X has density

$$f(x) = \begin{cases} 0 & 0 > x \quad \text{or} \quad 2 < x \\ \dfrac{x}{2} & 0 < x < 2 \end{cases}$$

Find $E(X^3)$ and $E(e^X + 3)$.

    Solution Directly from the definition in the box,

$$E(X^3) = \int_0^2 x^3 \frac{x}{2}\, dx = \left.\frac{x^5}{10}\right|_0^2 = 3.2$$

$$E(e^x + 3) = \int_0^2 (e^x + 3) \frac{x}{2}\, dx$$

$$= \frac{1}{2} \left[xe^x - e^x + \frac{3}{2}x^2 \right]_0^2$$

$$= \frac{1}{2}(e^2 + .7) \quad \blacksquare$$

Note that if X is a continuous random variable and $Z = h(X)$, then we now have *two methods* for finding $E(Z)$. The *first* uses the formula in the box above. The *second* finds the density of the random variable Z using the methods of Section 5.7. That is, Z is itself a random variable whose density $g(z)$ can be found and used to compute $E(Z)$ directly. Thus

$$E(Z) = \int_{-\infty}^{\infty} zg(z) \, dz$$

That these two methods always yield the same value of $E(Z)$ is shown in Problem 9.13.

Example 2

Let X be as in Example 1. Show that $E(X^3) = 3.2$ by first finding the density function of $Z = h(X) = X^3$.

Solution Since X is concentrated on $[0, 2]$, $Z = X^3$ is concentrated on $[0, 8]$. For $z \in [0, 8]$,

$$F_Z(z) = P(Z \leqslant z)$$

$$= P(X^3 \leqslant z)$$

$$= P(X \leqslant z^{1/3})$$

$$= \int_0^{z^{1/3}} \frac{x}{2} \, dx$$

$$= \frac{z^{2/3}}{4}$$

where the fourth equality uses the density function of X from Example 1. Differentiating the distribution function to find the density g for Z yields

$$g(z) = \begin{cases} 0 & z < 0 \quad \text{or} \quad 8 < z \\ \dfrac{z^{-1/3}}{6} & 0 < z < 8 \end{cases}$$

Therefore,

$$E(Z) = \int_0^8 z \frac{z^{-1/3}}{6} \, dz = \frac{z^{5/3}}{10} \Big|_0^8 = 3.2$$

in agreement with $E(X^3)$ found in Example 1. $\quad \blacksquare$

Example 3

Let X be uniformly distributed on $[a, b]$. Find $E(X^n)$ for positive integer n.

Solution The density for X is $1/(b - a)$ on the interval $[a, b]$. Thus

$$E(X^n) = \int_a^b x^n \frac{1}{b - a} \, dx$$

$$= \frac{1}{b - a} \int_a^b x^n \, dx$$

$$= \frac{1}{n + 1} \frac{b^{n+1} - a^{n+1}}{b - a}$$

Note that when $n = 1$,

$$E(X) = E(X^1) = \frac{1}{2} \frac{b^2 - a^2}{b - a} = \frac{b + a}{2}$$

which is the expectation of X found in Section 5.4 ∎

Example 4

Let X be exponentially distributed with parameter λ. Find $E(X^n)$ for positive integer n.

Solution Using the boxed formula above,

$$E(X^n) = \int_0^\infty x^n \lambda e^{-\lambda x} \, dx$$

Therefore,

$$E(X^n) = \frac{1}{\lambda^n} \int_0^\infty u^n e^{-u} \, du \qquad (*)$$

after the change of variable $u = \lambda x$. Integrate by parts with $u' = e^{-u}$ and $v = u^n$:

$$E(X^n) = \frac{1}{\lambda^n} \left[-u^n e^{-u} \Big|_0^\infty + n \int_0^\infty u^{n-1} e^{-u} \, du \right]$$

The first term in brackets is zero since it is clearly 0 at the lower limit; and at ∞,

$$\lim_{u \to \infty} u^n e^{-u} = \lim_{u \to \infty} \frac{u^n}{e^u} = 0$$

using L'Hôpital's rule for the second equality. Thus

$$E(X^n) = \frac{1}{\lambda^n} \int_0^\infty u^n e^{-u} \, du = \frac{n}{\lambda^n} \int_0^\infty u^{n-1} e^{-u} \, du$$

Now factor out n/λ from the coefficient in front of the second integral to obtain

$$E(X^n) = \frac{n}{\lambda} \left(\frac{1}{\lambda^{n-1}} \int_0^\infty u^{n-1} e^{-u} \, du \right)$$

The expression inside the parentheses is exactly $E(X^{n-1})$ since the expression is the right-hand side of equation (*) with n replaced by $n - 1$. Thus we have derived the **recursion relation**

$$E(X^n) = \frac{n}{\lambda} E(X^{n-1})$$

$$= \frac{n}{\lambda} \frac{n-1}{\lambda} E(X^{n-2})$$

$$= \frac{n}{\lambda} \frac{n-1}{\lambda} \frac{n-2}{\lambda} \cdots \frac{2}{\lambda} E(X^1)$$

$$= \frac{n!}{\lambda^n}$$

where we have used the fact that $E(X^1) = E(X) = 1/\lambda$ for an exponentially distributed random variable. Consequently, if X is exponentially distributed with parameter λ, then

$$E(X^n) = \frac{n!}{\lambda^n}$$

for $n = 1, 2, 3, \ldots$ ■

The special case of a *linear function* is of particular importance. Suppose that X is a random variable and

$$Y = aX + b$$

where a and b are constants. Then Y is a *change of scale* applied to X. If X represents an amount won in gambling, then for $b = 0$ and an appropriate choice of a, Y represents the same amount in rubles. It seems clear that if one plays the game many times with dollars, computes the average winnings, and *then* converts that average to rubles, this number should be the same as if one played many games with rubles rather than dollars from the start. This is to say that the expectation should be preserved.

Expectation is preserved under a change of scale:
$$E(aX + b) = aE(X) + b$$

Note the special case when $a = 0$:

The expectation of a constant is itself:
$$E(b) = b$$

Intuitively, if one *must* win $\$b$ by playing the game, one can *expect* to win $\$b$.

Formal Proof of Foregoing Result. For definiteness, suppose that X has density function f (although a similar proof works if X is discrete). Then

$$E(aX + b) = \int_{-\infty}^{\infty} (ax + b)f(x) \, dx$$

$$= a \int_{-\infty}^{\infty} xf(x) \, dx + b \int_{-\infty}^{\infty} f(x) \, dx$$

$$= aE(X) + b \cdot 1$$

since the first integral is by definition $E(X)$ and the second integral is the total area under the density function f, which is 1. ∎

How is the expectation of a function of *more than one* random variable computed? For examples, $X + Y$ or $X \sin Y$ or the maximum of X and Y? Let $g(x, y)$ be a real-valued function of two variables. [For example, to find $E(X \sin Y)$ the function $g(x, y) = x \sin y$ would be used.] Let $h(x, y)$ be the joint density function of X and Y. Using the heuristic idea that the expectation is the *sum of the values times the probabilities* leads to:

Definition

1. If X, Y are discrete, then

$$E(g(X, Y)) = \sum_{x,y} g(x,y)P(X = x \text{ and } Y = y)$$

where the sum extends over all x, y in the ranges of X, Y, respectively.

2. If X, Y are continuous with joint density function h, then

$$E(g(X, Y)) = \int_{-\infty}^{\infty} \int_{-\infty}^{\infty} g(x, y)h(x, y) \, dx \, dy$$

Example 5

Suppose that the joint density function for X and Y is concentrated on the square with vertices $(0, 0)$, $(0, 1)$, $(1, 0)$, and $(1, 1)$. For $0 \leqslant x, y \leqslant 1$,

$$h(x, y) = \frac{3}{2} (x^2 + y^2)$$

Find $E(XY)$, $E(X + Y)$, and $E(X)$ using the joint density function.

Solution

$$E(XY) = \int_0^1 \int_0^1 xy \cdot \frac{3}{2} (x^2 + y^2) \, dx \, dy$$

$$= \int_0^1 \frac{3}{2} \left(\frac{1}{4}x^4 y + \frac{1}{2}x^2 y^3 \right) \Big|_{x=0}^{x=1} dy$$

$$= \int_0^1 \left(\frac{3}{8}y + \frac{3}{4}y^3 \right) dy$$

$$= \frac{3}{8}$$

$$E(X + Y) = \int_0^1 \int_0^1 (x + y) \cdot \frac{3}{2} (x^2 + y^2) \, dx \, dy = \frac{5}{4}$$

$$E(X) = \int_0^1 \int_0^1 x \cdot \frac{3}{2} (x^2 + y^2) \, dx \, dy = \frac{5}{8} \quad \blacksquare$$

Example 6

Two cards are selected without replacement from a standard deck of 52. Let X = number of hearts and Y = number of spades. Find $E(XY)$ and $E(X + Y)$.

Solution   Let us first construct a probability table with the values of X along the top and the values of Y along the left.

$$P(X = 0 \text{ and } Y = 0) = P(\text{no hearts or spades in 2 cards})$$

$$= \frac{\binom{26}{2}}{\binom{52}{2}}$$

$$= .2451$$

$$P(X = 1 \text{ and } Y = 0) = P(1 \text{ heart and no spades})$$

$$= \frac{\binom{13}{1}\binom{13}{0}\binom{26}{1}}{\binom{52}{2}}$$

$$= .2549$$

Similarly, the other entries in the table are computed:

		X		
		0	1	2
	0	.2451	.2549	.0588
Y	1	.2549	.1275	0
	2	.0588	0	0

Using the fact that an expectation is the sum of the values times the probabilities:

$$E(XY) = 0 \cdot 0 \cdot (.2451) + 1 \cdot 0 \cdot (.2549) + 2 \cdot 0 \cdot (.0588)$$
$$+ 0 \cdot 1 \cdot (.2549) + 1 \cdot 1 \cdot (.1275) + 0 \cdot 2 \cdot (.0588)$$
$$= .1275$$

$$E(X + Y) = (0 + 0)(.2451) + (1 + 0)(.2549) + (2 + 0)(.0588)$$
$$+ (0 + 1)(.2549) + (1 + 1)(.1275) + (0 + 2)(.0588)$$
$$= 1.000$$

[Can you see an intuitive reason why $E(X + Y) = 1$?] ∎

PROBLEMS

9.1. Suppose that X has density

$$f(x) = \begin{cases} 0 & x < 0 \quad \text{or} \quad 1 < x \\ 2x & 0 < x < 1 \end{cases}$$

Find **(a)** $E(X)$, **(b)** $E(X^2)$, **(c)** $E(1/X)$, **(d)** $E(\sin X)$, and **(e)** $E(aX + b)$, where a and b are constants.

9.2. (*Continuation*) Let $U = X^2$, $V = 1/X$, where X is as in Problem 9.1. Use the methods of Section 5.7 to find the densities of U and V. Use them to find $E(U)$ and $E(V)$. Do they agree with the answers to Problem 9.1?

9.3. Suppose that Y has density

$$g(y) = \begin{cases} 0 & y < 1 \\ \dfrac{1}{y^2} & 1 < y \end{cases}$$

Find **(a)** $E(Y)$; **(b)** $E(1/Y)$; **(c)** $E(1/Y^2)$.

9.4. (*Continuation*) Let $U = 1/Y$, $V = 1/Y^2$, where Y is as in Problem 9.3. Find the densities of U and V and use them to find $E(U)$ and $E(V)$.

9.5. Suppose that F and C are Fahrenheit and Celsius temperatures so that $F = (9/5)C + 32$. Assume that C has density

$$f(x) = \begin{cases} \dfrac{2x}{7500} & 50 < x < 100 \\ 0 & \text{elsewhere} \end{cases}$$

(a) Find $E(C)$. **(b)** Also find the density function of F and use it to find $E(F)$. **(c)** Verify that $E(F) = 9E(C)/5 + 32$.

9.6. Flip a fair coin three times. Let X = number of heads and Y = the number of the flip on which the first head appeared. (If no heads on all three flips, set $Y = 0$.) **(a)** Construct a probability table in which the values of X are along the top and the values of Y are along the left. Compute **(b)** $E(XY)$, **(c)** $E(X + Y)$, **(d)** $E(X - Y)$, and **(e)** $E(X)$ from the table.

9.7. A bin contains 5 apples, 4 bananas, and 3 cantaloupes. Let A be the number of apples and B the number of bananas in a sample of size 3 taken without replacement. **(a)** Construct a probability table in which the values of A appear along the top and the values of B appear along the left. Use the table to find **(b)** $E(A + B)$; **(c)** $E(A)$; **(d)** $E(B)$; **(e)** $E(AB)$.

9.8. Suppose that X and Y have joint density function

$$h(x, y) = \begin{cases} x + y & 0 < x, y < 1 \\ 0 & \text{elsewhere} \end{cases}$$

Find **(a)** $E(X)$, **(b)** $E(Y)$, **(c)** $E(XY)$, and **(d)** $E(X + Y)$ using the joint density function. **(e)** Find the marginal density functions for X and Y and use them to find $E(X)$ and $E(Y)$ and verify the above.

9.9. Suppose that X and Y have joint density function

$$h(x, y) = \begin{cases} \dfrac{4}{5}(xy + 1) & 0 < x, y < 1 \\ 0 & \text{otherwise} \end{cases}$$

Find **(a)** $E(X)$, **(b)** $E(Y)$, and **(c)** $E(\text{Max }\{X, Y\})$, where Max $\{X, Y\}$ is the maximum of X and Y.

9.10. Suppose that X has exponential density with parameter λ. Find **(a)** $E(h_1(X))$; **(b)** $E(h_2(X))$. h_1 is the function

$$h_1(x) = \begin{cases} x & 0 < x < L \\ 0 & \text{otherwise} \end{cases}$$

where L is a fixed number. h_2 is the function

$$h_2(x) = \text{minimum of } x \text{ and } 1$$

Can you interpret these expectations?

9.11. Let $a < b$ be fixed real numbers. Let $h(x)$ be the "indicator function" of the interval $[a, b]$. That is,

$$h(x) = \begin{cases} 0 & x < a \quad \text{or} \quad b < x \\ 1 & a \leqslant x \leqslant b \end{cases}$$

Assume that X has density function f. Show that

$$E(h(X)) = P(a \leqslant X \leqslant b)$$

and interpret this result in gambling terms.

9.12. Show that in general $E(1/X)$ is *not* $1/E(X)$ by considering this special case: Suppose that X is uniformly distributed on the interval $[1, 2]$. Find $E(X), E(1/X)$, and compare $E(1/X)$ with $1/E(X)$.

9.13. Here is an outline of a proof that the two methods for finding $E(h(X))$ for X continuous result in the same value in one important case: *Assume* that h is an *increasing* function. Let X have density f_X and distribution F_X. The distribution of $Z = h(X)$ is

$$F_Z(z) = P(Z \leqslant z) = P(X \leqslant h^{-1}(z)) = F_X(h^{-1}(z))$$

Differentiate to obtain the density of Z;

$$f_Z(z) = (h^{-1})'\,(z)f_X(h^{-1}(z))$$

Therefore,

$$E(Z) = \int_{-\infty}^{\infty} zf_Z(z)\,dz$$

$$= \int_{-\infty}^{\infty} z((h^{-1})'(z))f_X(h^{-1}(z))\,dz$$

$$= \int_{-\infty}^{\infty} h(x)f_X(x)\,dx$$

Fill in all the steps.

9.2 EXPECTATIONS OF SUMS AND INDEPENDENT PRODUCTS

Suppose that $X_1, \ldots, X_n$ are random variables and

$$S = X_1 + \cdots + X_n$$

For example, X_i might be the lifetime of the ith component in a renewal process and S would therefore be the total lifetime of all n components used sequentially. Then the relation between $E(S)$ and the individual $E(X_i)$'s is

> The expectation of a sum is the sum of the expectations:
> $$E(X_1 + \cdots + X_n) = E(X_1) + \cdots + E(X_n)$$

Example 7

In Example 5 $E(X)$ was computed to be 5/8. By symmetry (or a similar calculation), $E(Y) = 5/8$ also. Thus

$$E(X) + E(Y) = \frac{5}{4}$$

in agreement with the result found in Example 5. ∎

Proof of the Foregoing Formula. Suppose that X and Y have joint density function $h(x, y)$. Then

$$E(X + Y) = \int_{-\infty}^{\infty}\int_{-\infty}^{\infty} (x + y)h(x, y)\,dx\,dy$$

$$= \int_{-\infty}^{\infty}\int_{-\infty}^{\infty} xh(x, y)\,dx\,dy + \int_{-\infty}^{\infty}\int_{-\infty}^{\infty} yh(x, y)\,dx\,dy$$

$$= \int_{-\infty}^{\infty} x\left(\int_{-\infty}^{\infty} h(x, y)\,dy\right)dx + \int_{-\infty}^{\infty} y\left(\int_{-\infty}^{\infty} h(x, y)\,dx\right)dy$$

$$= \int_{-\infty}^{\infty} xf(x)\, dx + \int_{-\infty}^{\infty} yg(y)\, dy$$

$$= E(X) + E(Y)$$

Note that the fourth equality follows from the fact that integrating $h(x, y)$ with respect to y yields the density function for X, and similarly, integrating $h(x, y)$ out with respect to x yields the marginal density function for Y.

Now consider the case for general n: Represent the entire sum as the sum of two random variables and apply the result we have just proved:

$$E(X_1 + \cdots + X_n) = E((X_1 + \cdots + X_{n-1}) + X_n)$$

$$= E(X_1 + \cdots + X_{n-1}) + E(X_n)$$

and continue the process starting with the sum of $n - 1$ rather than with n to conclude that

$$E(X_1 + \cdots + X_n) = E(X_1 + \cdots + X_{n-2}) + E(X_{n-1}) + E(X_n)$$

$$= \cdots$$

$$= E(X_1) + \cdots + E(X_n)$$

which proves the result. The proof for discrete rather than continuous random variables is similar and only involves replacing integral signs by summation signs. ■

The result is very useful; it allows calculation of $E(S)$ in situations in which S has a complicated distribution, but the X_i's have simple distributions.

Example 8

In Section 4.6 a binomially distributed random variable S was found to have expectation np, where n is the number of trials and p is the probability of success on any one trial. This result can be derived *much more simply by decomposing S as a sum.* Let (as in Chapter 8, Example 18)

$$X_i = \begin{cases} 1 & \text{ith trial results in a success} \\ 0 & \text{ith trial results in a failure} \end{cases}$$

in a succession of n Bernoulli trials. Then the number of successes on all n trials is *exactly* the sum

$$S = X_1 + \cdots + X_n$$

since each X_i adds 1 to S if trial i resulted in success. Consequently,

$$E(S) = E(X_1) + \cdots + E(X_n)$$

But each X_i is a Bernoulli random variable that assumes the value 1 with probability p and the value 0 with probability q. Thus

$$E(X_i) = 1 \cdot p + 0 \cdot q = p$$

for each i. Consequently,

$$E(S) = P + P + \cdots + p = np$$

(Look back at the derivation in Section 4.6 to see how much easier this method is!) ∎

Example 9

Let S_n be gamma distributed: S_n is the waiting time until the nth failure in a renewal process in which each component has an exponentially distributed lifetime with parameter λ. In Section 6.6, $E(S_n)$ was shown to be n/λ using an involved inte-gration by parts. Let T_i be the lifetime of the ith component. Since T_i is expo-nentially distributed with parameter λ, $E(T_i) = 1/\lambda$. But

$$S_n = T_1 + \cdots + T_n$$

implies that

$$E(S_n) = E(T_1) + \cdots + E(T_n) = \frac{1}{\lambda} + \cdots + \frac{1}{\lambda} = \frac{n}{\lambda}$$

with no difficult integration! ∎

Another random variable associated with a succession of Bernoulli trials is the *number of runs R*. For example, if a succession of 12 trials resulted in *SSSFFSSFSFFF*, then $R = 6$—the number of distinct runs in either success or failure. To find $E(R)$, the random variable R is decomposed as a sum. Let

$$\xi_i = \begin{cases} 1 & i\text{th result is different than } (i - 1)^{\text{st}} \\ 0 & i\text{th and } (i - 1)^{\text{st}} \text{ results are the same} \end{cases}$$

for $i = 2, 3, \ldots, n$. For example, with 8 Bernoulli trials:

Sequence	R	ξ_2	ξ_3	ξ_4	ξ_5	ξ_6	ξ_7	ξ_8
SSFFFSSS	3	0	1	0	0	1	0	0
SSSFFFFF	2	0	0	1	0	0	0	0
SSSSSSSS	1	0	0	0	0	0	0	0
SFSSFFSF	6	1	1	0	1	0	1	1

Thus, to repeat, ξ_i is 1 if and only if there was a *change* between the $(i - 1)$st and the ith Bernoulli trials; that is, one of them was a success and the other was a failure. The sum

$$\xi_2 + \xi_3 + \cdots + \xi_n$$

is the number of times there was a switch from success to failure *or* from failure to success. This is one less than the total number of runs. That is,

$$R = \xi_2 + \cdots + \xi_n + 1$$

(Check that this is true in the examples above.) Let us compute $E(\xi_i)$ for any $i = 2, 3, \ldots, n$:

$$P(\xi_i = 1) = P(i\text{th result different than } (i - 1)\text{st})$$
$$= P(S \text{ on } (i - 1)\text{st trial and } F \text{ on } i\text{th})$$
$$+ P(F \text{ on } (i - 1)\text{st trial and } S \text{ on } i\text{th})$$
$$= pq + qp$$
$$= 2pq$$

Therefore, since the expectation of a sum is the sum of the expectations,

$$E(R) = E(\xi_2) + \cdots + E(\xi_n) + E(1)$$
$$= 2pq + \cdots + 2pq + 1$$
$$= 2(n - 1)pq + 1$$

In a succession of n Bernoulli trials the expected number of runs is

$$E(R) = 2(n - 1)pq + 1$$

Note that if $p = 1/2 = q$ (fair coin), then

$$E(R) = 2(n - 1) \cdot \frac{1}{2} \cdot \frac{1}{2} + 1 = \frac{n + 1}{2}$$

about half as many expected runs as trials.

The expectation of a sum is the sum of the expectations. Is the same true for products? Is the expectation of a product equal to the product of the expectations?

Assume that $X_1, \ldots, X_n$ are *independent* random variables. Then the expectation of the product is the product of the expectations:

$$E(X_1 \cdots X_n) = E(X_1) \cdots E(X_n)$$

Let us emphasize the difference between sums and products. It is *always* true that the expectation of a (finite) sum is the sum of the expectations, but *only under the assumption of independence* is it in general true that the expectation of a (finite) product is the product of the expectations. Still, the result has important applications.

Proof. We will prove the result in the continuous case; the discrete case is similar. Suppose that X and Y have joint density function $h(x, y)$. By independence $h(x, y)$ is the product of the marginal densities f and g for X and Y, respectively. Thus

$$E(XY) = \int_{-\infty}^{\infty} \int_{-\infty}^{\infty} xyh(x, y)\, dx\, dy$$

$$= \int_{-\infty}^{\infty} \int_{-\infty}^{\infty} xf(x)yg(y)\, dx\, dy$$

$$= \int_{-\infty}^{\infty} \left(\int_{-\infty}^{\infty} xf(x)\, dx \right) yg(y)\, dy$$

$$= \int_{-\infty}^{\infty} E(X)yg(y)\, dy$$

$$= E(X)E(Y)$$

For products of more than two random variables,

$$E(X_1 \cdots X_n) = E((X_1 \cdots X_{n-1})X_n)$$

$$= E(X_1 \cdots X_{n-1})E(X_n)$$

$$= \cdots$$

$$= E(X_1) \cdots E(X_n)$$

The second equality uses the fact that the *two* random variables $X_1 \cdots X_{n-1}$ and X_n are independent combined with the result already proved for two random variables. Then the same technique is applied again and again to obtain the last equality. (Or use induction.) ∎

PROBLEMS

9.14. The expected number of runs $E(R) = 2(n - 1)pq + 1$ in a succession of n Bernoulli trials. With the number n of trials fixed, graph $E(R)$ as a function of p for $0 \leqslant p \leqslant 1$.

9.15. Machine B makes bolts. Two percent are defective. To see whether a defective bolt tends to be followed by another defective bolt or whether they are independent, the results of 1000 bolts are recorded. Assuming independence from one bolt to the next (and so successive bolts constitute successive Bernoulli trials), what is the expected number of runs?

9.16. A shelf has 7 cans, 3 of which are dented. **(a)** You choose 2 without replacement. Let X be the number of dented cans in the sample. What is $E(X)$? **(b)** Suppose that sampling was done with replacement. What is $E(X)$ now?

9.17. (*Continuation*) Suppose that 3 cans are selected. What is $E(X)$ when sampling is done **(a)** without replacement; **(b)** with replacement?

9.18. (*The Hypergeometric Distribution: Continuation*) A bin contains G green and R red blocks. $N = G + R$. n blocks are selected without replacement. Let X be the number of green blocks in the sample. Let

$$\eta_i = \begin{cases} 1 & \text{ith selection results in a green block} \\ 0 & \text{ith selection results in a red block} \end{cases}$$

(a) Show that $X = \eta_1 + \cdots + \eta_n$. (b) What is $P(\eta_i = 1)$? (See Section 3.3.) (c) What is $E(X)$? (d) What is $E(X)$ if sampling is performed with replacement?

Let X be the number of green blocks in a sample of size n from a bin of N blocks, G of which are green. For $n \le G$,

$$E(X) = n\,\frac{G}{N}$$

regardless of whether sampling is performed with or without replacement.

9.19. Let X be the number of aces Stan receives in a game of bridge. (Each player receives 13 cards.) (a) Show that

$$P(X = j) = \frac{\dbinom{4}{j}\dbinom{48}{13 - j}}{\dbinom{52}{13}}$$

(b) Find $E(X)$ directly from the definition as

$$\sum_{j=0}^{4} jP(X = j)$$

9.20. (*Continuation*) Here is a tricky way to find $E(X)$: Let $X_1, \ldots, X_4$ be the number of aces that each of the four players receives. Reason that $E(X_i) = E$ is the same for each $i = 1, 2, 3, 4$ and that $E(X_1 + X_2 + X_3 + X_4) = 4$ since $X_1 + X_2 + X_3 + X_4$ is the total number of aces received by all the players. Conclude that $E(X_i) = 1$.

9.21. Generalize the result about the expected number of runs: Suppose that n trials are performed; they are independent and each can result in A with probability p, B with probability q, and C with probability r where $p + q + r = 1$. Find the expected number of runs.

9.3 THE VARIANCE

The expectation is one number associated with a random variable. The variance is another; it is a measure of the variation of the random variable from the mean. Random variables X and Y with the density functions in Fig. 9.1 have the same mean μ. But the values of X are distributed more closely to $E(X)$ than are the values of Y to $E(Y)$. That is, in any *realization* (in the result of a random experiment) the probability is greater that X will be closer to μ than Y will be. To find a single number that will be an indication of the possibility for variation from μ, consider the values $X - \mu$ and $Y - \mu$. $X - \mu$ will tend to be close to 0, but

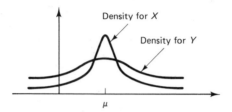

Density for X

Density for Y

Figure 9.1

$Y - \mu$ will vary far from 0 either positively or negatively. To avoid cancellation, consider the squares: $(X - \mu)^2$ will tend to be close to 0, but with greater probability $(Y - \mu)^2$ will be a large positive number. Consequently, $E[(X - \mu)^2]$ will be less than $E[(Y - \mu)^2]$.

Definition

Let X have mean μ. The **variance** of X is

$$\sigma^2 = \text{Var}\,(X) = E((X - \mu)^2)$$

The **standard deviation** is the square root of the variance:

$$\sigma = \sqrt{\text{Var}\,(X)}$$

That is, μ is subtracted from each value of X to obtain the new *random variable* $X - \mu$. Then Var (X) is the expectation of the square.

Example 10

Recall that if X denotes the result of a die roll, then $E(X) = 7/2$. Find Var (X).

Solution A probability table for $(X - 7/2)^2$ is formed:

X	1	2	3	4	5	6
$(X - 7/2)^2$	25/4	9/4	1/4	1/4	9/4	25/4
Probability	1/6	1/6	1/6	1/6	1/6	1/6

Thus

$$\text{Var}\,(X) = E\left(\left(X - \frac{7}{2}\right)^2\right)$$

$$= \frac{1}{6}\left(\frac{25}{4} + \frac{9}{4} + \frac{1}{4} + \frac{1}{4} + \frac{9}{4} + \frac{25}{4}\right)$$

$$= \frac{35}{12}$$

Here is a program that simulates the variance of a die roll: First N die rolls are simulated. The result of the ith is stored in DIE[I]. Then the average of all N

is computed as an estimate of μ (although in fact we know that $\mu = 3.5$). Then the average deviation is formed as an estimate of σ^2.

$$\frac{1}{N} \cdot \sum_{I=1}^{N} (DIE[I] - AVERAGE)^2$$

```
const NORM = 10000;
      ADDR =  4857;
      MULT =  8601;

var SEED,I,N: integer;.
    RND,AVERAGE,VARIANCE: real;
    DIE: array [1..1000] of integer;

begin
    readln(N);
    SEED: = 0;

    for I: = 1 to N do
        begin
            SEED: = (MULT*SEED + ADDR) mod NORM;
            RND: = SEED/NORM;

            DIE[I]: = trunc(6*RND + 1);
        end;

    AVERAGE: = 0.0;
    for I: = 1 to N do AVERAGE: = AVERAGE + DIE[I];
    AVERAGE: = AVERAGE/N;

    VARIANCE: = 0.0;
    for I: = 1 to N do
        VARIANCE: = (DIE[I]-AVERAGE)*(DIE[I]-AVERAGE);
    VARIANCE: = (VARIANCE/N);

    writeln(AVERAGE:10:4,VARIANCE:10:4)
end.   ■
```

Example 11

Let X be a Bernoulli random variable. Find Var (X).

Solution $X = 1$ with probability p and 0 with probability q. Thus

$$\mu = E(X) = 1 \cdot p + 0 \cdot q = p$$

Construct the probability table for $(X - \mu)^2$:

X	0	1
$(X - \mu)^2$	p^2	$(1 - p)^2$
Probability	q	p

Therefore,

$$\text{Var } (X) = E((X - \mu)^2) = p^2q + (1 - p)^2p = p^2q + q^2p = pq \quad \blacksquare$$

Example 12

Let X be uniformly distributed on $[a, b]$. Find Var (X).

Solution Recall that $E(X) = (b + a)/2$. Therefore,

$$\text{Var } (X) = E\left(\left(X - \frac{b + a}{2}\right)^2\right)$$

$$= \int_a^b \left(x - \frac{b + a}{2}\right)^2 \frac{1}{b - a} \, dx$$

$$= \frac{1}{b - a} \cdot \frac{1}{3} \left(x - \frac{b + a}{2}\right)^3 \Big|_a^b$$

$$= \frac{1}{b - a} \cdot \frac{1}{3} \cdot 2 \frac{(b - a)^3}{8}$$

$$= \frac{(b - a)^2}{12} \quad \blacksquare$$

Finding Var (X) directly from the definition as was done in the last three examples can be complicated. Another formula is usually used instead. Noting that the expectation of a sum is the sum of the expectations, we see that

$$\text{Var } (X) = E((X - \mu)^2)$$

$$= E(X^2 - 2\mu X + \mu^2)$$

$$= E(X^2) - 2\mu E(X) + E(\mu^2)$$

$$= E(X^2) - 2\mu \cdot \mu + \mu^2$$

Or, finally,

$$\boxed{\text{Var } (X) = E(X^2) - \mu^2}$$

This formula provides the computationally easiest method for finding variances.

Example 13

Let X be exponentially distributed with parameter λ. Find Var (X).

Solution By Example 4 $E(X^n) = n!/\lambda^n$. Consequently,

$$\text{Var } (X) = E(X^2) - \mu^2 = \frac{2}{\lambda^2} - \left(\frac{1}{\lambda}\right)^2 = \frac{1}{\lambda^2} \quad \blacksquare$$

Example 14

Compute the variance of W where W is geometrically distributed. From Section 4.6 $E(W) = 1/p$. To find $E(W^2)$ involves a similar technique of interchanging a derivative and a sum. In fact, $E(W(W - 1))$ is easier to find. So first this quantity is computed and then $E(W)$ is added to it to find $E(W^2)$. To find $E(W(W - 1))$, note that if W takes on the value j, then $W(W - 1)$ takes on the value $j(j - 1)$.

$$E(W(W - 1)) = \sum_{j=1}^{\infty} j(j - 1)pq^{j-1}$$

$$= pq \sum_{j=1}^{\infty} j(j - 1)q^{j-2}$$

$$= pq \sum_{j=0}^{\infty} \frac{d^2}{dq^2}(q^j)$$

$$= pq \frac{d^2}{dq^2}\left(\sum_{j=0}^{\infty} q^j\right)$$

$$= pq \frac{d^2}{dq^2}\left(\frac{1}{1 - q}\right)$$

$$= \frac{2pq}{(1 - q)^3}$$

$$= \frac{2q}{p^2}$$

Thus

$$E(W^2) = E(W^2 - W + W)$$
$$= E(W^2 - W) + E(W)$$
$$= E(W(W - 1)) + E(W)$$
$$= \frac{2q}{p^2} + \frac{1}{p}$$

Finally,

$$\text{Var}(W) = E(W^2) - \mu^2$$
$$= \frac{2q}{p^2} + \frac{1}{p} - \left(\frac{1}{p}\right)^2$$
$$= \frac{2q + p - 1}{p^2}$$
$$= \frac{q}{p^2} \quad \blacksquare$$

Given a random variable X, Var (X) is the expectation of the *positive* random variable $(X - \mu)^2$. Since $(X - \mu)^2$ *cannot* take on negative values, the farther this random variable is from 0, the larger will be its expectation. That is, the farther X can be from its expectation μ with large probability, the larger will be the variance of X. In fact, multiplying X by a factor of 2 will result in multiplying the variance by a factor of 4. More generally, let us see what the effect of a *change of scale* is on the variance:

Let a and b be constants. Then

$$\text{Var } (aX + b) = a^2 \text{ Var } (X)$$

$$\sigma_{aX+b} = |a|\sigma_X$$

Of course, the result about the standard deviation is simply the square root of the first equality. Before proving the first equality, note that the result is intuitive; the *values* of the random variable $aX + b$ vary from the expectation $E(aX + b)$, as do the *values* of aX from its expectation $E(aX)$. Note also the special case when $a = 0$:

The variance of a constant is 0:

$$\text{Var } (b) = 0$$

In gambling terminology: Suppose that you are *paid* $\$b$ for playing the game. Then your winnings will be $\$b$ with 0 variance.

To prove the change-of-scale formula, let $\mu = E(X)$. Note that

$$E(aX + b) = aE(X) + b = a\mu + b$$

Thus

$$\begin{aligned}
\text{Var } (aX + b) &= E((aX + b)^2) - (E(aX + b))^2 \\
&= E(a^2X^2 + 2abX + b^2) - (a\mu + b)^2 \\
&= a^2E(X^2) + 2abE(X) + b^2 - (a^2\mu^2 + 2ab\mu + b^2) \\
&= a^2(E(X^2) - \mu^2) \\
&= a^2 \text{ Var}(X)
\end{aligned}$$

Computations of the variance can get fairly involved. But there is a basic result that can be applied to sums of *independent* random variables which simplifies difficult sums and integrals. Recall how in Example 8 the mean of a binomially distributed random variable was found by decomposing it as a sum of other random variables; and later, the same technique was used to find the expected number of runs in n Bernoulli trials. In fact, a similar technique can *sometimes* be used to compute variances.

The variance of an *independent* sum is the sum of the variances: If $X_1, \ldots, X_n$ are independent, then

$$\text{Var} \,(X_1 + \cdots + X_n) = \text{Var} \,(X_1) + \cdots + \text{Var} \,(X_n)$$

Proof. The result is proved for two random variables X and Y. The proof for more than two is similar. Assume that X and Y are independent. Thus $E(XY) = \mu_X \mu_Y$, where μ_X and μ_Y are the expectations of X and Y, respectively. Then

$$\text{Var} \,(X + Y) = E((X + Y)^2) - (\mu_X + \mu_Y)^2$$

$$= E(X^2 + 2XY + Y^2) - (\mu_X^2 + 2\mu_X \mu_Y + \mu_Y^2)$$

$$= E(X^2) - \mu_X^2 + E(Y^2) - \mu_Y^2 + 2E(XY) - 2\mu_X \mu_Y$$

after a reordering of the terms to produce the last line. Since the expectation of XY is the product of the expectations as noted above, the last two terms cancel. The first two terms are $\text{Var} \,(X)$, the next two terms are $\text{Var} \,(Y)$. ∎

Example 15

Suppose that S is binomially distributed n, p. Decompose S as the sum of n Bernoulli variables as in Example 8:

$$S = X_1 + \cdots + X_n$$

where X_i is 1 or 0 if the ith trial resulted in success or failure, respectively. *Since* $X_1, \ldots, X_n$ are independent,

$$\text{Var} \,(S) = \text{Var} \,(X_1) + \cdots + \text{Var} \,(X_n)$$

But $\text{Var} \,(X_i) = pq$ by Example 11. Therefore,

$$\text{Var} \,(S) = pq + \cdots + pq = npq$$ ∎

Example 16

Suppose that X is Poisson distributed with parameter λ. Problem 9.29 asks you to compute a series to show that $\text{Var} \,(X) = \lambda$. Thus the variance *and* the expectation of a Poisson distributed random variable are *both* equal to the parameter λ. But here is a way to see this fact using Example 15. Suppose that S is binomially distributed, n trials, p = probability of success. Then the distribution of S approximates the distribution of X if

$$n \text{ large} \qquad p \cong 0 \qquad \lambda = np$$

But $\text{Var} \,(S) = npq = (np)q = \lambda q \cong \lambda$ since p close to 0 implies that q is close to 1. Hence we should not be surprised to find that the formal proof in Problem 9.29, shows that the variance of X is λ. ∎

> If X is binomially distributed, n = number of trials, then
>
> $$\text{Var}(X) = npq$$
>
> If Y is Poisson distributed with parameter λ, then
>
> $$\text{Var}(Y) = \lambda$$

$E(X)$ determines where X is "centered" and $\text{Var}(X)$ measures how the values of X are spread about that center. A change of scale changes both of these.

> Let μ be the expectation of X and σ^2 be the variance. Then the random variable Z obtained by a change of scale
>
> $$Z = \frac{X - \mu}{\sigma}$$
>
> is **standardized**. That is,
>
> $$E(Z) = 0 \qquad \text{Var}(Z) = 1$$

To see why this is so, we apply the results concerning changes of scale:

$$E(Z) = E\left(\frac{X - \mu}{\sigma}\right) = \frac{1}{\sigma}(E(X) - \mu) = 0$$

$$\text{Var}(Z) = \text{Var}\left(\frac{1}{\sigma}X - \frac{\mu}{\sigma}\right) = \frac{1}{\sigma^2}\text{Var}(X) = \frac{1}{\sigma^2}\sigma^2 = 1$$

Example 17

Let X be uniformly distributed on $[a, b]$. Let Z be the standardized version of X. That is, $Z = (X - \mu)/\sigma$, where μ and σ are the mean and standard deviation of X. Find the density of Z.

Solution Example 12 shows that

$$\mu = E(X) = \frac{a + b}{2}$$

$$\sigma = \sqrt{\text{Var}(X)} = \frac{b - a}{\sqrt{12}}$$

Thus

$$Z = \frac{X - (a + b)/2}{(b - a)/\sqrt{12}}$$

When $X = a$, $Z = -\sqrt{12}/2 = -\sqrt{3}$. And when $X = b$, $Z = +\sqrt{12}/2 =$

$\sqrt{3}$. Thus Z is concentrated on the interval $[-\sqrt{3}, +\sqrt{3}]$. For z in this interval,

$$P(Z \leqslant z) = P\left(\frac{X - (a + b)/2}{(b - a)/\sqrt{12}} \leqslant z\right)$$

$$= P\left(X \leqslant z\,\frac{b - a}{\sqrt{12}} + \frac{a + b}{2}\right)$$

$$= \frac{1}{b - a}\left(z\,\frac{b - a}{\sqrt{12}} + \frac{a + b}{2} - a\right)$$

Note that this last expression has been obtained by the fact that the probability that X resides in an interval is *proportional to the fraction* of the entire interval $[a, b]$ occupied by the subinterval. (see Fig. 9.2)

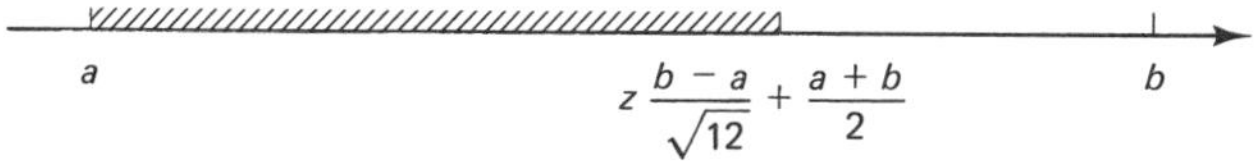

Figure 9.2 $P(Z \leqslant z)$ is the fraction of the total length taken by the hashed segment.

Taking derivatives implies that the density of Z is

$$f(z) = \begin{cases} 0 & z < -\sqrt{3} \quad \text{or} \quad +\sqrt{3} < z \\ \dfrac{1}{\sqrt{12}} & -\sqrt{3} < z < +\sqrt{3} \end{cases}$$

Note that not only is Z uniformly distributed (constant density on the interval), but Z does *not* depend on the endpoints a and b defining the density of the original random variable X. Thus *every* uniformly distributed random variable, when standardized, has the density of Z. ∎

PROBLEMS

9.22. For the random variable in Problem 9.1, find **(a)** Var (X); **(b)** Var (X^2); **(c)** Var (e^X).

9.23. (*Continuation*) Find the density of the standardized version of the random variable X of Problem 9.22. That is, find the density of $(X - \mu)/\sigma$.

9.24. Let X be exponentially distributed with parameter λ. Find the density of the standardized version of X. Show that it does not depend on the parameter λ.

9.25. (a) For the random variables F and C of Problem 9.5, find Var (C). **(b)** Also find Var (F) using the density function of F. **(c)** Verify that Var $(F) = (9/5)^2$ Var (C).

9.26. Let $Y = 3X - 4$, where X is as in Problem 9.1. Find the density function for Y and use it to find **(a)** $E(Y)$; **(b)** Var (Y). Verify that **(c)** $E(Y) = 3E(X) - 4$; **(d)** Var $(Y) = 9$ Var (X).

9.27. Suppose that W is the waiting time until the first success in a series of Bernoulli trials or $N + 1$, whichever comes first (see Problem 4.38). Find Var (W) and show that Var $(W) \to q/p^2$ as $N \to \infty$.

9.28. For any random variable X, show that

$$\text{Var } (X) = E(X(X - 1)) + E(X) - (E(X))^2$$

9.29. Let X be Poisson distributed with parameter λ. Evaluate

$$E(X(X - 1)) = \sum_{j=1}^{\infty} j(j - 1) \frac{\lambda^j}{j!} e^{-\lambda}$$

Use the result of Problem 9.28 to conclude that Var $(X) = \lambda$.

9.30. Let X be a random variable and let t be a *fixed* real number. Define the function g by

$$g(t) = E((X - t)^2)$$

Thus when $t = \mu$, $g(t) = $ Var (X). Show that

$$g(t) = E(X^2) - 2t\mu + t^2$$
$$= \text{Var } (X) + (\mu - t)^2$$

Conclude that g is minimized for $t = \mu$. Thus the smallest value of $E((X - t)^2)$ is Var (X), which occurs when $t = \mu$.

9.4 THE COVARIANCE AND CORRELATION COEFFICIENT

In seeking a few numbers that summarize how a random variable is distributed, we developed the expectation and the variance. For *two* random variables X and Y, is there a number that summarizes their relationship? At one extreme X and Y are independent so that knowledge of the value of X indicates *nothing* about the value of Y; at the other extreme, $Y = X$.

Suppose that large values of X tend to be associated with large values of Y. For example, let X be the temperature and Y equal the number of molecular reactions between chemicals for which heat acts as a catalyst. More specifically, suppose that whenever X is larger than its mean, μ_X, Y is also larger than μ_Y; and conversely, whenever X is smaller than μ_X, Y is also smaller than μ_Y. Then the product $(X - \mu_X)(Y - \mu_Y)$ is *always* nonnegative since *both* factors are either positive or negative. Thus the expectation of the product will be positive. On the other hand, if values of X larger than μ_X tend to be associated with values of Y smaller than μ_Y, the product $(X - \mu_X)(Y - \mu_Y)$ will tend to be negative and will therefore have a negative expectation.

Definition

Suppose X and Y are two random variables with expectations μ_X and μ_Y. The **covariance** between X and Y is

$$\text{Cov } (X, Y) = E((X - \mu_X)(Y - \mu_Y))$$

Example 18

Let X be the number of heads in three flips of a fair coin and Y be the number of runs. Find Cov (X, Y).

Solution Let us construct a probability table with first row the sample points:

Outcome	TTT	TTH	THT	HTT	HHT	HTH	THH	HHH
X	0	1	1	1	2	2	2	3
Y	1	2	3	2	2	3	2	1
Probability	1/8	1/8	1/8	1/8	1/8	1/8	1/8	1/8

μ_X can be calculated *without* reference to the table since X is binomially distributed $n = 3, p = 1/2$, so $E(X) = np = 3/2$. Also,

$$\mu_Y = \frac{1 + 2 + 3 + 2 + 2 + 3 + 2 + 1}{8} = 2$$

[Note that Y is the number of runs in $n = 3$ Bernoulli trials with $p = 1/2$; therefore, from Section 9.2, $E(Y) = 2(n - 1)pq + 1 = 2$.] Thus

$$\text{Cov}\,(X, Y) = E\left(\left(X - \frac{3}{2}\right)(Y - 2)\right)$$

$$= \frac{1}{8}\left[(-3/2)(-1) + \left(-\frac{1}{2}\right)(0) + \left(-\frac{1}{2}\right)(1) + \left(-\frac{1}{2}\right)(0)\right.$$

$$\left. + \left(\frac{1}{2}\right)(0) + \left(\frac{1}{2}\right)(1) + \left(\frac{1}{2}\right)(0) + \left(\frac{3}{2}\right)(-1)\right]$$

$$= 0 \quad \blacksquare$$

Note that if $X = Y$, then

$$\boxed{\text{Cov}\,(X, X) = E((X - \mu_X)^2) = \text{Var}\,(X)}$$

by definition. Thus the covariance is actually a *generalization of the variance to more than one random variable*. And just as the variance is computed using the fact that it is the expectation of the square minus the square of the expectation, the covariance has an expression which allows for *easier computation*:

$$\boxed{\text{Cov}\,(X, Y) = E(XY) - \mu_X\mu_Y}$$

In words, the covariance is the *expectation of the product minus the product of the expectations*. To see this expand the definition:

$$\text{Cov}\,(X, Y) = E((X - \mu_X)(Y - \mu_Y))$$

$$= E(XY - \mu_X Y - \mu_Y X + \mu_X\mu_Y)$$

$$= E(XY) - \mu_X E(Y) - \mu_Y E(X) + E(\mu_X\mu_Y)$$

$$= E(XY) - \mu_X\mu_Y - \mu_Y\mu_X + \mu_X\mu_Y$$

$$= E(XY) - \mu_X\mu_Y$$

Example 19 (*Continuation of Example 6*)

Two cards are selected. $X =$ number of hearts, $Y =$ number of spades. In Example 6 we showed that $E(XY) = .1275$. Also from the table,

$$E(X) = 1(.3824) + 2(.0588) = .5$$

$$E(Y) = 1(.3824) + 2(.0588) = .5$$

after computing the marginals. Thus

$$\text{Cov } (X, Y) = E(XY) - E(X)E(Y) = .1275 - .25 = -.1225$$

The covariance is negative because there is a negative association between X and Y: The presence of one suit tends to *decrease* the likelihood of cards of the other suits. ∎

Suppose that X and Y are *independent* random variables. Then in Section 9.2 we showed that the expectation of XY is the *product of the expectations*, that is, that $E(XY) = \mu_X\mu_Y$. Thus

---

If X and Y are independent, then

$$\text{Cov } (X, Y) = 0$$

The converse of this result is **false**. The random variables X and Y of Example 18 have covariance 0, but they are *not* independent. For the two values $X = 2$ and $Y = 2$,

$$P(X = 2 \text{ and } Y = 2) = P(\text{HHT or THH}) = \frac{1}{4}$$

$$P(X = 2)P(Y = 2) = P(\text{two heads})P(\text{two runs})$$

$$= \frac{3}{8} \cdot \frac{4}{8}$$

$$\neq \frac{1}{4}$$

Thus covariance 0 does *not* imply independence. ∎

Still, Cov (X, Y) can be used as a measure of how *nonindependent* X and Y are. Cov $(X, Y) = 0$ if X and Y are independent. So the larger Cov (X, Y) is, either positively or negatively, the less independent X and Y will be. On the other hand, if the values of X and/or Y happen to be large, even though X and Y might be "nearly" independent, the covariance might be large simply because X and/or Y take on large values. To remedy this situation and define a quantity that truly measures how closely X and Y are associated, *first* X and Y are standardized and *then* the covariance is taken.

Before going into the details and examples, let's see how a *change of scale* affects the covariance.

> Let a, b, c, d be constants. Then
> $$\text{Cov}(aX + b, cY + d) = ac\, \text{Cov}\,(X, Y)$$

Note that the special case $X = Y$, $a = c$, and $b = d$ is the old result about the *effect of a change of scale on the variance*:

$$\text{Cov}(aX + b, aX + b) = \text{Var}\,(aX + b)$$
$$= a^2\, \text{Var}\,(X)$$
$$= a^2\, \text{Cov}\,(X, X)$$

To prove the result *in general* involves using the basic formula for computing covariances:

$\text{Cov}(aX + b, cY + d)$

$$= E((aX + b)(cY + d)) - E(aX + b)E(cY + d)$$
$$= E(acXY + adX + bcY + bd) - (a\mu_X + b)(c\mu_Y + d)$$
$$= acE(XY) + ad\mu_X + bc\mu_Y + bd - (ac\mu_X\mu_Y + ad\mu_X + bc\mu_Y + bd)$$
$$= ac(E(XY) - \mu_X\mu_Y)$$
$$= ac\, \text{Cov}\,(X, Y)$$

Now we are ready to define a measure of association between X and Y. We start with the derivation and then summarize in a formula that can be used for computations. Let X and Y be random variables and let

$$Z_1 = \frac{X - \mu_X}{\sigma_X} \qquad Z_2 = \frac{Y - \mu_Y}{\sigma_Y}$$

be the *standardizations* of X and Y. That is, Z_1 and Z_2 are obtained from X and Y by *changes of scale* so that Z_1, Z_2 have 0 expectations and variances 1. The *correlation coefficient* between X and Y is *defined to be* $\text{Cov}\,(Z_1, Z_2)$. But it is almost never computed using this definition. In fact,

$$\text{Cov}\,(Z_1, Z_2) = \text{Cov}\left(\frac{X - \mu_X}{\sigma_X}, \frac{Y - \mu_Y}{\sigma_Y}\right)$$

$$= \text{Cov}\left(\left(\frac{1}{\sigma_X}X + \frac{\mu_X}{\sigma_X}\right), \left(\frac{1}{\sigma_Y}Y + \frac{\mu_Y}{\sigma_Y}\right)\right)$$

$$= \frac{1}{\sigma_X\sigma_Y}\, \text{Cov}\,(X, Y)$$

by the change-of-scale formula for the covariance: $a = 1/\sigma_X$, $b = \mu_X/\sigma_X$, $c = 1/\sigma_Y$, and $d = \mu_Y/\sigma_Y$. So we arrive at a new definition equivalent to the one above.

Definition

The **correlation coefficient** between X and Y is

$$\rho(X, Y) = \frac{\text{Cov } (X, Y)}{\sigma_X \sigma_Y}$$

Example 20

Find $\rho(X, Y)$ where X and Y are as in Example 19.

    Solution By that example Cov $(X, Y) = -.1225$. The variances are needed; the marginal distribution of X is (from Example 6)

X	0	1	2
Probability	.5588	.3824	.0588

Therefore,

$$E(X^2) = 0^2(.5588) + 1^2(.3824) + 2^2(.0588)$$
$$= .6176$$

Since $E(X) = .5$ (either from the table or Example 19),

$$\text{Var } (X) = .6176 - (.5)^2 = .3676$$

By symmetry in the original joint probability table, the marginal distribution of Y is the same as the distribution of X. Thus Var $(Y) = $ Var (X). Finally,

$$\rho(X, Y) = \frac{\text{Cov } (X, Y)}{\sigma_X \, \sigma_Y} = \frac{-.1225}{\sqrt{.3676} \cdot \sqrt{.3676}} = -.3332 \quad \blacksquare$$

    Using the correlation coefficient as the measure of association between X and Y has a very convenient property: It is unchanged as the result of a change in scale. For example, if X is the temperature at noon on Saturday and Y is the temperature at noon on Sunday, then $\rho(X, Y)$ is the same whether Celsius or Fahrenheit temperatures are used. Or suppose that X records the chickens crossing the road from right to left and Y records the chickens crossing from left to right. Then $\rho(X, Y)$ is the same whether the actual *numbers* of chickens are measured or whether the number of *tons* of chickens is measured (assuming that the chickens crossing in either direction weigh the same).

The correlation coefficient is invariant under changes in scale: Let a, b, c, d be constants. Then

$$\rho(aX + b, cY + d) = \pm \rho(X, Y)$$

where the sign is $\begin{cases} + & \text{if } a \text{ and } c \text{ have the } same \text{ sign} \\ - & \text{if } a \text{ and } c \text{ have } opposite \text{ signs} \end{cases}$

The technicalities about the sign are a result of the calculations in the proof below. But note that if *one* change of scale is applied to both X and Y, then $a = c$, $b = d$ and

$$\rho(aX + b, aY + b) = + \rho(X, Y)$$

Proof. Use the definition of ρ in terms of Cov and the effect of changes of scale on the covariance:

$$\rho(aX + b, cY + d) = \frac{\text{Cov } (aX + b, cY + d)}{\sigma_{aX+b}\sigma_{cY+d}}$$

$$= \frac{ac \text{ Cov } (X, Y)}{|a|\sigma_X|c|\sigma_Y}$$

$$= \pm \frac{\text{Cov } (X, Y)}{\sigma_X\sigma_Y}$$

which completes the proof since this is $\rho(X, Y)$ by definition. ■

We showed that if X and Y are independent random variables, then Cov $(X, Y) = 0$ and consequently $\rho(X, Y) = 0$. Thus the correlation coefficient is a measure of the degree of nonindependence. In fact, much more can be said.

Result

For any two random variables X and Y,

$$-1 \leqslant \rho(X, Y) \leqslant +1$$

If $\rho(X, Y) = \pm 1$, one of the random variables is a linear function of the other.

Thus we see that a *large* value of the correlation coefficient implies a direct relationship between X and Y.

Proof of the Result. We can assume that X and Y are *standardized* with
$$E(X) = 0 = E(Y) \qquad \text{Var } (X) = 1 = \text{Var } (Y)$$

This is so since if X and Y are not standardized, then replace them with their standardizations X' and Y'; we know that the correlation coefficient will remain the same:

$$\rho(X', Y') = \rho(X, Y)$$

Since X and Y are standardized, we also have these relationships:

$$E(X^2) = E(X^2) - (E(X))^2 = \text{Var}(X) = 1$$
$$E(Y^2) = E(Y^2) - (E(Y))^2 = \text{Var}(Y) = 1$$
$$\sigma_X = 1 = \sigma_Y$$
$$\text{Cov}(X, Y) = E(XY) - E(X)E(Y) = E(XY)$$
$$\rho(X, Y) = \frac{\text{Cov}(X, Y)}{\sigma_X \sigma_Y} = E(XY)$$

But the random variable

$$Z = (X - Y)^2$$

is nonnegative. Consequently, its expectation is nonnegative. In fact, since *all* the values of Z are greater than or equal to zero, $E(Z) \geq 0$ and $E(Z) = 0$ implies that $Z = 0$ and thus $X = Y$. That is,

$$E((X - Y)^2) \geq 0$$

and

$$E((X - Y)^2) = 0$$

impies that $X = Y$. However,

$$0 \leq E((X - Y)^2)$$
$$= E(X^2) - 2E(XY) + E(Y^2)$$
$$= 1 - 2\rho(X, Y) + 1$$
$$= 2(1 - \rho(X, Y))$$

Thus

$$\rho(X, Y) \leq 1$$

with equality holding *if and only if* $X = Y$. By considering the random variable $Z_1 = X + Y$ rather than $Z = X - Y$, similar reasoning implies that

$$\rho(X, Y) \geq -1$$

with equality holding *if and only if* $X = -Y$. Thus always

$$-1 \leq \rho(X, Y) \leq +1$$

If $\rho(X, Y) = +1$, then $X = Y$; if $\rho(X, Y) = -1$, then $X = -Y$. Now suppose that X and Y are not necessarily standardized. By what we have just shown, if

X' denotes the standardization for X and Y' the standardization for Y, then

$$-1 \leqslant \rho(X', Y') = \rho(X, Y) \leqslant +1$$

But

$$X' = \frac{X - \mu_X}{\sigma_X} \qquad Y' = \frac{Y - \mu_Y}{\sigma_Y}$$

And if $\rho(X', Y') = \pm 1$, then

$$X' = \pm Y'$$

$$\frac{X - \mu_X}{\sigma_X} = \pm \frac{Y - \mu_Y}{\sigma_Y}$$

Solving this last equation for X shows that X is a linear function of Y. In fact,

$$X = \pm \left(\frac{\sigma_X}{\sigma_Y} \right) Y + \left(\mu_X \mp \mu_Y \frac{\sigma_X}{\sigma_Y} \right) \qquad \blacksquare$$

What does the value of the correlation coefficient $\rho(X, Y)$ allow us to conclude? If $\rho(X, Y)$ is ± 1, then one is a linear function of the other. If $\rho(X, Y)$ is close to ± 1, then X is "close" to being a linear function of Y. For example, perhaps X is the number of people entering a theater and Y is the number of tickets sold. Then on any one day X is *nearly* Y: All people entering the theater buy tickets except for a few who are picking up kids or who are using the phone, and so on. How close to ± 1 is close enough. Values of $\pm .9$ are considered to be highly significant in the more exact sciences. Values of $\pm .7$ are considered significant in the social sciences. Now suppose that the value of $\rho(X, Y) = 0$. It is tempting to leap to the conclusion that X and Y must be independent. But recall Example 18: There Cov $(X, Y) = 0$; thus $\rho(X, Y) = 0$. But X and Y are *not* independent.

If X and Y are independent, then $\rho(X, Y) = 0$. But if $\rho(X, Y) = 0$, then *no conclusion* as to the independence of X and Y can be drawn.

In fact, Y might be a function of X and still $\rho(X, Y) = 0$ (see Problem 9.38).

Here is an example which shows how partially correlated random variables $(0 < \rho < 1)$ can arise from independent random variables:

Example 21

Suppose that U, V, and W are *independent* random variables each with mean $\mu = 3$ and variance $\sigma^2 = 5$. Let

$$X = U + V \qquad Y = U + W$$

Find $\rho(X, Y)$.

Solution

$$E(X) = E(U + V) = E(U) + E(V) = 6$$

$$E(Y) = E(U + W) = E(U) + E(W) = 6$$

$$E(XY) = E[(U + V)(U + W)]$$

$$= E(U^2) + E(U)E(W) + E(V)E(W) + E(V)E(W)$$

$$= E(U^2) + 3 \cdot 3 + 3 \cdot 3 + 3 \cdot 3$$

$$= E(U^2) + 27$$

where the second equality uses the fact that the expectation of a product of *independent* random variables is the product of the expectations.

$$E(U^2) = [(E(U^2) - (E(U))^2] + (E(U))^2$$

$$= \text{Var}(U) + (E(U))^2$$

$$= 5 + 9$$

$$= 14$$

Thus

$$\text{Cov}(X, Y) = E(XY) - E(X)E(Y)$$

$$= (14 + 27) - 6 \cdot 6$$

$$= 5$$

Also, since U, V, and W are independent,

$$\text{Var}(X) = \text{Var}(U) + \text{Var}(V) = 5 + 5 = 10$$

$$\text{Var}(Y) = \text{Var}(U) + \text{Var}(W) = 5 + 5 = 10$$

Therefore,

$$\rho(X, Y) = \frac{\text{Cov}(X, Y)}{\sigma_X \sigma_Y} = \frac{5}{\sqrt{10}\sqrt{10}} = \frac{1}{2} \quad \blacksquare$$

Thus random variables with correlation coefficients in $(-1, 1)$ often arise when they are "combinations" (sums, products, . . .) of partially overlapping sets of independent random variables. For example, the number of tickets sold at the theater on Monday "partially correlates" (has a value of $|\rho|$ between 0 and 1) with the number sold on Tuesday because *some* of the variables determining each are the same (season of the year, same movie on both days, . . .) and *some* are independent (weather, different groups of people on the two days, . . .).

PROBLEMS

In Problems 9.31 to 9.35, find $E(X)$, $E(Y)$, Var (X), Var (Y), Cov (X, Y), and $\rho(X, Y)$ for the random variables X and Y in

9.31. Example 5.

9.32. Problem 9.8.

9.33. Problem 9.9.

9.34. Problem 9.6.

9.35. Problem 9.7. Let $X = A =$ number of apples and $Y = B =$ number of bananas.

9.36. Suppose that U, V, and W are independent, each with mean μ and variance σ^2. Let $X = U + V$ and $Y = U + W$. Find $\rho(X, Y)$ in terms of μ and σ.

9.37. (*Continuation*) With U and V as in Problem 9.36, suppose that $X = aU + bV$ and $Y = \alpha U + \beta V$, where a, b, α, β are constants. Find $\rho(X, Y)$ in terms of a, b, α, β, μ, and σ.

9.38. Let X be uniformly distributed on $[-1, 1]$. Let $Y = X^2$. Show that $\rho(X, Y) = 0$ even though X and Y are as far from being independent as two random variables can get: Given the value of X, $Y = X^2$ is completely determined!

9.39. (*A Time-Series Model*) Each day an amount of pollutant X is dumped into the river. This amount decays (dissipates and degenerates) at an exponential rate so that t days after dumping there will be an amount $\alpha^t X$ still active, where $0 < \alpha < 1$. On day t assume that X_t was dumped where

$$\ldots, X_{-2}, X_{-1}, X_0, X_1, X_2, \ldots$$

are IIDRVs. Since they are identically distributed, they have a common mean μ and variance σ^2. Show that the amount of pollutant still active in the river on day t is

$$S_t = \sum_{i=0}^{\infty} \alpha^i X_{t-i}$$

Show that

$$E(S_t) = \frac{\mu}{1 - \alpha}$$

$$E(S_t^2) = \frac{\mu^2}{(1 - \alpha)^2} + \frac{\sigma^2}{1 - \alpha^2}$$

$$\text{Var } (S_t) = \frac{\sigma^2}{1 - \alpha^2}$$

For $t \geq s$,

$$E(S_t \cdot S_s) = \frac{\mu^2}{(1 - \alpha)^2} + \frac{\sigma^2 \alpha^{t-s}}{1 - \alpha^2}$$

$$\text{Cov } (S_t, S_s) = \frac{\sigma^2 \alpha^{t-s}}{1 - \alpha^2}$$

$$\rho(S_t, S_s) = \alpha^{t-s}$$

(In your computations assume that the expectation of the *infinite* sums are the sums of the expectations, and similarly the variance of the *infinite* sums of independent random variables are the sums of the variances.)

9.40. Show that

$$\text{Var}(X + Y) = \text{Var}(X) + 2\,\text{Cov}(X, Y) + \text{Var}(Y)$$

for any random variables X and Y.

9.41. (*Continuation*) Show that

$$\text{Var}(X + Y + Z) = \text{Var}(X) + \text{Var}(Y) + \text{Var}(Z)$$
$$+ 2\,\text{Cov}(X, Y) + 2\,\text{Cov}(X, Z) + 2\,\text{Cov}(Y, Z)$$

9.5 SUMMARY OF E, VAR, COV, AND ρ PROPERTIES

Let a, b, c, d be constants. Then

1. $E(c) = c$.
2. $E(aX + b) = aE(X) + b$.
3. $E(X_1 + \cdots + X_n) = E(X_1) + \cdots + E(X_n)$.
4. If $X_1, \ldots, X_n$ are independent, then

$$E(X_1 \cdots X_n) = E(X_1) \cdots E(X_n)$$

5. $\text{Var}(c) = 0$.
6. $\text{Var}(aX + b) = a^2\,\text{Var}(X)$.
7. $\text{Var}(X) = E(X^2) - (E(X))^2$.
8. If $X_1, \ldots, X_n$ are independent, then

$$\text{Var}(X_1 + \cdots + X_n) = \text{Var}(X_1) + \cdots + \text{Var}(X_n)$$

9. If X has expectation μ and variance σ^2, then

$$Z = \frac{X - \mu}{\sigma}$$

is the standardized version of X:

$$E(Z) = 0 \qquad \text{Var}(Z) = 1$$

10. $\text{Cov}(X, X) = \text{Var}(X)$.
11. $\text{Cov}(X, Y) = E(XY) - E(X)E(Y)$.
12. $\text{Cov}((aX + b), (cY + d)) = ac\,\text{Cov}(X, Y)$.
13. If X and Y are independent, then

$$\text{Cov}(X, Y) = 0 \qquad \text{and} \quad \rho(X, Y) = 0$$

14. $-1 \leqslant \rho(X, Y) \leqslant +1$.

15. $\rho(aX + b, cY + d) = \pm \rho(X, Y)$.

16. If $\rho(X, Y) = \pm 1$, one is a linear function of the other.

DISCRETE RANDOM VARIABLES

Random variable	Distribution	Expectation	Variance
Bernoulli	$\begin{cases} 0 & \text{with prob } q \\ 1 & \text{with prob } p \end{cases}$	p	pq
Binomial	$j \quad$ with prob $\binom{n}{j} p^j q^{n-j}$ $j = 0, 1, 2, \ldots, n$	np	npq
Geometric	$j \quad$ with prob $q^{j-1} p$ $j = 1, 2, 3, \ldots$	$\dfrac{1}{p}$	$\dfrac{q}{p^2}$
Poisson	$j \quad$ with prob $\dfrac{\lambda^j}{j!} e^{-\lambda}$ $j = 0, 1, 2, \ldots$	λ	λ

CONTINUOUS RANDOM VARIABLES

Random variable	Density	Expectation	Variance
Uniform	$\dfrac{1}{b - a} \quad a < x < b$	$\dfrac{a + b}{2}$	$\dfrac{(b - a)^2}{12}$
Exponential	$\lambda e^{-\lambda x} \quad x > 0$	$\dfrac{1}{\lambda}$	$\dfrac{1}{\lambda^2}$
Gamma	$\dfrac{\lambda^n x^{n-1}}{n!} e^{-\lambda x} \quad x > 0$	$\dfrac{n}{\lambda}$	$\dfrac{n}{\lambda^2}$

Oft expectation fails, and most oft there
Where most it promises

William Shakespeare, 1564–1610, All's Well that Ends Well

— Chapter 10 ——————————

The Normal Distribution, Central Limit Theorem, and Law of Large Numbers

The normal distribution with its associated "bell-shaped" density function is one of the most useful distributions; it forms the basis of much of statistical analysis. The reason for this is the **central limit theorem**, which states that many distributions can be approximated by the normal distribution. The theorem was first proved by Abraham de Moivre (1667–1754) and extended to the general binomial distribution by Pierre-Simon de Laplace (1749–1827). In many ways, de Moivre and Laplace were opposites; de Moivre was unpretentious, of modest means, unable to find a university position, living on his earnings as a tutor; Laplace was well established, a monarchist during the time of the French revolution. Laplace was the foremost contributor to probability theory during its early years.

10.1 THE NORMAL DISTRIBUTION

Almost simultaneously Carl Friedrich Gauss (1777–1855) and the American Robert Adrain (1775–1843) in the early nineteenth century developed a "theory of errors." Suppose a quantity is measured several times; each observation has a slight error due to inexactness in measurement. How are the errors distributed? They will be random, but what is the specific distribution function? Both Gauss and Adrain were led to the normal distribution, a variant of which is still called the *error function*.

Suppose that the random variable X is due to very many small contributions; X might be the temperature or the total winnings after many gambling games or a student's exam score or the number of people in the bus depot or. . . . As we saw in Chapter 9, the random variable

$$Z = \frac{X - \mu}{\sigma}$$

obtained by subtracting the mean of X and dividing by the standard deviation is *standardized*: $E(Z) = 0$, Var $(Z) = 1$. The "law of errors" states that Z is normally distributed:

The *normal distribution mean 0, variance 1* (abbreviated as $N_{0,1}$) has *density function*

$$\phi(x) = \frac{1}{\sqrt{2\pi}} e^{-x^2/2}$$

and *distribution function*

$$\Phi(x) = \frac{1}{\sqrt{2\pi}} \int_{-\infty}^{x} e^{-u^2/2} \, du$$

Example 1

Graph ϕ.

    Solution ϕ is a function of x^2; hence the graph of ϕ is *symmetric about the y axis*.

$$\phi'(x) = \frac{1}{\sqrt{2\pi}} (-x)e^{-x^2/2}$$

$$\phi''(x) = \frac{1}{\sqrt{2\pi}} (x^2 - 1)e^{-x^2/2}$$

Therefore, the slope of the tangent to the graph of ϕ is 0 for $x = 0$. Inflection points ($\phi''(x) = 0$) occur at $x = \pm 1$. (see Fig. 10.1) ∎

    To check that ϕ is in fact a density function requires showing that the total area under the graph of ϕ is 1. This requires a tricky maneuver with polar co-

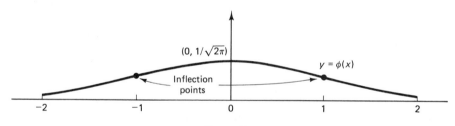

$(0, 1/\sqrt{2\pi})$

$y = \phi(x)$

Inflection points

Figure 10.1

ordinates due to Laplace. Let

$$I = \int_{-\infty}^{\infty} e^{-x^2/2}\, dx$$

We need to show that $I = \sqrt{2\pi}$ or, equivalently, that $I^2 = 2\pi$.

$$I^2 = I \cdot I$$

$$= \int_{-\infty}^{\infty} e^{-x^2/2}\, dx \int_{-\infty}^{\infty} e^{-y^2/2}\, dy$$

$$= \int_{-\infty}^{\infty} \int_{-\infty}^{\infty} e^{-x^2/2}\, dx\, e^{-y^2/2}\, dy$$

$$= \int_{-\infty}^{\infty} \int_{-\infty}^{\infty} e^{-x^2/2}\, e^{-y^2/2}\, dx\, dy$$

$$= \int_{-\infty}^{\infty} \int_{-\infty}^{\infty} e^{-(x^2+y^2)/2}\, dx\, dy$$

The second equality is true because whether we use the dummy variable x or y as the variable of integration is immaterial to the actual value. The third equality follows from interpreting x and y as coordinates in two-dimensional xy space; *since* $e^{-x^2/2}$ is a *constant* with respect to the variable y, $e^{-x^2/2}$ and the integral sign for the y variable can be interchanged. The fourth equality holds since $e^{-y^2/2}$ is a constant with respect to x, so $e^{-y^2/2}$ and dx can be interchanged.

Switch to polar coordinates; note that

$$x = r \cos \theta \qquad y = r \sin \theta$$

and the infinitesimal area element is

$$dx\, dy = r\, dr\, d\theta$$

As x and y both range from $-\infty$ to $+\infty$, the entire plane is spanned; thus r ranges from 0 to ∞ and θ ranges from 0 to 2π.

$$I^2 = \int_0^{2\pi} \int_0^{\infty} e^{-r^2/2}\, r\, dr\, d\theta$$

$$= \int_0^{2\pi} [-e^{-r^2/2}]_0^{\infty}\, d\theta$$

$$= \int_0^{2\pi} 1\, d\theta$$

$$= \theta\big|_0^{2\pi}$$

$$= 2\pi$$

This completes the demonstration that $I^2 = 2\pi$ and hence that $I = \sqrt{2\pi}$. Thus ϕ is normalized and therefore *is* a density function, as claimed.

To show that ϕ has mean 0 and variance 1 requires evaluating these integrals:

$$E(Z) = \int_{-\infty}^{\infty} x\phi(x)\, dx = \frac{1}{\sqrt{2\pi}} \int_{-\infty}^{\infty} xe^{-x^2/2}\, dx = 0$$

$$\text{Var}\,(Z) = E(Z^2) - E(Z)^2 = \frac{1}{\sqrt{2\pi}} \int_{-\infty}^{\infty} x^2 e^{-x^2/2}\, dx - 0 = 1$$

These two form the content of Problem 10.8.

Unfortunately, there is no technique of integration that will allow an indefinite integral of ϕ to be found in terms of a simple expression involving "ordinary" functions. That is, it is difficult to show, but nonetheless true that there *does not exist* a function F which is a relatively straightforward combination of familiar functions (polynomials, trig functions, exponentials, logarithms, . . .) such that $F' = \phi$. There *is* a function Φ which is the indefinite integral of ϕ, but it is a *new function*. The integral of ϕ from $-\infty$ to x is denoted by $\Phi(x)$. The **error function** is defined to be $2\Phi(x/\sqrt{2}) - 1$.

Values of $\Phi(x)$ must therefore be found using approximations to the integral. They are tabulated for values of x from 0.00 to 3.49 in Appendix 3. For $x \geq 3.50$, $\Phi(x)$ is nearly 1.

Example 2

Let Z be a random variable $N_{0,1}$ distributed. Find (a) $P(Z > 2.3)$, (b) $P(Z < -1.7)$, (c) $P(-.8 < Z < .8)$, and (d) $P(-.3 < Z < .7)$

Solution (a)

$$P(Z > 2.3) = 1 - P(Z \leq 2.3)$$
$$= 1 - \Phi(2.3)$$
$$= 1 - .9893$$
$$= .0107$$

(see Fig. 10.2)

(b) By symmetry,

$$P(Z < -1.7) = P(Z > 1.7)$$
$$= 1 - \Phi(1.7)$$
$$= 1 - .9554$$
$$= .0446$$

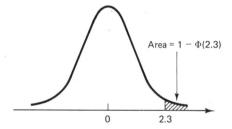

Area $= 1 - \Phi(2.3)$

0   2.3

Figure 10.2 Note exaggeration of vertical axis.

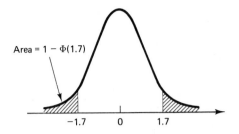

Area = $1 - \Phi(1.7)$

−1.7   0   1.7

Figure 10.3

(see Fig. 10.3)
  (c) Also by symmetry,

$$P(-.8 < Z < .8) = P(X < .8) - P(Z \leqslant -.8)$$
$$= \Phi(.8) - P(Z > .8)$$
$$= \Phi(.8) - [1 - P(Z \leqslant .8)]$$
$$= 2 \cdot \Phi(.8) - 1$$
$$= 2 \cdot .7881 - 1$$
$$= .5762$$

(see Fig. 10.4)

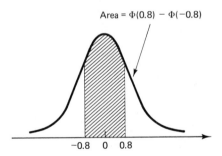

Area = $\Phi(0.8) - \Phi(-0.8)$

−0.8   0   0.8

Figure 10.4

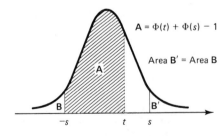

$A = \Phi(t) + \Phi(s) - 1$

Area B' = Area B

A

B   B'

−s   t   s

Figure 10.5

(d) Finally,

$$P(-.3 < Z < .7) = P(Z < .7) - P(Z \leqslant -.3)$$
$$= \Phi(.7) - [1 - \Phi(.3)]$$
$$= .7580 - [1 - .6179]$$
$$= .3759 \quad \blacksquare$$

Note: To find probabilities involving the $N_{0,1}$ distributed random variable Z, it is easier to remember *how to draw* a quick sketch and use it to find the required probability than it is to remember various formulas. For example, if s, $t \geqslant 0$, then $P(-s < Z < t) = \text{area } \mathbf{A} = \Phi(t) - \text{area } \mathbf{B} = \Phi(t) - (1 - \Phi(s)) = \Phi(t) + \Phi(s) - 1$ as in Fig. 10.5

10.2 PROPERTIES OF NORMALLY DISTRIBUTED RANDOM VARIABLES

In general, a normally distributed random variable need not have mean 0 and variance 1. For example, if Z is $N_{0,1}$ distributed, then $X = aZ + b$ obtained by a change of scale will still be normally distributed although $E(X) = b$ and Var $(X) = a^2$.

Definition

Suppose that X has mean μ and variance σ^2. X is normally distributed μ, σ^2 (abbreviated N_{μ,σ^2}) if the standardized random variable

$$Z = \frac{X - \mu}{\sigma}$$

is $N_{0,1}$ distributed.

Example 3

Past experience has shown that the number of cars entering a park on a summer's day is normally distributed with mean 200, variance 900. With Y equal to the number of cars, find

$$P(X \leqslant 220) \qquad P(X > 195) \qquad P(190 < X < 210)$$

Solution

$$Z = \frac{X - 200}{30}$$

is $N_{0,1}$ distributed. So we express the various events in terms of Z and then use the table.

$$P(X \leq 220) = P\left(\frac{X - 200}{30} \leq \frac{220 - 200}{30}\right) = P(Z \leq .6667)^* = .7486$$

$$P(X > 195) = P\left(\frac{X - 200}{30} > \frac{195 - 200}{30}\right) = P(Z > -.1667) = .5675$$

$$P(190 < X < 210) = P\left(\frac{-10}{30} < Z < \frac{10}{30}\right)$$

$$= P(-.3333 < Z < .3333)$$

$$= 2 \cdot .6293 - 1$$

$$= .2586 \quad \blacksquare$$

In finding a probability involving the N_{μ, σ^2} distributed random variable X, the general technique is to express the probability in terms of the $N_{0,1}$ distributed variable $Z = (X - \mu)/\sigma$ and use the table.

Example 4

Experience has shown that a certain small company uses its phones for a random time T each month where T is normally distributed with mean 300 hours, variance 80. Find an interval centered around 300 hours so that we can be 90% sure that the time T for the next month will fall in this interval.

Solution A constant c is sought which satisfies the equation

$$.90 = P(300 - c < T < 300 + c)$$

$$= P\left(\frac{-c}{\sqrt{80}} < \frac{T - 300}{\sqrt{80}} < \frac{c}{\sqrt{80}}\right)$$

$$= P\left(\frac{-c}{\sqrt{80}} < Z < \frac{c}{\sqrt{80}}\right)$$

From the table and Fig. 10.6

$$\frac{c}{\sqrt{80}} = 1.645$$

$$c = 14.71$$

Conclusion: Ninety percent of the time (9 out of 10 months) the total phone usage Y will satisfy $300 - 14.71 < T < 300 + 14.71$ or $T \in (285.3, 314.7)$ $\blacksquare$

Let us find the density function for an N_{μ, σ^2} random variable X. Since $Z =$

---

*For simplicity, interpolation is not used in the table. For example, to find $P(Z \leq z)$, z is simply rounded to the nearest one-one hundredth.

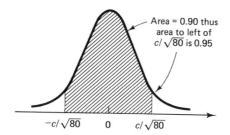

Area = 0.90 thus
area to left of
$c/\sqrt{80}$ is 0.95

$-c/\sqrt{80}$ 0 $c/\sqrt{80}$

Figure 10.6

$(X - \mu)/\sigma$ is $N_{0,1}$, the distribution function for X is

$$F_X(x) = P(X \leq x)$$

$$= P\left(\frac{X - \mu}{\sigma} \leq \frac{x - \mu}{\sigma}\right)$$

$$= P\left(Z \leq \frac{x - \mu}{\sigma}\right)$$

$$= \Phi\left(\frac{x - \mu}{\sigma}\right)$$

since Z has distribution function Φ. Differentiate using the *chain rule*:

$$f_X(x) = \frac{1}{\sigma} \phi\left(\frac{x - \mu}{\sigma}\right)$$

$$= \frac{1}{\sqrt{2\pi}\sigma} \exp\left[-\frac{1}{2}\left(\frac{x - \mu}{\sigma}\right)^2\right]$$

$$= \frac{1}{\sqrt{2\pi}\sigma} \exp\left[-\frac{(x - \mu)^2}{2\sigma^2}\right]$$

Alternative definition of a normal mean μ, variance σ^2 random variable: X is N_{μ,σ^2} distributed if its density function is

$$\phi_{\mu,\sigma^2}(x) = \frac{1}{\sqrt{2\pi}\sigma} \exp\left[-\frac{(x - \mu)^2}{2\sigma^2}\right]$$

However, this formula is of limited usefulness since when dealing with an N_{μ,σ^2} random variable X, it is almost always *simplest to express all computations in terms of the $N_{0,1}$ distributed random variable $Z = (X - \mu)/\sigma$ obtained by standardizing X*. Note that the formula does in fact become the $N_{0,1}$ density function when μ is taken to be 0 and σ^2 is taken to be 1. Fig. 10.7 shows normal density curves with various values of μ and σ.

A distinguishing feature of the normal distribution is that independent sums of normally distributed random variables are again normally distributed. (Recall

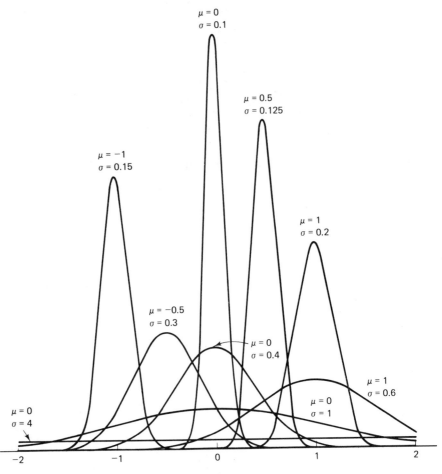

$\mu = 0$
$\sigma = 0.1$

$\mu = 0.5$
$\sigma = 0.125$

$\mu = -1$
$\sigma = 0.15$

$\mu = 1$
$\sigma = 0.2$

$\mu = -0.5$
$\sigma = 0.3$

$\mu = 0$
$\sigma = 0.4$

$\mu = 1$
$\sigma = 0.6$

$\mu = 0$
$\sigma = 4$

$\mu = 0$
$\sigma = 1$

-2   -1   0   1   2

Figure 10.7

from Chapter 8 that this property is also true of Poisson distributed random variables.)

Let $X_1, \ldots, X_n$ be independent; suppose that X_i is normally distributed μ_i, σ_i^2. Then

$$X_1 + \cdots + X_n$$

is normally distributed with mean $\mu_1 + \cdots + \mu_n$ and variance $\sigma_1^2 + \cdots + \sigma_n^2$.

The mean of the sum of the random variables is the sum of the means; the variance of the sum (*not* the standard deviation) is the sum of the variances.

The proof involves intricate computations with integrals. First the result is proved for two normally distributed random variables X and Y; then the result is extended by induction to more (see Problems 10.10 and 10.11). Thus the bell-shaped normal density curve "propagates itself" in sums of variables each having the bell-shaped normal density curve.

Example 5

Suppose the time until a construction crew completes a building is normally distributed with mean 90 days and standard deviation 10 days. After completion, it takes an additional time to install the plumbing, electricity, and finish the interior. Assume that the additional time is independent of the building completion time and is normally distributed with mean 30 days and standard deviation 5 days. Let T be the time from the beginning until the interior is finished. Find $P(T \leqslant 130$ days).

Solution T is normally distributed with

$$E(T) = 90 + 30 = 120$$

$$\text{Var } (T) = 10^2 + 5^2 = 125$$

Hence

$$Z = \frac{T - 120}{\sqrt{125}}$$

is $N_{0,1}$ distributed. Thus

$$P(T \leqslant 130) = P\left(Z \leqslant \frac{130 - 120}{\sqrt{125}}\right)$$

$$= P(Z \leqslant .8944)$$

$$= .8133 \quad \blacksquare$$

Generalizing from Example 5: A random experiment is performed n times and the same quantity is measured each time. Call the result of the ith measurement X_i. For examples, X_i could be the temperature at noon on the ith day of the week or X_i could be the height of the ith person. Note that $X_1, \ldots X_n$ are IIDRVs. The collection $\{X_i\}_{i=1}^n$ is called a **random sample**. Since they are identically distributed, they have a common mean and standard deviation

$$\mu = E(X_i)$$

$$\sigma^2 = \text{Var } (X_i)$$

The **sample mean** is the average

$$\overline{X} = \frac{1}{n} (X_1 + \cdots + X_n)$$

Note that

$$E(\overline{X}) = \frac{1}{n} E(X_1 + \cdots + X_n) = \frac{1}{n} n\mu = \mu$$

$$\text{Var } (\overline{X}) = \frac{1}{n^2} \text{Var } (X_1 + \cdots + X_n) = \frac{1}{n^2} n \text{ Var } (X_i) = \frac{\sigma^2}{n}$$

The sample mean $\overline{X}$ has mean and variance

$$E(\overline{X}) = \mu \qquad \text{Var}(\overline{X}) = \frac{\sigma^2}{n}$$

In words, the sample mean has expectation equal to the population mean μ, but the variance is *decreased* by a factor equal to the sample size n. This confirms intuition: If a quantity is to be measured, it is better to take several measurements and use the average. Why? Because, as stated above, the average will have a smaller variance than the individual measurements. This property is very important; it explains why the sample mean is used widely in statistical estimation.

Now suppose that each X_i is normally distributed with mean μ, and standard deviation σ. Then the mean of $\overline{X}$ is also μ, but Var $(\overline{X}) = \sigma^2/n$. But the sum $X_1 + \cdots + X_n$ is normal distributed; thus $\overline{X}$, which is the sum divided by n, is also normally distributed.

Let $\{X_i\}_{i=1}^n$ be a random sample, each N_{μ,σ^2} distributed. Then the sample mean $\overline{X}$ is $N_{\mu,\sigma^2/n}$ distributed.

The normal distribution reappears as the distribution of the sample mean if each X_i is normally distributed.

Example 6

Assume that the temperature for a random day in July is normally distributed with average $77°$ and standard deviation $9°$. Let $\overline{X}$ be the average temperature for a week. Find $P(72 \leqslant \overline{X} \leqslant 80)$.

Solution Under the assumption of independence $\overline{X}$ is $N_{77,81/7}$ distributed. Thus

$$P(72 \leqslant \overline{X} \leqslant 80) = P\left(\frac{72 - 77}{\sqrt{81/7}} \leqslant \frac{\overline{X} - 77}{\sqrt{81/7}} \leqslant \frac{80 - 77}{\sqrt{81/7}}\right)$$

$$= P(-1.470 \leqslant Z \leqslant 0.8819)$$

$$= .7398 \quad \blacksquare$$

PROBLEMS

10.1. Z is $N_{0,1}$ distributed. Find **(a)** $P(Z < .6)$; **(b)** $P(Z \leqslant -.03)$; **(c)** $P(.12 < Z \leqslant 2.14)$; **(d)** $P(-1.67 \leqslant Z < 1.20)$.

10.2. X is $N_{-10,16}$ distributed. Find **(a)** $P(X > -12)$; **(b)** $P(-11 < X \leqslant -8)$; **(c)** $P(|X + 10| < 2)$; **(d)** $P(|X + 11| > 1.5)$.

10.3. With Φ denoting the $N_{0,1}$ distribution function and Z $N_{0,1}$ distributed, show that **(a)**

The Normal Distribution, Central Limit Theorem   Chap. 10

$P(Z > z) = 1 - \Phi(z)$; **(b)** $P(Z > -z) = \Phi(z)$; **(c)** $P(-z < Z < z) = 2\Phi(z) - 1$; **(d)** $P(-z_1 < Z < z_2) = \Phi(z_1) + \Phi(z_2) - 1$, where z, z_1, and z_2 are nonnegative.

10.4. Suppose that the length X of a random bolt produced by machine A is 1.2 cm, on the average, with a standard deviation of .3 cm. Assuming that the length X is normally distributed, find **(a)** $P(X < 1.4)$; **(b)** $P(X > 1.3)$; **(c)** $P(|X - 1.2| > .2)$.

10.5. Suppose that the number of brand X cornflakes in a box is $N_{2000, 40000}$ distributed. Let Y be the number of flakes in *four* boxes. What is **(a)** $E(Y)$; **(b)** Var (Y)? **(c)** What is the distribution of Y? Find **(d)** $P(Y < 8200)$; **(e)** $P(|Y - 8000| > 300)$.

10.6. X is the *actual* weight of a bag of concrete (labeled "80-lb bag"). Suppose that $E(X) = 81$ and $\sigma_X = 2$. Let Y be the average weight of 10 bags bought: $Y = (X_1 + \cdots + X_{10})/10$. **(a)** What is the distribution of Y assuming that each bag's weight is normally distributed? Find **(b)** $P(Y \geq 80)$; **(c)** $P(|Y - 81.5| < 1)$.

10.7. Let X be N_{μ, σ^2} distributed. Find **(a)** $P(|X - \mu| < \sigma/2)$; **(b)** $P(|X - \mu| < \sigma)$; **(c)** $P(|X - \mu| < 1.5\sigma)$. **(d)** Let the function g be defined by $g(t) = P(|X - \mu| < t\sigma)$. Show that $g(t) = 2\Phi(t) - 1$. Plot $g(t)$ as a function of t. **(e)** What is $g'(0)$?

10.8. Actually show that an $N_{0,1}$ random variable has mean 0 and variance 1. That is, assume that Z has density $e^{-x^2/2}/\sqrt{2\pi}$. Show that

$$E(Z) = \frac{1}{\sqrt{2\pi}} \int_{-\infty}^{\infty} x e^{-x^2/2}\, dx = 0$$

$$E(Z^2) = \frac{1}{\sqrt{2\pi}} \int_{-\infty}^{\infty} x^2 e^{-x^2/2}\, dx = 1$$

(For the second integral use integration by parts: $u = x$, $v' = xe^{-x^2/2}$.)

10.9. (*Continuation*) Show that the third and fourth moments of Z are $E(Z^3) = 0$ and $E(Z^4) = 3$.

10.10. Let X be N_{0,σ^2} and Y be N_{0,ρ^2} distributed. Show that $X + Y$ is $N_{0,\sigma^2+\rho^2}$ distributed.

10.11. Let X be N_{μ,σ^2} and Y be N_{ν,ρ^2} distributed. What are the distributions of $X - \mu$ and $Y - \nu$? Show that $(X + Y) - (\mu + \nu)$ is $N_{0,\sigma^2+\rho^2}$ distributed using Problem 10.10. Conclude that $X + Y$ is $N_{\mu+\nu,\sigma^2+\rho^2}$ distributed. Extend this result to prove the boxed result before Example 5.

10.3 THE CENTRAL LIMIT THEOREM

Consider a *random sample* of measurement $\{X_i\}_{i=1}^n$. Then the fact that the X_i's are identically distributed implies that they have a common distribution—the **population distribution**. In the preceding section we showed that *if* the population distribution is normal, *then* the sample mean $\overline{X}$ is also normally distributed. The **central limit theorem** states that *even though* the population distribution may be far from being normal, *still* for large sample size n, the distribution of the sample mean $\overline{X}$ is approximately normal with better approximations obtained the larger the sample size n. The central limit theorem is truly remarkable; it allows calculations of probabilities involving $\overline{X}$ even when the individual X_i's have a very complicated and unknown distribution. Only the population mean μ and standard deviation σ are required to obtain the approximate distribution of $\overline{X}$.

The central limit theorem will be stated twice, once for sums and then sample means.

Let $X_1, \ldots, X_n$ be IIDRVs with common mean μ and standard deviation σ. Then the sum

$$S_n = X_1 + \cdots + X_n$$

has mean and variance

$$E(S_n) = E(X_1 + \cdots + X_n) = n\mu$$

$$\text{Var}(S_n) = n\sigma^2$$

Thus $(S_n - n\mu)/\sqrt{n}\sigma$ is *standardized*.

The Central Limit Theorem for Sums

$X_1, \ldots, X_n$ are IIDRVs with common mean μ and standard deviation σ. Let

$$S_n = X_1 + \cdots + X_n$$

Then the distribution of

$$Z = \frac{S_n - n\mu}{\sqrt{n}\sigma}$$

approaches the $N_{0,1}$ distribution as $n \to \infty$.

Thus $Z = (S_n - n\mu)/\sqrt{n}\sigma$ will have a distribution that is approximately $N_{0,1}$ for n large. How large is large enough? That depends on the individual distributions of the X_i's as well as the accuracy required. The closer the distribution of X_i is to the bell-shaped normal curve, the smaller n needs to be to provide good accuracy. Specific values of n will be given in the next two sections, but in general, surprisingly small ($n \geqslant 20$) values of n provide reasonable accuracy for most applications.

Example 7

Light bulbs are installed successively into a socket. Assume that each has a mean life of 2 months with a standard deviation of 1/4 month. Find $P(40$ bulbs last at least 7 years).

Solution Let X_i denote the lifetime of the ith bulb installed. Then n bulbs last a total time of $S_n = X_1 + \cdots + X_n$. With $n = 40$, $\mu = 2$, and $\sigma = 1/4$

$$\frac{S_{40} - 40 \cdot 2}{\sqrt{40} \cdot .25}$$

is approximately $N_{0,1}$ distributed *assuming* that $n = 40$ is large enough.

$$P(S_{40} \geqslant 7 \cdot 12 \text{ months}) = P\left(\frac{S_{40} - 80}{\sqrt{40} \cdot .25} \geqslant \frac{84 - 80}{\sqrt{40} \cdot .25}\right)$$

$$\cong P(Z > 2.530)$$

$$= .0057 \quad \blacksquare$$

Example 8 *(Continuation)*

How many bulbs n should be bought so that one can be 95% sure that the supply of n will last 5 years?

Solution Note that $n = 30$ bulbs have a total expected life span of $30 \cdot 2 = 60$ months $= 5$ years. For general n, the total life span S_n has

$$E(S_n) = 2n \qquad \sigma_{S_n} = \sqrt{n} \cdot .25$$

Using the Central Limit Theorem, we seek that value of n so that

$$.95 = P(S_n \geqslant 60)$$

$$= P\left(\frac{S_n - 2n}{\sqrt{n} \cdot .25} \geqslant \frac{60 - 2n}{\sqrt{n} \cdot .25}\right)$$

Thus a table look-up implies that

$$\frac{60 - 2n}{\sqrt{n} \cdot .25} = -1.645$$

This is a *quadratic equation* in root n:

$$60 - 2n = -1.645\sqrt{n} \cdot .25 = -.4113 \sqrt{n}$$

$$2n - .4113 \sqrt{n} - 60 = 0$$

$$\sqrt{n} = \frac{.4113 \pm \sqrt{(.4113)^2 + 4 \cdot 2 \cdot 60}}{2 \cdot 2} = -5.375, 5.581$$

Eliminating the negative root, we have

$$n = 31.15$$

So we should buy 32 bulbs. In this example the number 32 is fairly large, so that the central limit theorem can apply. Purely on the basis of the number 32 calculated *by means of* the central limit theorem are we *afterward* justified in using the central limit theorem. The logic of this is strange, but nonetheless valid. $\blacksquare$

A proof of the central limit theorem is beyond the scope of this book, but the next two examples show *how* the bell-shaped density curve emerges in specific cases:

Example 9

Suppose that each X_i is uniformly distributed on $[0, 1]$. Then $\mu = 1/2$ and $\sigma^2 = 1/12$ from the results of Chapter 9. Thus

$$Z = \frac{S_n - n/2}{\sqrt{n/12}}$$

will be approximately $N_{0,1}$ distributed for n large. For $n = 50$, 500 simulations of S_{50} were generated by computer and a histogram of total area 1 was drawn from the 500 values of $(S_{50} - 25)/\sqrt{50/12}$. The $N_{0,1}$ density function ϕ is overlaid in Fig. 10.8. ■

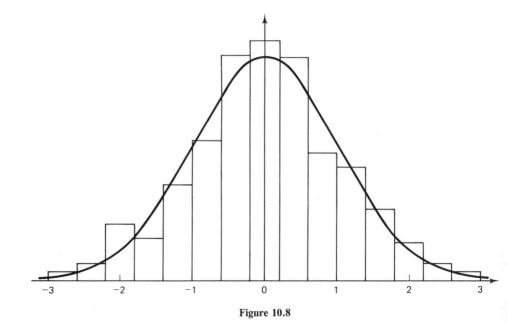

Figure 10.8

Example 10

Let $T_1, \ldots, T_n$ be IIDRVs, each exponentially distributed with parameter λ. Then $S_n = T_1 + \cdots + T_n$ is gamma distributed. Thus the central limit theorem claims that S_n, once standardized, has a density that is approximately $N_{0,1}$ for n large. Since $E(T_i) = 1/\lambda$ and $\text{Var}(T_i) = 1/\lambda^2$ from Chapter 9,

$$Z = \frac{S_n - n/\lambda}{\sqrt{n}/\lambda}$$

is standardized. For several values of n Fig. 10.9 shows the density of Z with the $N_{0,1}$ density superimposed: ■

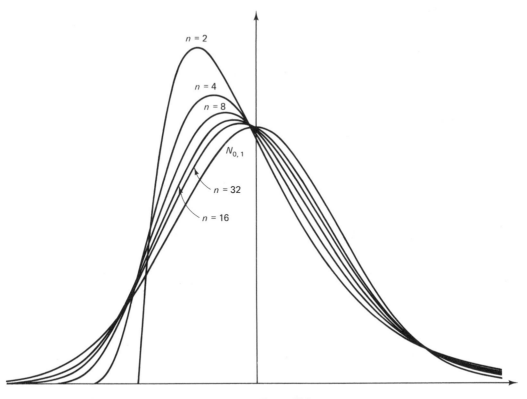

Figure 10.9

The central limit theorem can be phrased in terms of the sample mean rather than the sum S_n. Note that with $S_n = X_1 + \cdots + X_n$, $\overline{X} = S_n/n$. Therefore,

$$\frac{S_n - n\mu}{\sqrt{n}\sigma} = \frac{\overline{X} - \mu}{\sigma/\sqrt{n}}$$

is standardized.

The Central Limit Theorem for Sample Means

$X_1, \ldots, X_n$ are IIDRVs with common mean μ, standard deviation σ, and sample mean $\overline{X}$. Then the distribution of

$$Z = \frac{\overline{X} - \mu}{\sigma/\sqrt{n}}$$

approaches the $N_{0,1}$ distribution as $n \to \infty$.

Example 11 (*Continuation of Example 7*)

Let $\overline{S}$ be the average life of a package of 25 light bulbs.   (a) Find $P(\overline{S} > 1.9$ months).   (b) Also find an interval $(2 - c, 2 + c)$ about the mean $\mu = 2$ so that we can be 95% sure that the average lifetime $\overline{S}$ will fall into this interval.

   Solution   (a) Applying the central limit theorem,

$$Z = \frac{\overline{S} - 2}{.25/5}$$

is approximately $N_{0,1}$ distributed.   Thus

$$P(\overline{S} > 1.9) \cong P\left(Z > \frac{1.9 - 2}{.25/5}\right)$$

$$= P(Z > -2)$$

$$= .9772$$

(b) To find c, note that

$$.95 = P(2 - c < \overline{S} < 2 + c)$$

$$= P\left(\frac{-c}{.25/5} < Z < \frac{+c}{.25/5}\right)$$

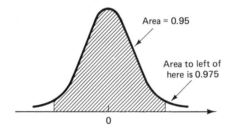

Area = 0.95

Area to left of here is 0.975

0

Figure 10.10

Therefore, c must satisfy

$$\frac{c}{.25/5} = 1.96$$

$$c = .098$$

Thus 95% of the packages with 25 bulbs will have average life in (1.902, 2.098).
■

PROBLEMS

10.12. Suppose that wildflowers occur at distances along a path X apart where $E(X) = 100$ feet and $\sigma_X = 50$ feet.   Let $S_n =$ distance until the nth clump of wildflowers. S_n

$= X_1 + \cdots + X_n$. Find (a) $P(30$ clumps within 2700 feet of start$) = P(S_{30} \le 2700)$; (b) $P($fewer than 15 clumps within 1800 feet of start$) = P(S_{15} > 1800)$.

10.13. (*Continuation*) Find the largest number n so that one can be 90% sure that there will be at least n clumps within 1 mile of the start of the path. That is, find the largest n so that $.90 \le P(S_n \le 5280)$.

10.14. (*Continuation*) Suppose that $\sigma = 10$ feet rather than 50 feet. Now find the n in Problem 10.13. Is the result reasonable? Should a *decrease* in σ cause an increase or a decrease in n?

10.15. Benjy can hit a nail an average of 1/4 centimeter per hammer blow with a standard deviation of .1 centimeter. To be 90% sure of driving a 5-centimeter nail all the way, how many hammer blows must Benjy do? Find n so that $.90 \le P(S_n \ge 5)$, where S_n is the distance the nail is driven in n blows. (First show that $.90 = P(S_n \ge 5)$ implies $(5 - n/4)/.1\sqrt{n} = -1.28$.)

10.16. Batteries last an average of 2 months with a standard deviation of 10 days (assume 30 days/month). Twenty-five batteries are bought. Find (a) $P($average life of all $25 > 61$ days$)$; (b) $P($average life differs from 2 months by more than 3 days$)$. (c) How many batteries n must be bought so that the average life of all n is 2 months to within 1 day with probability at least .95?

10.4 THE CENTRAL LIMIT THEOREM APPLIED TO THE BINOMIAL DISTRIBUTION

Perform n Bernoulli trials each with probability p of success. With $X_i = 1, 0$ if the ith trial results in success, failure, respectively, the sum

$$S_n = X_1 + \cdots + X_n$$

is binomially distributed. From Chapter 9,

$$\mu = E(X_i) = p$$

$$\sigma^2 = \text{Var}\ (X_i) = pq$$

Consequently, the central limit theorem applied to S_n implies:

> If S_n is binomially distributed n, p, then for n large,
> $$Z = \frac{S_n - np}{\sqrt{npq}}$$
> is approximately $N_{0,1}$ distributed.

Example 12

In $n = 100$ flips of a fair coin, find $P(45 \le S \le 55)$, where $S = S_{100}$ is the total number of heads.

Solution 1 $np = 100/2 = 50$ and $\sqrt{npq} = \sqrt{100/4} = 5$.

$$P(45 \leq S \leq 55) = P\left(-\frac{5}{5} \leq \frac{S - 50}{5} \leq \frac{5}{5}\right)$$

$$\cong P(-1 \leq Z \leq +1)$$

$$= .6826$$

Solution 2 Since it is impossible to obtain a nonintegral number of heads,

$$(\text{answer}) = P(44 < S < 56)$$

$$= P\left(-\frac{6}{5} < \frac{S - 50}{5} < \frac{6}{5}\right)$$

$$\cong P(-1.2 < Z < 1.2)$$

$$= .7698$$

Solution 3 Or perhaps since the discrete random variable S_n is being approximated by a continuous one, the boundary of the event might better be taken at half-integer points:

$$(\text{answer}) = P(44\tfrac{1}{2} \leq S \leq 55\tfrac{1}{2})$$

$$= P\left(-\frac{5\tfrac{1}{2}}{5} \leq \frac{S - 50}{5} \leq \frac{5\tfrac{1}{2}}{5}\right)$$

$$= P(-1.1 \leq Z \leq 1.1)$$

$$= .7286$$

Intuition suggests that Solution 3 is best. The exact probability is

$$P(45 \leq S \leq 55) = \sum_{j=45}^{55} \binom{100}{j} \frac{1}{2^{100}} = .7281 \quad \blacksquare$$

Continuity Correction

Let $j < k$ be integers and let S be an integer-valued random variable. In using the central limit theorem to find $P(j \leq S \leq k)$, apply the theorem to

$$P\left(j - \frac{1}{2} \leq S \leq k + \frac{1}{2}\right)$$

Example 13

Of the bolts made by machine A, 10% are defective. The first 1000 produced after a tune-up produced only 80 defective bolts. (Expected number 100.) Is this sufficient evidence to conclude that the tune-up improved performance?

Solution *Each* of the 1000 tested bolts constitutes one Bernoulli trial. Under the assumption that the tune-up had no effect, the number of defective bolts S is binomially distributed, $n = 1000, p = .1$. Therefore,

$$Z = \frac{S - np}{\sqrt{npq}} = \frac{S - 100}{\sqrt{90}}$$

is approximately $N_{0,1}$ distributed. Assuming that the tune-up had no effect,

$$P(S \leq 80) = P(S \leq 80.5)$$

$$\cong P\left(Z \leq \frac{80.5 - 100}{\sqrt{90}}\right)$$

$$= P(Z \leq -2.06)$$

$$= .0197$$

using the continuity correction to obtain the first equality.

    Conclusion: Assuming that the tune-up had no effect, so few defective bolts would have been produced in about 2% of all samples of size 100. We are justified, tentatively, in assuming that the tune-up worked. ∎

    The central limit theorem can be applied to the sample mean $\overline{X}$ rather than the total number of successes S_n in n Bernoulli trials. In fact, $\overline{X} = S_n/n$ is the fraction of the number of trials resulting in success.

n Bernoulli trials are performed. $\overline{X}$ equals the fraction of them which resulted in success. Then

$$Z = \frac{\overline{X} - p}{\sqrt{pq/n}}$$

is approximately $N_{0,1}$ distributed for n large.

Example 14

A pollster wants to find the proportion p of adults who favor gun control. How many adults n must be sampled to find the value of p? In more detail: The *exact* value of p cannot be known unless *all* the adults in the entire population are sampled. How many n must be sampled to find p to within one-one hundredth? Again, depending on the *exact composition* of the particular sample of size n, the estimate of p will differ; some samples will even have an estimate of p equal to 0. (No one favored gun control in that sample.) But (and the final restatement of the question) how many n must be sampled so that the fraction $\overline{X}$ in the sample who favored gun control is within .01 of p with probability .95?

    Solution With $p = $ true fraction of the adults who favor gun control, $S_n = $ number of adults favoring gun control in a sample of size n is binomially distributed.

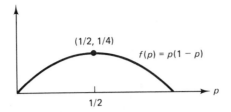

Figure 10.11

Thus the sample mean $\overline{X} = S_n/n$ is in fact an estimate of p. n satisfies

$$.95 \le P(|\overline{X} - p| \le .01)$$

$$= P\left(-\frac{.01}{\sqrt{pq/n}} \le \frac{\overline{X} - p}{\sqrt{pq/n}} \le \frac{.01}{\sqrt{pq/n}}\right)$$

$$= P\left(-\frac{.01}{\sqrt{pq/n}} \le Z \le \frac{.01}{\sqrt{pq/n}}\right)$$

where Z is $N_{0,1}$ distributed.   A table look-up implies that

$$\sqrt{n} = \frac{1.96\sqrt{pq}}{.01} = 196\sqrt{pq}$$

At this point it is not altogether clear how to proceed. We wanted a *specific* value of n. If the pollster had hired us to compute the value of n and tell him how many adults need to be sampled, we cannot very well present $(196\sqrt{pq})^2$ as the answer. If we do, the pollster will simply say that in order to find the specific number of adults to sample, $pq = p(1 - p)$ must be known. But this entails knowing p, which is what the pollster really *wants to know in the first place*. If our answer is $(196\sqrt{pq})^2$, our answer is useless!

Consider the graph of the function $f(p) = pq = p(1 - p)$ in Fig. 10.11. $pq = p(1 - p)$ is a quadratic in p with maximum value $1/4$. [Differentiate $p(1 - p)$ and set derivative equal to 0.] *Therefore*, in order that the number n be independent of the true proportion p of adults who favor gun control, the number to be sampled is

$$n = 196^2 \cdot pq \le 196^2 \cdot \frac{1}{4} = 9604$$

Conclusion: To be 95% sure of "capturing" the correct proportion p, sample about 9600 adults. Fewer may have been necessary, but this many will *always* (regardless of the true value of p) be enough. ∎

For p close to $1/2$, the distribution of binomially distributed S_n will be close to symmetric with respect to its mean np. Thus given a value of n, the normal approximation will be better the closer p is to $1/2$. In general,

> The normal approximation to the binomial distribution is accurate for $npq > 5$.

The Normal Distribution, Central Limit Theorem   Chap. 10

The value 5 is somewhat arbitrary. But consider this comparison of values: For $n = 21$ and $p = 1/2 = q$, let S be the number of successes in n Bernoulli trials. Then S is binomially distributed with $np = 10.5, npq = 5.25$. The exact probability that $S = j$ is

$$P(S = j) = \binom{21}{j} \frac{1}{2^{21}}$$

Using the central limit theorem, the approximation is

$$P(S = j) = P(j - .5 < S < j + .5)$$
$$= P\left(\frac{j - 11}{\sqrt{5.25}} < Z < \frac{j - 10}{\sqrt{5.25}}\right)$$

where Z is $N_{0,1}$ distributed.

j	$P(S = j)$	$P\left(\dfrac{j - 11}{\sqrt{5.25}} < Z < \dfrac{j - 10}{\sqrt{5.25}}\right)$
3	.0006	.0009
4	.0029	.0033
5	.0097	.0101
6	.0259	.0259
7	.0554	.0548
8	.0970	.0948
9	.1402	.1399
10	.1682	.1687
11	.1682	.1687
12	.1402	.1399
13	.0970	.0948
14	.0554	.0548
15	.0259	.0259
16	.0097	.0101
17	.0029	.0033
18	.0006	.0009

PROBLEMS

10.17. Let S be binomially distributed with $n = 24, p = .6$. Compute the exact value of $P(S = j)$ and compare it with the approximation using the central limit theorem to compute $P(j - .5 < S < j + .5)$ for $j =$ **(a)** 10; **(b)** 15; **(c)** 20. Note that

$$P(j - .5 < S < j + .5) \cong P\left(\frac{j - 14.4 - .5}{\sqrt{5.76}} < Z < \frac{j - 14.4 + .5}{\sqrt{5.76}}\right)$$

where Z is $N_{0,1}$ since $np = 24 \cdot .6 = 14.4$ and $npq = 24 \cdot .6 \cdot .4 = 5.76$. To compute the approximation, compute the right-hand side for $j = 10, 15,$ and 20.

10.18. Suppose that 40 people in 100 favor candidate C. In a randomly selected group of

100 people, let $S = $ #(who favor C). Find the central limit theorem approximations to **(a)** $P(38 \leqslant S \leqslant 42)$; **(b)** $P(37 < S < 43)$; **(c)** $P(37\frac{1}{2} \leqslant S \leqslant 42\frac{1}{2})$.

10.19. Roll a fair die 1000 times. Let X equal the fraction of the times that either a 1 or a 2 occurs. Find **(a)** $P(X < 340)$; **(b)** $P(330 < X \leqslant 337)$. Make sure to use the continuity correction.

10.20. Let S be the number of success in 10,000 Bernoulli trials. What is $E(S)$? Find

$$P(10,000p - 20 < S < 10,000p + 20)$$

for $p = $ **(a)** .1; **(b)** .25; **(c)** .50; **(d)** .75; and **(e)** .9. **(f)** Plot this probability as a function of p.

10.21. Perform n Bernoulli trials with $p = 1/2$. Use the central limit theorem to find an interval about $n/2$—$(n/2 - c, n/2 + c)$ so that the actual number of successes will fall into this interval with probability .90. What is the length of this interval? How does it depend on n?

10.22. Let $S_n = $ #(heads on n flips on a fair coin). How many flips must be performed so that with probability at least .95 the average number of heads per flip is 1/2 to within .01? That is, solve for n in

$$.95 = P\left(\left|\frac{S_n}{n} - \frac{1}{2}\right| < .01\right)$$

10.23. A marketing research analyst wants to find the proportion p of people who like brand X cereal. He/she sets up shop in a busy mall. n people are interviewed and S_n are found to like brand X cereal. Given p, why is S_n binomially distributed? Find n so that the analyst can be 99% sure that S_n/n is within .1 of p.

10.24. A certain fraction p of seeds cast to the wind germinate. A sample of n seeds were scattered and S_n germinated. If $\overline{X} = S_n/n$ is taken to be the estimator for p, how large should n be so that $\overline{X}$ will be within .05 of p with probability .95? Obtain n as a function of p and graph it.

10.5 THE CENTRAL LIMIT THEOREM APPLIED TO THE POISSON DISTRIBUTION

The normal distribution also approximates the Poisson distribution for a large value of the parameter λ. To see how this is so, let X be Poisson distributed with parameter $\Lambda > 0$. Since the mean and the variance of X are *both* equal to the parameter Λ,

$$Z = \frac{X - \Lambda}{\sqrt{\Lambda}}$$

is standardized.

Consider this model: Calls arrive at an exchange according to a Poisson stream with $\lambda = 1$ call per minute, on the average. Let

$$X_i = \text{#(calls registered in the interval } (i - 1, i])$$

Then the number of calls registered in $(0, t]$ is

$$X = X_1 + \cdots + X_t$$

The Normal Distribution, Central Limit Theorem   Chap. 10

But

$$\mu = E(X_i) = \lambda = 1$$

$$\sigma^2 = \text{Var}(X_i) = \lambda = 1$$

since each X_i is itself Poisson distributed with parameter $\lambda = 1$. Also, the X_i's are *independent by the first* **Poisson postulate**, *which states that the number of calls registered in nonoverlapping time intervals are independent.* Thus we can conclude:

1. X is Poisson distributed with parameter $t\lambda = t$.
2. $(X - t)/\sqrt{t} = (X - t\lambda)/\sqrt{t\lambda}$ is approximately $N_{0,1}$ distributed for large t by the central limit theorem.

Now set $t = \Lambda$ and the general result can be phrased without reference to the reasoning—the model—used to derive it:

If X is Poisson distributed with parameter Λ, then

$$Z = \frac{X - \Lambda}{\sqrt{\Lambda}}$$

is approximately $N_{0,1}$ distributed for Λ large.

Example 15

Calls arrive at the rate of $\lambda = 2$ calls per minute. In an 8-hour day, therefore, 2 $\cdot$ 60 $\cdot$ 8 $= 960$ calls are expected. Let $X = \#$(calls actually registered). Find

$$P(X < 1000) \qquad P(X > 900)$$

and an interval around 960—$[960 - c, 960 + c]$—so that with probability 1/2, X will fall in this interval.

Solution $\Lambda = E(X) = 960$. Therefore, $Z = (X - 960/\sqrt{960}$ is approximately $N_{0,1}$ distributed. Using the *continuity correction*,

$$P(X < 1000) = P(X \leqslant 999.5)$$

$$= P\left(\frac{X - 960}{\sqrt{960}} \leqslant \frac{999.5 - 960}{\sqrt{960}}\right)$$

$$= P(Z \leqslant 1.275)$$

$$= .8997$$

$$P(Z > 900) = P(Z \geqslant 900.5)$$

$$= P\left(\frac{X - 960}{\sqrt{960}} \geqslant \frac{900.5 - 960}{\sqrt{960}}\right)$$

$$= P(Z \geqslant -1.920)$$

$$= .9726$$

Finally, the number c satisfies

$$.5 = P(960 - c \leqslant X \leqslant 960 + c)$$

$$= P\left(- \frac{c}{\sqrt{960}} \leqslant Z \leqslant \frac{c}{\sqrt{960}}\right)$$

Therefore,

$$\frac{c}{\sqrt{960}} = .675$$

$$c = 20.91$$

Thus with 50% probability there will be 940 or 941 or . . . or 980 calls. ∎

Example 16

A snack bar sells hot dogs at the rate of 1 per every 7 minutes. How many minutes must the snack bar stay open so that with probability 90% all of the 6 dozen hot dogs are sold?

    Solution Calls coming into an exchange—hot dogs being sold. The same three Poisson postulates apply to each. Hence the number of hot dogs sold in t minutes X_t is Poisson distributed with parameter $\lambda t = t/7$. (In t minutes we *expect* to sell $t/7$ hot dogs.) We seek that value of t that solves the equation

$$.90 = P(X_t \geqslant 6 \cdot 12) = P(X_t \geqslant 72)$$

With $\Lambda = t/7$ the central limit theorem states that

$$\frac{X_t - t/7}{\sqrt{t/7}}$$

is approximately $N_{0,1}$ distributed for large t.

$$.90 = P(X_t \geqslant 72)$$

$$= P\left(\frac{X_t - t/7}{\sqrt{t/7}} \geqslant \frac{72 - t/7}{\sqrt{t/7}}\right)$$

$$= P\left(Z \geqslant \frac{72 - t/7}{\sqrt{t/7}}\right)$$

A table look-up allows us to continue:

$$\frac{72 - t/7}{\sqrt{t/7}} = -1.28$$

$$\frac{t}{7} - 1.28 \sqrt{\frac{t}{7}} - 72 = 0$$

$$\frac{t}{7} - .4838 \sqrt{t} - 72 = 0$$

$$\sqrt{t} = \frac{.4838 \pm \sqrt{(.4838)^2 + 4 \cdot 72/7}}{2/7} = -20.82, 24.21$$

Discarding the negative root gives us

$$t = 24.21^2 = 586.1 \text{ minutes} \cong 9\tfrac{3}{4} \text{ hours}$$

Note that in 586.1 minutes the snack bar can *expect* to sell

$$\frac{586.1}{7} = 83.7 \cong 7 \text{ dozen}$$

hot dogs. But according to our calculations, we can be only 90% sure of selling 6 dozen. ■

The normal approximation to the Poisson distribution is accurate for $\Lambda > 15$.

The number 15 is somewhat arbitrary. Suppose that X is Poisson distributed with $\Lambda = 16$. The following table compares the exact probabilities $P(X = j)$ with the approximation using the central limit theorem with the continuity correction. Note that

$$P(X = j) = e^{-16} \frac{16^j}{j!}$$

is the exact probability; the approximation is

$$P(X = j) = P(j - .5 < X < j + .5) = P\left(\frac{j - .5 - 16}{4} < Z < \frac{j + .5 - 16}{4}\right)$$

where Z is $N_{0,1}$.

j	$P(X = j)$	$P\left(\dfrac{j - .5 - 16}{4} < Z < \dfrac{j + .5 - 16}{4}\right)$
5	.0010	.0023
6	.0026	.0045
7	.0060	.0080
8	.0120	.0136
9	.0213	.0217
10	.0341	.0325
11	.0496	.0458
12	.0661	.0605
13	.0814	.0752
14	.0930	.0889
15	.0992	.0954
16	.0992	.0995
17	.0934	.0954
18	.0830	.0889
19	.0699	.0752
20	.0559	.0605
21	.0426	.0458
22	.0310	.0325
23	.0216	.0217
24	.0144	.0136

PROBLEMS

10.25. On a given day 1000 cars can be expected to pass a certain toll booth. Why should the actual number of cars X be Poisson distributed with parameter $\Lambda = 1000$? Use the normal approximation to find **(a)** $P(X > 960)$; **(b)** $P(X \leqslant 1050)$; **(c)** $P(980 < X \leqslant 1020)$. Make sure to use the continuity correction.

10.26. Let the parameter Λ be 15 for Poisson distributed X. Compute $P(X = j)$ and the normal approximation to $P(j - 1/2 < X < j + 1/2)$ for $j = 10, 15$, and 20.

10.27. Raindrops collect on the window pane at the average rate of $\lambda = 20$ per minute. **(a)** What is the exact distribution of $N_t = \#(\text{drops in } t \text{ minutes})$? Find **(b)** $P(N_5 \leqslant 105)$; **(c)** $P(91 < N_5 < 109)$; **(d)** $P(92 \leqslant N_5 \leqslant 108)$; **(e)** $P(91\frac{1}{2} \leqslant N_5 \leqslant 108\frac{1}{2})$ using the central limit theorem.

10.28. A business has 5 telephone lines. The first rings every minute on the average, the second every 1/2 minute, the third every 2 minutes, the fourth every 5 minutes, and the fifth every 1/10 minute, on the average. Let $X_t = \#(\text{calls in } [0, t])$. **(a)** What is the exact distribution of X_t? Find **(b)** $E(X_{60})$ and **(c)** $P(X_{60} < 850)$ using the normal approximation. **(d)** Find a number c so that with 95% probability the number of calls will be less than c in 1 hour.

10.29. Let $X_t = \#(\text{events in } [0, t])$ for a Poisson stream with parameter λ. Suppose that $\lambda = 100$. **(a)** What is the exact distribution of X_t? Find $g(t) = P(X_t \leqslant 2000)$ for these values of t: **(b)** 19; **(c)** 19.5; **(d)** 20; **(e)** 20.5; **(f)** 21; **(g)** Plot $g(t)$ as a function of t.

10.30. A switchboard receives orders at the rate of 1 every 2 minutes. **(a)** What is the exact distribution of $X_t = \#(\text{orders in } [0, t])$? **(b)** How long must the switchboard plan on staying open so that with 90% probability at least 100 orders will have been made in $[0, t]$?

10.6 CHEBYSHEV'S INEQUALITY AND THE LAW OF LARGE NUMBERS

Of less computational applicability than the central limit theorem, but with as much theoretical interest, is the **law of large numbers**. In Chapter 1 the frequency interpretation of probability was used as the intuitive ground for developing the entire axiomatic structure of probability theory. In Chapter 4 the frequency interpretation was again used to develop the definition of the expectation. *The law of large numbers is actually the frequency interpretation phrased as a theorem.* In stating and proving the law of large numbers, we come full circle: The whole structure of probability is based on the frequency interpretation the axioms of which can be used to *prove* the frequency interpretation.

The law of large numbers uses a technical tool called **Chebyshev's inequality**. Pafnutii Lvovich Chebyshev (1821–1894) performed path-breaking work in many areas of applied mathematics. Under his supervision Russia came into the forefront of probability theory. He felt that only mathematics that arose out of real applications was of value, although he was particularly able in generalizing from particular cases to general theories.

Let W be a random variable with mean 0. Although the expectation of W is 0, any single *realization* of W may be very far from 0. The variance measures how far the values of W are dispersed from 0. The larger the value of Var (W), the less surprised one would be to find the *actual* value of W far from 0. Chebyshev's inequality makes this idea precise. The question is: Given the variance σ^2, how close to $\mu = 0$ are the values of W likely to be?

To try to answer this, fix a number $\varepsilon > 0$ and let us ask for the probability that W is farther than ε away from its mean $\mu = 0$. In fact, we expect that this probability $P(|W| \geq \varepsilon)$ should get *larger* as Var $(W) = \sigma^2$ gets *larger*; for then the values of W will be spread over a larger interval. Let us suppose that W has density f. (A similar derivation applies when W is discrete rather than continuous.) Then for *fixed* number $\varepsilon > 0$,

$$P(|W| \geq \varepsilon) = \int_{|x| \geq \varepsilon} f(x)\, dx$$

$$= \int_{x^2 \geq \varepsilon^2} \frac{\varepsilon^2}{\varepsilon^2} f(x)\, dx$$

$$\leq \int_{x^2 \geq \varepsilon^2} \frac{x^2}{\varepsilon^2} f(x)\, dx$$

$$\leq \int_{-\infty}^{\infty} \frac{x^2}{\varepsilon^2} f(x)\, dx$$

$$= \frac{1}{\varepsilon^2} \int_{-\infty}^{\infty} x^2 f(x)\, dx$$

$$= \frac{E(W^2)}{\varepsilon^2}$$

$$= \frac{\sigma^2}{\varepsilon^2}$$

Note that the first inequality follows from the fact that the interval of integration is the points x where $x^2 \geq \varepsilon^2$, and hence the integrand can only be larger if ε^2 is replaced by x^2 in the numerator. The second inequality follows from increasing the interval of integration from the points x where $x^2 \geq \varepsilon^2$ to the *entire* line from $-\infty$ to ∞. The second-to-last equality follows from the definition of $E(W^2)$.

Hence we have shown that if $E(W) = 0$ and given any positive number ε, the event that W differs by at least ε from 0 is bounded:

$$P(|W| \geq \varepsilon) \leq \frac{\sigma^2}{\varepsilon^2}$$

Now suppose that X is *any* random variable; and let $\mu = E(X)$. Then $W = X - \mu$ has $E(W) = 0$, so the above applies to W. To summarize:

Chebyshev's Inequality

Let X have finite mean μ and finite variance σ^2. Then for $\varepsilon > 0$ a fixed number, the chance that X differs by at least ε from its mean is bounded:

$$P(|X - \mu| \geq \varepsilon) \leq \frac{\sigma^2}{\varepsilon^2}$$

In terms of the complementary event,

$$P(|X - \mu| < \varepsilon) \geq 1 - \frac{\sigma^2}{\varepsilon^2}$$

Example 17

Boxes of bolts have an average of 100 bolts with a standard deviation of 3. Find the probability that the number of bolts in the box I buy is between 95 and 105.

Solution 1: Using Chebyshev's inequality. Let X be the number of bolts in the box. Then

$$\mu = 100 \qquad \sigma = 3$$

Hence

$$P(95 < X < 105) = P(|X - 100| < 5) \geq 1 - \frac{3^2}{5^2} = \frac{14}{25}$$

With *at least* chance $14/25 = .56$, the box contains between 95 and 105 bolts.

Solution 2: Using the central theorem *Assuming* that the central limit theorem applies to the random variable X (that X is due to many small causes, in other words), then X is approximately $N_{100,9}$ distributed. Hence

$$P(95 < X < 105) = P(95.5 \leq X \leq 104.5)$$

$$= P\left(\frac{95.5 - 100}{3} \leq Z \leq \frac{104.5 - 100}{3}\right)$$

$$= P(-1.5 \leq Z \leq 1.5)$$

$$= .8664$$

For large sample size the probability is approximated to better accuracy using the central limit theorem than using Chebyshev's inequality. This is so since Chebyshev's inequality is a general result that holds true for every distribution with the same mean and variance. If, however, the distribution is known to be approximately normal, *then* the specific details of that distribution can be used. ∎

But the weakness of Chebyshev's inequality due to its generality is precisely what is required to prove the law of large numbers and the consistency of the frequency interpretation of probability.

Let $\{X_i\}_{i=1}^n$ be a random sample. Then the X_i's are IIDRVs with common mean μ and variance σ^2. One intuitively expects that the sample mean $\overline{X}$ should be close to the population mean μ for n large. Mathematically, this is expressed by

$$\lim_{n \to \infty} \overline{X} = \lim_{n \to \infty} \frac{S_n}{n} = \mu$$

where

$$S_n = X_1 + \cdots + X_n$$

is the sum. More precisely, we will show that the *probability* that $\overline{X}$ differs by any nonzero amount from μ tends to 0 as n becomes large. What is surprising is not that this result holds (it must hold in any reasonable theory of probability), but that our mathematical machinery allows us to *prove* it.

Let $\varepsilon > 0$ be a fixed number. By independence of the sequence $X_1, \ldots,$ X_n in the random sample,

$$E(S_n) = n\mu$$

$$\text{Var }(S_n) = n\sigma^2$$

Chebyshev's inequality applied to S_n states that

$$P(|S_n - n\mu| \geq n\varepsilon) \leq \frac{\text{Var }(S_n)}{(n\varepsilon)^2} = \frac{n\sigma^2}{n^2\varepsilon^2} = \frac{\sigma^2}{n\varepsilon^2}$$

In terms of the sample mean $\overline{X}$,

$$P(|\overline{X} - \mu| \geq \varepsilon) = P\left(\left| \frac{S_n}{n} - \mu \right| \geq \varepsilon \right)$$

$$= P(|S_n - n\mu| \geq n\varepsilon)$$

$$\leq \frac{\sigma^2}{n\varepsilon^2}$$

Now let $n \to \infty$. Then the bound on the right tends to 0 and the following conclusion follows:

Law of Large Numbers

Let $\{X_i\}_{i=1}^n$ be a random sample with common mean μ and variance σ^2. Let

$$S_n = X_1 + \cdots + X_n$$

Then

$$P\left(\left| \frac{S_n}{n} - \mu \right| \geq \varepsilon \right) \to 0$$

as $n \to \infty$ for *each* fixed $\varepsilon > 0$.

Example 18

Perform n Bernoulli trials with probability p of success. The fraction of the times resulting in success is

$$\overline{X} = \frac{1}{n}(X_1 + \cdots + X_n) = \frac{S_n}{n}$$

where X_i is 1, 0 with probability p, q respectively. Since $\mu = E(X_i) = p$,

$$P(|\overline{X} - p| \geq \varepsilon) \to 0$$

as $n \to \infty$ for each fixed $\varepsilon > 0$. ■

To show how the law of large numbers leads to the frequency interpretation of probability, consider an event A associated with a random experiment. Perform the random experiment a large number n of times. Define random variable X_i by

$$X_i = \begin{cases} 1 & i\text{th experiment results in event } A \\ 0 & \text{otherwise} \end{cases}$$

Then $S_n = X_1 + \cdots + X_n$ is the total number of times A has occurred on all n experiments. Since

$$E(X_i) = 1 \cdot P(X_i = 1) + 0 \cdot P(X_i = 0) = P(A)$$

the law of large numbers states that

$$P\left(\left|\frac{S_n}{n} = P(A)\right| < \varepsilon\right) \to 1$$

as $n \to \infty$ for fixed $\varepsilon > 0$.

The law of large numbers says this: A random experiment is performed and X_1 is measured, then the experiment is repeated and X_2 is measured, and so on.

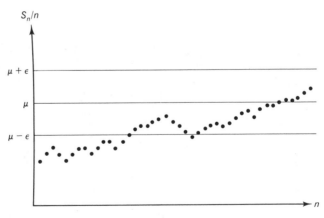

Figure 10.12

With $S_n = X_1 + \cdots + X_n$, S_n/n is the sample average of the X_i's over the first n experiments. The law of large numbers says that for n *large*, we can be as sure as we like that S_n/n is close to μ. That is, if an error ε is set, *the chance that S_n/n differs from μ by more than the error ε goes to 0 as $n \to \infty$*. Or, stated differently, *the chance that S_n/n is within ε of μ tends to 1 as $n \to \infty$*. (In Fig. 10.12, with large probability the value of S_n/n will be within the horizontal lines distance ε from μ.)

If each repetition of the random experiment takes 1 minute, then S_n/n is the average of the X_i values over the course of the first n minutes. Thus the *time average S_n/n* approaches the *population average μ* as the time tends to ∞.

Example 19

Consider a Poisson stream with parameter λ. With $N_t = \#(\text{calls in } [0, t])$, $E(N_t) = \lambda t$ and Var $(N_t) = \lambda t$ since the counting variable N_t is Poisson distributed with parameter λt. By Chebyshev's inequality, therefore,

$$P\left(\left|\frac{N_t}{t} - \lambda\right| \geq \varepsilon\right) = P(|N_t - \lambda t| > \varepsilon t)$$

$$\leq \frac{\text{Var } (N_t)}{(\varepsilon t)^2}$$

$$= \frac{\lambda t}{(\varepsilon t)^2}$$

$$= \frac{\lambda}{\varepsilon^2 t}$$

$$\to 0$$

as $t \to \infty$. Thus the *temporal average* number of calls per unit time N_t/t tends to λ as the time $t \to \infty$. ■

10.7 THE CHI-SQUARE DISTRIBUTION AND SAMPLING FROM THE NORMAL DISTRIBUTION (OPTIONAL)

Assume throughout that $Z_1, \ldots, Z_n$ are IIDRVs, each with the normal distribution with mean 0 and variance 1. Then by *definition*, the random variable

$$Y_n = Z_1^2 + \cdots + Z_n^2$$

has the **chi-square distribution** *with n degrees of freedom* (often denoted "χ^2 distribution," using the Greek lowercase letter chi). Note that Y_n is a continuous random variable concentrated on the positive real axis $(0, \infty)$. Why?

Example 20

Find the density f_1 for the χ^2 random variable Y_1 with one degree of freedom.

　　Solution $f_1(y) = 0$ for $y < 0$. $Y_1 = Z^2$, where Z is $N_{0,1}$. Thus the distribution function for Y_1 is

$$P(Y_1 \leqslant y) = P(Z^2 \leqslant y)$$
$$= P(|Z| \leqslant \sqrt{y})$$
$$= \frac{1}{\sqrt{2\pi}} \int_{-\sqrt{y}}^{\sqrt{y}} e^{-z^2/2} \, dz$$
$$= \sqrt{\frac{2}{\pi}} \int_0^{\sqrt{y}} e^{-z^2/2} dz$$

Differentiate to find the density function:

$$f_1(y) = \sqrt{\frac{2}{\pi}} e^{-(\sqrt{y})^2/2} \cdot \frac{1}{2} y^{-1/2}$$

using the chain rule to differentiate the integral in which the top limit is a *function* of y. To summarize:

$$
f_1(y) =
\begin{cases}
1 & y < 0 \\
\dfrac{1}{\sqrt{2\pi}} y^{-1/2} e^{-y/2} & y > 0
\end{cases}
$$

Example 21

Find the density for Y_2.

Solution   Use the *convolution formula* for the density of a sum of independent random variables derived in Section 8.5. $Y_2 = Z_1^2 + Z_2^2$, where Z_1^2 and Z_2^2 are each χ^2 *distributed with one degree of freedom*; their density functions were derived in Example 20.   Consequently, since they are concentrated on $(0, \infty)$,

$$f_2(y) = \int_0^y f_1(t) f_1(y - t) \, dt$$
$$= \int_0^y \frac{1}{2\pi} t^{-1/2} e^{-t/2}(y - t)^{-1/2} e^{-(y-t)/2} \, dt$$
$$= \frac{1}{2\pi} e^{-y/2} \int_0^y t^{-1/2}(y - t)^{-1/2} \, dt$$

Now use the substitution $t = u^2$ in the integral:

$$f_2(y) = \frac{1}{2\pi} e^{-y/2} \int_0^{\sqrt{y}} u^{-1}(y - u^2)^{-1/2} \cdot 2u \, du$$
$$= \frac{1}{2\pi} e^{-y/2} \int_0^{\sqrt{y}} \frac{2 \, du}{\sqrt{y - u^2}}$$

$$= \frac{1}{\pi} e^{-y/2} \sin^{-1} \frac{u}{\sqrt{y}} \Bigg|_{u=0}^{u=\sqrt{y}}$$

$$= \frac{1}{\pi} e^{-y/2} (\sin^{-1} 1 - \sin^{-1} 0)$$

$$= \frac{1}{2} e^{-y/2}$$

where the integration of $1/\sqrt{y - u^2}$ was done using a table of integrals.   *This*
density function you may recognize: Mysteriously enough:

Y_2 has the exponential density with parameter 1/2:

$$f_2(y) = \begin{cases} 0 & y < 0 \\ \frac{1}{2} e^{-y/2} & y > 0 \end{cases}$$

For degrees of freedom $n > 2$, the exact density function for Y_n is derived
in the problems.   To summarize:

The density function for the chi-square distributed random variable Y_n with
n degrees of freedom is

$$f_n(y) = \begin{cases} 0 & y < 0 \\ C_n y^{(n/2)-1} e^{-y/2} & y > 0 \end{cases}$$

where C_n is a constant.   (See Problems 10.31 to 10.33 for the exact
value of C_n.)

Fig. 10.13 depicts graphs of the chi-square density functions for various values of
the parameter n.

Here is a *method for simulating an* $N_{0,1}$ *distributed random variable* using the
χ^2 distribution with two degrees of freedom: Let a two-dimensional coordinate
system have horizontal and vertical axes labeled s and t, respectively.   A point is
chosen at random with coordinates (S, T).   Assume that the random variables S
and T are independent, each $N_{0,1}$ distributed.   Then the distance of the point from
the origin is $R = \sqrt{S^2 + T^2}$.   From Example 21 we know that the random variable
R^2 is χ^2 distributed with two degrees of freedom, which is to say that R^2 is exponentially distributed with parameter 1/2.   Let the angle Φ be the angle $0 \leq \Phi <
2\pi$ the line segment from the origin to the point (S, T) subtends with respect to
the positive horizontal axis as in Fig. 10.14.

Let us show that Φ is uniformly distributed on the interval $[0, 2\pi)$.   In fact,
if u is a fixed number with $0 \leq u < 2\pi$, then $\Phi \leq u$ if and only if (S, T) is contained
in the wedge **A** of Fig. 10.15.

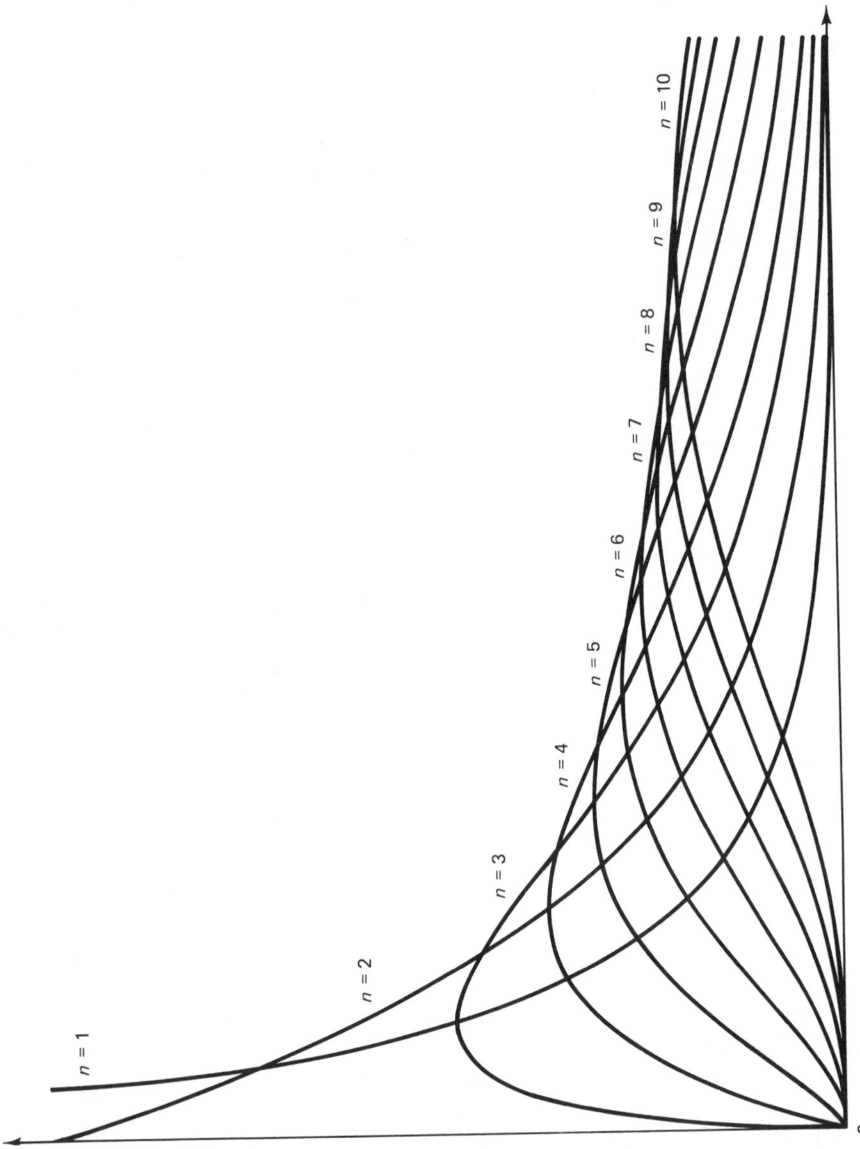

Figure 10.13 The chi-square density functions.

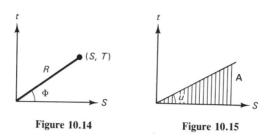

Figure 10.14   Figure 10.15

Thus the distribution function for the random angle Φ is

$$P(\Phi \le u) = P((S, T) \in A)$$

$$= \iint_A \frac{1}{\sqrt{2\pi}} e^{-s^2/2} \frac{1}{\sqrt{2\pi}} e^{-t^2/2} \, ds \, dt$$

$$= \frac{1}{2\pi} \iint_A e^{-(s^2+t^2)/2} \, ds \, dt$$

Now switch to polar coordinates:

$$s = r \cos \theta \qquad t = r \sin \theta$$

$$r^2 = s^2 + t^2 \qquad ds \, dt = r \, dr \, d\theta$$

$$P(\Phi \le u) = \frac{1}{2\pi} \int_0^u \int_0^\infty e^{-r^2/2} r \, dr \, d\theta$$

$$= \frac{1}{2\pi} \int_0^u 1 \, d\theta$$

$$= \frac{u}{2\pi}$$

which proves that Φ is uniformly distributed on the interval $[0, 2\pi)$ since its distribution function has that form. Let us summarize:

If a point (S, T) is chosen so that S and T are independent, each $N_{0,1}$ distributed, then R^2 is exponentially distributed with parameter $1/2$ and Φ is uniformly distributed on $[0, 2\pi)$, where R is the distance from the origin and Φ is the angle subtended by (S, T).

To simulate an $N_{0,1}$ value, turn this reasoning around: *First* simulate an exponentially distributed random variable E with parameter $1/2$ and a uniformly distributed random variable U on $[0, 2\pi)$ and then set

$$S = \sqrt{E} \cos U$$

From Chapter 7, Example 15, E is set equal to $-2 \ln (1 - \text{RND})$, where RND is uniform on $[0, 1)$.

> To simulate an $N_{0,1}$ value X, first simulate RND_1 and RND_2 uniformly distributed in $[0, 1)$ and set
> $$X = \sqrt{-2 \ln(1 - \text{RND}_1)} \cdot \cos (2\pi \, \text{RND}_2)$$

Example 22

Write a program to simulate 100 $N_{0,1}$ values.

Solution The body of the program is

```
begin
    SEED: = 0;

    for I: = 1 to 100 do
        begin
            SEED: = (MULT*SEED + ADDR) mod NORM;
            RND: = SEED/NORM;
            E: = - 2*ln(1-RND);

            SEED: = (MULT*SEED + ADDR) mod NORM;
            RND: = SEED/NORM;
            U: = 2*3.14159*RND;

            X: = (E**0.5)*cos(U);

            write(X:10:4);
        end;
    end.   ■
```

PROBLEMS

10.31. (*Derivation of* χ^2 *Density with n Degrees of Freedom for* $n = 2k$ *Even*) Show that
$$Y_{2k} = (Z_1^2 + Z_2^2) + \cdots + (Z_{2k-1}^2 + Z_{2k}^2)$$

is the sum of k independent random variables, *each* exponentially distributed with parameter $1/2$ by Example 21. Conclude that Y_{2k} is gamma distributed with $n = k$ and $\lambda = 1/2$. Thus conclude that
$$f_{2k}(y) = \begin{cases} 0 & y < 0 \\ \dfrac{1}{2^k(k-1)!} \, y^{k-1} e^{-y/2} & y > 0 \end{cases}$$

10.32. (*Derivation of χ^2 Density with n Degrees of Freedom for $n = 2k + 1$ Odd*) Show that

$$Y_{2k+1} = Y_{2k} + Z^2$$

where Y_{2k} and Z are independent, Z $N_{0,1}$ distributed, and Y_{2k} with the density of Problem 10.31. Conclude that the density for Y_n is

$$f_n(y) = \int_0^y Ct^{k-1}(y - t)^{-1/2}e^{-y/2}\,dt$$

$$= Ce^{-y/2}y^{k-1/2} \cdot \int_0^1 u^{k-1}(1 - u)^{-1/2}\,du$$

where C is a constant. Note that the integral in the last expression *is itself* a constant independent of y. Thus

$$f_n(y) = C_n y^{k-1/2}e^{-y/2}$$

for some constant C_n. Note that $n = 2k + 1$, so $k = (n - 1)/2$.

10.33. To find C_n of Problem 10.32, show that

$$C_n^{-1} = \int_0^\infty y^{(n/2)-1}e^{-y/2}\,dy$$

$$= (n - 2)C_{n-2}^{-1}$$

What is C_1? Successively find C_3, C_5, and then C_n for n odd.

10.34. (*The Rayleigh Distribution*) **(a)** Let R^2 be χ^2 distributed with two degrees of freedom. Find the density function for R. **(b)** Let $S = \alpha R$. Find the density function for S.

10.35. Let Y_n be χ^2 distributed with n degrees of freedom. Show that $E(Y_n) = n$ and Var $(Y_n) = 2n$.

10.36. Write a program that will input N, then generate 100 simulated values of a χ^2 random variable with N degrees of freedom. Use the technique of Example 22 to generate $N_{0,1}$ values first.

— Chapter 11

Continuous-Time Birth and Death Processes

In Chapter 6 we studied one stochastic process in detail—the Poisson stream in which the "event counting" random variable N_t equals the number of arrivals in $[0, t]$. N_t can only increase with time: $N_t \geq N_s$ for $t \geq s$. There are situations in which the "state of the system" can fluctuate up and down. One of the most important applications is queuing theory, in which the state of the system at time t is the length of a waiting line of customers.

Understanding the exponential distribution is indispensable to grasping this chapter. Recall that if T is the lifetime of a component that is exponentially distributed with parameter α, then T has density

$$f(t) = \begin{cases} 0 & t < 0 \\ \alpha e^{-\alpha t} & 0 < t \end{cases}$$

The *expectation* of T is the *reciprocal* of the parameter:

$$E(T) = \frac{1}{\alpha}$$

Recall also from Section 5.5 that T has the *lack of memory* or *aging property* [and exponentially distributed random variables are the *only* continuous random variables concentrated on $(0, \infty)$ that do]. This property states that regardless of how old the component is, it operates as though brand new; mathematically,

$$P(T > t + s \mid T > t) = P(T > s)$$

for times $t, s \geqslant 0$. Recall also that

$$P(T > t) = e^{-\alpha t}$$

for $t \geqslant 0$.

11.1 TWO FACTS ABOUT THE EXPONENTIAL DISTRIBUTION

We will extensively use two additional results not proved in Chapter 5. Suppose that $T_1, T_2, \ldots, T_n$ are independent, each exponentially distributed, but possibly with different parameters. Suppose that T_i has parameter α_i. Think of n components all plugged in at time $t = 0$; T_i is the lifetime of the ith component. Let M be the minimum of all the T_i's. Thus M is the time that the first component fails. M is itself a random variable. Let $t \geqslant 0$. Then $M = \text{Min }\{T_1, \ldots, T_n\}$ is larger than t if and only if every $T_i > t$. Thus

$$P(M > t) = P(\text{Min }\{T_1, \ldots, T_n\} > t)$$

$$= P(T_1 > t \quad \text{and} \quad T_2 > t \quad \text{and} \quad \cdots \quad \text{and} \quad T_n > t)$$

$$= P(T_1 > t) \cdot P(t_2 > t) \cdots P(T_n > t)$$

$$= e^{-\alpha_1 t} \, e^{-\alpha_2 t} \cdots e^{-\alpha_n t}$$

$$= \exp\left(-(\alpha_1 + \alpha_2 + \cdots + \alpha_n)t\right)$$

Note that the third equality follows by independence. The last expression shows that M is exponentially distributed, so we have proved

---

Fact 1

$M = \text{Min}\{T_1, \ldots, T_n\}$ is *exponentially distributed* with parameter $\alpha_1 + \alpha_2 + \cdots + \alpha_n$ and mean $1/(\alpha_1 + \alpha_2 + \cdots + \alpha_n)$.

In words, the minimum of n independent exponentially distributed random variables is exponentially distributed with parameter equal to the sum of the individual parameters.

Example 1

Assume that a machine needs three parts, which must be operating simultaneously. Each has an exponentially distributed lifetime with mean 2 days. The machine arrives with three installed parts plus one spare. What is the expected time until the spare needs to be installed? What is the expected time until the machine breaks down because of a lack of parts?

Solution The lifetime of the equipment before failure is the *minimum* of three exponentially distributed random variables each with *parameter* 1/2. Hence by Fact 1 the lifetime of the equipment is exponentially distributed with *parameter*

$$\frac{1}{2} + \frac{1}{2} + \frac{1}{2} = \frac{3}{2}$$

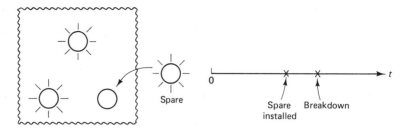

Figure 11.1

and *mean* 2/3. This is the mean time until the spare needs to be installed. Once the spare is installed, because of the lack of memory property, the original two operate as brand new. Hence the time until one of the three wears out (the original two and the spare) is again exponentially distributed with mean 2/3. Thus the expected lifetime of the machine is $2 \cdot (2/3) = 4/3$. (see Fig. 11.1) ■

Fact 1 shows that the time until the first burnout is exponentially distributed with parameter equal to the sum of the individual parameters. Let us now ask for the probability that *when* the first burnout occurs, it is the jth component. That is, we are asking for the probability that among the n T_i's, the *minimum* is T_j.

Fact 2

$$P(T_j = \text{Min}\{T_1, T_2, \ldots, T_n\})$$

$$= \frac{\alpha_j}{\alpha_1 + \alpha_2 + \cdots + \alpha_n}$$

Example 2

Consider a system consisting of two components; the first has mean lifetime 2 months, the second 7 months. If they operate independently each with an exponential distribution, what is the probability that the second breaks before the first?

Solution Here T_1 has parameter 1/2 and T_2 has parameter 1/7. We are asking for the probability that $T_2 < T_1$, which is to say that T_2 is the *minimum* of the two. Hence

$$P(T_2 < T_1) = P(T_2 = \text{Min}\{T_1, T_2\})$$

$$= \frac{1/7}{1/2 + 1/7}$$

$$= \frac{2}{9}$$

Note that this makes sense because it is intuitively reasonable that the odds in favor of the second breaking before the first is 2:7. This does not prove that the result is true, but it reinforces its plausibility. ∎

Example 3

Incoming calls at a business form a Poisson stream. Assume that correct calls arrive at the rate of 1.5 per minute, but wrong numbers at the rate of 1 per half hour, on the average. What is the probability that the first call after noon will be a wrong number?

Solution The time T_1 until the first correct number is exponentially distributed with parameter 1.5. The time T_2 until the first wrong number is also exponentially distributed; the parameter is 1/30 in terms of minutes. Thus Fact 2 implies that

$$P(\text{first call after noon is a wrong number})$$
$$= P(T_2 = \text{Min } \{T_1, T_2\})$$
$$= \frac{1/30}{1.5 + 1/30}$$
$$= 1/46 \quad \blacksquare$$

Proof of Fact 2. The proof is a good review of the joint distribution methods of Chapter 8. Suppose that T_1, T_2 are independent, each exponentially distributed with respective parameters α and β. The joint density function is therefore the product

$$h(s, t) = \alpha e^{-\alpha s} \beta e^{-\beta t}$$

for $s, t > 0$. With s and t, respectively, corresponding to the values of T_1 and T_2, Fig. 11.2 shows that

$$P(T_1 = \text{Min}\{T_1, T_2\}) = P(T_1 \leq T_2)$$
$$= \iint_A h(s,t) \, ds \, dt$$
$$= \int_0^\infty \int_0^t \alpha e^{-\alpha s} \beta e^{-\beta t} \, ds \, dt$$
$$= \int_0^\infty (1 - e^{-\alpha t}) \beta e^{-\beta t} \, dt$$
$$= 1 - \frac{\beta}{\alpha + \beta}$$
$$= \frac{\alpha}{\alpha + \beta}$$

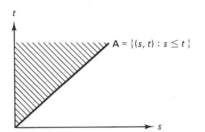

$A = \{(s, t) : s \le t\}$

Figure 11.2

which proves Fact 2 for $n = 2$ random variables. The general case involves no more calculation: Suppose that there are n independent random variables $T_1, \ldots, T_n$. Then $M = \mathrm{Min}\{T_2, \ldots, T_n\}$ is itself *exponentially distributed* with parameter $\alpha_2 + \cdots + \alpha_n$ by Fact 1; M is also independent of T_1. Why? Therefore, by the result that we have just shown for two random variables,

$$P(T_1 = \mathrm{Min}\{T_1, \ldots, T_n\}) = P(T_1 = \mathrm{Min}\{T_1, M\})$$

$$= \frac{\alpha_1}{\alpha_1 + \alpha_2 + \cdots + \alpha_n}$$

Using arbitrary j rather than $j = 1$ proves Fact 2 in general. ∎

PROBLEMS

11.1. A certain piece of equipment needs three parts. Each part lasts for a time that is exponentially distributed; the first part has mean lifetime 3 days, the second 4 days, and the third 5 days. Assume that their lifetimes are independent. **(a)** What is the distribution until the time of first failure? **(b)** What is the probability that the second part wears out before either of the other two?

11.2. Assume that bus arrivals form a Poisson stream. Buses to White Plains arrive every 15 minutes, on the average, but buses to Chappaqua arrive every 25 minutes on the average. Let T be the waiting time until a bus of either type arrives after you arrive at the bus stop. **(a)** What is the distribution of T? **(b)** What is the probability that the next bus to arrive is a White Plains bus?

11.3. Let T_1, T_2 be uniformly distributed on the interval $[0, 1]$. Let $Z = \mathrm{Min}\{T_1, T_2\}$. Show that Z is *not* uniformly distributed by computing the density function for Z.

11.4. Let T_1, T_2 be independent, each exponentially distributed with respective parameters α and β. Find $P(\mathrm{Max}\{T_1, T_2\} \le t)$ and use this expression to find the density function for $\mathrm{Max}\{T_1, T_2\}$. Is the maximum exponentially distributed?

11.2 THE BIRTH AND DEATH PROCESS IN CONTINUOUS TIME

Consider a machine that can be in any one of a number of states at each instant of time $t \ge 0$. The set of possible states, the *state space* S, will always be *discrete*. For definiteness, S will be taken to be $\{0, 1, 2, \ldots, N\}$, although $S = \{0, 1, 2,$

. . .} in several important examples. At time t the state of the machine is denoted X_t.

For example, X_t could denote the number of animals at a watering hole. Here the "machine" consists of the watering hole together with the animals. The state of the machine is the number X_t of animals at time t. Thus $X_t \in \{0, 1, 2, \dots\}$ for each $t \geq 0$. The arrival of an animal at time t_0 will increase X_t by 1 at t_0; the departure of an animal will decrease X_t.

The *stochastic process* $\{X_t\}_{t=0}^{\infty}$ is a complete record of the states occupied by the machine for all times $t \geq 0$. (see Fig. 11.3) Here are the assumptions of a **birth and death process**: If at time t the machine is in state i, it remains in state i for a random time that is *exponentially distributed* with parameter Ω_i; thus the expected waiting time in state i is the reciprocal $1/\Omega_i$. Ω_i can depend on the state i, but it does *not* depend on any other features; for example, Ω_i does not depend on whether the machine was last in state k or state j. State i might be *absorbing*: This means that once the machine enters state i, it stays there forever. (Perhaps state i corresponds to "broken beyond repair.") If this is so, then $\Omega_i = 0$; that is, the expected waiting time in state i is $1/\Omega_i = \infty$.

The second assumption of a birth and death process is that *when* the machine shifts out of state i, it shifts to either state $i + 1$ or to state $i - 1$ with probabilities that do *not* depend on how long the machine occupied state i or on other details such as the time t or on the state of the machine before it shifted into state i. Set

$$p_i = P(\text{next state is } i + 1 \mid \text{last state was } i)$$

$$q_i = 1 - p_i = P(\text{next state is } i - 1 \mid \text{last state was } i)$$

The second assumption is that p_i and q_i depend *only* on the state i and not on any other details of the process.

These two assumptions embody a generalization of the lack of memory property. *Given* the present state X_t of the system at time t, the future states of the machine do *not* depend on the past states. In particular, if the state at time t is $X_t = i$, then whether the machine has been in state i for several years or whether it just shifted into state i is completely irrelevant to predicting *when* it will next shift out of state i. This is so since the times spent in each state are exponentially distributed. Since the exponential distribution obeys the lack of memory property, the machine behaves as though it has just shifted into state i regardless of how

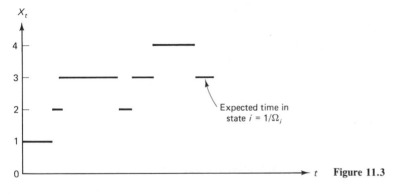

Figure 11.3

long it has actually occupied state i. The exponential distribution is the *only* continuous distribution concentrated on $(0, \infty)$ for the waiting times that has this property. The assumption that *given* the present state, the future of the process is independent of the past is called the **Markov assumption**. (In Chapter 12 we consider the discrete analog in considerable detail.)

Note that if $\Omega_i = 0$ for state i, then the values of p_i, q_i are unnecessary to specify since the machine can *never* shift out of state i once entered.

> A *birth and death process in continuous time* consists of a machine that can shift between states in a state space S. X_t denotes the state occupied at time t for $t \geq 0$. The machine remains in state i (the *waiting* or *sojourn time*) for a period of time that is exponentially distributed with parameter Ω_i (expected waiting time $1/\Omega_i$). When the machine shifts, it shifts to states $i + 1, i - 1$ with respective probabilities p_i, $q_i = 1 - p_i$.

Example 4

The very simplest example of a birth and death process in continuous time is in fact defined by the exponential distribution. Suppose that T denotes the lifetime of a component that is exponentially distributed with parameter α. Let $S = \{0, 1\}$. The state of the machine is 1 as long as the component is operational. Once the component fails, the machine shifts into state 0, there to remain forever. (see Fig. 11.4) Thus

$$\Omega_0 = 0 \qquad \Omega_1 = \alpha \qquad p_1 = 0 \qquad q_1 = 1$$

Note that state 0 is absorbing. Note also that p_1 must be zero; otherwise, there would be a positive probability of shifting into state 2. ∎

Example 5

The Poisson process can be seen as an example of a birth and death process. Let X_t denote the number of arrivals in the time interval $[0, t]$. Recall that X_t is Poisson distributed with parameter λt and that the interarrival times are exponentially distributed with the same parameter λ.

$$P(X_t = i) = \frac{(\lambda t)^i}{i!} e^{-\lambda t}$$

$$P(\text{interarrival time} > s) = e^{-\lambda s}$$

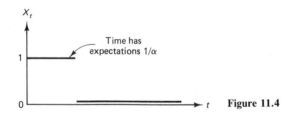

Continuous-Time Birth and Death Processes   Chap. 11

The "machine" is said to be in state i at time t if $X_t = i$—if i calls have arrived in $[0, t]$. As soon as another call arrives, the machine shifts into state $i + 1$. Thus the waiting time in state i is the interarrival time between the ith and the $(i + 1)$st arrival; this is exponentially distributed with parameter λ. Therefore,

$$\Omega_i = \lambda \qquad p_i = 1 \qquad q_i = 0$$

for all i in the state space $S = \{0, 1, 2, \ldots\}$ Note that this is a **pure birth process** since the machine can never shift downward: $p_i = 1$ for all i. ■

Example 6: *The Two-State Device*

The machine is *on* or *operational* for a time that is exponentially distributed with parameter α (mean lifetime $1/\alpha$) and *off* or *down* for a time that is exponentially distributed with parameter β (mean fix-it time $1/\beta$). For example, the machine needs a part that has an exponentially distributed lifetime; once it burns out, the fix-it time is the time required to install a new part. The state space is $S = \{0, 1\}$ with 0, 1 corresponding respectively to off, on. Then

$$\Omega_0 = \beta \qquad p_0 = 1 \qquad q_0 = 0$$

$$\Omega_1 = \alpha \qquad p_1 = 0 \qquad q_1 = 1 \quad ■$$

11.3 QUEUES

Queues are a very important subclass of birth and death processes. Here the "machine" consists of customers and servers (cars pulling up to toll booths, customers at a grocery checkout counter, children lining up at an arcade game, airplanes circling an airport waiting to land, . . .) (see Fig. 11.5) There may be one or more servers. *Customers are assumed to arrive according to a Poisson stream with parameter* λ. That is, λ customers arrive, on the average, per unit time. Service times are random, but are assumed to be exponentially distributed with parameter ν. Thus the mean service time is $1/\nu$. Let X_t denote the length of the queue at time t; this is the number of customers *including* the one (or more than one if there is more than one server) being serviced at time t. Then the stochastic process $\{X_t\}_{t=0}^{\infty}$ is a birth and death process. To see this note that both the incoming

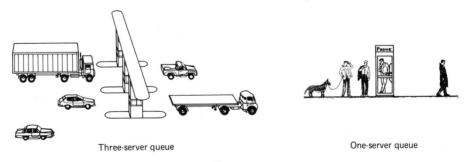

Three-server queue   One-server queue

Figure 11.5

stream of customers as well as the outgoing stream of customers who have finished service obey the lack of memory property. Whether another customer joins the queue is independent of the number of customers in line or of any past details about the queue; since the service times are exponentially distributed, whether a customer finishes service in some period of time is independent of any details of the history of the queue, including how long that customer has been receiving service.

Example 7: *The One-Server Queue*

Suppose that there is one checkout counter at the grocery store and, as above, the incoming customers form a Poisson stream with parameter λ and the service time is exponentially distributed with parameter v. The state X_t at time t is the length of the queue. Thus $S = \{0, 1, 2, \ldots\}$. A shift from 0 customers to 1 customer occurs at a random time exponentially distributed with parameter λ. Thus

$$\Omega_0 = \lambda \qquad p_0 = 1$$

If the state at time t is $X_t = i \geq 1$, a shift to *either* state $i - 1$ or to $i + 1$ can occur. Let T be the arrival time of the next customer and S be the service time of the customer presently receiving service. Then T and S are independent, and each is exponentially distributed with respective parameters λ and v. A shift occurs out of state i at time equal to Min $\{T, S\}$. By Fact 1 in Section 11.1, Min $\{T, S\}$ is exponentially distributed with parameter $\lambda + v$. A shift occurs to state $i + 1$ if $T = $ Min $\{T, S\}$; by Fact 2 this occurs with probability $\lambda/(\lambda + v)$. Similarly, the shift is to $i - 1$ customers if $S = $ Min $\{T, S\}$, which occurs with probability $v/(\lambda + v)$ by Fact 2. To summarize:

> For the *One-Server Queue*,
>
> $$\Omega_0 = \lambda \qquad p_0 = 1$$
>
> $$\Omega_i = \lambda + v \qquad p_i = \frac{\lambda}{\lambda + v} \qquad q_i = \frac{v}{\lambda + v}$$
>
> for $i \geq 1$.

∎

Example 8: *The ∞- Server Queue*

Now suppose that customers arrive according to a Poisson stream with parameter λ as in the one-server queue, but each customer receives *instant service*, although the service time is still exponentially distributed with parameter v. That is, there are *infinitely many* checkout counters in the grocery store. More realistically, the customers could be "self-servicing"; for example, picnickers arrive at a park at the rate of λ per hour; they remain a random length of time, then leave. As in the one-server queue, $\Omega_0 = \lambda$. If there are i customers at time t, they are each receiving service. Let their respective service times be $S_1, \ldots, S_i$. Let T be the time of arrival of the next customer. Then a shift out of state i occurs at time equal to Min $\{S_1, \ldots, S_i, T\}$. Since each S_j is exponentially distributed with parameter v and T is exponentially distributed with parameter λ, the time to shift from state i

is exponentially distributed with parameter equal to the sum $v + \cdots + v + \lambda = iv + \lambda$. The shift will be to $i + 1$ customers if $T = \text{Min } \{S_1, \ldots, S_i, T\}$. By Fact 2 the probability of this is the ratio $\lambda/(iv + \lambda)$. The shift will be to $i - 1$ customers if *any one* of the i customers finishes service. The probability that the jth customer finishes before the others and also before an arrival is $v/(iv + \lambda)$ by Fact 2. *Any* of the i customers could finish for the shift to be to $i - 1$ customers. Thus the probability of a shift to $i - 1$ is $iv/(iv + \lambda)$. [Note that this can be obtained as $1 - \lambda/(iv + \lambda)$.] To summarize:

For the ∞-*Server Queue*

$$\Omega_0 = \lambda \qquad p_0 = 1$$

$$\Omega_i = iv + \lambda \qquad p_i = \frac{\lambda}{iv + \lambda} \qquad q_i = \frac{iv}{iv + \lambda}$$

for $i \geq 1$.

■

Example 9

A business office has a phone with a hold button. Assume that incoming calls form a Poisson stream with parameter λ. Also assume that each call takes an exponentially distributed time with average $1/v$ minutes. If a call arrives during a time the phone is busy, it is placed on hold. If another call arrives, it receives a busy tone and must hang up. Let the state of the system be the number of calls either receiving service or on hold. What are the parameters Ω_i and the transition probabilities p_i, q_i?

Solution The state space is $S = \{0, 1, 2\}$. A shift from state 0 to state 1 occurs with the arrival of a call. Thus

$$\Omega_0 = \lambda \qquad p_0 = 1$$

If the state is 2, a shift occurs to state 1 as soon as the call receiving service finishes. Thus

$$\Omega_2 = v \qquad q_2 = 1$$

If the state is 1, a shift occurs if *either* another call arrives (exponentially distributed with parameter λ) *or* the call being serviced finishes (exponentially distributed with parameter v). By Facts 1 and 2 as in Examples 7 and 8,

$$\Omega_1 = \lambda + v \qquad p_1 = \frac{\lambda}{\lambda + v} \qquad q_1 = \frac{v}{\lambda + v} \qquad ■$$

Example 10 (*Continuation*)

Suppose that the office has two phones neither of which has a hold button. If a call arrives while one phone is busy, the call is answered by the other phone. The state is the number of phones currently busy. Now what are the parameters Ω_i and the transition probabilities p_i, q_i?

Solution Ω_0, p_0, Ω_1, p_1, and q_1 are the same as in the previous example. Why? If the state is 2, both lines are busy. A shift into state 1 occurs with the termination of one of the two calls. This time is the *minimum* of the two service times. Since each is exponentially distributed with parameter v, Fact 1 implies that the minimum is exponentially distributed with parameter $v + v = 2v$. Thus

$$\Omega_2 = 2v \qquad q_2 = 1 \quad \blacksquare$$

Finding Ω_i, p_i, and q_i for a Queue

First represent the waiting time in state i as Min $\{S, T, U, \ldots\}$, where S, T, U, $\ldots$ are independent, each exponentially distributed (they are either arrival times or service times.) Then

Ω_i = sum of all the parameters,

p_i = sum of arrival time parameters divided by Ω_i, and

q_i = sum of service time parameters divided by Ω_i.

Example 11: *The Two-Server Queue*

Arrivals form a Poisson stream with parameter λ. There is one line formed, but *two* servers. Each service time is exponentially distributed with parameter v. When a customer completes service, a customer from the one line begins service and the queue becomes one less. What are S, Ω_i, p_i, and q_i?

Solution S is the number of customers in line *or* receiving service. Thus $S = \{0, 1, 2, \ldots\}$. Let $i \geq 2$. Then *both* servers are busy and the waiting time in state i is Min $\{S_1, S_2, T\}$, where S_1, S_2 are the respective service times for servers 1, 2; T is the arrival time for a new customer. S_1, S_2, T are each exponentially distributed with respective parameters v, v, λ. By the foregoing method,

$$\Omega_i = 2 \cdot v + \lambda \qquad p_i = \frac{\lambda}{2v + \lambda} \qquad q_i = \frac{2v}{2v + \lambda}$$

for $i \geq 2$. If $i = 1$, the waiting time in state $i = 1$ is Min $\{S, T\}$, where S is the *one* service time of the one customer receiving service. Thus, as before,

$$\Omega_1 = v + \lambda \qquad p_1 = \frac{\lambda}{v + \lambda} \qquad q_1 = \frac{v}{v + \lambda}$$

Finally, the waiting time in state 0 is the time T of arrival (or Min $\{T\}$); thus

$$\Omega_0 = \lambda \qquad p_0 = 1 \quad \blacksquare$$

Before leaving this section, let us emphasize that in a queue *only one* shift can occur at a time. For example, in the ∞-server queue, if there are 100 customers currently receiving service, a shift to either 101 customers or to 99 customers only can occur at one time. To see this, let (as above) $S_1, \ldots, S_{100}$ be the respective service times of the customers and T be the arrival time of the next customer.

Since each S_j and T are exponentially distributed, they are continuous random variables. The probability that any two of them have the same value is 0. But this would have to be the case for more than one shift to occur at the same time.

> In a queue, only one shift can occur at a time.

Here is a program to simulate the one-server queue. Inputs are LAMBDA (for λ), NU (for ν), the initial length of the queue QUEUE, and the total time for the simulation TMAX. Outputs are the length QUEUE of the queue every time a change in the length occurs. The waiting time in state i is exponentially distributed with parameter OMEGA (for Ω). OMEGA = L if $i = 0$ and LAMBDA + NU if $i > 0$. An exponentially distributed random variable with parameter OMEGA is generated (see Chapter 7, Example 15) and added to TIME. This is the time that the queue changes. If the length QUEUE > 0, another random number is generated to determine whether a customer arrives or one departs [with respective probabilities LAMBDA/(LAMBDA + NU) and NU/(LAMBDA + NU)]. The length QUEUE of the queue is printed every time it changes.

```
const NORM = 10000;
      ADDR = 4857;
      MULT = 8601;
var QUEUE,SEED: integer;
    RND,TMAX,LAMDBA,NU,OMEGA,TIME: real;

begin
    readln(LAMBDA,NU,QUEUE,TMAX);

    TIME: = 0.0; SEED: = 0;

    while TIME < TMAX do
        begin
            SEED: = (MULT*SEED + ADDR) mod NORM;
            RND: = SEED/NORM;

            if QUEUE = 0 then OMEGA: = LAMBDA
                         else OMEGA: = LAMBDA+NU;

            TIME: = TIME − ln(1-RND)/OMEGA;

            if QUEUE = 0
                then QUEUE: = 1
                else begin
                        SEED: = (MULT*SEED + ADDR) mod NORM;
                        RND: = SEED/NORM;
                        if RND< LAMBDA/OMEGA then QUEUE: = QUEUE+1
                                             else QUEUE: = QUEUE -1;
                    end;
            writeln(TIME:10:4,QUEUE);
        end;
    end.
```

PROBLEMS

11.5. A radio uses one battery. Assume that the battery lifetime is exponentially distributed with parameter β. When the battery dies, another is bought, but the buying time is exponentially distributed with parameter α. Let the state of the system be either 0 (for no good batteries) or 1 (for 1 good battery) so that $S = \{0, 1\}$. What are the parameters Ω_i and the transition probabilities p_i, q_i for $i =$ **(a)** 0; **(b)** 1?

11.6. There are two machines and one repair person. The *state is the number of functioning machines*. Each machine operates for an exponentially distributed time with mean $1/\alpha$. After breakdown the machine goes to the shop. The fix-it time is exponentially distributed with parameter β, but if both are broken, the second machine must wait until the first is fixed before receiving service. With $S = \{0, 1, 2\}$, what are the parameters Ω_i and the transition probabilities p_i, q_i?

11.7. (*Continuation*) Suppose that there are two repair people so that each machine gets instant service regardless of whether the other is broken or not. Now what are the Ω_i's, p_i's, and q_i's?

11.8. Solve Example 9 except now assume that there are two hold buttons, so that the number of people either being serviced or waiting is either 0, 1, 2, or 3. When a call terminates, one of the calls on hold begins service (if there are any); if there are two on hold, the other remains on hold.

11.9. Solve Example 10 except now assume that there are three rather than two phones.

11.10. An ornament consists of N light bulbs. Each is on for an exponentially distributed length of time with mean $1/\alpha$; each is off an exponentially distributed length of time with mean $1/\beta$. Assume that the light bulbs operate independently of each other. Let the state of the system X_t at time t be the number of lit bulbs. What is the state space S? Use Fact 1 to find the expected length of time that state i is occupied. What are Ω_i, p_i, and q_i?

11.11. A parking lot has N spaces. The incoming traffice forms a Poisson stream with parameter λ, but only as long as spaces are available. Each car remains in its spot a time that is exponentially distributed with parameter v. Let X_t be the number of occupied spots at time t. What are S, Ω_i, p_i, and q_i?

11.12. Generalize Problem 11.6 to the case of N machines and one repair person.

11.13. Write a computer simulation for the two-state device of Example 6. Inputs should be A (for α), B (for β), and TMAX. Start at time 0 in state 1. Then generate successive on and off times and output them until the total time $\geq$ TMAX.

11.14. Write a simulation for the infinite server queue. Input L (for λ), NU (for v), the initial length of the QUEUE, and the total time TMAX. Output the length of the queue every time it changes.

11.15. Write a simulation for the two-server queue. Output should be as in Problem 11.14.

11.4 THE STEADY-STATE PROBABILITY VECTOR

After the birth and death process evolves for some time, one expects stability to set in. This means that the state of the machine becomes less and less dependent on the initial state X_0 of the machine at time 0. The machine will still be shifting states, but there will be a well-defined probability ϕ_i with which the machine is in state i.

Throughout this section we assume that the state space S is either the finite set $S = \{0, 1, 2, \ldots, N\}$ or the countably infinite set $S = \{0, 1, 2, \ldots\}$. At time 0 the birth and death process starts in a certain state X_0. X_0 may be completely determined or it may be known only up to probabilities. Let $\rho_i = P(X_0 = i)$ for all $i \in S$. If X_0 is known to be some specific state k, then $\rho_k = 1$ and $\rho_i = 0$ for $i \neq k$.

A **probability vector** $\rho = (\rho_0, \rho_1, \rho_2, \ldots)$ on the state space S satisfies

1. $0 \leqslant \rho_i \leqslant 1$ for all $i \leqslant S$.
2. $\displaystyle\sum_{i \in S} \rho_i = 1$.

Note that Property 2 must hold for an *initial probability vector* ρ with $\rho_i = P(X_0 = i)$ since the process must start *somewhere* at time 0.

Mathematically, the steady state means exactly this: Regardless of the initial probability vector ρ at time 0,

$$P(X_t = i \mid \text{initial vector } \rho) \to \phi_i$$

as $t \to \infty$ for *each* state i. In words, this means that the machine settles down into the various states with probabilities given by the vector $\phi = (\phi_0, \phi_1, \ldots, \phi_N)$. During the first few minutes after the grocery store opens, the fact that the checkout counters were empty at 8:00 is important to predicting the number of customers in line, but as the day progresses, this fact has less and less influence on the actual numbers in line. Intuitively, one expects a certain probability ϕ_i of i customers for times late in the day regardless of the number in line at the start.

In general, ϕ is a vector of probabilities that specifies how likely the machine is to be in the various states when all the particularities of the initial probability vector ρ at time 0 have been swamped by the effects of randomness as the machine evolves in time.

In fact, there are birth and death processes that do not have such a steady state of probabilities. But let us now *assume* that ϕ exists and derive formulas it must satisfy. Later we present conditions for the existence of ϕ.

The *waiting* or *sojourn time* in state i is exponentially distributed with parameter Ω_i. Let $f_i(t) = \Omega_i e^{-\Omega_i t}$ for $t > 0$ be the density for this waiting time. Therefore, the machine will shift *out of* state i in a time interval of length Δt with probability

$$P(\text{shift out of } i \text{ in } [t, t + \Delta t) \mid \text{in state } i \text{ at time } t)$$

$$= P(\text{shift out of } i \text{ in } [0, \Delta t) \mid \text{in state } i \text{ at time } 0)$$

$$= \int_0^{\Delta t} f_i(t) \, dt$$

$$= 1 - e^{-\Omega_i \Delta t}$$

$$= 1 - \left(1 + \Omega_i \, \Delta t + \frac{(\Omega_i \, \Delta t)^2}{2!} + \cdots \right)$$

$$\cong \Omega_i \, \Delta t$$

for small Δt. The first equality uses the lack of memory property of the exponential distribution: *Given* that the machine is in state i, whether it shifts out in the next Δt time units does not depend on how long it has been there. The third equality is a straightforward integration. The next-to-last equality uses the Taylor series expansion of the exponential function. The conclusion is that the probability that the machine will shift out of state i during the next Δt time units is approximately $\Omega_i \Delta t$ for $\Delta t \cong 0$.

Suppose that there is a large number of machines each shifting states according to the same parameters Ω_i and transition probabilities p_i, q_i for $i \in S$. Suppose that n_i of these machines are in state i. Then approximately $n_i \Omega_i \, \Delta t$ will shift *out of* state i during the next Δt time units. Where will they shift *into*? A fraction p_i will shift into state $i + 1$ and fraction q_i into $i - 1$. Thus the approximate number of machines that shift *from* state i *into* state $i - 1$ at time t during the next Δt time units is $n_i \Omega_i \, \Delta t q_i$. In the steady state this number must be balanced by an equivalent number of machines shifting up from state $i - 1$ into state i. This must be the case since otherwise numbers of machines would be accumulating on one side or the other of state i. For similar reasons, the number of machines shifting from $i - 1$ to i at time t during the next Δt time units is $n_{i-1} \Omega_{i-1} \, \Delta t \, p_{i-1}$. In the steady state,

$$n_i \Omega_i \, \Delta t \, q_i \cong n_{i-1} \Omega_{i-1} \, \Delta t \, p_{i-1}$$

Assume that there is a large number n of machines. Then the probability that any one of them is in state i is $n_i / n = \phi_i$. Dividing the equation above by n and canceling Δt implies that the steady-state probabilities ϕ_i satisfy

$$\phi_i \Omega_i q_i = \phi_{i-1} \Omega_{i-1} p_{i-1}$$

for $i = 1, 2, \ldots$.

Example 12

Consider the two-state device of Example 6. For $i = 1$ the equation above is

$$\phi_1 \, \Omega_1 \, q_1 = \phi_0 \, \Omega_0 \, p_0$$

$$\phi_1 \alpha = \phi_0 \beta$$

This is one equation in the two unknowns ϕ_0 and ϕ_1. The other equation is the *normalization* that must be satisfied by any probability vector:

$$1 = \phi_0 + \phi_1 = \phi_0 \left(1 + \frac{\beta}{\alpha} \right)$$

Thus

$$\phi_0 = \frac{\alpha}{\alpha + \beta} \qquad \phi_1 = \frac{\beta}{\alpha + \beta} \qquad \blacksquare$$

In summarizing, assume that the state space is $S = \{0, 1, \ldots , N\}$ or $S = \{0, 1, 2, \ldots\}$. Assume also that no state is absorbing and that it is possible to reach every state from every other state; that is, assume that

$$p_0 = 1$$

$$0 < p_i < 1 \qquad \text{for } i \in S, i > 0$$

$$q_N = 1 \qquad \text{if } S = \{0, \ldots , N\}$$

$$\Omega_i > 0 \qquad \text{for } i \in S$$

Finding the Steady-State Probability Vector for a Birth and Death Process

Use the recursive formula

$$\phi_i = \frac{\Omega_{i-1}p_{i-1}}{\Omega_i q_i} \phi_{i-1}$$

for $i = 1, 2, \ldots$ to express each ϕ_i in terms of ϕ_0. Then use normalization

$$\sum_i \phi_i = 1$$

Example 13

Solve for the steady-state probabilities ϕ_0, ϕ_1, ϕ_2 for the phone with a hold button of Example 9. Find the expected number of people on the line or on hold in the steady state.

Solution Using the recursive formula with the values of the parameters Ω_i and the transition probabilities p_i, q_i for $i = 0, 1, 2$ yields

$$\phi_1 = \frac{\Omega_0 p_0}{\Omega_1 q_1}\phi_0 = \frac{\lambda \cdot 1}{(\lambda + \nu)\nu/(\lambda + \nu)}\phi_0 = \frac{\lambda}{\nu}\phi_0$$

$$\phi_2 = \frac{\Omega_1 p_1}{\Omega_2 q_2}\phi_1 = \frac{(\lambda + \nu)\lambda/(\lambda + \nu)}{\nu \cdot 1}\phi_1 = \frac{\lambda}{\nu}\phi_1 = \left(\frac{\lambda}{\nu}\right)^2\phi_0$$

Now use normalization:

$$1 = \phi_0 + \phi_1 + \phi_2 = \phi_0\left(1 + \frac{\lambda}{\nu} + \left(\frac{\lambda}{\nu}\right)^2\right) = \frac{\phi_0(\lambda^2 + \lambda\nu + \nu^2)}{\nu^2}$$

Therefore,

$$\phi_0 = \frac{v^2}{C} \qquad \phi_1 = \frac{\lambda v}{C} \qquad \phi_2 = \frac{\lambda^2}{C}$$

where $C = (\lambda^2 + \lambda v + v^2)$. There are i people with probability ϕ_i in the steady state. Thus the expected number is

$$0\phi_0 + 1\phi_1 + 2\phi_2 = \frac{\lambda v + 2\lambda^2}{C} \qquad \blacksquare$$

Example 14

Solve for the steady-state probability vector ϕ for the one-server queue of Example 7.

Solution Using the values of Ω_i, p_i, and q_i from that example, check that

$$\Omega_{i-1}p_{i-1} = \lambda \qquad \Omega_i q_i = v$$

for every $i \geq 1$. Thus

$$\phi_i = \frac{\Omega_{i-1}p_{i-1}}{\Omega_i q_i}\phi_{i-1} = \frac{\lambda}{v}\phi_{i-1}$$

Thus

$$\phi_i = \frac{\lambda}{v}\phi_{i-1} = \left(\frac{\lambda}{v}\right)^2 \phi_{i-2} = \cdots = \left(\frac{\lambda}{v}\right)^i \phi_0$$

for $i = 0, 1, 2, \ldots$. Normalization implies that

$$1 = \sum_{i=0}^{\infty} \phi_i = \phi_0 \sum_{i=0}^{\infty} \left(\frac{\lambda}{v}\right)^i = \phi_0 \frac{1}{1 - \lambda/v}$$

for $\lambda/v < 1$. If $\lambda/v \geq 1$, the normalization condition cannot be met. This means that there is no steady-state probability vector. (see Fig. 11.6)

For the one-server queue:

1. If $\lambda < v$, the steady-state probabilities are

$$\phi_i = \left(1 - \frac{\lambda}{v}\right)\left(\frac{\lambda}{v}\right)^i$$

for $i = 0, 1, 2, \ldots$.

2. If $\lambda \geq v$, the queue tends to become longer and longer without reaching a steady state.

In case 2 the queue becomes longer and longer, but not necessarily uniformly. There may be periods of time where the queue becomes shorter, but eventually

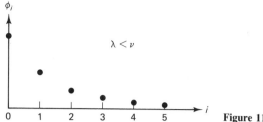

Figure 11.6

the queue will become larger than any prespecified length. The result is certainly plausible: For a steady state to exist, the departure rate ν must be greater than the arrival rate λ. ∎

Example 15

For the one-server queue with $\lambda < \nu$, find the expected length of the queue in the steady state.

Solution In the steady state the length L of the queue is i with probability ϕ_i for $i = 0, 1, 2, \ldots$. Note that the random variable $X = L + 1$ is *geometrically distributed*: For $j \geqslant 1$,

$$P(X = j) = P(L = j - 1) = \phi_{j-1} = (1 - q)q^{j-1}$$

where $q = \lambda/\nu$. Thus (see Section 4.6)

$$E(X) = \frac{1}{1 - q} = \frac{1}{1 - \lambda/\nu} = \frac{\nu}{\nu - \lambda}$$

$$E(L) = E(X - 1) = E(X) - 1 = \frac{\lambda}{\nu - \lambda}$$

The expected length of the one-server queue for $\lambda < \nu$ is

$$\frac{\lambda}{\nu - \lambda}$$

Example 16

Solve for the steady-state probability vector ϕ for the ∞-server queue of Example 8.

Solution Using the values of Ω_i, p_i, and q_i from that example, check that

$$\Omega_{i-1}p_{i-1} = \frac{((i - 1)\nu + \lambda)\lambda}{(i - 1)\nu + \lambda} = \lambda$$

$$\Omega_i q_i = \frac{(i\nu + \lambda)i\nu}{i\nu + \lambda} = i\nu$$

Therefore,

$$\phi_i = \frac{\Omega_{i-1} p_{i-1}}{\Omega_i q_i} \phi_{i-1} = \frac{\lambda}{i\nu} \phi_{i-1}$$

for $i = 1, 2, \ldots$. Using this relation recursively implies

$$\phi_i = \frac{\lambda}{i\nu} \phi_{i-1}$$

$$= \frac{\lambda}{i\nu} \frac{\lambda}{(i-1)\nu} \phi_{i-2}$$

$$= \cdots$$

$$= \frac{1}{i!} \left(\frac{\lambda}{\nu}\right)^i \phi_0$$

Using normalization yields

$$1 = \sum_{i=0}^{\infty} \phi_i = \phi_0 \sum_{i=0}^{\infty} \frac{(\lambda/\nu)^i}{i!} = \phi_0 e^{\lambda/\nu}$$

Consequently,

$$\phi_0 = e^{-\lambda/\nu}$$

and

For the ∞-server queue the steady-state probabilities are

$$\phi_i = \frac{(\lambda/\nu)^i}{i!} e^{-\lambda/\nu}$$

for $i = 0, 1, 2, \ldots$.

(see Fig. 11.7) This distribution should be familiar: *The steady-state probabilities for the ∞-server queue are Poisson distributed with parameter λ/ν.* Consequently,

---

The expected length of the ∞-server queue is λ/ν.

Note that a steady state always exists; this makes sense because there are infinitely many servers. ∎

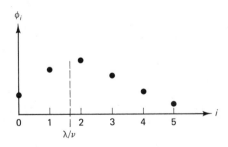

Figure 11.7

Example 17

For the ∞-server queue with arrival rate λ and mean service time $1/v$, find the smallest number N so that 90% of the time there will be N or fewer customers in the steady state.

Solution   In the steady state the probability of i customers is

$$\phi_i = \frac{(\lambda/v)^i}{i!} e^{-\lambda/v}$$

N is the smallest integer satisfying

$$\phi_0 + \phi_1 + \cdots + \phi_N \geq .90$$

or

$$\sum_{i=0}^{N} \frac{(\lambda/v)^i}{i!} \geq .90 e^{\lambda/v}$$

In the following program LAMBDA (for λ) and NU (for v) are input.

```
var LAMBDA,NU,SUM,NEXTERM: real;
    N: integer;

begin
    readln(LAMBDA,NU);

    N: = 0; SUM: = 1.0; NEXTERM: = 1.0;

    while SUM < 0.90*exp(LAMBDA/NU) do
        begin
            N: = N+1;
            NEXTTERM: = NEXTERM*LAMBDA/(NU*N);
            SUM: = SUM + NEXTERM;
        end;
    writeln(N);
end.
```

Note that the value of N depends *only* on the ratio λ/v and not on their individual values beyond this ratio.   With the following values of λ/v, these values of N were output:

λ/v	N
0.5	1
1	2
5	8
10	14
20	26
50	59
100	113

The result is surprising: The expected number of customers for the ∞-server queue is λ/ν, but only slightly more than this number of customers will be present 10% of the time. ∎

We have found conditions that the steady-state probability vector must satisfy. The following theorem is of considerable interest since it shows the *meaning* of the steady-state vector.

Limit Theorem

Suppose that

$$p_0 = 1$$

$$0 < p_i < 1 \quad \text{for} \quad i = 1, 2, \ldots$$

$$q_N = 1 \quad \text{if } S = \{0, 1, \ldots, N\}$$

$$\Omega_i > 0 \text{ for } i \in S$$

for the birth and death process. Suppose that ϕ is a probability vector satisfying

$$\phi_i = \frac{\Omega_{i-1} p_{i-1}}{\Omega_i q_i} \phi_{i-1}$$

for $i = 1, 2, \ldots.$ Then

1. Given any initial probability vector ρ,

$$P(X_t = i \mid \text{intial vector } \rho) \to \phi_i$$

as $t \to \infty$ for each $i \in S$.
2. If the initial probability vector is $\rho = \phi$, then

$$P(X_t = i \mid \text{initial vector } \phi) = \phi_i$$

for all $t \geq 0$ for each $i \in S$.

Result 1 states that regardless of the initial state at time 0, the machine will be found in state i with probability ϕ_i as the time t becomes large. Result 2 states that if ϕ is used as the initial probability vector, then ϕ will be the probability vector for all times $t \geq 0$. The conditions of the theorem on Ω_i, p_i, q_i are essential. They guarantee that no state is absorbing and that any state can be reached from any other state. For example, if $S = \{0, 1, 2, 3\}$ and $p_2 = 1, q_1 = 1$, the process would "decompose": If the machine starts in states 0 or 1, it will remain in these states forever; but if it starts in states 2 or 3, it will remain in *those* states forever.

The proof would take us too far afield; you can find it in several of the books listed in the Bibliography.

PROBLEMS

Solve for the steady-state probability vector φ for the birth and death processes of the following; also find the expectation $\Sigma\ i\phi_i$.

11.16. Example 10.

11.17. Problem 11.5.

11.18. Problem 11.6.

11.19. Problem 11.7.

11.20. Problem 11.8.

11.21. Problem 11.9.

11.22. Problem 11.10.

11.23. Problem 11.11.

11.24. Problem 11.12.

11.25. (*Saturation*) We have all experienced situations in which a store or highway is crowded, but traffic is still moving swiftly. But then an addition of only a few customers (or cars or whatever) jams up the entire system. In the one-server queue, graph the expected length of the queue as a function of $x = \lambda/v$. That is, graph the function $f(x) = x/(1 - x)$ for $0 \leqslant x < 1$. Saturation can be defined for the one-server queue as the case $\lambda \geqslant v$—the case in which the arrival rate is too large for a steady state to exist. What is the expected length of the queue for these ratios $x = \lambda/v$ of arrival to departure rates: **(a)** .9; **(b)** .95; **(c)** .99; **(d)** .999? Thus at near saturation level ($\lambda/v \cong 1$) a very *slight increase* in λ/v implies an *enormous* increase in the expected length of the queue.

11.26. For the one-server queue with $\lambda < v$, show that the probability of at least N customers in the steady state is $(\lambda/v)^N$. Given λ and v, find N so that 90% of the time there will be fewer than N customers.

11.27. (*Continuation of Problem 11.14*) Now output the fraction of the total time TMAX during which the length of the queue was i for $i = 0, 1, \ldots$ These should be close to the steady-state probabilities ϕ_i for large TMAX.

11.5 THE PURE DEATH PROCESS: SYSTEMS THAT AGE (OPTIONAL)

One drawback in using the exponential distribution to model the lifetime of a system is that it embodies the lack of aging property. In reality, most systems degrade with time and have a higher failure rate. In this section we show how a generalization of the exponential distribution—the pure death process—can be used to model complex systems.

Consider a system consisting of N identical components. They are all installed and begin operating at time $t = 0$. Let T_i be the lifetime of the ith component. Assume that $T_1, \ldots, \ldots, T_n$ are IIDRVs each exponentially distributed with parameter δ (mean lifetime $1/\delta$). The state of the system at time t is $X_t = $ number of operational components at time t. Thus $X_0 = N$ and X_t can only decrease with time. With fewer and fewer components operating, the system finally becomes absorbed in state 0. Here are two applications: First, consider a set of N dishes. As we saw in Section 5.5 the exponential distribution is a good model for the lifetime of each dish in the set. X_t then denotes the number of unbroken dishes t time units after buying the set. Another application is a movie marquee consisting of N light bulbs; X_t = number of operating bulbs at time t after the sign is first turned on.

This process is a **pure death process**: Since only a transition from i components operating to $i - 1$ operating is possible,

$$p_i = 0 \qquad q_i = 1$$

for $i = 1, 2, \ldots$. Note also that state 0 is absorbing. Ω_i is readily computed using Fact 1 of Section 11.1: If the system is in state i at time t, each of the i operating components behaves as brand new by the lack of aging property implied by the exponential distribution. Thus a transition to state $i - 1$ occurs at time Min $\{T_1, \ldots, T_i\}$, where T_j is the lifetime of component j. By Fact 1 this time is exponentially distributed with parameter equal to the sum $\delta + \cdots + \delta = i\delta$. Thus

$$\Omega_i = i\delta$$

for $i \geqslant 1$.

$$\Omega_0 = 0$$

(see Fig. 11.8)

Let U_i denote the time spent in state i for $i = N, N - 1, \ldots, 1$. Then U_i is exponentially distributed with parameter Ω_i. It is also true that $U_N, U_{N-1}, \ldots,$ U_1 are independent. This is so by the lack of aging property of the individual components: Once the system enters state i, the i components then operating continue to operate as though brand new. Hence the time U_i to shift to state $i - 1$ (the time of the first of the failures of the remaining i components) is independent of $U_N, \ldots, U_{i+1}$.

Let S_N = time for all components to burn out. Note that

$$S_N = \text{Max } \{T_1, \ldots, T_N\}$$

since the system goes dead when all the components have burned out (see Problems

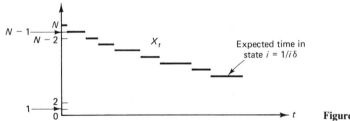

Expected time in state i = $1/i\delta$

Figure 11.8

Continuous-Time Birth and Death Processes   Chap. 11

11.28 and 29). Another expression for S_N is

$$S_N = U_1 + \cdots + U_N$$

since S_N is the total time for N burnouts and U_i is the time *between* burnouts. (see Fig. 11.9)

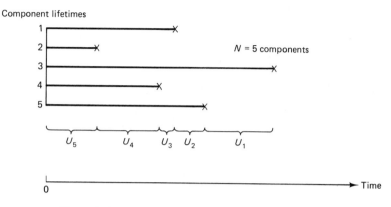

Figure 11.9 $N = 5$ components start operation at time 0. *x*'s mark time of failure.

Each U_i is exponentially distributed with mean $1/\Omega_i = 1/i\delta$ and variance $1/\Omega_i^2 = 1/i^2\delta^2$. Since they are also independent and S_N is their sum,

---

The expectation and variance of the system of N components are

$$E(S_N) = \frac{1}{\delta}\left(1 + \frac{1}{2} + \cdots + \frac{1}{N}\right)$$

$$\text{Var}(S_N) = \frac{1}{\delta^2}\left(1 + \frac{1}{2^2} + \cdots + \frac{1}{N^2}\right)$$

Example 18

We are familiar with such situations as a set of dishes in which the first few break within a relatively short period of time, but the last few seem to linger for years. Assume that the component (dish) lifetimes are exponentially distributed with parameter δ. Starting with N dishes, find that value of J so that

$$E(S_J) \cong \frac{1}{2} E(S_N)$$

that is, the number J so that *for half the expected lifetime of the entire set, J or fewer can be expected to be unbroken.*

Solution Note that there will not necessarily be a J that solves the equation exactly. We will find the smallest J so that

$$E(S_J) \geq \frac{1}{2} E(S_N)$$

$$\frac{1}{\delta} \left(\frac{1}{1} + \frac{1}{2} + \cdots + \frac{1}{J} \right) \geq \frac{1}{2} \frac{1}{\delta} \left(\frac{1}{1} + \frac{1}{2} + \cdots + \frac{1}{N} \right)$$

$$2 \left(1 + \frac{1}{2} + \cdots + \frac{1}{J} \right) \geq 1 + \frac{1}{2} + \cdots + \frac{1}{J} + \frac{1}{J+1} + \cdots + \frac{1}{N}$$

$$1 + \frac{1}{2} + \cdots + \frac{1}{J} \geq \frac{1}{J+1} + \cdots + \frac{1}{N}$$

There is no way to solve directly for J in terms of the total number of dishes N. Some numerical method must be used; an approximation formula forms the content of Problem 11.32. Here is a program:

```
        var S,SJ: real;
            I,J,N: integer

    begin
        readln(N);

        S:= 0.0;
        for I:= 1 to N do S:= S + 1/I;

        SJ:= 0.0; J:= 0;

        while 2*SJ < S do
            begin
                J:= J+1;
                SJ:= SJ + 1/J;
            end;

        writeln(N,J);
    end.
```

These are the results for several values of N:

N	J
2	1
4	2
10	2
50	5
100	8
500	17
1,000	24
10,000	75
100,000	237
1,000,000	749

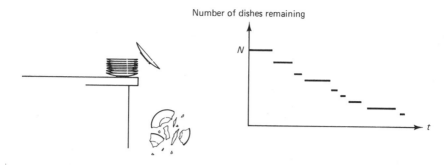

Number of dishes remaining

Figure 11.10

Note that J is slightly less than, but of order of magnitude $\sqrt{N}$. The conclusion that the expected lifetime of $\sqrt{N}$ many dishes is *roughly half* the expected lifetime of N is startling: It shows why the last few tend to linger long after the rest have broken. (see Fig. 11.10) ∎

Here is another way in which exponentially distributed components can be used to model system lifetimes:

Example 19: *Lifetime of a Taut Rope or Cable*

Suppose that a rope is composed of a total of N fibers, *each* of which obeys the lack of aging property; assume also that each fiber wears independently of the others. Assume that the stress remains constant through time until the fibers break one by one and the rope snaps as the last remaining fiber breaks. We make the reasonable assumption that if at time t there are i fibers intact, then the stress is shared equally; it is S/i on each. Hence an intuitively reasonable model is the following: The lifetime of each fiber obeys lack of aging with *mean lifetime proportional* to some power of the stress on it. That is, there is a constant $v \geq 0$ so that the the mean lifetime on each unbroken fiber is $C(S/i)^{-v}$. That is, the larger the stress, the shorter the mean lifetime. Thus the *parameter* for each fiber is $C^{-1}(S/i)^{v}$. Let the state of the system X_t be the number of intact fibers. The time spent in state i is the *minimum* of the snapping times for each of the i fibers and hence by Fact 1 is exponentially distributed with parameter

$$C^{-1} i \left(\frac{S}{i}\right)^{v} = \delta i^{1-v}$$

where δ is a constant of proportionality depending on the stress. That is,

$$\Omega_i = \delta i^{1-v} \qquad p_i = 0 \qquad q_i = 1$$

Since the *waiting time in state i has expectation*

$$\frac{1}{\Omega_i} = \frac{i^{v-1}}{\delta}$$

there are three cases that naturally arise:

Case 1: $v > 1$. Expected waiting time *decreases* as fibers break.
snap........snap....snap..snap.snapsnpsnpspspp

Case 2: $v = 1$. Expected waiting time *remains constant.*

Case 3: $v < 1$. Expected waiting time *increases* as fibers break.
spsnpsnap.snap..snap....snap......snap.......

One would expect the first case to arise when the stress is severe compared with the ability of each strand to withstand it. On the other hand, the third case would result if the stress were small so that each strand breaks in response to other influences in addition to the stress.

Starting with N fibers, the expected time until the rope breaks is

$$E(\text{rope lifetime}) = \sum_{i=1}^{N} E(\text{waiting time in state } i)$$

$$= \frac{1}{\delta}(1^{v-1} + 2^{v-1} + \cdots + N^{v-1})$$

Question: Is it better to wait until one rope breaks and then replace it? Or is it better to start with a rope twice as thick? Compute the expected lifetime in each case.

Solution In the first case let U_1, U_2 be the lifetimes of two ropes used successively—each with N fibers. In the second case let V be the lifetime of one rope with $2N$ fibers. From the formula above

$$E(U_1 + U_2) = 2\frac{1}{\delta}(1 + 2^{v-1} + \cdots + N^{v-1})$$

$$E(V) = \frac{1}{\delta}(1 + 2^{v-1} + \cdots + (2N)^{v-1})$$

And the question is whether or not $E(U_1 + U_2) \geq E(V)$? Working backward yields

$$2\frac{1}{\delta}(1 + 2^{v-1} + \cdots + N^{v-1}) > \frac{1}{\delta}(1 + 2^{v-1} + \cdots + N^{v-1} + \cdots + (2N)^{v-1})$$

$$1 + 2^{v-1} + \cdots + N^{v-1} > (N+1)^{v-1} + \cdots + (2N)^{v-1}$$

$$\sum_{i=1}^{N} i^{v-1} > \sum_{i=1}^{N}(N+i)^{v-1}$$

Each of the terms in the *second* sum is smaller than the corresponding term in the *first* sum if and only if $v - 1 < 0$. Hence $E(U_1 + U_2) > E(V)$ if and only if $v - 1 < 0$.

Conclusion: If $v > 1$ (waiting time decreases as fibers break), it is better to use a rope twice as thick. If $v < 1$ (waiting time increases as fibers break), it is better to use two ropes one after the other. ∎

Figure 11.11

PROBLEMS

11.28. Assume that $T_1, \ldots, T_N$ are IIDRVs each exponentially distributed with parameter δ. **(a)** Find $P(S_N \leq t)$ where $S_N = \text{Max}\{T_1, \ldots, T_N\}$. **(b)** Find the density function for S_N.

11.29. (*Continuation*) In the text we showed that $E(S_N) = (1 + 1/2 + \cdots + 1/N)/\delta$. Show this directly from the density for S_N: Show that

$$E(S_N) = \int_0^\infty (1 - (1 - e^{-\delta t})^N) \, dt$$

using Problem 5.12. Use this expression to show that $E(S_N) - E(S_{N-1}) = 1/\delta N$. Why is $E(S_1) = 1/\delta$?

11.30. Use the diagrams to show that

$$\int_1^{N+1} \frac{1}{x} \, dx < 1 + \frac{1}{2} + \cdots + \frac{1}{N} < 1 + \int_1^N \frac{1}{x} \, dx$$

or

$$\ln(N + 1) < 1 + \frac{1}{2} + \cdots + \frac{1}{N} < 1 + \ln(N)$$

Conclude that

$$\frac{1}{\delta} \ln(N + 1) < E(S_N) < \frac{1}{\delta}[1 + \ln(N)]$$

where $E(S_N)$ is the expected system lifetime in the formula before Example 18.

11.31. (*Continuation*) Given a value of E, what must be the value of N so that $E(S_N)$ is at least as large as E? What must N be if E is taken to be **(a)** 5; **(b)** 10; **(c)** 100?

11.32. In Example 18, the integer J that approximately solves the equation $E(S_J) = E(S_N)/2$ was obtained using a program. Now derive J as a function of N in closed form: We seek that J so that $E(S_{J-1}) < E(S_N)/2 \leq E(S_J)$. Show that Problem 11.30 implies that $\ln(N + 1)/2 - 1 < \ln(J) < (1 + \ln(N))/2$. Show that $\sqrt{N + 1}/e < J < \sqrt{e}\sqrt{N}$ and hence that J is of order of magnitude $\sqrt{N}$.

11.33. In Example 18, let the initial set consist of N dishes and X_t be the number of dishes at time t. Fix time t and set $D_i = 0, 1$, respectively, if the ith dish is broken, intact at time t. Show that $E(D_i) = e^{-\delta t}$. Show that this implies that $E(\#(\text{intact dishes at time } t)) = Ne^{-\delta t}$.

11.34. Write a program that will input N and a fraction α, $0 < \alpha < 1$. Output should be the smallest J, so that $E(S_J) \geqslant \alpha E(S_N)$ as in Example 18.

11.35. Write a program to simulate the times of component failures in the system of Example 18. Input the number of components N and the parameter δ. Output should be the successive times $U_N, \ldots, U_1$ of component failures. (Note that U_i is exponentially distributed with parameter $i\delta$.)

11.36. (*Continuation*) Modify the program of Problem 11.35 so that MAX is input (as well as N and δ); MAX many simulations of $S_N = U_N + \cdots + U_1$ should be performed. Output the average of the MAX many S_N values. Is it close to $E(S_N)$?

Again I saw under the sun the race is not to the swift,
nor the battle to the strong, nor bread to the wise, nor riches
to the intelligent, nor favor to the men of skill, but time
and chance happen to them all.

Ecclesiastes

— Chapter 12 —————————

Discrete-Time Markov Chains

12.1 THE MARKOV CHAIN ASSUMPTIONS AND THE TRANSITION MATRIX

A store stocks floppy disks. The disks are sold one by one and an inventory is taken at the end of each month. Let X_t denote the number in stock at the end of the tth month. (X_0 is the number in stock when the store first opened; X_1 is the number at the end of the first month; . . . .) If X_t falls below a fixed critical level, more disks are ordered. X_{t+1} can be larger than X_t if enough disks are sold during the month so that more than that number are ordered. X_{t+1} depends on two quantities: X_t and the number sold between time t and time $t + 1$. Since the number sold is random, X_t does not completely determine X_{t+1}. *But the basic assumption is that given the value of X_t, in trying to predict what X_{t+1} will be, all the past records $X_{t-1}, X_{t-2}, \ldots, X_0$ are irrelevant; X_{t+1} depends *only* on the number X_t now in stock at time t and the number sold during *this* month. This is the *Markov assumption that the future is independent of the past given the state of affairs in the present.*

Here is a more abstract formulation keeping all the essentials intact: Consider a "system" (the shelf and the floppy disks in stock) that can be in any of a number of "states" (the actual number of items in stock). The set of states is called the *state space S* and we will assume in general that $S = \{0, 1, 2, \ldots, N\}$, although sometimes other state spaces will be used, for example, $S = \{1, 2, \ldots, N\}$ or the *infinite* state space $S = \{0, 1, 2, \ldots\}$. Now suppose that a "particle" is free to jump among the states of the state space S; its location at time t is X_t. In this way

349

we have a *stochastic process* $\{X_t\}_{t=0}^{\infty}$. The location X_t is measured only at the discrete times $t = 0, 1, 2, \ldots$ X_0 is the starting location at time 0.

The following Markov chain assumptions will be assumed to hold throughout the chapter:

1. Suppose that the particle is in state (or location) i at time t. Then regardless of its history prior to time t, the probability that it will jump next to another state j depends only on i. In other words: At time t we see that the particle is occupying state i ($X_t = i$). Then whether it was in that state for 500 years or whether it just jumped to i does not matter; in trying to predict the particle's future state after *time t*, only the present state i is what counts. Mathematically, this can be expressed as follows: Let $i, j, i_{t-1}, \ldots, i_0 \in S$. Then for any time t,

$$P(X_{t+1} = j \mid X_t = i, X_{t-1} = i_{t-1}, \ldots, X_0 = i_0) = P(X_{t+1} = j \mid X_t = i)$$

That is, the future (time $t + 1$), given the present (time t), is *independent* of the past (times $t - 1, \ldots, 0$). The probability above is the *transition* or *jump probability* from state i to state j.

2. Not only are the transition probabilities independent of the past states of the particle once it is known where the particle is *now*, but the transition probabilities are independent of t:

$$P(X_{t+1} = j \mid X_t = i) = \Pi_{i,j}$$

This assumption is called **homogeneity in time**.

A (homogeneous) **Markov chain in discrete time** consists of a particle that jumps at each unit of time between states in a state space S. X_t denotes the state occupied at time t for $t = 0, 1, 2, \ldots$. If the particle is in state i at time t, it will be in state j at time $t + 1$ regardless of the states occupied before time t with probability

$$\Pi_{i,j} = P(X_{t+1} = j \mid X_t = i)$$

Andrei Andreevich Markov (1856–1922) was Chebyshev's most outstanding student. Markov was most involved in proving limit theorems—extending both the central limit theorem and the law of large numbers of Chapter 10. Although Markov originally used Markov chains in abstract settings to prove various theorems, they were quickly applied. Markov himself illustrated the ideas by examining vowel–consonant interchanges in 20,000 letters of Pushkin's poetry.

Example 1

Let $S = \{0, 1\}$ and the transition probabilities be

$$\Pi_{0,0} = \frac{1}{3} \quad \Pi_{0,1} = \frac{2}{3} \quad \Pi_{1,0} = \frac{1}{4} \quad \Pi_{1,1} = \frac{3}{4}$$

Figure 12.1 depicts this.

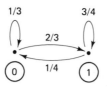

Figure 12.1

A table or *matrix* that displays the jump probabilities is

$$\Pi = \begin{bmatrix} 1/3 & 2/3 \\ 1/4 & 3/4 \end{bmatrix} \quad \blacksquare$$

There is a standard way of writing the jump probabilities $\Pi_{i,j}$ as a table. This is called the **transition matrix** Π. The element in the *i*th *row* and *j*th *column* is $\Pi_{i,j}$—the probability that the particle jumps *from i to j*.

$$\Pi = \begin{bmatrix} \Pi_{0,0} & \Pi_{0,1} & \Pi_{0,2} & \cdots & \Pi_{0,N} \\ \Pi_{1,0} & \Pi_{1,1} & \Pi_{1,2} & \cdots & \Pi_{1,N} \\ \cdot\cdot & \cdot\cdot & \cdot\cdot & \cdots & \cdot\cdot \\ \Pi_{N,0} & \Pi_{N,1} & \Pi_{N,2} & \cdots & \Pi_{N,N} \end{bmatrix}$$

Using matrix terminology, the *ij* entry of Π, is $\Pi_{i,j}$. Note that the *i*th *row* of Π displays the jump probabilities *from* state *i*; the *j*th *column* displays the jump probabilities *to* state *j*. For example, if the third column consisted of all 0's, that is, if

$$\Pi_{i,3} = 0$$

for all states *i* in the state space *S*, the particle could never enter state 3. This is so since if the particle *could* jump from some state i_0 to state 3, then $\Pi_{i_0,3} > 0$.

> Let Π be a Markov chain transition matrix. Then
>
> 1. $0 \le \Pi_{i,j} \le 1$ for all i, j in the state space S
> 2. Π has row sums 1:
>
> $$\sum_{j=0}^{N} \Pi_{i,j} = \sum_{j=0}^{N} P(X_{t+1} = j | X_t = i) = 1$$

Property 2 is true since at time $t + 1$ the particle must be located *somewhere*. (If it could disappear, the state of disappearance would have to included as a state in the state space.)

Example 2

In this chain there are three states; $S = \{0, 1, 2\}$. From state 0 the particle jumps to states 1 or 2 with equal probability 1/2. From state 2 the particle must next jump to state 1. State 1 is *absorbing*; that is, once the particle enters state 1, it cannot leave. Draw the diagram and write down the transition matrix.

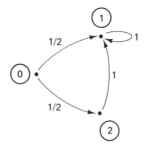

Figure 12.2

Solution Fig. 12.2 depicts the transition probabilities. The zeroth row of Π consists of the jump probabilities *from* state 0 and similarly for the other two rows. Check that

$$\Pi = \begin{bmatrix} 0 & \frac{1}{2} & \frac{1}{2} \\ 0 & 1 & 0 \\ 0 & 1 & 0 \end{bmatrix} \quad \blacksquare$$

> State i is absorbing if $\Pi_{i,i} = 1$.

Example 3: *A Random Walk on* $S = \{0, 1, 2, \ldots, N\}$

From any of the *interior* states $1, 2, \ldots$, or $N - 1$ the particle jumps to the *right* to state $i + 1$ with probability p and to the *left* to state $i - 1$ with probability $q = 1 - p$. That is, for $1 \le i \le N - 1$,

$$\Pi_{i,i+1} = p \qquad \Pi_{i,i-1} = q \qquad \Pi_{i,j} = 0 \quad \text{for } j \ne i \pm 1$$

This corresponds in the language of gambling to the following game: Flip a coin; if heads, then I win \$1; if tails, then I lose \$1. Consequently, at each flip I jump to state $i + 1$ with probability p or to state $i - 1$ with probability q, assuming that I presently have \$$i$. Various assumptions can be made about the behavior of the particle at the *boundary* states 0 and N.

Case 1. They could both be *absorbing*, in which case

$$\Pi_{0,0} = 1 \qquad \Pi_{N,N} = 1$$

This corresponds to the fact that the game is over once I have \$0 *or* if I win all the opponent's money.

$$\Pi = \begin{bmatrix} 1 & 0 & 0 & 0 & \cdot & \cdot & \cdot & 0 \\ q & 0 & p & 0 & \cdot & \cdot & \cdot & 0 \\ 0 & q & 0 & p & \cdot & \cdot & \cdot & 0 \\ \cdot & \cdot & \cdot & \cdot & \cdot & \cdot & \cdot & \cdot \\ 0 & 0 & 0 & 0 & \cdot & q & 0 & p \\ 0 & 0 & 0 & 0 & \cdot & \cdot & \cdot & 1 \end{bmatrix}$$

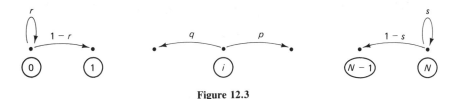

Figure 12.3

Case 2. They could be *reflecting*, in which case

$$\Pi_{0,1} = 1 \qquad \Pi_{N,N-1} = 1$$

This corresponds to having my opponent give me one of his/her dollars when I run out and conversely.

Case 3. They could be *partially reflecting*, as depicted in Fig. 12.3 in which case

$$\Pi_{0,0} = r \qquad \Pi_{0,1} = 1 - r \qquad \Pi_{N,N} = s \qquad \Pi_{N,N-1} = 1 - s$$

$$\Pi = \begin{bmatrix} r & 1-r & 0 & 0 & 0 & \cdot & \cdot & & \cdot & 0 \\ q & 0 & p & 0 & 0 & \cdot & \cdot & & \cdot & 0 \\ 0 & q & 0 & p & 0 & \cdot & \cdot & \cdot & & \cdot \\ \cdot & \cdot & \cdot & \cdot & \cdot & \cdot & \cdot & \cdot & & \cdot \\ 0 & 0 & 0 & 0 & 0 & \cdot & \cdot & q & 0 & p \\ 0 & 0 & 0 & 0 & 0 & \cdot & \cdot & \cdot & 1-s & s \end{bmatrix}$$

Note that case 3 includes cases 1 and 2 for particular choices of r and s. ∎

Example 4: *A Renewal Process*

Consider a component whose age can be 0 or 1 or 2 or . . . . Age 0 means "just installed." Assume that no matter how old the component is, it will burn out during the next interval of time with probability q or continue operating with probability $p = 1 - q$. Thus the component obeys the lack of aging property. The state space is $S = \{0, 1, 2, . . .\}$ and the state of the system is the *age of the component presently installed*. Assume that as soon as the component burns out, it is instantly replaced and then the state of the system becomes 0. Notice that the transition from state 0 to state 0 occurs if the component just installed immediately burns out.

$$\Pi = \begin{bmatrix} q & p & 0 & 0 & \cdot & \cdot & \cdot \\ q & 0 & p & 0 & 0 & \cdot & \cdot \\ q & 0 & 0 & p & 0 & \cdot & \cdot \\ \cdot & \cdot & \cdot & \cdot & \cdot & \cdot & \cdot \end{bmatrix}$$

Note that the state space S, while discrete, has infinitely many states. (This model is also called a *birth or disaster model*; see Problem 12.26.) Certain applications of this model are clear from the terminology—component lifetimes. But here is one that is not so obvious: Notices pile up on a bulletin board at a more-or-less constant rate until someone decides to throw them all away. The state of the system is the number of days since the bulletin board was last cleared. *If the clearing of the board is done at random independent of how many notices or the time since the last clearing, the bulletin board will be cleared at the next unit of time with a constant probability q.* ∎

12.2 THE tth-ORDER TRANSITION MATRIX

The transition matrix Π displays at a glance the transition probabilities $\Pi_{i,j}$. Suppose that we need to find probabilities such as

$$P(X_{t+3} = j \mid X_t = i)$$

that the particle will be in state j *three* jumps from now. The *one-step* probabilities $\Pi_{i,j}$ are the entries of the matrix Π. From these, how can one find the three-step probabilities, and more generally the t-step probabilities?

Definition

The tth-order transition matrix is Π^t, whose ijth entry is

$$\Pi^t_{i,j} = P(X_t = j \mid X_0 = i)$$

which is the probability of jumping *from i to j* in t steps.

Note that $\Pi^1 = \Pi$. Why? It should be clear that homogeneity in time (that the transition probabilities do not depend on t) implies that regardless of the time $u \geq 0$,

$$P(X_{t+u} = j \mid X_u = i) = \Pi^t_{i,j}$$

That is, the t-step transition probabilities depend only on the *time difference.*

A general algorithm is needed to find the tth-order transition matrix Π^t for any given Markov chain matrix Π.

To find the $(t + 1)$st-order transition matrix from the tth, use the basic Markov assumptions: Suppose that the particle starts in state i at time 0. For the particle to be in state j at time $t + 1$, it must have traveled through *some* state k at the intermediate time t. Consequently, *where* the particle was at time t *partitions* the *event* "in state j at time $t + 1$ given start in state i at time 0."

$$\Pi^{t+1}_{i,j} = P(X_{t+1} = j \mid X_0 = i)$$

$$= \sum_{k=0}^{N} P(X_{t+1} = j \ \text{ and } \ X_t = k \mid X_0 = i)$$

$$= \sum_{k=0}^{N} P(X_{t+1} = j \mid X_t = k \ \text{ and } \ X_0 = i)P(X_t = k \mid X_0 = i)$$

$$= \sum_{k=0}^{N} P(X_{t+1} = j \mid X_t = k)P(X_t = k \mid X_0 = i)$$

$$= \sum_{k=0}^{N} \Pi_{k,j} \, \Pi_{i,k}^{t}$$

$$= \sum_{k=0}^{N} \Pi_{i,k}^{t} \, \Pi_{k,j}$$

The second equality follows by partitioning on *where* the particle was at time t. The third equality follows from this identity

$$P(A \cap B \mid C) = P(A \mid B \cap C)P(B \mid C)$$

which follows from the definition of conditional probability (see Problem 3.8). The fourth equality uses the Markov chain assumption that the chance that the particle is at j at time $t + 1$ *given* that it was at k at time t is *independent* of the fact that it was at i at time 0.

In terms of *matrix multiplication** we have shown that

$$\Pi^{t+1} = \Pi^{t}\Pi$$

The result can be generalized:

$$\Pi^{t+2} = \Pi^{t+1}\Pi = (\Pi^{t} \cdot \Pi)\Pi = \Pi^{t}\Pi^{2}$$

using what we have just proved together with the fact that matrix multiplication is associative. In general, we have proved the

---

Chapman–Kolmogorov Equations

Let times $t, s \geq 0$. Then for all states i, j

$$\Pi_{i,j}^{t+s} = \sum_{k=0}^{N} \Pi_{i,k}^{t} \, \Pi_{k,j}^{s}$$

In terms of matrix multiplication, the $(t + s)$th-order transition matrix is the product of the tth and the sth:

$$\Pi^{t+s} = \Pi^{t}\Pi^{s}$$

In words: For the particle to start at i at time 0 and be in j at time $t + s$, it must be in *some* state k at the intermediate time t.

Example 5

Convert the jump probability diagram of Fig. 12.4 into the corresponding Markov chain and find the probability that the particle will be in state 1 after three jumps given it started in state 1.

---

*The mechanics of matrix multiplication are explained in Appendix 2.

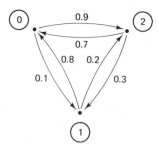

Figure 12.4

Solution

$$\Pi = \begin{bmatrix} 0 & .1 & .9 \\ .8 & 0 & .2 \\ .7 & .3 & 0 \end{bmatrix}$$

$$\Pi^2 = \Pi^1\Pi^1 = \begin{bmatrix} .71 & .27 & .02 \\ .14 & .14 & .72 \\ .24 & .07 & .69 \end{bmatrix}$$

$$\Pi^3 = \Pi^2\Pi = \begin{bmatrix} .230 & .077 & .693 \\ .616 & .230 & .154 \\ .539 & .231 & .230 \end{bmatrix}$$

Consequently,

$$P(X_3 = 1 \mid X_0 = 1) = \Pi^3_{1,1} = .230 \quad \blacksquare$$

PROBLEMS

In Problems 12.1 to 12.3, draw the transition diagrams corresponding to the transition matrices given.

12.1.
$$\Pi = \begin{bmatrix} .2 & .8 \\ .6 & .4 \end{bmatrix}$$

12.2.
$$\Pi = \begin{bmatrix} .1 & 0 & .9 \\ 0 & .9 & .1 \\ .1 & 0 & .9 \end{bmatrix}$$

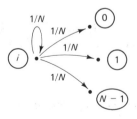

Figure 12.5

Discrete-Time Markov Chains   Chap. 12

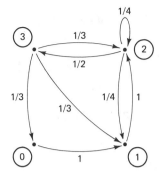

Figure 12.6   **Figure 12.7**

12.3.

$$\Pi = \begin{bmatrix} p_0 & p_i & \cdot & \cdot & \cdot & p_N \\ 1 & 0 & \cdot & \cdot & \cdot & 0 \\ \cdot & \cdot & & \cdot & \cdot & \cdot \\ 1 & 0 & \cdot & \cdot & \cdot & 0 \end{bmatrix}$$

In Problems 12.4 to 12.6, what are the transition matrices corresponding to the diagrams?

12.4. N states; $S = \{0, 1, 2, \ldots, N - 1\}$. For *each* pair of states i, j, $\Pi_{i,j} = 1/N$. Fig. 12.5.

12.5. Fig. 12.6.

12.6. Fig. 12.7.

Find the second- and third-order transition matrices for Problems 12.7 to 12.10 and the second-order transition matrix for Problems 12.11 and 12.12:

12.7. Problem 12.1.

12.8. Problem 12.2.

12.9. Problem 12.3.

12.10. Problem 12.4.

12.11. Problem 12.5.

12.12. Problem 12.6.

12.13. Write a program that will input N, then the $(N + 1) \times (N + 1)$ transition matrix P[I,J]; input should also be a positive integer MAX. Output should be the tth-order transition matrices P^t for $t = 1, 2, \ldots,$ MAX. Do this as follows: Set each entry of the matrix C equal to the corresponding entry of P. Then in a nested loop compute the new value of the transition matrix P as the matrix product of C times the old value of P. Test your program on the Markov chain of Problem 12.1.

12.3 THE PROBABILITY VECTOR ρ^t

So far we have seen how to compute conditional probabilities of the form $P(X_t = j \mid X_0 = i)$. But now suppose that it is known for a fact that the particle started in state i_0 at time 0. Then what is $P(X_t = j)$? More generally, assume that the particle starts in state i with probability ρ_i at time $t = 0$. We want to answer the question: With the starting probabilities $\rho_0, \rho_1, \ldots, \rho_N$, what is $P(X_t = j)$ for any state j?

Let the **initial probability vector** be defined

$$\rho = (\rho_0, \rho_1, \rho_2, \ldots, \rho_N)$$

Note that $0 \leqslant \rho_i \leqslant 1$ for all states i in the state space S and

$$\rho_0 + \rho_1 + \cdots + \rho_N = 1$$

since the particle must start *somewhere* at time 0. The *probability vector at time t* is defined as

$$\rho^t = (\rho_0^t, \rho_1^t, \rho_2^t, \ldots, \rho_N^t)$$

where

$$\rho_j^t = P(X_t = j \mid \text{initial probability vector } \rho)$$

That is, ρ_j^t is *the chance that the particle will be found in state j given that at time 0 it started in the various states with probability ρ_i for $i = 0, 1, \ldots, N$.* Note that

$$\rho^0 = \rho$$

and

$$\sum_{j=0}^{N} \rho_j^t = \sum_{j=0}^{N} P(X_t = j) = 1$$

That is, for each t, ρ^t is a *probability vector*.

Definition

A probability vector $\rho = (\rho_0, \rho_1, \ldots, \rho_N)$ satisfies

1. $0 \leqslant \rho_i \leqslant 1$ for each $i = 0, 1, 2, \ldots, N$
2. $\rho_0 + \rho_1 + \cdots + \rho_N = 1$

There is a straightforward method for obtaining the probability vector ρ^t at time t given the initial probability vector ρ^0 at time 0 and the tth-order transition matrix Π^t:

$$\rho_j^t = \sum_{i=0}^{N} \rho_i \Pi_{i,j}^t$$

Expressed as multiplication between a vector and a matrix, the probability vector at time t is

$$\rho^t = \rho \Pi^t = \rho^0 \Pi^t$$

To see why this result is true, we compute

$$\rho_j^t = P(X_t = j)$$

$$= \sum_{i=0}^{N} P(X_t = j \mid X_0 = i)P(X_0 = i)$$

$$= \sum_{i=0}^{N} \Pi_{i,j}^t \rho_i$$

where the first and second equalities are the definitions of ρ^t, Π^t, and ρ. The second equality follows from the law of total probability.

Example 6

For the Markov chain in Fig. 12.8 find the chance that the particle will be in state 0 at time 3 if it started in state 0 with probability 1/3 and in state 1 with probability 2/3 at time 0.

Solution

$$\Pi = \begin{bmatrix} \dfrac{1}{4} & \dfrac{3}{4} \\[2ex] 1 & 0 \end{bmatrix}$$

and

$$\rho = (1/3, 2/3)$$

Consequently

$$\Pi^2 = \Pi \cdot \Pi = \begin{bmatrix} \dfrac{13}{16} & \dfrac{3}{16} \\[2ex] \dfrac{1}{4} & \dfrac{3}{4} \end{bmatrix}$$

$$\Pi^3 = \Pi \cdot \Pi^2 = \begin{bmatrix} \dfrac{25}{64} & \dfrac{39}{64} \\[2ex] \dfrac{13}{16} & \dfrac{3}{16} \end{bmatrix}$$

$$\rho^3 = \rho\Pi^3$$

$$= \left(\dfrac{1}{3}, \dfrac{2}{3}\right)\Pi^3$$

$$= \left(\dfrac{129}{192}, \dfrac{63}{192}\right)$$

from which we conclude that

$$P(X_3 = 0) = \rho_0^3 = \dfrac{129}{192} \quad \blacksquare$$

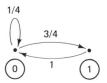

Figure 12.8

Suppose that the particle starts at time $t = 0$ in state i. In the terminology of probability vectors, this means that

$$\rho^0 = (0, \ldots, 0, 1, 0, \ldots, 0)$$

$\nwarrow$*i*th entry

Therefore, the probability vector at time t is

*i*th entry$\searrow$

$$\rho^t = (0, \ldots, 0, 1, 0, \ldots, 0)\Pi^t$$

$$= (\Pi^t_{i,0}, \Pi^t_{i,1}, \Pi^t_{i,2}, \ldots, \Pi^t_{i,N})$$

which implies that *given* that the particle started in state i,

$$P(X_t = j) = \rho^t_j = \Pi^t_{i,j}$$

which confirms what we *already know*: The ij entry of the matrix Π^t is the chance of being in state j at time t given in state i at time 0.

PROBLEMS

In Problems 12.14 to 12.16, find the probability vector ρ^t at the times t for the Markov chains indicated:

12.14. At $t = 1, 2,$ and 3 for the Markov chain of Problem 12.1 with **(a)** $\rho = (1, 0)$; **(b)** $\rho = (0, 1)$; **(c)** $\rho = (3/7, 4/7)$.

12.15. At $t = 1, 2,$ and 3 for the Markov chain of Problem 12.2 with **(a)** $\rho = (1, 0, 0)$; **(b)** $\rho = (0, 1, 0)$; **(c)** $\rho = (1/3, 1/3, 1/3)$.

12.16. For all $t \geqslant 0$ for the Markov chain of Problem 12.4 for *any* initial probability vector ρ.

12.17. Assume that the transition matrix also has *column* sums 1 in addition to having row sums 1. Such a Markov chain is called *doubly* stochastic. Suppose that $\rho^0 = (1/(N + 1), 1/(N + 1), \ldots, 1/(N + 1))$. (There are $N + 1$ states: $0, 1, 2, \ldots, N$.) Show that $\rho^t = \rho^0$ for all $t \geqslant 0$.

12.18. (*Continuation of Problem 12.13*) Revise your program so that it will also input the initial probabilities R[0], R[1], ..., R[N]. Output should be the vectors ρ^t for $t = 1, 2, \ldots,$ MAX. Test the program on the Markov chains of Problems 12.14 to 12.16.

12.4 THE STEADY-STATE PROBABILITY VECTOR

Suppose that there is a large number n of particles each jumping from state to state among the states of S guided by the transition matrix Π of jump probabilities. If all n particles start in state 0 at time $t = 0$, then after one jump some will remain in state 0 (if $\Pi_{0,0} > 0$) and others will jump to other states. In fact, we can expect $n\Pi_{0,j}$ particles to be in state j after one jump. (Why?) On the other hand, suppose that we distribute the n so that n_j start in state j at time 0 for $j = 0, 1, \ldots, N$. Since $n_j\Pi_{j,i}$ of those particles starting in state j can be expected to jump to state i, the *total* number of particles that can be expected to be in state i after one jump is

$$\sum_{j=0}^{N} n_j\Pi_{j,i}$$

It may just happen that *this* number is the same as the number n_i of particles that *started* in state i at time 0. Each of the particles might change states, but the *overall number* in state i would remain constant. If this were true for *each* state $i \in S$, the entire system of n particles would be in a steady state; for each particle that leaves a state, one would replace it from another state.

$$n_i = \sum_{j=0}^{N} n_j\Pi_{j,i}$$

Rather than the *absolute* number n_i of particles in state i, let us phrase the equation in terms of the *relative* number n_i/n of particles in state i; this is the *probability that any one particle* occupies state i.

$$\frac{n_i}{n} = \sum_{j=0}^{N} \frac{n_j}{n} \Pi_{j,i}$$

If this were the case, the entire system of n particles would be in the steady state.
A probability vector ϕ represents the steady state if

$$\phi_i = \sum_{j=0}^{N} \phi_j\Pi_{j,i}$$

that is, if $\phi^1 = \phi \cdot \Pi = \phi$. Thus the probability that a particle is in state i is the *same* at time 1 as at time 0. Note that if ϕ has this property of "reproducing itself" after one jump, this will also be true for all times t:

$$\phi^1 = \phi\Pi = \phi$$

implies

$$\phi^2 = \phi^1\Pi = \phi\Pi = \phi$$
$$\phi^3 = \phi^2\Pi = \phi\Pi = \phi$$

and in general,

$$\phi^t = \phi^{t-1}\Pi = \phi\Pi = \phi$$

We call any probability vector with the property that $\phi = \phi\Pi$ a *steady-state probability vector*. If the particle starts in state i with probability ϕ_i for each state i, then at *every* time t it will be in state i with probability ϕ_i.

Procedure for Finding the Steady-State Probability Vector

1. Set up and solve these equations:

$$\phi_j = \sum_{i=0}^{N} \phi_i \Pi_{i,j}$$

for $j = 0, 1, 2, \ldots, N$ or alternatively, in matrix notation,

$$\phi = \phi\Pi$$

2. *Normalize* by insisting that

$$\sum_{i=0}^{N} \phi_i = 1$$

Step 1 involves solving $N + 1$ equations in the $N + 1$ unknowns $\phi_0, \phi_1, \ldots, \phi_N$. As we will see in the examples, there will always be redundancy; one of the equations will be a combination of the others. The equation of step 2 is actually the $(N + 1)$st.

Example 7

Find the steady-state probability vector of the Markov chain in Fig. 12.9:

Solution

$$\phi = \phi\Pi$$

$$(\phi_0, \phi_1) = (\phi_0, \phi_1)\Pi = (\phi_0, \phi_1) \begin{bmatrix} \dfrac{1}{2} & \dfrac{1}{2} \\ 1 & 0 \end{bmatrix}$$

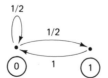

Figure 12.9

which yields two equations in the two unknowns ϕ_0 and ϕ_1:

$$\phi_0 = \frac{1}{2}\phi_0 + \phi_1$$

$$\phi_1 = \frac{1}{2}\phi_0$$

Both these equations are really the same:

$$\phi_1 = \frac{\phi_0}{2}$$

Using the normalization condition,

$$1 = \phi_0 + \phi_1 = \phi_0 + \frac{\phi_0}{2} = 3\frac{\phi_0}{2}$$

Thus

$$\phi_0 = \frac{2}{3} \qquad \phi_1 = \frac{1}{3}$$

Consequently, two-thirds of the time the particle will be found in state 1; one-third of the time will it be found in state 2 in the steady state. A simulation was run in which 66 particles were started in state 0 and 33 in state 1. *Each* jumped according to the transition probabilities. Here are the results: The first column n is the number of transitions performed by each of the 99 particles; the second column is the fraction in state 0.

n	Fraction in state 0
1	.667
2	.667
3	.717
4	.636
5	.677
6	.667
7	.647
8	.707

There are random fluctuations, but about 2/3 of the particles are found in state 0 at *any time t* if *2/3 start* in state 0. ∎

Example 8

Consider the Markov chain in Fig. 12.10. Find the steady-state probability vector ϕ.

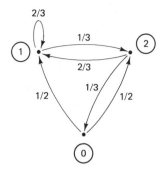

Figure 12.10

Solution

$$\Pi = \begin{bmatrix} 0 & 1/2 & 1/2 \\ 0 & 2/3 & 1/3 \\ 1/3 & 2/3 & 0 \end{bmatrix}$$

$$(\phi_0, \phi_1, \phi_2) = (\phi_0, \phi_1, \phi_2) \begin{bmatrix} 0 & 1/2 & 1/2 \\ 0 & 2/3 & 1/3 \\ 1/3 & 2/3 & 0 \end{bmatrix}$$

results in these equations:

$$\phi_0 = \frac{1}{3}\phi_2$$

$$\phi_1 = \frac{1}{2}\phi_0 + \frac{2}{3}\phi_1 + \frac{2}{3}\phi_2$$

$$\phi_2 = \frac{1}{2}\phi_0 + \frac{1}{3}\phi_1$$

Clearing the fractions and combining factors of each ϕ_i:

$$-3\phi_0 \qquad + \phi_2 = 0$$

$$3\phi_0 - 2\phi_1 + 4\phi_2 = 0$$

$$3\phi_0 + 2\phi_1 - 6\phi_2 = 0$$

Adding the second and third equations results in

$$6\phi_0 \qquad - 2\phi_2 = 0$$

which is essentially the same as the first equation. Hence the third equation is redundant. From the first two equations

$$\phi_2 = 3\phi_0$$

$$\phi_1 = \frac{1}{2}(3\phi_0 + 4\phi_2) = \frac{15}{2}\phi_0$$

Now use the normalization condition

$$1 = \phi_0 + \phi_1 + \phi_2 = \left(1 + \frac{15}{2} + 3\right)\phi_0 = \frac{23}{2}\phi_0$$

Consequently,

$$\phi_0 = \frac{2}{23}$$

$$\phi_1 = \frac{15}{2}\phi_0 = \frac{15}{23}$$

$$\phi_2 = 3\phi_0 = \frac{6}{23} \quad \blacksquare$$

Example 9

Consider the *cyclic process* depicted in Fig. 12.11. There are $N + 1$ states 0, 1, 2, . . . , N. For each state i, $0 < q_i < 1$. The particle remains in state i with probability q_i. Otherwise, it jumps to the next state $i + 1$ with probability $p_i = 1 - q_i$. If $i = N$, then $i + 1$ is taken to be state 0. That is, there is a "wraparound" from state N to state 0.

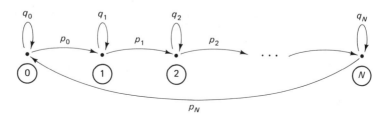

Figure 12.11

Solve for the steady-state probability vector ϕ.

Solution

$$\Pi = \begin{bmatrix} q_0 & p_0 & 0 & \cdot & \cdot & \cdot & 0 \\ 0 & q_1 & p_1 & 0 & \cdot & \cdot & 0 \\ 0 & 0 & q_2 & p_2 & & & \\ \cdot & \cdot & \cdot & \cdot & \cdot & \cdot & \cdot \\ p_N & 0 & \cdot & \cdot & \cdot & 0 & q_N \end{bmatrix}$$

The equation $\phi = \phi\Pi$ implies that

$$(\phi_0, \phi_1, \ldots, \phi_N) = (\phi_0, \phi_1, \ldots, \phi_N)\Pi$$

which "uncouples" to these $N + 1$ equations:

$$\phi_0 = q_0\phi_0 \qquad\qquad\qquad + p_N\phi_N$$

$$\phi_1 = p_0\phi_0 \qquad + q_1\phi_1$$

$$\phi_2 = \qquad\qquad p_1\phi_1 + q_2\phi_2$$

$$\cdots\cdots\cdots$$

or

$$p_0\phi_0 = p_N\phi_N$$

$$p_1\phi_1 = p_0\phi_0$$

$$p_2\phi_2 = p_1\phi_1$$

$$\cdots\cdot$$

Solve successively for each ϕ_i in terms of ϕ_0 starting with the second equation:

$$\phi_1 = \frac{p_0}{p_1}\phi_0$$

$$\phi_2 = \frac{p_1}{p_2}\phi_1 = \frac{p_0}{p_2}\phi_0$$

$$\phi_3 = \frac{p_2}{p_3}\phi_2 = \frac{p_0}{p_3}\phi_0$$

$$\cdots\cdots$$

$$\phi_N = \frac{p_0}{p_N}\phi_0$$

Use the normalization condition:

$$1 = \phi_0 + \phi_1 + \cdots + \phi_N$$

$$= \left(1 + \frac{p_0}{p_1} + \frac{p_0}{p_2} + \cdots + \frac{p_0}{p_N}\right)\phi_0$$

$$= \left(\frac{1}{p_0} + \frac{1}{p_1} + \frac{1}{p_2} + \cdots + \frac{1}{p_N}\right)p_0\phi_0$$

Let

$$C = \frac{1}{p_0} + \frac{1}{p_1} + \cdots + \frac{1}{p_N}$$

Then $1 = Cp_0\phi_0$, which determines ϕ_0. From the equations (*), we have:

> For the cyclic process,
>
> $$\phi_i = \frac{1}{Cp_i}$$
>
> where
>
> $$C = \sum_{j=0}^{N} \frac{1}{p_j}$$

The Markov chains in the last three examples have each had unique steady-state probability vectors. This need not always be the case, as the next two examples show.

Example 10

Let

$$\Pi = \begin{bmatrix} \dfrac{1}{2} & \dfrac{1}{2} & 0 & 0 \\[2mm] \dfrac{1}{2} & \dfrac{1}{2} & 0 & 0 \\[2mm] 0 & \dfrac{1}{3} & \dfrac{1}{3} & \dfrac{1}{3} \\[2mm] 0 & 0 & 0 & 1 \end{bmatrix}$$

Here are two distinct steady-state probability vectors:

$$\phi = \left(\frac{1}{2}, \frac{1}{2}, 0, 0, 0\right)$$

$$\psi = (0, 0, 0, 0, 1)$$

These can be verified simply by checking that $\phi\Pi = \phi$ and $\psi\Pi = \psi$. ∎

Example 11

Consider a random walk on the integers $S = \{0, 1, 2, \ldots\}$ in which transitions only to the right can occur as in Fig. 12.12. Assume that $0 < p < 1$ and $q = 1 - p$.

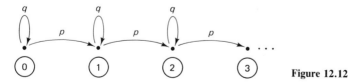

Figure 12.12

This chain is similar to the cyclic process of Example 9. Here $p_i = p$ is constant and $N = \infty$.

$$\Pi = \begin{bmatrix} q & p & 0 & 0 & 0 & \cdot & \cdot & \cdot \\ 0 & q & p & 0 & 0 & \cdot & \cdot & \cdot \\ 0 & 0 & q & p & 0 & \cdot & \cdot & \cdot \\ \cdot & \cdot & \cdot & \cdot & \cdot & \cdot & \cdot & \cdot \end{bmatrix}$$

$\phi = \phi\Pi$ implies that

$$q\phi_0 = \phi_0$$

$$p\phi_0 + q\phi_1 = \phi_1$$

$$p\phi_1 + q\phi_2 = \phi_2$$

$$\cdot \quad \cdot \quad \cdot \quad \cdot \quad \cdot$$

Since $0 < p, q < 1$, the first equation, and then the second, and then the third, ... imply

$$\phi_0 = 0$$

$$\phi_1 = 0$$

$$\phi_2 = 0$$

Consequently, there is *no* steady state: ■

Why didn't the Markov chain in Example 10 have a *unique* steady state? Why did it have two? And why didn't the Markov chain in Example 11 have any steady state at all?

Looking at what happens in the chain in Example 10 reveals the reason. If the particle starts in states 0 or 1, it stays in these two states forever. If it starts in state 3, it stays *there* forever. If, finally, it starts in state 2, sooner or later it will jump to *either* state 3 *or* to the combination of states 0 and 1. Consequently, the entire chain "splits" into two separate pieces, each with its own steady state. The chain is said to be *decomposable*. (But more about that later.)

How about Example 11? The particle has a "drift" to the right. Consequently, there is no steady state. Start with a million particles and eventually they will all be very far to the right of state 0.

There is also another complication in finding the steady state:

Example 12

With

$$\Pi = \begin{bmatrix} 0 & 1/2 & 1/2 \\ 1 & 0 & 0 \\ 1 & 0 & 0 \end{bmatrix}$$

it is a straightforward verification to check that $\phi = (1/2, 1/4, 1/4)$ is a steady-state probability vector, and in fact it is the only one. For a large number of particles, there is a steady state: If $n/2$ start in state 0 and $n/4$ in each of states 1 and 2, there will be approximately this many in each of the states at all subsequent times. But for *one* particle, there is no steady state. If it starts in state 0, it *must* jump to $\{1, 2\}$, from which it *must* jump to state 0, from which . . . . At even times it will be in state 0; at odd times in either 1 or 2. There is a *periodicity* problem. ■

In Section 12.6 we will see how eliminating these complications leads to a very useful result.

PROBLEMS

Find the steady-state probability vectors (if they exist) for the Markov chains of:

12.19. Problem 12.1.

12.20. Problem 12.2.

12.21. Problem 12.3.

12.22. Problem 12.4.

12.23. Problem 12.5.

12.24. Problem 12.6.

12.25. Consider this model: A shelf starts with N items for sale. An item is sold each hour with probability p. Hence $\Pi_{i,i-1} = p$, $\Pi_{i,i} = q = 1 - p$. As soon as there are 0 items on the shelf, the shelf is restocked with N so that $\Pi_{0,N} = 1$. Note that this is similar to the cyclic process except that the "direction" is reversed. Draw the probability diagram and solve for ϕ. Do the steady-state probabilities ϕ_i make intuitive sense?

12.26. Consider the birth or disaster model shown in Fig. 12.13:

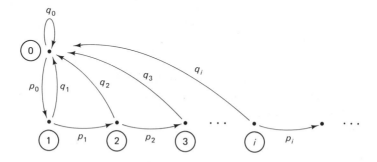

Figure 12.13

(a) What is the transition matrix Π? (b) Show that $\phi_i = p_{i-1} \cdots p_0 \cdot \phi_0$. (c) Show that a steady-state probability vector exists only if

$$C = 1 + p_0 + p_0 p_1 + p_0 p_1 p_2 + \cdots < \infty$$

(d) If $C < \infty$, find ϕ. **(e)** If $p_i = p$ is constant, what is ϕ? **(f)** What is the interpretation if $C = \infty$?

12.5 BIRTH AND DEATH PROCESSES IN DISCRETE TIME: RANDOM WALKS

If the state space S is $\{0, 1, 2, \ldots, N\}$, the vector equation $\phi = \phi\Pi$ yields $N + 1$ equations in the $N + 1$ unknowns $\phi_0, \ldots, \phi_N$. For N larger than four or five, solutions can be time consuming. Fortunately, there is a fast method for finding ϕ in one of the most important special cases.

Definition

A *birth and death process* in discrete time is a Markov chain with this property: From any state $i \in S$ transitions in one jump to $i - 1$, i, or $i + 1$ only can occur.

There may be infinitely many states in S or S may be finite. For some states a transition to the right only or to the left only may be possible. But for *all* states, the particle can jump at most one unit to the right or to the left.

All random walk models of Example 3 are birth and death chains.

To simplify notation, set

$$b_i = \Pi_{i,i+1} \qquad r_i = \Pi_{i,i} \qquad d_i = \Pi_{i,i-1}$$

(for birth, remain, and death) as in Fig. 12.14.

For each i

$$b_i + r_i + d_i = 1$$

The transition matrix is

$$\Pi = \begin{bmatrix} r_0 & b_0 & 0 & 0 & 0 & \cdot & \cdot & \cdot \\ d_1 & r_1 & b_1 & 0 & 0 & \cdot & \cdot & \cdot \\ 0 & d_2 & r_2 & b_2 & 0 & \cdot & \cdot & \cdot \\ \cdot & \cdot & \cdot & \cdot & \cdot & \cdot & & \\ \cdot & \cdot & \cdot & \cdot & \cdot & 0 & d_N & r_N \end{bmatrix}$$

Note that $d_0 = 0$ and $b_N = 0$ (for N finite). Why?

Now suppose that there is a large number n of particles each jumping according to the birth and death chain. Then assuming that the entire system of n particles is in the steady state, there will be $n\phi_i$ particles in state i at any instant

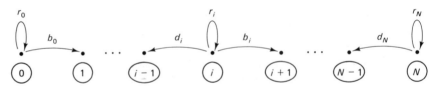

Figure 12.14

of time. The number of these that will jump *next* to state $i + 1$ is therefore $(n\phi_i)b_i$. But in the *steady state* this must be compensated for an equal number of particles moving *down* from $i + 1$. This is $(n\phi_{i+1})d_{i+1}$. Otherwise, particles would "bunch up" to the left or to the right of state i and the system would not be in the steady state. Consequently (after canceling the factor n),

$$\phi_{i+1}d_{i+1} = \phi_i b_i$$

Procedure for finding the Steady-State Probability Vector ϕ

Use the equations

$$\phi_{i+1} = \frac{b_i}{d_{i+1}} \phi_i$$

to solve for each ϕ_i in terms of ϕ_0. Then use normalization

$$1 = \phi_0 + \phi_1 + \cdots + \phi_N$$

Example 13

Solve for ϕ for the Markov chain in Fig. 12.15:

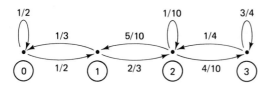

Figure 12.15

Solution Using the procedure

$$\phi_1 = \frac{b_0}{d_1} \phi_0 = \frac{1/2}{1/3} \phi_0 = \frac{3}{2} \phi_0$$

$$\phi_2 = \frac{b_1}{d_2} \phi_1 = \frac{2/3}{5/10} \phi_1 = \frac{4}{3} \phi_1 = \frac{4}{3} \cdot \frac{3}{2} \phi_0 = 2 \phi_0$$

$$\phi_3 = \frac{b_2}{d_3} \phi_2 = \frac{4/10}{1/4} \phi_2 = \frac{8}{5} \phi_2 = \frac{8}{5} \cdot 2 \phi_0 = \frac{16}{5} \phi_0$$

Use normalization:

$$1 = \phi_0 + \phi_1 + \phi_2 + \phi_3 = \left(1 + \frac{3}{2} + 2 + \frac{16}{5}\right)\phi_0 = \frac{77}{10}\phi_0$$

Thus

$$\phi_0 = \frac{10}{77} \qquad \phi_1 = \frac{3\phi_0}{2} = \frac{15}{77}$$

$$\phi_2 = 2\phi_0 = \frac{20}{77} \qquad \phi_3 = \frac{16\phi_0}{5} = \frac{32}{77} \qquad \blacksquare$$

Example 14: *The Random Walk on* $\{0, \ldots, N\}$ *with Partially Reflecting Boundaries*

For $i = 1, \ldots, N - 1$, $b_i = b$, $r_i = r$, and $d_i = d$ are constant as in Fig. 12.16. $b_0 = b$ and $d_N = d$.

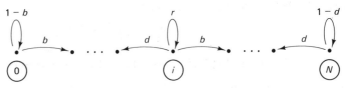

Figure 12.16

Note that $b_i = b$ for $i = 0, 1, \ldots, N - 1$ and $d_i = d$ for $i = 1, 2, \ldots, N$. Thus

$$\phi_{i+1} = \frac{b_i}{d_{i+1}} \phi_i = \frac{b}{d} \phi_i$$

for $i = 0, 1, \ldots, N - 1$. Using this relation *recursively*,

$$\phi_i = \frac{b}{d} \phi_{i-1} = \left(\frac{b}{d}\right)^2 \phi_{i-2} = \cdots = \left(\frac{b}{d}\right)^i \phi_0$$

Now use normalization:

$$1 = \phi_0 + \phi_1 + \cdots + \phi_N$$

$$= \left(1 + \frac{b}{d} + \left(\frac{b}{d}\right)^2 + \cdots + \left(\frac{b}{d}\right)^N\right) \phi_0$$

There are two cases:

Case 1: The asymmetric random walks, $b \neq d$. Then this normalization sum is a geometric series whose sum we know from Section 4.3.

$$1 = \frac{1 - (b/d)^{N+1}}{1 - b/d} \phi_0$$

With constant

$$C = \frac{1 - b/d}{1 - b/d^{N+1}}$$

$$\phi_i = \left(\frac{b}{d}\right)^i C$$

for $i = 0, 1, 2, \ldots, N$

Case 2: The symmetric random walk, $b = d$. Then the normalization sum is

$$1 = (1 + 1 + 1^2 + \cdots + 1^N)\phi_0 = (N + 1)\phi_0$$

Consequently,

$$\phi_0 = \frac{1}{N + 1}$$

$$\phi_i = \left(\frac{b}{d}\right)^i \phi_0 = 1^i \phi_0 = \phi_0 = \frac{1}{N + 1}$$

for each i. *In the symmetric random walk the chance of finding the particle at any state i is the same $1/(N + 1)$ regardless of i.* ■

In the assymmetric random walk the steady-state probabilities ϕ_i appear to be fairly complicated. But they make sense—at least qualitatively. Suppose, for example, that $b > d$. Then the ratio $b/d > 1$. Thus

$$\phi_i = \left(\frac{b}{d}\right)^i C$$

shows that ϕ_i is *increasing* with i. That is, the particle will be found with higher probability closer to the right boundary than to the left. This is certainly what we would expect since the right boundary "attracts" the particle ($b > d$). Here are the actual probabilities for $N = 10$ for several values of b/d:

STEADY-STATE PROBABILITY ϕ_i

State i	$b/d = 1$	$b/d = 1.2$	$b/d = 1.5$	$b/d = 2$	$b/d = 5$
0	.0909	.0311	.0058	.0005	.0000
1	.0909	.0373	.0088	.0010	.0000
2	.0909	.0448	.0132	.0020	.0000
3	.0909	.0537	.0197	.0039	.0000
4	.0909	.0645	.0296	.0078	.0001
5	.0909	.0774	.0444	.0156	.0003
6	.0909	.0929	.0666	.0313	.0013
7	.0909	.1115	.0999	.0625	.0064
8	.0909	.1337	.1499	.1251	.0320
9	.0909	.1605	.2248	.2501	.1600
10	.0909	.1926	.3372	.5002	.8000

Here is a program to simulate a random walk. Inputs are p, the starting position S, the boundary N, and the number of jumps JUMP to perform. For definiteness, states 0 and N are completely reflecting.

```
const NORM = 10000;
      ADDR =  4857;
      MULT =  8601;
var SEED,JUMP,I,S,N: integer;
    RND,P: real;
```

```
begin
        readln(P,S,N,JUMP); SEED: = 0;

        for I: = 1 to JUMP do
                begin
                        if S = 0 then S: = 1;
                        if S = N then S: = N − 1;
                        if (S < N) and (S > 0)
                                then begin
                                        SEED: = (MULT∗SEED + ADDR) mod NORM;
                                        RND: = SEED/NORM;

                                        if RND < P then S: = S+1
                                                    else S: = S−1;
                                end;
                        write(S);
                end;
        end.
```

PROBLEMS

12.27. Solve for the steady-state probability vector for the Markov chain in Fig. 12.17:

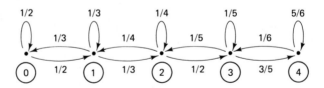

Figure 12.17

12.28. Consider the random walk on $\{0, 1, 2, \ldots\}$ with a partially reflecting boundary at state 0 in Fig. 12.18.

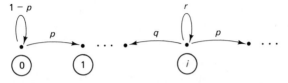

Figure 12.18

Show that a steady-state probability vector exists only if $p < q$. What is it in this case?

12.29. Write a program that will input N, then input b_i, r_i, and d_i for $i = 0, \ldots, N$. Output should be the steady-state probability components $\phi_0, \ldots, \phi_N$. Test your program on Problem 12.27.

Discrete-Time Markov Chains   Chap. 12

12.6 APERIODICITY, INDECOMPOSABILITY, AND THE APPROACH TO THE STEADY STATE

The Markov chain in Example 12 is *periodic*; from state 0 the particle must jump to either state 1 or 2; from state 1 and 2 it must next jump to state 0. Thus

$$\{0\} \rightarrow \{1, 2\} \rightarrow \{0\} \rightarrow \{1, 2\} \rightarrow \cdots$$

The reason why there is no steady state in the intuitive sense, *although* a vector ϕ with $\phi\Pi = \phi$ exists is that the chain has a periodicity.

Definition

Suppose that the sets $A_1, A_2, \ldots, A_r$ *partition* the state space S. That is, suppose that

$$S = \bigcup_{i=1}^{r} A_i$$

disjointly. Assume that a transition from A_i to A_{i+1} must occur in one jump (where $r + 1$ is taken to be 1: The particle "wraps around" to A_1 from A_r)— pictorially

$$A_1 \rightarrow A_2 \rightarrow \cdots \rightarrow A_r$$

That is, if at time t the particle is in one of the states of A_i, then at time $t + 1$ it must be in one of the states of A_{i+1}. Then the Markov chain is said to be *periodic with period r*. If the chain is not periodic, it is said to be *aperiodic*.

Example 15

(a) The random walk infinite in both directions is periodic with period 2: Let A_1 = set of even integers and A_2 = set of odd integers. Then

$$A_1 \rightarrow A_2 \rightarrow A_1 \rightarrow A_2 \rightarrow \cdots$$

(b) The random walk with a boundary at 0 is periodic with period 2 *if* the reflecting probability at 0 is $r = 1$. If $r < 1$, the chain is aperiodic. This is the case since state 0 can be in one and only one partition set.

(c) The random walk with completely reflecting boundaries at 0 and N is periodic with period 2 just as in part (a). ∎

In looking for conditions implying existence of a steady state, we ought to exclude periodic chains. Fortunately, there's an easy criterion to use to determine if a Markov chain is aperiodic:

Suppose that

$$\Pi_{k,k} > 0$$

for *any* state k. Then the chain is aperiodic.

This may not always apply; that is, there are chains with $\Pi_{k,k} = 0$ for all states k which *are* periodic. But it is easy to spot entries $\Pi_{k,k}$ along the main diagonal of Π which are nonzero; *if* there are any, the chain *must be* aperiodic.

To see why the boxed result is true, suppose that $A_1, \ldots, A_r$ is a periodic decomposition of the state space S; thus the A_i's are *disjoint*. But $k \in A_i$ for some i; if $\Pi_{k,k} > 0$, then $k \in A_{i+1}$, which contradicts the fact that $A_i \cap A_{i+1} = \emptyset$.

The Markov chain in Example 10 failed to have a *unique* steady-state vector because the state-space split into two disjoint subsets—$\{0, 1\}$ and $\{3\}$—from each of which it was impossible to reach the other. In general, we use the notation $i \leadsto j$ to denote the fact that the particle can make a transition from i to j in *some* number of steps, no matter how many other intermediate states are involved or how low the probability (as long as it is greater than 0).

Definition

A Markov chain is indecomposable if for every pair i, j of states, either $i \leadsto j$ or $j \leadsto i$ or both.

Example 16

The random walk on $S = \{0, 1, \ldots, N\}$ with absorbing barriers at 0 and N is *not* indecomposable since neither $0 \leadsto N$ nor $N \leadsto 0$. If N is partially reflecting, the chain *is* indecomposable since $N \leadsto 0$, although $0 \not\leadsto N$ still. ∎

Example 17

Is the chain in Fig. 12.19 (a) aperiodic? (b) indecomposable? (The arrows indicate positive transition probabilities.)

Solution (a) Note that $i \not\leadsto 2$ for all states i. Let us start at state 2 and see where it leads:

$$\{2\} \to \{1\} \to \{0, 3\} \to \{0, 3, 4\} \to \{0, 1, 3, 4\} \to \{0, 1, 3, 4\} \to \cdots$$

where the *next* set is obtained by placing into it all the states that the states in the *previous* set can jump to in one transition. Thus the chain is aperiodic.

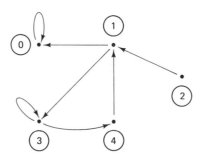

Figure 12.19

(b) The chain is also indecomposable since for all pairs i, j either $i \rightsquigarrow j$ or $j \rightsquigarrow i$ even though $i \not\rightsquigarrow 2$ for every i. ∎

Suppose that ρ is an initial probability vector specifying the probabilities with which the particle occupies the various states at time $t = 0$. Then the probability vector at time t is $\rho' = \rho\Pi'$, which quite clearly depends on the initial probability vector ρ. On the other hand, the Markov assumption that the future is independent of the past given the present suggests that after *many* jumps, the particle will "forget" where it started at time 0. If a particle starts at one of the interior states in a random walk, then after one jump, it is absolutely certain to have been at one of its neighboring states at the *previous* time. After several jumps, however, we begin to lose track of where it was originally. In the inventory model with which Section 12.1 began, the number of disks on the shelf at time 0 is crucial in knowing how many will be on the shelf at the end of the first month. But after a few years go by, the number of disks currently in stock depends less and less on the number originally stocked because of the unpredictability in the number sold each month.

Given a transition matrix Π and an initial probability vector ρ, what will be the steady state? What will be the limit of $\rho' = \rho\Pi'$ as $t \to \infty$ regardless of ρ? Since we have dwelt at length on the steady-state probability vector ϕ, it should come as no surprise that the limit is ϕ. But we must exclude the types of complications that can arise due to periodicity and decomposability. With these chains excluded, the following theorem is extremely useful:

Limit Theorem

Suppose that Π is the transition matrix for an aperiodic and indecomposable Markov chain. Assume that the vector equation

$$\phi\Pi = \phi$$

has a solution ϕ that is a probability vector with

$$0 < \phi_i < 1 \qquad \text{for all } i \in S$$

$$\sum_{i=0}^{N} \phi_i = 1$$

Then the following hold:

1. ϕ is unique: it is the only probability vector satisfying $\phi\Pi = \phi$.
2. Regardless of the initial probability vector ρ,

$$\rho' = \rho\Pi' \to \phi$$

   as $t \to \infty$.
3. If the initial probability vector is ϕ, then for all t,

$$\phi' = \phi\Pi' = \phi$$

The theorem applies whether S is finite or not. It is very useful because solving for the steady-state probability vector ϕ is often relatively straightforward (especially if one is willing to use a computer), although perhaps tedious.

Note that property 2 can be phrased as

$$P(X_t = j \mid \text{initial vector } \rho) \to \phi_j$$

as $t \to \infty$ for all $j \in S$. And property 3 states

$$P(X_t = j \mid \text{initial vector } \phi) = \phi_j$$

for *all* t and all $j \in S$.

Example 18

The general Two-State Process of Fig. 12.20.

$$\Pi = \begin{bmatrix} 1 - \alpha & \alpha \\ \beta & 1 - \beta \end{bmatrix}$$

Case 1: $\alpha = 0$ and $\beta = 0$. The particle will not move; the chain is decomposable.

Case 2: $\alpha = 1$ and $\beta = 1$. The particle jumps back and forth; the chain is periodic with period 2.

Case 3: Either $0 < \alpha < 1$ or $0 < \beta < 1$ or both.

$$(\phi_0, \phi_1) \begin{bmatrix} 1 - \alpha & \alpha \\ \beta & 1 - \beta \end{bmatrix} = (\phi_0, \phi_1)$$

implies that

$$\phi_0(1 - \alpha) + \phi_1\beta = \phi_0$$

$$\phi_0\alpha + \phi_1(1 - \beta) = \phi_1$$

Both of these are the *same* equation:

$$\alpha\phi_0 = \beta\phi_1$$

Using normalization,

$$1 = \phi_0 + \phi_1 = \left(1 + \frac{\alpha}{\beta}\right)\phi_0$$

Therefore,

$$\phi_0 = \frac{\beta}{\alpha + \beta} \qquad \phi_1 = \frac{\alpha}{\alpha + \beta}$$

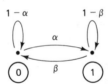

Figure 12.20

The conclusion of the limit theorem is that *regardless* of the starting probabilities, after many jumps the particle will be in states 0 and 1 with respective probabilities ϕ_0 and ϕ_1. (See Problem 12.32 for more details.) ∎

As a special case of the limit theorem, let us see the implications for the initial probability vector

$$\rho = (0, \ldots, 0, 1, 0, \ldots, 0)$$
$$\uparrow ith \text{ entry}$$

That is, the particle starts in state i with probability 1. We have already seen in Section 12.3 that

$$\rho_j^t = \Pi_{i,j}^t$$

for all states j. Therefore, if the particle starts in state i, *the probability vector at time t is the ith row of Π^t*. Hence the limit theorem states that the ith row of Π^t approaches the steady-state probability vector ϕ as $t \to \infty$.

Corollary to the Limit Theorem

Under the same assumptions, the tth-order transition matrix Π^t has a limit matrix

$$\lim_{t \to \infty} \Pi^t = M$$

where M has *constant rows* each equal to the steady-state probability vector ϕ.

Example 19

For the Markov chain of Example 8, successive powers of the transition matrix Π yield

$$\Pi = \begin{bmatrix} 0 & 1/2 & 1/2 \\ 0 & 2/3 & 1/3 \\ 1/3 & 2/3 & 0 \end{bmatrix} \qquad \Pi^2 = \begin{bmatrix} .1667 & .6667 & .1667 \\ .1111 & .6667 & .2222 \\ 0 & .6111 & .3889 \end{bmatrix}$$

$$\Pi^4 = \begin{bmatrix} .0876 & .6524 & .2600 \\ .0872 & .6523 & .2605 \\ .0861 & .6519 & .2620 \end{bmatrix} \qquad \Pi^8 = \begin{bmatrix} .0870 & .6522 & .2609 \\ .0870 & .6522 & .2609 \\ .0870 & .6522 & .2609 \end{bmatrix}$$

which agrees exactly to four significant digits with the steady-state probability vector ϕ found in Example 10 (that is, *each row* of Π^t approaches ϕ). ∎

Example 20

Consider this cyclic process—a special case of Example 9: (see Fig. 12.21)

$$\Pi = \begin{bmatrix} \dfrac{1}{10} & \dfrac{9}{10} & 0 \\ 0 & \dfrac{3}{4} & \dfrac{1}{4} \\ \dfrac{5}{7} & 0 & \dfrac{2}{7} \end{bmatrix}$$

Using the notation of Example 9 yields

$$p_0 = \frac{9}{10} \qquad p_1 = \frac{1}{4} \qquad p_2 = \frac{5}{7}$$

$$C = (p_0^{-1} + p_1^{-1} + p_2^{-1}) = 6.511$$

$$\phi_0 = \frac{1}{Cp_0} = .1706$$

$$\phi_1 = \frac{1}{Cp_1} = .6143$$

$$\phi_2 = \frac{1}{Cp_2} = .2150$$

Computing powers successively implies

$$\Pi^2 = \begin{bmatrix} .01 & .765 & .225 \\ .1786 & .5625 & .2589 \\ .2755 & .6429 & .0816 \end{bmatrix}$$

$$\Pi^4 = \begin{bmatrix} .1712 & .6133 & .2154 \\ .1710 & .6142 & .2148 \\ .1692 & .6156 & .2152 \end{bmatrix}$$

$$\Pi^8 = \begin{bmatrix} .1706 & .6143 & .2150 \\ .1706 & .6143 & .2150 \\ .1706 & .6143 & .2150 \end{bmatrix} \quad \blacksquare$$

The proof of the limit theorem would take us too far afield of our primary goal of developing techniques for dealing with random models. Proofs can be found in the books listed in the Bibliography.

A final note about the steady-state probability vector ϕ: In the limit theorem we *assumed* that ϕ exists with $\phi\Pi = \phi$. Recall that in Example 11 no such ϕ exists because the particle "dribbles" off to infinity without ever returning. For finitely many states this cannot happen.

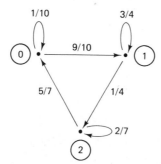

Figure 12.21

Existence Theorem

An aperiodic and indecomposable Markov chain with finite state space has one and only one steady-state probability vector.

If there is a steady-state probability vector, the limit theorem implies that there is only one. The existence theorem guarantees one. The proof can be found in books listed in the Bibliography.

PROBLEMS

Are the Markov chains with the given diagrams in Problems 12.30 and 12.31 aperiodic? indecomposable? If periodic, find the period and the period decomposition. Arrows denote positive transition probabilities.

12.30. (a) Fig. 12.22; (b) Fig. 12.23.

12.31. (a) Fig. 12.24; (b) Fig. 12.25.

12.32. For the general two-state process

$$\Pi = \begin{bmatrix} 1 - \alpha & \alpha \\ \beta & 1 - \beta \end{bmatrix}$$

show that

$$\Pi^t = \frac{1}{\alpha + \beta} \begin{bmatrix} \beta + \alpha C^t & \alpha - \alpha C^t \\ \beta - \beta C^t & \alpha + \beta C^t \end{bmatrix}$$

where

$$C = 1 - \alpha - \beta$$

Do this by induction. That is, is the formula above true for $t = 1$? Assume that the formula is true for time $t - 1$; that is, assume that Π^{t-1} is given by the formula above with $t - 1$ replacing t on the right-hand side. Show that $\Pi^{t-1}\Pi$ is then given by the formula above. Conclude that Π^t is given by the formula above for all $t > 0$.

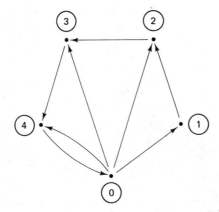

Figure 12.22

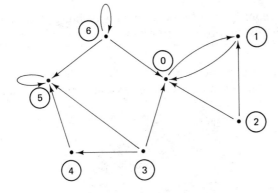

Figure 12.23

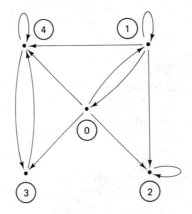

Figure 12.24

12.33. (*Continuation*) Assuming that $0 \leq \alpha, \beta \leq 1$, show that

$$-1 \leq C = 1 - \alpha - \beta \leq +1$$

with strict inequalities for *either* $0 < \alpha < 1$ *or* $0 < \beta < 1$ or both. Conclude that

$$\Pi^t \to \frac{1}{\alpha + \beta} \begin{bmatrix} \beta & \alpha \\ \beta & \alpha \end{bmatrix} \qquad \text{as } t \to \infty$$

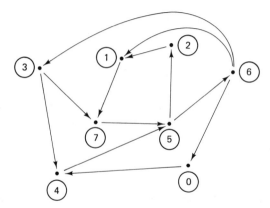

Figure 12.25

12.34. (*The Gambler's Ruin Problem*) Consider the random walk on $\{0, 1, \ldots, N\}$ with absorbing boundaries at 0 and N. (The gambler starts with $\$i$; the game continues until either the gambler or the casino goes broke.) The problem is to calculate

$$\eta_i = P(\text{particle hits } N \text{ before } 0 \mid \text{start in state } i)$$

$$= P(\text{gambler wins all } \$N \mid \text{gambler starts with } \$i)$$

By conditioning on whether the particle first jumps to the right or the left, show that

$$\eta = p\eta_{i+1} + q\eta_{i-1}$$

for $i = 1, 2, \ldots, N - 1$ and that

$$\eta_0 = 0 \qquad \eta_N = 1$$

To solve these equations, set

$$\delta_i = \eta_i - \eta_{i-1}$$

for $i = 1, 2, \ldots, N$. Show that $\delta_i = (q/p) \cdot \delta_{i-1}$. Show that this implies $\delta_i = (q/p)^{i-1} \cdot \delta_1$ for $i = 1, 2, \ldots, N$. Now show that

$$\eta_i = \eta_0 + (\eta_1 - \eta_0) + (\eta_2 - \eta_1) + \cdots + (\eta_i - \eta_{i-1})$$

$$= \eta_0 + \delta_1 + \delta_2 + \cdots + \delta_i$$

$$= \left(1 + \frac{q}{p} + \cdots + \left(\frac{q}{p}\right)^{i-1}\right)\delta_1$$

There are two cases:

> *Case 1: $p = q$* (*symmetric random walk*). Show that $\eta_i = i\delta_1$ $\eta_i = i/N$ using the boundary condition $\eta_N = 1$.
> *Case 2: $p \neq q$* (*asymmetric random walk*). Show that

$$\eta_i = C\left(1 - \left(\frac{q}{p}\right)^i\right)$$

for $i = 0, 1, \ldots, N$ where $C^{-1} - (q/p)^N$ using the formula for the sum of a finite geometric series together with the fact that $\eta_N = 1$.

12.35. (*Continuation*) Also of interest in the gambler's ruin problem is the expected time of the game—the expected number of jumps until absorption in either the right or the left boundaries. Let

$$\tau_i = E(\text{time until absorption} \mid \text{particle starts in state } i)$$

Now, on the *first* jump from state i, the particle jumps to the right with probability p or to the left with probability q. In either case the *additional* time until absorption is as though the particle started from its present state Show that

$$\tau_i = 1 + p\tau_{i+1} + q\tau_{i-1}$$

for $i = 1, 2, \ldots, N - 1$. Show that the boundary conditions are $\tau_0 = 0$ and $\tau_N = 0$.

12.36. (*Continuation*) Show that for the symmetric random walk ($p = 1/2 = q$) that $\tau_i = Ni - i^2$ satisfies all the equations of Problem 12.35. Fix N and graph τ_i as a function of i.

12.37. Write a program to simulate the symmetric random walk. Inputs p, the position N of the right boundary, the starting position S, and an integer MAX. MAX many simulations should be performed, *each* with initial position S. *Each* simulation should continue until the particle hits 0 or N. Output the fraction of the simulations that resulted in absorption in N. Also print out the average time (number of jumps) until absorption. Do these agree with the results of Problems 12.34 and 12.36?

12.7 RANDOM COMMENTS AND PROBLEMS: RETURN TIMES (OPTIONAL)

There is a remarkable relation between the steady-state probability ϕ_i and the times between visits to state i. Suppose that the particle starts in state i at time 0. Let T denote the *time that it next returns to state i*. Thus $T = 1$ if the particle jumps back immediately to state i at time 1; if the particle jumps to state 2, then 14, then 7, then back to state i, then $T = 4$. If the particle *never* returns to state i, set $T = \infty$. In this way T itself is a random variable. Let $\tau_i = E(T) = $ *expected return time to state i*.

> Under the hypotheses of the limit theorem, the expected return time to state i is the reciprocal of the steady-state probability:
>
> $$\tau_i = \frac{1}{\phi_i}$$

Here is an *intuitive* reason why this is so: Assume that the particle starts in state i. Let T_1 be the time of *first* return back to state i. ($T_1 \geqslant 1$.) Let T_2 be the time *between* the first return and the second return to state i. Thus the actual time that the particle returns to i for the second time is $T_1 + T_2$. In general, let T_n be *the time between the $n - 1$st and the nth return to state i*. Over the course of n returns the quotient

$$\frac{T_1 + \cdots + T_n}{n}$$

is *the average time between visits to state i.* For n large this should be very close to τ_i = expected time between visits to state i by the law of large number of Section 10.7. Note that $T_1, \ldots, T_n$ are IIDRVs. Why? Thus

$$\frac{T_1 + \cdots + T_n}{n} \rightarrow \tau_i \qquad \text{as } n \rightarrow \infty$$

The reciprocal of the fraction on the left-hand side is

$$\frac{n}{T_1 + \cdots + T_n}$$

which can be interpreted as the number of visits to state i per time required; or *the number of visits to state i per unit time.* Averaged over a long interval of time this is the chance of finding the particle in state i at any one instant of time. And *this* quantity is the steady-state probability ϕ_i. Consequently,

$$\frac{n}{T_1 + \cdots + T_n} \rightarrow \phi_i \qquad \text{as } n \rightarrow \infty$$

so

$$\tau_i = \frac{1}{\phi_i}$$

Example 21: *The Ehrenfest Diffusion Model*

Around the turn of the century a paradox arose in statistical physics. The equations of motion of particles obey Newton's equations; these equations are time reversible. This means that if a system of particles evolves in a certain way through time, the evolution backward in time is also a physical possibility. In other words, if a movie is made of a real physical system of particles, the movie shown in *reverse* is also physically realizable. It is clear, however, that complex systems we see in the world do not have this property. Slide a book across the table; it comes slowly to rest. But no matter how long you wait, you will not see a motionless book begin to move faster and faster toward your hand. How can this obvious feature of the world be reconciled with the time reversibility of physical laws? The following model, though a vast oversimplification to real systems, helps explain how this can be.

Consider N tags labeled from 1 to N distributed in two containers—urn I and urn II. At each instant I choose *one* of the tags at random and *switch* the urn in which it is located. The state of the system at time t is X_t = *number* of tags in urn I. The state space S is the set of possible *numbers* of tags in urn I; thus $S =$

$\{0, 1, 2, \ldots, N\}$. This is a birth and death chain with

$$b_i = P(X_{t+1} = i + 1 \mid X_t = i)$$

$$= P(\text{choose a tag from urn II} \mid i \text{ tags in urn I})$$

$$= \frac{N - i}{N}$$

$$d_i = P(X_{t+1} = i - 1 \mid X_t = i)$$

$$= P(\text{choose a tag from urn I} \mid i \text{ tags in urn I})$$

$$= \frac{i}{N}$$

$$r_i = 0$$

since it is impossible that the system *not* change at the next choosing of a tag.
Problem 12.38 asks you to show that the steady-state probabilities are

$$\phi_i = \binom{N}{i} \cdot 2^{-N}$$

Now suppose that the system starts in state 0 with 0 tags in urn I. The expected return time is

$$\tau_0 = \frac{1}{\phi_0} = 2^N$$

which is enormously large for even moderate values of N. To get an idea of the order of magnitude we switch from base 2 to base 10:

$$\tau_0 = 2^N = 10^{\log_{10}(2^N)} = 10^{N \log_{10}(2)} = 10^{.3010N}$$

For example, if there are $N = 100$ tags and we start with all 100 in urn II (that is, the system is started in state 0), it will take an expected number of random tag switches equal to 10^{30} approximately, to return to state 0. (That's about 3×10^{20} centuries at the rate of 1 switch per second!)

Here's the idea: The systems around us *are* time reversible, but the time required to restore the initial condition of an *ordered* system is inconceivably long. Urn I is your apartment; urn II is the rest of the city. Each tag is a speck of dirt. After cleaning the apartment, the state of the system is 0—0 dirt specks in the apartment. Every time someone enters the apartment and leaves, one (or several) "tags" are switched. According to the model, it *is* possible that all the tags will be shifted back again outside the apartment simply due to randomness, but do not count on it happening soon!

PROBLEMS

12.38. Let ϕ_i for $0 \le i \le N$ denote the steady-state probabilities for the Ehrenfest model. Use the procedure for finding the steady-state probability vector from Section 12.5

to show that

$$\phi_i = \frac{N - i + 1}{i} \phi_{i-1}$$

for $1 \leq i \leq N$. Show that these equations are satisfied with

$$\phi_i = \binom{N}{i} \cdot 2^{-N}$$

Also show that $\phi_0 + \phi_1 + \cdots + \phi_N = 1$.

12.39. In the random walk model with partially reflecting boundaries of Example 14, let $N = 10$ and assume that the particles starts in state 0. Find the expected return time τ_0 to state 0 for these values of b/d; **(a)** .1; **(b)** .5; **(c)** 1; **(d)** 2; **(e)** 5; **(f)** 10. **(g)** If jumps occur each second, how many *years* can one expect to wait until the particle returns to state 0 for $b/d = 10$?

12.40. In the cyclic process of Example 9, find the expected cycle time: Assume that the particle starts in state 0 and $p_0 = 1$ (so that it *must* jump to state 1 at time 1). Find τ_0.

Bibliography

There are numerous introductory texts in probability. The following cover many of the same topics in more depth.

BREIMAN, LEO, *Probability and Stochastic Processes with a View Toward Applications*, Houghton Mifflin Company, Boston, 1969.

FELLER, WILLIAM, *An Introduction to Probability Theory and Its Applications*, John Wiley & Sons, Inc., New York. Volume 1 (1968) covers discrete random variables; Volume 2 (1966) covers continuous random variables. The two together form a classic in probability texts.

TRIVEDI, KISHOR, *Probability and Statistics with Reliability, Queuing, and Computer Science Applications*, Prentice-Hall, Inc., Englewood Cliffs, NJ, 1982.

These cover stochastic processes and applications for which this course is a prerequisite:

HOEL, P., S. PORT, and C. STONE, *Introduction to Stochastic Processes*, Houghton Mifflin Company, Boston 1972.

PARZEN, EMANUEL, *Stochastic Processes*, Holden-Day, Inc., San Francisco, 1962.

ROSS, SHELDON, *Introduction to Probability Models*, Academic Press, Inc., Orlando, 1985.

Here are two on the history of probability:

DAVID, F. N., *Games, Gods and Gambling*, Hafner, London, 1962.

MAISTROV, L. E., *Probability Theory, A Historical Sketch*, Academic Press, Inc., New York, 1974.

These four volumes contain a wealth of historical information on all aspects of mathematics:

NEWMAN, JAMES, *The World of Mathematics*, Simon & Schuster, New York, 1956.

— Appendix 1 ————————

Programming Terminology

Probability is an applied subject; this entails using formulas to compute numbers. To do this, the computer is helpful, but not essential. In a more significant way programs are used to *simulate* random processes beginning in Chapter 7. This means that the details of the process are represented in a computer language.

For both these purposes we will be using a language that expresses the algorithm. The language used consists of a subset of Pascal for two reasons: First, programs written in Pascal are relatively easy to read and understand without knowing the specifics of the language. Second, Pascal programs reveal the *logic* of algorithms better than most languages. If you know and prefer another language, such as FORTRAN or BASIC, you should be able to understand all the algorithms in this book and translate them into your own language without much effort.

In fact only a minimum of the Pascal language is used—just enough to write the programs needed. Here is a summary of what is used:

1. Words that have predefined meanings in Pascal are in lowercase; for example, array, begin, while, if, var, ... Words that the programmer defines are in UPPERCASE; these are *constant* and *variable* names. This convention is purely for readability and is not essential for the program to run.

2. *Constants*. At the beginning of the program are the constant definitions if there are any. These create synonyms for specific numbers. For example, the

beginning of a program might be

```
const PI = 3.1415927;
      E  = 2.7182818;
```

Then in the program whenever PI is used, its actual value as defined is substituted. The word "const" appears once, as indicated, to flag the beginning of the constant definitions.

3. *Variables.* After the constants come the variable declarations. Only the types integer, real, and array are used in this book. For example, after the constant definitions, this might appear:

```
var I,J,MAX: integer;
    X: real;
    A: array [0..10] of integer;
    B,C: array [-10..10] of real;
```

I, J, and MAX are storage areas able to hold one integer each. X can hold a real [floating-point number (number with a decimal point)]. A is an array of 11 integer storage areas; thus A[0], A[1], . . ., A[10] are each able to hold one integer. B and C are both arrays of 21 real storage areas. The *indices* for both B and C range from -10 to $+10$.

4. The actual series of instructions (the body of the program) starts with the word "begin" and ends with "end."

5. *Semicolons* separate logical units or "thoughts."

6. *Indentation* and *line skipping* are used for better legibility, although they are not essential for the actual running of the program. They allow one to see at a glance the overall logical structure.

7. *Assignment operator.* The symbol $:=$ is used to assign values.

$$A := 4; \quad B := 4.3; \quad B := B+1; \quad C[13] := 45;$$

A can be either an integer or a real variable, B must be real, and C can be either an array of integers or reals whose range of indices includes 13. A is set equal to 4, then B is assigned the value 4.3, then B is incremented to 5.3, and finally C[13] is assigned the value 45.

8. *Arithmetic operators.* $+$, $-$, $*$, and $/$ mean, respectively, addition, subtraction, multiplication, and division. $**$ is used for exponentiation (although it is not part of standard Pascal). For example,

$$A := 4.3*A + 1; \quad B := B/A**5 - 2;$$

Exponentiation precedes multiplication and division, which precede addition and subtraction in the order of precedence. Thus the above is equivalent to

$$A := (4.3*A) + 1; \quad B := (B/(A**5)) - 2;$$

Spaces and parentheses, while not essential, add to legibility. Note that the *square root* operator is

$$A := A**0.5$$

If N and I are integers, then N div I is the integer obtained by dividing N by I and N mod I is the remainder. Thus 17 div 5 is 3 while 17 mod 5 is 2. If A is a real number, then trunc(A) is the integer part of A. (Strip off what is to the right of the decimal point.) Thus trunc(53.2109) = 53. Trunc, div, and mod are connected by these relations: For N and I integers,

```
trunc(N/I) = N div I;
N − trunc(N/I)*I = N mod I
```

For example, trunc(17/5) = 3 and 17 − trunc(17/5)*5 = 17 − 3*5 = 2.

9. *System-Defined Functions.* We use the following:

```
A := exp(B+3);    C := cos(A);    D := sin(D−2);    E := ln(D**4);
```

as notations for the exponential function, cosine, sine, and natural logarithm (base *e*).

10. *For loops*

```
for I: = 1 to 100 do            for I: = 1 to 100 do ....
    begin

    . . . . .

    end;
```

In the first example each of the instructions between the "begin" and "end" are executed 100 times. The *loop counter* I must be declared to be an integer. In the second example the *one* instruction after "do" is executed 100 times. Thus if there is only one instruction to be performed in a for loop, the "begin" and "end" are optional.

11. *While loops*

```
I: = 1; SUM: = 0;               I: = 1;
while A[I]< = 50 do             while A[I]< = 50 do I: = I+1;
    begin
        SUM: = SUM+A[I];
        I: = I+1;
    end;
```

In the first example the two instructions between the "begin" and "end" are executed *until* an array element A[I] is found so that A[I] > 50. Suppose that A[1], A[2], . . . have the values 5, 10, 32, 67. Then at the termination of the loop, SUM = 47 and I = 4. In the second example there is only one instruction to be performed, so the "begin" and "end" are optional. At the termination of the loop, I will have the value 4.

12. *Repeat loops*. These begin with the word "repeat" and end with the word "until." The two examples in (11) are written

```
I: = 1; SUM: = 0;          I: = 0;
repeat                     repeat
    SUM: = SUM + A[I];         I: = I + 1;
    I: = I + 1;            until A[I] > 50;
until A[I] > 50;
```

But there is a minor difference. If A[1] is larger than 50, the first example of the while loop in (11) will leave SUM with the value 0 (zero times through the while loop), but the first example of the repeat loop in (12) will add the value A[1] into SUM and continue through the loop since A[1] is never compared to 50.

13. *Input*. To read in (input) numbers and place them in the storage areas A, I, and X, use this instruction (read "read line")

```
readln(A,I,X);
```

14. *Output*. To write out the values of the variables A, I, and C[3], either of these will suffice:

```
write(A,I,C[3]);     writeln(A,I,C[3]);
```

The difference between *write* and *writeln* is that *writeln* will jump to the *next* line for the *next* output operation whereas *write* will not.

If X is a real storage area, *field widths* are used:

```
write(X:10:3);     writeln (X:10:3);
```

will both output the value of X right justified in a field width of size 10 with three digits printed to the *right* of the decimal point.

15. *If then*:

```
If ...   then          If ...   then .....;
         begin
            .....
         end;
```

If the condition is satisfied, all instructions between the "begin" and "end" are executed. If the condition is false, these instructions are not executed. If *only one* instruction is to be executed if the condition is satisfied, the "begin" and "end" are optional.

16. *If then else*:

```
If . . .   then
              begin
                  A: = 1; B: = 3;
              end
          else
              begin
                  X: = 1.2; write(Z);
              end;
```

If the condition is met, then A is set equal to 1 and B is set equal to 3. If the condition is *not* met, X is set equal to 1.2 and the value of Z is output. There is *never* a semicolon before an "else." As with the previous instructions, for either the "then" part or the "else" part, if there is *only one* instruction to be performed, the corresponding "begin" and "end" are optional.

— Appendix 2 ——————————

Multiplying Square Matrices and a Vector Times a Matrix

In Chapter 12 these techniques are required. Let A be an $n \times n$ matrix. This means that A is an array of n rows and n columns containing n^2 numbers. The entry in the ith row and jth column is denoted $A_{i,j}$ and is called the ij entry of A.

Let A and B both be $n \times n$ matrices. Then the product AB is an $n \times n$ matrix. The ij entry of AB is obtained by multiplying corresponding entries in the ith row of A by the jth column of B and summing all the products.

Suppose that

$$A = \begin{bmatrix} 2 & 3 \\ 1 & -4 \end{bmatrix} \qquad B = \begin{bmatrix} -3 & 1 \\ 5 & -6 \end{bmatrix}$$

Then both A and B are 2×2 matrices. The 1,1 entry of AB is obtained by multiplying the first row of A by the first column of B:

$$(2 \quad 3) \begin{bmatrix} -3 \\ 5 \end{bmatrix} = 2(-3) + 3(5) = 9$$

The 1,2 entry of AB is

$$(2 \quad 3) \begin{bmatrix} 1 \\ -6 \end{bmatrix} = 2(1) + 3(-6) = -16$$

The other two entries of AB are found in the same way: Check that

$$AB = \begin{bmatrix} 2 & 3 \\ 1 & -4 \end{bmatrix} \begin{bmatrix} -3 & 1 \\ 5 & -6 \end{bmatrix} = \begin{bmatrix} 9 & -16 \\ -23 & 25 \end{bmatrix}$$

394

As another example, check that

$$\begin{bmatrix} 1 & 2 & 3 \\ 4 & 5 & 6 \\ 7 & 8 & 9 \end{bmatrix} \begin{bmatrix} 0 & -1 & -3 \\ 4 & -3 & 0 \\ 10 & 6 & 3 \end{bmatrix} = \begin{bmatrix} 38 & 11 & 6 \\ 80 & 17 & 6 \\ 122 & 23 & 6 \end{bmatrix}$$

In general, it is *not* true that $AB = BA$. For example, with A and B the 2×2 matrices above, check that

$$BA = \begin{bmatrix} -3 & 1 \\ 5 & -6 \end{bmatrix} \begin{bmatrix} 2 & 3 \\ 1 & -4 \end{bmatrix} = \begin{bmatrix} -5 & -13 \\ 4 & 39 \end{bmatrix} \neq AB$$

That is, matrix multiplication is *not commutative* (although AB might equal BA for some specific matrices A and B).

Matrix multiplication is always *associative*, however. Thus if A, B, and C are matrices, then always

$$A(BC) = (AB)C$$

For example,

$$\left(\begin{bmatrix} 1 & 2 \\ 3 & 4 \end{bmatrix} \begin{bmatrix} 0 & 1 \\ 1 & -1 \end{bmatrix} \right) \begin{bmatrix} -1 & 1 \\ 0 & 1 \end{bmatrix} = \begin{bmatrix} 2 & -1 \\ 4 & -1 \end{bmatrix} \begin{bmatrix} -1 & 1 \\ 0 & 1 \end{bmatrix} = \begin{bmatrix} -2 & 1 \\ -4 & 3 \end{bmatrix}$$

and

$$\begin{bmatrix} 1 & 2 \\ 3 & 4 \end{bmatrix} \left(\begin{bmatrix} 0 & 1 \\ 1 & -1 \end{bmatrix} \begin{bmatrix} -1 & 1 \\ 0 & 1 \end{bmatrix} \right) = \begin{bmatrix} 1 & 2 \\ 3 & 4 \end{bmatrix} \begin{bmatrix} 0 & 1 \\ -1 & 0 \end{bmatrix} = \begin{bmatrix} -2 & 1 \\ -4 & 3 \end{bmatrix}$$

The integer power of a matrix is defined

$$A^n = A \cdots A$$

n times. Because of associativity, it does not matter in what order the matrices are multiplied. With A as above,

$$A^2 = AA = \begin{bmatrix} 1 & 2 \\ 3 & 4 \end{bmatrix} \begin{bmatrix} 1 & 2 \\ 3 & 4 \end{bmatrix} = \begin{bmatrix} 7 & 10 \\ 15 & 22 \end{bmatrix}$$

$$A^3 = AA^2 = \begin{bmatrix} 1 & 2 \\ 3 & 4 \end{bmatrix} \begin{bmatrix} 7 & 10 \\ 15 & 22 \end{bmatrix} = \begin{bmatrix} 37 & 54 \\ 81 & 118 \end{bmatrix}$$

By associativity this is also A^2A, as can easily be checked. A^4 can be obtained in any of these ways:

$$A^3A \qquad AA^3 \qquad A^2A^2$$

The ij entry of AB is obtained by multiplying the kth entry in *row i* of A by the kth entry of *column j* of B and adding for each k. Thus a formula for the ij entry of AB is

$$(AB)_{i,j} = \sum_{k=1}^{n} A_{i,k} B_{k,j}$$

Let $v = (v_1, v_2, \ldots, v_n)$ be a (row) vector with n components. If A is an

$n \times n$ matrix, the product vA is defined and is a row vector with n components. The jth component of vA is obtained by taking each component of v, multiplying it by the corresponding entry in the jth column of A, and adding. For example,

$$(2 \quad 3) \begin{bmatrix} 1 & 4 \\ 5 & 6 \end{bmatrix} = (17 \quad 26)$$

Thus the first component of the product is obtained by multiplying each entry in $(2 \quad 3)$ by the corresponding entry in $\begin{bmatrix} 1 \\ 5 \end{bmatrix}$ and adding to obtain 17. As another example,

$$(1 \quad 2 \quad 3) \begin{bmatrix} 1 & -1 & 5 \\ 0 & 3 & 4 \\ 6 & -7 & 0 \end{bmatrix} = (19 \quad -16 \quad 13)$$

Let the ith entry of the vector v be v_i as above. Then the jth entry of the product

$$(vA)_j = \sum_{k=1}^{n} v_k A_{k,j}$$

Associativity also holds for multiplication of a vector by several matrices. Thus

$$(vA)B = v(AB)$$

where v is a vector with n components and A and B are $n \times n$ matrices. For example,

$$\left((2 \quad 3) \begin{bmatrix} 2 & 3 \\ 1 & -4 \end{bmatrix} \right) \begin{bmatrix} -3 & 1 \\ 5 & -6 \end{bmatrix} = (7 \quad -6) \begin{bmatrix} -3 & 1 \\ 5 & -6 \end{bmatrix} = (-51 \quad 43)$$

and

$$(2 \quad 3) \left(\begin{bmatrix} 2 & 3 \\ 1 & -4 \end{bmatrix} \begin{bmatrix} -3 & 1 \\ 5 & -6 \end{bmatrix} \right) = (2 \quad 3) \begin{bmatrix} 9 & -16 \\ -23 & 25 \end{bmatrix} = (-51 \quad 43)$$

Therefore, if v is a vector with n components and A is an $n \times n$ matrix, vA^m can be obtained in two ways: First, find A^m, then multiply to obtain vA^m. Second, obtain vA, then vA^2 as $(vA)A$, and continue to obtain vA^m as $(vA^{m-1})A$.

— Appendix 3

Table of the Cumulative Distribution Function for the Normal $N(0,1)$ Distribution

$$F(x) = \int_{-\infty}^{x} \frac{1}{\sqrt{2\pi}} e^{-t^2/2}\, dt$$

x	.00	.01	.02	.03	.04	.05	.06	.07	.08	.09
.0	.5000	.5040	.5080	.5120	.5160	.5199	.5239	.5279	.5319	.5359
.1	.5398	.5438	.5478	.5517	.5557	.5596	.5636	.5675	.5714	.5753
.2	.5793	.5832	.5871	.5910	.5948	.5987	.6026	.6064	.6103	.6141
.3	.6179	.6217	.6255	.6293	.6331	.6368	.6406	.6443	.6480	.6517
.4	.6554	.6591	.6628	.6664	.6700	.6736	.6772	.6808	.6844	.6879
.5	.6915	.6950	.6985	.7019	.7054	.7088	.7123	.7157	.7190	.7224
.6	.7257	.7291	.7324	.7357	.7389	.7422	.7454	.7486	.7517	.7549
.7	.7580	.7611	.7642	.7673	.7704	.7734	.7764	.7794	.7823	.7852
.8	.7881	.7910	.7939	.7967	.7995	.8023	.8051	.8078	.8106	.8133
.9	.8159	.8186	.8212	.8238	.8264	.8289	.8315	.8340	.8365	.8389
1.0	.8413	.8438	.8461	.8485	.8508	.8531	.8554	.8577	.8599	.8621
1.1	.8643	.8665	.8686	.8708	.8729	.8749	.8770	.8790	.8810	.8830
1.2	.8849	.8869	.8888	.8907	.8925	.8944	.8962	.8980	.8997	.9015
1.3	.9032	.9049	.9066	.9082	.9099	.9115	.9131	.9147	.9162	.9177
1.4	.9192	.9207	.9222	.9236	.9251	.9265	.9279	.9292	.9306	.9319
1.5	.9332	.9345	.9357	.9370	.9382	.9394	.9406	.9418	.9429	.9441
1.6	.9452	.9463	.9474	.9484	.9495	.9505	.9515	.9525	.9535	.9545
1.7	.9554	.9564	.9573	.9582	.9591	.9599	.9608	.9616	.9625	.9633
1.8	.9641	.9649	.9656	.9664	.9671	.9678	.9686	.9693	.9699	.9706
1.9	.9713	.9719	.9726	.9732	.9738	.9744	.9750	.9756	.9761	.9767
2.0	.9772	.9778	.9783	.9788	.9793	.9798	.9803	.9808	.9812	.9817
2.1	.9821	.9826	.9830	.9834	.9838	.9842	.9846	.9850	.9854	.9857
2.2	.9861	.9864	.9868	.9871	.9875	.9878	.9881	.9884	.9887	.9890
2.3	.9893	.9896	.9898	.9901	.9904	.9906	.9909	.9911	.9913	.9916
2.4	.9918	.9920	.9922	.9925	.9927	.9929	.9931	.9932	.9934	.9936
2.5	.9938	.9940	.9941	.9943	.9945	.9946	.9948	.9949	.9951	.9952
2.6	.9953	.9955	.9956	.9957	.9959	.9960	.9961	.9962	.9963	.9964
2.7	.9965	.9966	.9967	.9968	.9969	.9970	.9971	.9972	.9973	.9974
2.8	.9974	.9975	.9976	.9977	.9977	.9978	.9979	.9979	.9980	.9981
2.9	.9981	.9982	.9982	.9983	.9984	.9984	.9985	.9985	.9986	.9986
3.0	.9987	.9987	.9987	.9988	.9988	.9989	.9989	.9989	.9990	.9990
3.1	.9990	.9991	.9991	.9991	.9992	.9992	.9992	.9992	.9993	.9993
3.2	.9993	.9993	.9994	.9994	.9994	.9994	.9994	.9995	.9995	.9995
3.3	.9995	.9995	.9995	.9996	.9996	.9996	.9996	.9996	.9996	.9997
3.4	.9997	.9997	.9997	.9997	.9997	.9997	.9997	.9997	.9997	.9998

Leo Breiman, *Probability and Stochastic Processes*, Houghton Mifflin Company, New York, 1969.

Solutions and Hints
to Selected Problems

CHAPTER 1

1.1. $\Omega = \{H1, H2, H3, H4, H5, H6, T1, T2, T3, T4, T5, T6\}$
$A = \{H1, H5\}$, $B = \{H1, H2, H3, H4, H5, H6\}$, $C = \{H2, H4, H6, T2, T4, T6\}$

1.3. $\Omega = \{H1, H2, H3, H4, H5, H6, TH, TT\}$
$A = \{TT\}$, $B = \{H1, H2, H3, H4, H5, H6\}$, $C = \{H2, H4, H6\}$

1.5. $\Omega = \{t : 0 \leqslant t \leqslant 10\} \cup \{never\} = [0, 10] \cup \{never\}$
where t is in hours and the sample point "never" represents the event "none observed."
$A = [0, 5/60)$ $B = (3, 5)$ $C = \{never\}$

1.7. $\Omega = \{(S,T) : 0 \leqslant S \leqslant 1, 0 \leqslant T \leqslant 1\}$
$A = \{(S,T) \in \Omega : 0 \leqslant S < 1/3\}$
$B = \{(S,T) \in \Omega : 11/12 < T \leqslant 1\}$
$C = \{(S,T) \in \Omega : 0 \leqslant S \leqslant 1/4, 0 \leqslant T \leqslant 1/4\}$
$D = \{(S,T) \in \Omega : T < S\}$
$E = \{(S,T) \in \Omega : 0 < S - T < 1/6\}$
$F = \{(S,T) \in \Omega : |T - S| < 1/4\}$

1.9. **(a)** $A \cup B$ = "coin was heads" = $\{H1, H2, H3, H4, H5, H6\}$
(b) $B \cap C$ = "coin was heads, die was even" = $\{H2, H4, H6\}$
(c) A^c = "coin was a tail or die was 2, 3, 4, or 6"
= $\{H2, H3, H4, H6, T1, T2, T3, T4, T5, T6\}$

1.17. **(a)** $P(A \cap B) = .4$; **(b)** $P(A^c \cup B) = .9$; **(c)** $P(A \cap B^c) = .1$

1.19. $P(B^c) = .4$; **(b)** $P(A \cap B \cap C^c) = .2$; **(c)** $P(A) = .6$; **(d)** $P(B - (B \cap C)) = .3$

1.20. First find $P(A \cap B^c \cap C^c)$, $P(A^c \cap B \cap C^c)$, and $P(A^c \cap B^c \cap C)$ noting that $P(A \cup B \cup C) = 1$.

1.21. (a) .1; (b) .4; (c) .5

1.23. (a) .2; (b) .4; (c) 0; (d) .4

1.25. $P(A \cup B \cup C) = P(A \cup B) + P(C) - P((A \cup B) \cap C)$
$\qquad = P(A) + P(B) - P(A \cap B) + P(C) - P((A \cap C) \cup (B \cap C))$
$\qquad = P(A) + P(B) + P(C) - P(A \cap B) - P(A \cap C) - P(B \cap C) + P(A \cap B \cap C)$
using Property 7 for each equality.

1.26. Let $B = A_2 \cup A_3 \cup A_4$. $P(A_1 \cup A_2 \cup A_3 \cup A_4) = P(A_1 \cup B) = P(A_1) + P(B) - P(A_1 \cap B)$. Apply Problem 1.25 to $P(B)$ and to $P(A_1 \cap B) = P((A_1 \cap A_2) \cup (A_1 \cap A_3) \cup (A_1 \cap A_4))$.

1.27. Ω and $\emptyset$ are disjoint. Therefore Axiom 3 implies that $P(\Omega) = P(\Omega \cup \emptyset) = P(\Omega) + P(\emptyset)$. Subtract $P(\Omega)$ to obtain $P(\emptyset) = 0$.

1.29. Assume Axiom 3'. Let $A_1, \ldots, A_n$ be disjoint. Set $A_i = \emptyset$ for $i > n$. Then $A_1, A_2, \ldots$ are disjoint. Thus

$$P(\overset{n}{\underset{i=1}{\cup}} A_i) = P(\overset{\infty}{\underset{i=1}{\cup}} A_i) = \overset{\infty}{\underset{i=0}{\sum}} P(A_i) = \overset{n}{\underset{i=1}{\sum}} P(A_i)$$

where the second equality follows from Axiom 3' and the third from Axiom 1.

CHAPTER 2

2.1. (a) $\Omega = \{H1, H2, H3, H4, H5, H6, T1, T2, T3, T4, T5, T6\}$; (b) 6/12; (c) 6/12; (d) 3/12

2.3. (a) $HRD, HRC, HRS, HDC, HDS, HCS, RDC, RDS, RCS, DCS$; (b) 6/10; (c) 3/10; (d) 3/10

2.5. 962

2.7. (a) 15; (b) 60

2.9. (a) 10; (b) 270; (c) 720; (d) 120; (e) as many ways as there are to select n from the 10 digits; the smallest will be placed on the left, the next smallest in the next position, $\ldots$.

2.11. (a) $\binom{20}{2} = 190$; (b) 18!; (c) 190 · 18!

2.13. (a) $\binom{30}{8}8!$; (b) $\binom{15}{8} \cdot 2^8 \cdot 8!$

2.15. (a) 7^5; (b) 6^5; (c) $(7)_5$; (d) $(7)_5/7^5 = .1499$

2.17. (a) (1, 2, 3), (1, 3, 2), (2, 1, 3), (2, 3, 1), (3, 1, 2), (3, 2, 1); (b) (1, 2, 3), (1, 3, 2), (1, 2, 2), (1, 3, 3), (2, 1, 3), (3, 1, 2), (2, 1, 2), (3, 1, 3), (2, 3, 1), (3, 2, 1), (2, 2, 1), (3, 3, 1); (c) For part (a): As many ways as to line up 3 ping pong balls − 3! For part (b): Task 1. Choose ball for can 1: 3 ways. Task 2. Distribute other two balls in other two cans: 4 ways.

2.19. (a) .3902; (b) .05522; (c) .3049

2.21. (a) .25; (b) .05882; (c) .01294; (d) $((13)_3 + 39(13)_2)/(52)_3$

2.22. (a) Task 1: choose a suit; task 2: choose 5 cards from that suit. (b) Task 1: choose a denomination for the "three;" task 2: choose two denominations, each to have one card in the hand; task 3:

choose 3 cards from the first denomination; task 4: choose 1 card apiece from each denomination in task 2.

2.23. (a) Ω = Set of all permutations of size 13 from the 52 cards; **(b)** $\binom{4}{2}\binom{48}{11}\Big/ D$;

(c) $\binom{13}{7}\binom{39}{6}\Big/ D$; **(d)** $\binom{13}{7}\binom{13}{6}\Big/ D$; **(e)** $\binom{13}{7}\binom{13}{4}\binom{13}{2}\Big/ D$; **(f)** $\binom{39}{13}\Big/ D$;

(g) $\binom{4}{3}\binom{4}{2}\binom{44}{8}\Big/ D$; **(h)** $\binom{4}{2}\binom{4}{3}\binom{4}{1}\binom{40}{7}\Big/ D$ where $D = \binom{52}{13}$

2.25. (a) $\binom{10}{3}\Big/ D$; **(b)** $\binom{10}{2}\binom{10}{1}\Big/ D$; **(c)** $10^3\Big/ D$; **(d)** $\binom{40}{3}\Big/ D$; **(e)** $\binom{5}{3}10^3\Big/ D$ where $D = \binom{50}{3}$

2.26. (e) Task 1: choose the pocket to be empty; task 2: choose the pocket to have 2 balls; task 3: choose 2 balls to go into the pocket selected in task 2; task 4: place the remaining 4 balls into the remaining 4 pockets, one ball per pocket.

2.27. For parts (c) and (d) there are $\binom{52}{13}\binom{39}{13}$ ways to deal 13 cards to you (task 1) and 13 cards to your partner (task 2). This product is the denominator.

(a) $\binom{13}{7}\binom{39}{6}\Big/ \binom{52}{13}$; **(b)** $\binom{13}{10}\binom{39}{16}\Big/ \binom{52}{26}$; **(c)** $\binom{13}{7}\binom{39}{6}\binom{6}{4}\binom{33}{9}\Big/ \binom{52}{13}\binom{39}{26}$;

(d) $\binom{4}{3}\binom{48}{10}\binom{1}{1}\binom{38}{12}\Big/ \binom{52}{13}\binom{39}{26}$

2.29. (a) $\binom{9}{3}$; **(b)** .09524

2.31. (a) $\binom{10}{2}\Big/ \binom{12}{4}$; **(b)** $\binom{10}{3}\Big/ \binom{12}{4}$; **(c)** $3\binom{10}{2}\Big/ \binom{12}{4}$

2.32. The denominator is $\binom{25}{5}\binom{20}{4}$.

2.33. $\binom{40}{4}\Big/ \binom{200}{4}$ = .001413—about 1 in 1000 chance that the numbers would all be this high just due to randomness.

2.34. *Algebraic*: Use the binomial formula with $x = 1 = y$. *Combinatorial*: Right-hand side = #(subsets of set of size n). How many subsets of size k are there?

2.35. Right-hand side = #(ways to choose a subset of size n from a set of size $2n$). Suppose that n are green and n are red. A subset of size n can be chosen by selecting k green and $n - k$ red elements, where k can be 0 or 1 or 2 or . . . or n.

2.36. *Algebraic*: Differentiate the binomial formula with respect to y and then set $x = 1$ and $y = 1$. *Combinatorial*: How many ways to select a subset of any size and choose a president?

2.37. A set of size $n + 2$ has n green and 2 red elements. Left-hand side = # (subsets of size k). Can choose a subset of size k by choosing k green elements *or* by choosing $k - 1$ green and 1 red *or* by choosing $k - 2$ green and both red.

2.39. $\dfrac{12!}{5!\ 4!\ 3!} = 27{,}720$

2.41. $\dfrac{15!}{5!\ 4!\ 3!\ 2!\ 1!} = 37{,}837{,}800$

Solutions and Hints to Selected Problems

CHAPTER 3

3.1. (a) 1/3; **(b)** 1/2; **(c)** 4/7

3.3. (a) $2\binom{47}{1}/\binom{49}{2}$; **(b)** $2\cdot 3 /\binom{49}{2}$; **(c)** $3\cdot 44/\binom{49}{2}$

3.5. (a) 39/51; **(b)** 39/50 **(c)** 26/50; **(d)** 13/49; **(e)** $\dfrac{39\cdot 26\cdot 13}{51\cdot 50\cdot 49}$

3.7. (a) $1/N$; **(b)** $1/N$; **(c)** $1/(N-1)$; **(d)** $1/(N-j+1)$; **(e)** $1/N$; **(f)** $1/(N-1)$

3.9. $P(E \cup F|B) = P((E \cup F) \cap B)/P(B) = P((E \cap B)\cup(F \cap B))/P(B)$
$= P(E \cap B)/P(B) + P(F \cap B)/P(B) = P(E|B) + P(F|B)$

3.11. (a) $\dfrac{1}{2}\left(\dfrac{1}{845} + \dfrac{1}{3664}\right)$; **(b)** .8126

3.13. (a) 1/7; **(b)** 3/11; **(c)** 3/5; **(d)** 1

3.15. (b) 1/2; **(c)** 1/3

3.19. Let G_i, R_i be the events "green on ith," "red on ith," respectively. Then
$$P(G_3) = P(G_3|G_1\cap G_2)P(G_1\cap G_2) + P(G_3|G_1\cap R_2)$$
$$\cdot P(G_1\cap R_2) + P(G_3|R_1\cap G_2)P(R_1\cap G_2) + P(G_3|R_1\cap R_2)P(R_1\cap R_2)$$
$$= \dfrac{G-2}{N-2}\cdot\dfrac{G(G-1)}{N(N-1)} + \dfrac{G-1}{N-2}\cdot\dfrac{GR}{N(N-1)} + \dfrac{G-1}{N-2}\cdot\dfrac{RG}{N(N-1)} + \dfrac{G}{N-2}\cdot\dfrac{R(R-1)}{N(N-1)}$$
$$= \dfrac{G((G-2)(G-1) + R(G-1) + R(G-1) + R(R-1))}{N(N-1)(N-2)}$$
$$= \dfrac{G((G-1)(R+G-2) + R(G+R-2))}{N(N-1)(N-2)} = \dfrac{G(G+R-1)(G+R-2)}{N(N-1)(N-2)} = \dfrac{G}{N}$$
noting that $G + R = N$.

3.21. $P(A^c \cap B^c) = P((A \cup B)^c) = 1 - P(A \cup B) = 1 - (P(A) + P(B) - P(A \cap B))$
$= 1 - P(A) - P(B) + P(A)P(B) = (1 - P(A))(1 - P(B))$
$= P(A^c)P(B^c)$

3.23. (a) $n(1-p)^{n-1}p$; **(b)** $1/n$; **(c)** $1/n$

3.25. Right-hand side $= \dfrac{1}{2}(P(A)(2 - P(B) - P(C)) + P(B)(2 - P(A) - P(C))$
$$+ P(C)(2 - P(A) - P(B))) + P(A \cap B \cap C)$$
$$= P(A) + P(B) + P(C) - P(A)P(B) - P(A)P(C) - P(B)P(C) + P(A \cap B \cap C)$$
$$= P(A) + P(B) + P(C) - P(A \cap B) - P(A \cap C) - P(B \cap C) + P(A \cap B \cap C)$$
$$= P(A \cup B \cup C)$$

3.27. $P(A \cap (B \cup C)) = P((A \cap B) \cup (A \cap C)) = P(A \cap B) + P(A \cap C) - P(A \cap B \cap C)$
$$= P(A)P(B) + P(A)P(C) - P(A)P(B)P(C)$$
$$= P(A)(P(B) + P(C) - P(B \cap C)) = P(A)P(B \cup C)$$

3.29. .7604

3.31. (a) .7135; (b) 1151

3.35. .4096

3.37. $(.64)^n$

CHAPTER 4

4.1.

Outcome	11	12	13	14	15	16	21	22	$\cdots$	66
X	0	1	0	0	0	0	1	2	$\cdots$	0
Probability	1/36	1/36	1/36	1/36	1/36	1/36	1/36	1/36	$\cdots$	1/36

where ij denotes "i on first toss, j on second."

X	0	1	2
Probability	25/36	10/36	1/36

4.3.

Outcome	11	12	13	14	15	16	21	$\cdots$	66
Z	2	2	2	2	0	0	2	$\cdots$	0
Probability	1/36	1/36	1/36	1/36	1/36	1/36	1/36	$\cdots$	1/36

Z	0	2
Probability	20/36	16/36

4.5.

Outcome	R_1R_2	R_1R_3	R_1G_1	R_1G_2	R_2R_3	R_2G_1	R_2G_2	R_3G_1	R_3G_2	G_1G_2
X	2	2	1	1	2	1	1	1	1	0
Probability	.1	.1	.1	.1	.1	.1	.1	.1	.1	.1

where, for example, R_2G_1 denotes "red sock 2, green sock 1 selected."

X	0	1	2
Probability	.1	.6	.3

4.7.

Outcome	$B_1B_2R_1$	$B_1B_2R_2$	B_1B_2Y	$B_1R_1R_2$	B_1R_1Y	B_1R_2Y	$B_2R_1R_2$	B_2R_1Y	B_2R_2Y	R_1R_2Y
X	1	1	0	2	1	1	2	1	1	2
Y	2	2	2	1	1	1	1	1	1	0
Probability	.1	.1	.1	.1	.1	.1	.1	.1	.1	.1

where, for example, B_1R_2Y = "sample consists of first blue bulb, second red bulb, and the yellow bulb."

Z	2	3
Probability	.6	.4

Solutions and Hints to Selected Problems

4.9. (a) .01652; **(b)** .01887; **(c)** .5367

4.11. (a) .3599; **(b)** .2137; **(c)** .1066

4.13. (a) .8031; **(b)** .4557; **(c)** .1969

4.17. .8878

4.18. (a) Use the definition of conditional probability.
(b) Note that $\{W > j - 1\} = \{W > j\} \cup \{W = j\}$ disjointly.
(c) Use part (b) recursively.
(d) Use parts (a) and (c).

4.19. $p = 3/4 \cdot 60 = 1/80$
(a) $(79/80)^{60}$; **(b)** $1 - (79/80)^{120} - 120(19/80)^{119} (1/80)$

4.21. (a) Without:
(b)

X	0	1	2	3
Probability	21/252	105/252	105/252	21/252

4.23. (a) With: X is binomial, $n = 4$, $p = .4$.
(b) Without:

X	0	1	2	3	4
Probability	$\binom{60}{4} / D$	$40\binom{60}{3} / D$	$\binom{40}{2}\binom{60}{2} / D$	$60\binom{40}{3} / D$	$\binom{40}{4} / D$

where $D = \binom{100}{4}$.

4.24. Once the recursive formula is established, $P(X = j + 1) > P(X = j)$ if and only if $(G - j) (n - j) > (j + 1) (R - n + j + 1)$. Solve this inequality for j. Note that $G + R = N$.

4.27.

X	0	1	2
Probability	.1	.6	.3

$E(X) = 0(.1) + 1(.6) + 2(.3) = 1.2$

4.29. $E(X) = 1.2$, $E(Y) = 1.2$, $E(Z) = 2.4$

4.31. $\Omega = \{HH, HT, TH, TT\}$

Outcome	HH	HT	TH	TT
Probability	$p_1 p_2$	$p_1 q_2$	$q_1 p_2$	$q_1 q_2$

$E(X) = 2p_1 p_2 + p_1 q_2 + q_1 p_2 = 2p_1 p_2 + p_1 - p_1 p_2 + p_2 - p_1 p_2$

$\qquad = p_1 + p_2$

4.33. Three days. *On the third day (Wednesday) mail can be expected.*

4.35. 10

4.37. (a) $1 - (12/13)^5 = .3298$; **(b)** $500(12/13)$; **(c)** $100(.6702)$

4.38. $E(X) = \sum_{j=1}^{N} jq^{j-1}p + (N + 1)q^N = p \sum_{j=0}^{N} \frac{d}{dq} q^j + (N + 1)q^N$

$$= p \frac{d}{dq} \left(\frac{1 - q^{N+1}}{1 - q} \right) + (N + 1)q^N$$

Note that X becomes geometrically distributed as $N \to \infty$. Note also that $E(X) \to 0/0$ as $q \to 1$.

4.45. For $r = 1$, $P(W = j) = \binom{j-1}{0} p^1 q^{j-1} = pq^{j-1}$ for $j = 1, 2, \ldots$

CHAPTER 5

5.1. $c = 3$, $F(x) = 1 - 1/(x + 1)^3$ for $x > 0$, $P(X > 4) = 1/125$, $P(X < 2) = 26/27$, $P(1 \le X < 3) = 7/64$

5.3. $c = 1/3$, $F(x) = (x^3 + 1)/9$ for $-1 \le x \le 2$, $P(X > 0) = 8/9$, $P(X < 1) = 2/9$, $P(0 \le X < 1) = 1/9$

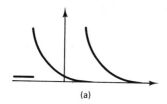

(a)

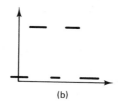

(b)

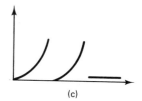

(c)

Figure A.1

5.5.

5.7. 5/4

5.9. $(\pi - 2)/2$

5.11. 1/2; use this method to compute the integral:

$$\int_0^\infty \frac{x}{(x + 1)^4} dx = \int_0^\infty \frac{(x + 1) - 1}{(x + 1)^4} dx = \int_0^\infty \frac{1}{(x + 1)^3} dx - \int_0^\infty \frac{1}{(x + 1)^4} dx$$

5.12. $E(X) = \int_0^\infty xf(x) dx = \int_0^\infty u(-v') dx = -xG(x) \Big|_0^\infty + \int_0^\infty G(x) dx$

$$= \int_0^\infty G(x) dx$$

5.13. $\int_0^\infty G(x) dx = \int_0^{\pi/2} (1 - \sin(x)) dx = \frac{\pi - 2}{2}$

5.15. $\int_0^\infty G(x) dx = \int_0^\infty \frac{dx}{(x + 1)^3} = \frac{1}{2}$

5.17. (a) 1/2; **(b)** 2/3; **(c)** 2/3

Solutions and Hints to Selected Problems

5.19. (a) 3/4; (b) 1/16; (c) X is binomial, $n = 10$, $p = 1/4$; (d) .1460; (e) .5256

5.21. (a) .4512; (b) .6376; (c) .2476

5.23. (a) $\lambda = .02390$/sec; (b) .3013; (c) .4544; (d) 125.3 sec

5.25. (a) $\lambda = \ln(2)/4 = .1733$/week; (b) .6465; (c) .2264; (d) .2494. Note that 1 month = 30/7 weeks.

5.27. $\dfrac{dG}{G} = -\lambda dt$. Integrate both sides to obtain

$\ln G = -\lambda t + C$

$G = e^{-\lambda t + C}$

$1 = G(0) = e^{0+C} = e^C$ implies that $C = 0$.

5.29. (a) $1/(t+1)$; (b) $e^{-t/(t+1)}$. (c) With probability e^{-1} the component never fails.

5.33. $f_X(t) = e^t$ for $-\infty < t < 0$, $f_Y(t) = (t-2)^{2/3}/3$ for $2 < t < 3$

$f_Z(t) = 1/t^2$ for $1 < t < \infty$

5.35. $P(Y \le t) = P(3\ln(T+1) \le t) = P(T \le e^{t/3} - 1) = 1 - \exp(-(e^{t/3} - 1)/200)$. $f_Y(t) = e^{t/3} \cdot \exp(-(e^{t/3} - 1)/200)/600$ for $0 < t < \infty$.

5.37. θ is concentrated on $(0, \pi/2)$. $P(\theta \le u) = P(X/R \le \tan u) = P(X \le R \tan u) = 1 - \exp(-R \tan u/50)$. $f_\theta(u) = R \sec^2 u \exp(-R \tan u/50)/50$ for $0 < u < \pi/2$.

5.39. $E(T) = \displaystyle\sum_{n=1}^{\infty} nP(T = n) = \sum_{n=1}^{\infty} 1/(n+1) = \infty$

5.41. $u = -(1-x)^{n-j+1}/(n-j+1)$. Therefore,

$$I_j = -x^j \left.\frac{(1-x)^{n-j+1}}{n-j+1}\right|_0^1 + \frac{j}{n-j+1} \int_0^1 x^{j-1}(1-x)^{n-(j-1)}\, dx$$

$$= \frac{j}{n-j+1} I_{j-1}$$

5.43. (a) .4034; (b) .1534

CHAPTER 6

6.1. (a) .03020; (b) .1850; (c) .6792

6.3. (a) Average number $= 2.1 \cdot t$; (b) .5916; (c) .6096; (d) .2953

6.5. (a) .03567; (b) .8454; (c) 10/3

6.7. (a) 200/160; (b) .2238; (c) .03827; (d) 5

6.9. (a) .2231; (b) .1353; (c) .2231

6.11. (a) .4724; (b) $\exp\left(-1.5 \cdot \dfrac{50^2 \pi}{10000}\right) = .3079$

6.13. (a) $P(j \text{ in } [t, t+\varepsilon]) = (\lambda\varepsilon)^j e^{-\lambda\varepsilon}/j!$ (b) $P(0 \text{ calls in } [t, t+\varepsilon]) = e^{-\lambda\varepsilon} \to 1$ as $\varepsilon \to 0$

6.15. (a) X is Poisson, $\lambda t = (1/.1)(.5) = 5$; (b) .1247; (c) .3158

6.17. (a) $e^{-5.5} (1 + 5.5 + 5.5^2/2 + 5.5^3/6) = .2017$ (b) $1 - e^{-3}(1 + 3 + 3^2/2 + 3^3/6) = .3528$

6.19. $\lambda = 4/3$. S_n = time to complete n tasks; S_n satisfies $P(S_n \leqslant 4) \geqslant .70$. That is, $P(N_4 \geqslant n) \geqslant .70$. $n \leqslant 4$.

6.22. Suppose that $S_n < t < S_{n+1}$. Then $\{S_n < t\}$ holds, but the event $\{N_t > n\}$ does not.

6.23. (a) Average time per sale = 7/4, thus $\lambda = 4/7$. (b) $P(S_4 \leqslant 6) = P(N_6 \geqslant 4) = .4479$; (c) $P(S_4 > 9) = P(N_9 < 4) = .2455$.

6.25. For S_n, the failure rate is

$$\frac{\lambda^n t^{n-1}/(n-1)!}{1 + \lambda t + \cdots + (\lambda t)^{n-1}/(n-1)!}$$

6.27. $P(S_n > t + s | S_n > t) = \dfrac{P(N_{t+s} < n)}{P(N_t < n)}$

$$= e^{-\lambda s} \frac{\displaystyle\sum_{j=0}^{n-1} \frac{(\lambda(t+s))^j}{j!}}{\displaystyle\sum_{j=0}^{n-1} \frac{(\lambda t)^j}{j!}}$$

If it is known that $S_n > t$ and t is large, it is more and more certain that the last component is operating. This is exponentially distributed.

6.29. Use integration by parts in the integral defining $\Gamma(\alpha)$ with $u = t^{\alpha-1}$, $v' = e^{-t}$ to derive the recursive formula $\Gamma(\alpha) = (\alpha - 1)\Gamma(\alpha - 1)$. $\Gamma(1) = 1$ directly by integration. Thus $\Gamma(2) = 1\Gamma(1) = 1$, $\Gamma(3) = 2\Gamma(2) = 2$, $\Gamma(4) = 3\Gamma(2) = 3!$ . . . .

6.31. Alice is correct.

6.33. Poisson, parameter $(1/2)(40.7)$ $(2/5)$

6.35. $P(n$ people waiting$) = \displaystyle\int_0^b P(n$ waiting$|$bus arrives at $t) \frac{1}{b} dt$

$$= \frac{1}{b} \int_0^b \frac{(\lambda t)^n}{n!} e^{-\lambda t} dt$$

To obtain the last integral, use the substitution $u = \lambda t$.

$$(\text{answer}) = \frac{1}{\lambda b} \left(1 - \sum_{j=0}^{n} (\lambda b)^j e^{-\lambda b}/j! \right)$$

CHAPTER 7

7.1. (a) 0 3 1 0 . . .
(b) 0 3 2 13 4 7 6 1 8 11 10 5 12 15 14 9 0 . . .
(c) 0 3 9 5 13 13 . . .
(d) 0 7 2 7 . . .
(e) 0 9 8 7 6 5 4 3 2 1 0 . . .
(f) 0 4 5 3 7 8 6 1 2 0 . . .
Parts (b) and (e) satisfy the conditions of the theorem.

7.3. M mod NORM = M_1 mod NORM if and only if M and M_1 have the same remainder when divided by NORM if and only if $M - M_1$ is a multiple of NORM. Consequently, if MULT-$MULT_1$ is a multiple of NORM, then (MULT-$MULT_1$)*SEED is a multiple of NORM for any integer SEED. Thus (MULT*SEED + ADDR) − ($MULT_1$*SEED + ADDR) is a multiple of NORM.

7.5 0 17 34 51 . . .

7.7. begin
       C: = 0; SEED: = 0; SUM: = 0.0;
      repeat
         SEED: = (MULT*SEED + ADDR) mod NORM;
         RND: = SEED/NORM;
         SUM: = SUM + RND;
         C: = C + 1;
      until SEED = 0;
      writeln(C,SUM/C);
    end.

7.11. Use Example 8 with P[0] := 1/35, P[1] := 12/35, P[2] := 18/35, P[3] := 4/35.

7.17. begin
       SUM: = 0; SEED: = 0; readln(P,K); Q: = 1 − P;
       for I: = 1 to 1000 do
         begin
           SEED: = (MULT*SEED + ADDR) mod NORM;
           RND: = SEED/NORM;
           if RND < Q**K then SUM: = SUM + 1;
         end;
       writeln(SUM/1000);
    end.

7.19. $F(x) = x^3$, $F^{-1}(x) = x^{1/3}$ for $0 \leqslant x \leqslant 1$

7.23. begin
       SUM: = 0; SEED: = 0; readln(MAX,U);
       for I: = 1 to MAX do
         begin
           SEED: = (MULT*SEED + ADDR) mod NORM; RND: = SEED/NORM;
           T: = RND;
           SEED: = (MULT*SEED + ADDR) mod NORM; RND: = SEED/NORM;
           S: = (1 − T)*RND + T;
           if S − T > U then SUM: = SUM + 1;
         end;
       writeln(SUM/MAX);
    end.

7.25. V := 0.8*RND + 0.2; then set L := 2/V. Then simulate the Poisson distribution with parameter L as in Example 12.

Solutions and Hints to Selected Problems

CHAPTER 8

8.1. (a) .39; **(b)** .91; **(c)** $P(X = i) = .52, .28, .09, .11$ for $i = 1, 2, 3, 4$, $P(Y = j) = .23, .36, .41$ for $j = 1, 3, 5$; **(d)** .89; **(e)** .41

8.3.

		\(X\)				
		0	1	2	3	
	0	5/495	30/495	30/495	5/495	70/495
	1	40/495	120/495	60/495	4/495	224/495
Y	2	60/495	90/495	18/495	0	168/495
	3	20/495	12/495	0	0	32/495
	4	1/495	0	0	0	1/495
		126/495	252/495	108/495	9/495	

8.5

.2	.24	.16	.6
.083	.1	.067	.25
.050	.06	.040	.15
.333	.4	.267	

8.7. (a) parameter $= 6.3$; .7531; **(b)** parameter $= 12.6$; .001438

8.9. (a) parameter $= 1.6$; .4751; **(b)** parameter $= 3.2$; .6201; **(c)** $\sum\limits_{j=3}^{5} P(j$ cars, $5 - j$ buses in 3 minutes)/ $P(5$ vehicles in 3 minutes) $= .9839$

8.10. Show that

$$P(X + Y = k) = \sum_{j} \binom{n}{j}\binom{m}{k - j} p^{j}q^{n-j} \cdot p^{k-j}q^{m-(k-j)}$$

$$= p^{k}q^{n+m-k} \sum_{j} \binom{n}{j}\binom{m}{k - j}$$

Use combinatorial reasoning to show that the sum is $\binom{n + m}{k}$. (A set has n green and m red objects. How many subsets of size k are there?) The intuitive way to see that $X + Y$ is binomially distributed is to note that $X + Y$ is the number of successes in $n + m$ Bernoulli trials with probability p of success at each trial.

8.11. (a) $c = 1$; **(b)** $f_X(x) = x + 1/2$ for $0 < x < 1$, $f_Y(y) = y + 1/2$ for $0 < y < 1$; **(c)** X and Y not independent; **(d)** $P(X \leq 1/3) = 2/9$; **(e)** $P(Y \geq 1/2) = 5/8$

8.13. $f_X(x) = \int_{-\infty}^{\infty} h(x, y)\, dy = \int_{-\infty}^{\infty} f(x)g(y)\, dy = cf(x)$. Similarly, $f_Y(y) = dg(y)$.

$cd = \int_{-\infty}^{\infty} f(x)\, dx \int_{-\infty}^{\infty} g(y)\, dy = \int_{-\infty}^{\infty}\int_{-\infty}^{\infty} h(x, y)\, dx\, dy = 1$. Finally, $f_X(x)f_Y(y) = cf(x)dg(y)$ $= cdh(x, y) = h(x, y)$, which implies that X and Y are independent.

8.15 (a) $h(x, y) = 9e^{-3x}e^{-3y}$ for $x > 0$ and $y > 0$; $h(x, y) = 0$; otherwise,

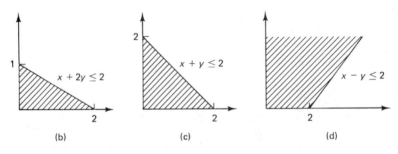

(b)   (c)   (d)

Figure A-2

(e) $P(X) + 2Y \leq 2) = 1 - 2e^{-3} + e^{-6}$; (f) $P(X + Y \leq 2) = 1 - 7e^{-6}$; (g) $P(X - Y \leq 2) = 1 - e^{-6}/2$

8.17. (a) $P(XY > 1) = (1 - e^{-5})/5$; (b) $P(\text{Max}\{X, Y\} < 2) = (1 - e^{-10})/2$;

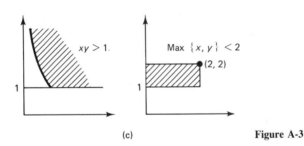

(c)   **Figure A-3**

8.19. The density is $6(e^{-2z} - e^{-3z})$ for $z > 0$; $1 - 3e^{-2} + 2e^{-3}$

8.21. $h(z) = 0$ unless $0 < z < 2$. For $0 < z < 1$, $h(z) = \int_0^z f(x)g(z - x)\, dx$ with both $f(x)$ and $g(z - x)$ equal to 1. For $1 < z < 2$, $h(z) = \int_0^z f(x)g(z - x)\, dx$; but $g(z - x) = 0$ if $x < z - 1$. The result: $h(z) = z$ for $0 < z < 1$ and $h(z) = 2 - z$ for $1 < z < 2$.

8.23. Let $f(x) = 2e^{-2x}$ for $x > 0$ and 0 otherwise. Let $g(x) = 1$ for $0 < x < 1$ and 0 otherwise. Then
$$h(z) = \int_0^z f(x)g(z - x)\, dx$$
The integrand is 0 unless $0 < z - x < 1$. Thus if $1 < z$, the limits of integration are from $z - 1$ to z. The result: $h(z) = 1 - e^{-2z}$ for $0 < z < 1$ and $h(z) = e^{-2z}(e^2 - 1)$ for $1 < z$.

8.25. (a) 3 glazed, 2 chocolate, 5 jelly; (b) at rate $\lambda = 1.3 + .6 + 2.8 = 4.7$, 8 total are needed.

8.27. (a) $p = .98^{24} = .6158$; (b) X_i is binomial, $n = 24$, $p = .02$; (c) S is binomial, $n = 120$, $p = .02$, $P(S = 2) = .2633$; (d) T is binomial, $n = 5$, $p = .3842$, $P(T < 2) = .3648$

8.29. (a) e^{-1}; (b) $e^{-2}(1 + 2 + 2^2/2)$; (c) $1 - 5e^{-2}$

8.31. (a) .05078; (b) .3125; (c) .7383

8.35. $E(B_{n,1}) = n \int_0^1 t^n \, dt = n/(n + 1)$

$$E(B_{n,m}) = \frac{(n + m - 1)!}{(n - 1)!(m - 1)!} \int_0^1 t^n (1 - t)^{m-1} \, dt$$

$$= \frac{(n + m - 1)!}{(n - 1)!(m - 1)!} \cdot \frac{1}{n + 1} \int_0^1 (1 - t)^{m-1} \frac{d}{dt}(t^{n+1}) \, dt$$

$$= \frac{1}{n + 1} \frac{(n + m - 1)!}{(n - 1)!(m - 1)!} \left[(1 - t)^{m-1} t^{n+1} \Big|_0^1 + (m + 1) \int_0^1 t^{n+1}(1 - t)^{m-2} \, dt \right]$$

$$= 0 + \frac{n}{n + 1} E(B_{n+1,m-1})$$

8.36. For $0 < x, y < 1$, $f(x|y) = (x + y)/(y + 1/2)$, $g(y|x) = (x + y)/(x + 1/2)$. $E(X|Y = y) = (2 + 3y)/(6y + 3)$, $E(Y|X = x) = (2 + 3x)/(6x + 3)$.

8.38. 7/20

CHAPTER 9

9.1. (a) 2/3; (b) 1/2; (c) 2; (d) $2(\sin(1) - \cos(1))$; (e) $2a/3 + b$

9.3. (a) ∞; (b) 1/2; (c) 1/3

9.5. (a) $E(C) = 700/9$; (b) $f_F(x) = (x - 32)/81 \cdot 150$ for $122 < x < 212$, $E(F) = 172$

9.7. (a)

		A				
		0	1	2	3	
	0	1/220	15/220	30/220	10/220	56/220
	1	12/220	60/220	40/220	0	112/220
B	2	18/220	30/220	0	0	48/220
	3	4/220	0	0	0	4/220
		35/220	105/220	70/220	10/220	

(b) $E(A + B) = 2.25$; (c) $E(A) = 1.25$; (d) $E(B) = 1$; (e) $E(AB) = 10/11$

9.9. (a) $E(X) = 8/15$; (b) $E(Y) = 8/15$;

(c) $E(\text{Max } \{X, Y\}) = \int_0^1 \int_y^1 xh(x, y) \, dx \, dy + \int_0^1 \int_0^y yh(x, y) \, dx \, dy$

$= 52/75$

9.11. $E(h(X)) = \int_{-\infty}^{\infty} h(x)f(x) \, dx = \int_a^b 1 \cdot f(x) \, dx = P(a \leqslant X \leqslant b)$

This expectation is the average winnings when the game is: "You win \$1 if X has a value in $[a, b]$; othewise, you win \$0."

9.13. To obtain the last integral from the next to last, use the substitution $z = h(x)$.

9.15. $p = .02$, $n = 1000$, $E(R) = 40.16$

9.17. (a) 9/7; (b) $np = 9/7$

9.19. (a) $E(X) = 1$

9.21. $E(R) = 2(n - 1)(pq + pr + qr) + 1$

9.23. Let $Z = (X - \mu)/\sigma = \sqrt{18}(X - 2/3)$

$$f_Z(z) = 2\left(\frac{2}{3} + \frac{z}{\sqrt{18}}\right) \Big/ \sqrt{18} \text{ for } -2\sqrt{18}/3 < z < \sqrt{18}/3$$

9.25. (a) $\text{Var}(C) = 200.62$; **(b)** $\text{Var}(F) = 650$

9.27. $E(X) = (1 - q^{N+1})/p$ from Problem 4.38. Following the technique used in Example 14 yields

$$E(X(X - 1)) = \sum_{j=1}^{N} j(j - 1)q^{j-1}p + (N + 1)Nq^N$$

$$= qp\frac{d^2}{dq^2}\left(\sum_{j=0}^{N} q^j\right) + (N + 1)Nq^N$$

$$= qp\frac{d^2}{dq^2}\left(\frac{1 - q^{N+1}}{1 - q}\right) + (N + 1)Nq^N$$

$$= -\frac{2Nq^{N+1}}{p} + \frac{2q(1 - q^N)}{p^2}$$

Therefore,

$$E(X^2) = E(X(X - 1)) + E(X) = -\frac{2Nq^{N+1}}{p} + \frac{2q(1 - q^N)}{p^2} + \frac{1 - q^{N+1}}{p}$$

and $\text{Var}(X) = E(X^2) - E(X)^2 = \frac{q}{p^2} - \frac{(2N + 1)q^{N+1}}{p} - \frac{q^{2N+2}}{p^2}$

$$\to \frac{q}{p^2} \text{ as } N \to \infty \text{ for } 0 < q < 1 \text{ by L'Hôspital's rule.}$$

9.29. $E(X(X - 1)) = \sum_{j=0}^{\infty} j(j - 1)\frac{\lambda^j}{j!}e^{-\lambda}$

$$= \lambda^2 e^{-\lambda}\sum_{j=2}^{\infty}\frac{\lambda^{j-2}}{(j - 2)!}$$

$$= \lambda^2 e^{-\lambda}e^{\lambda}$$

$$= \lambda^2$$

Since $E(X) = \lambda$, Problem 9.28 implies that

$$\text{Var}(X) = \lambda^2 + \lambda - \lambda^2 = \lambda$$

9.31. $E(X) = 5/8$, $E(Y) = 5/8$, $\text{Var}(X) = 73/960$, $\text{Var}(Y) = 73/960$, $\text{Cov}(X, Y) = -1/64$, $\rho(X, Y) = -15/73$

9.33. $E(X) = 8/15$, $E(Y) = 8/15$, $\text{Var}(X) = 37/450$, $\text{Var}(Y) = 37/450$, $\text{Cov}(X, Y) = 1/225$, $\rho(X, Y) = 2/37$

9.35. $E(X) = 1.25$, $E(Y) = 1$, $\text{Var}(X) = 105/176$, $\text{Var}(Y) = 6/11$, $\text{Cov}(X, Y) = -15/44$, $\rho(X, Y) = -5/\sqrt{70}$

9.37. $E(X) = (a + b)\mu$, $E(Y) = (\alpha + \beta)\mu$, $\text{Var}(X) = (a^2 + b^2)\sigma^2$, $\text{Var}(Y) = (\alpha^2 + \beta^2)\sigma^2$, $\text{Cov}(X, Y) = (a\alpha + b\beta)\sigma^2$, $\rho(X, Y) = (a\alpha + b\beta)/\sqrt{(a^2 + b^2)(\alpha^2 + \beta^2)}$

9.39. On day t the amount dumped i days *before* was X_{t-i}; the amount still active is $\alpha^i X_{t-i}$. Thus $S_t = \sum_{i=0}^{\infty} \alpha^i X_{t-i}$.

$$E(S_t) = \sum_{i=0}^{\infty} \alpha^i E(X_{t-i}) = \mu \sum_{i=0}^{\infty} \alpha^i = \frac{\mu}{1 - \alpha}$$

$$S_t^2 = \sum_{i,j} \alpha^i \alpha^j X_{t-i} X_{t-j} = \sum_{i \neq j} \alpha^i \alpha^j X_{t-i} X_{t-j} + \sum_i \alpha^{2i} X_{t-i}^2$$

$$E(S_t^2) = \sum_{i \neq j} \alpha^i \alpha^j \mu^2, + \sum_i \alpha^{2i} E(X_{t-i}^2)$$

$$= \sum_{i,j} \alpha^i \alpha^j \mu^2 - \sum_{i=j} \alpha^i \alpha^j \mu^2 + \sum_i \alpha^{2i}(\sigma^2 + \mu^2)$$

$$= \frac{\mu^2}{(1 - \alpha)^2} - \frac{\mu^2}{1 - \alpha^2} + \frac{\sigma^2 + \mu^2}{1 - \alpha^2}$$

$$= \frac{\mu^2}{(1 - \alpha)^2} + \frac{\sigma^2}{1 - \alpha^2}$$

$$\text{Var}(S_t) = E(S_t^2) - E(S_t)^2 = \frac{\sigma^2}{1 - \alpha^2}$$

For $t \geqslant s$
$$S_t = X_t + \alpha X_{t-1} + \cdots + \alpha^{t-s} X_s + \alpha^{t-s+1} X_{s-1} + \cdots$$

$$= \sum_{i=0}^{t-s-1} \alpha^i X_{t-i} + \alpha^{t-s} S_s$$

Thus

$$E(S_t S_s) = E\left(\sum_{i=0}^{t-s-1} \alpha^i X_{t-i} S_s + \sigma^{t-s} S_s^2 \right)$$

$$= E(S_s) E\left(\sum_{i=0}^{t-s-1} \alpha^i X_{t-i} \right) + \alpha^{t-s} E(S_s^2)$$

$$= \frac{\mu}{1 - \alpha} \mu \frac{1 - \alpha^{t-s}}{1 - \alpha} + \alpha^{t-s} \left(\frac{\mu^2}{(1 - \alpha)^2} + \frac{\sigma^2}{1 - \alpha^2} \right)$$

$$= \frac{\mu^2}{(1 - \alpha)^2} + \frac{\sigma^2 \alpha^{t-s}}{1 - \alpha^2}$$

$$\text{Cov}(S_t, S_s) = E(S_t S_s) - E(S_t) E(S_s)$$

9.41. $\text{Var}(X + Y + Z) = E((X + Y + Z)^2) - (\mu_X + \mu_Y + \mu_Z)^2$

$$= E(X^2) - \mu_X^2 + E(Y^2) - \mu_Y^2 + E(Z^2) - \mu_Z^2$$

$$+ 2(E(XY) - \mu_X \mu_Y) + 2(E(XZ) - \mu_X \mu_Z)$$

$$+ 2(E(YZ) - \mu_Y \mu_Z)$$

which agrees with the formula.

CHAPTER 10

10.1. (a) .7257, (b) .4880, (c) .4360, (d) .8374

10.3. (a) $P(Z > z) = 1 - P(Z \leqslant z) = 1 - \Phi(z)$

Solutions and Hints to Selected Problems

(b) $P(Z > -z) = 1 - P(Z \leqslant -z) = 1 - P(Z \geqslant z) = 1 - (1 - P(Z < z))$

$$= P(Z < z) = \Phi(z)$$

(c) $P(-z < Z < z) = P(Z < z) - P(Z \leqslant -z) = P(Z < z) - P(Z \geqslant z)$

$$= P(Z < z) - (1 - P(Z < z))$$

$$= 2P(Z < z) - 1$$

$$= 2\Phi(z) - 1$$

10.5. (a) $E(Y) = 4 \cdot 2000$; **(b)** Var $(Y) = (400)^2$; **(c)** Y is normally distributed with $\mu = 8000$, $\sigma = 400$; **(d)** .6915; **(e)** .4532

10.7. (a) .3830; **(b)** .6826; **(c)** .8664; **(d)** $g(t) = 2\Phi(t) - 1$; **(e)** $g'(0) = \sqrt{2/\pi}$

10.9. $\displaystyle\int_{-\infty}^{\infty} x^3 e^{-x^2/2}\, dx = -\int_{-\infty}^{\infty} x^2 \frac{d}{dx}(e^{-x^2/2})\, dx$

$$= \lim_{L \to \infty} \, [-x^2 e^{-x^2/2}]_{-L}^{L} + \int_{-\infty}^{\infty} e^{-x^2/2} \frac{d}{dx}(x^2)\, dx$$

$$= 0 + 2 \cdot \int_{-\infty}^{\infty} x e^{-x^2/2}\, dx = -2 \cdot \lim_{L \to \infty} \, [-e^{-x^2/2}]_{-L}^{L}$$

$$= 0$$

10.10. Let f, g be the densities of X, Y, respectively. From Section 8.5 the density for $X + Y$ is the *convolution*

$$h(z) = \int_{-\infty}^{\infty} f(x) g(z - x)\, dx$$

$$= \int_{-\infty}^{\infty} \frac{1}{\sqrt{2\pi}\sigma} \exp\left(-\frac{x^2}{2\sigma^2}\right) \frac{1}{\sqrt{2\pi}\rho} \exp\left(\frac{(z-x)^2}{2\rho^2}\right) dx$$

$$= \frac{1}{2\pi\sigma\rho} \int_{-\infty}^{\infty} \exp\left[-\frac{1}{2}\left(\left(\frac{1}{\sigma^2}+\frac{1}{\rho^2}\right)x^2 - \frac{2}{\rho^2}xz + \frac{1}{\rho^2}z^2\right)\right] dx$$

$$= \frac{1}{2\pi\sigma\rho} \int_{-\infty}^{\infty} \exp\left[-\frac{1}{2}\left(\frac{\sigma^2+P^2}{\sigma^2\rho^2}\right)\left(x^2 - 2\frac{\sigma^2}{\sigma^2+\rho^2}XZ\right)\right] dx \, \exp\left[-\frac{Z^2}{2\rho^2}\right]$$

$$= \frac{1}{2\pi\sigma\rho} \int_{-\infty}^{\infty} \exp\left[-\frac{1}{2}\left(\frac{\sigma^2+\rho^2}{\sigma^2\rho^2}\right)\left(x - \frac{\sigma^2}{\sigma^2+\rho^2}z\right)^2\right] dx$$

$$\cdot \exp\left[\frac{1}{2}\left(\frac{\sigma^2+\rho^2}{\sigma^2\rho^2}\right)\left(\frac{\sigma^2}{\sigma^2+\rho^2}z\right)^2 - \frac{z^2}{2\rho^2}\right]$$

$$= \frac{1}{2\pi\sigma\rho} \int_{-\infty}^{\infty} \exp\left[-\frac{1}{2}\left(\frac{\sigma^2+\rho^2}{\sigma^2\rho^2}\right)\cdot u^2\right] du \, \exp\left[-\frac{z^2}{2(\sigma^2+\rho^2)}\right]$$

$$= \frac{1}{2\pi\sigma\rho} \frac{\sigma\rho}{\sqrt{\sigma^2+\rho^2}} \int_{-\infty}^{\infty} \exp\left(-\frac{v^2}{2}\right) dv \, \exp\left[-\frac{z^2}{2(\sigma^2+\rho^2)}\right]$$

$$= \frac{1}{\sqrt{2\pi}\sqrt{\sigma^2+\rho^2}} \exp\left[-\frac{z^2}{2(\sigma^2+\rho^2)}\right]$$

10.11. $X - \mu$ is N_{0,σ^2} and $Y - \nu$ is N_{0,ρ^2}. Therefore, Problem 10.10 implies that $(X + Y) - (\mu + \nu)$ is $N_{0,\sigma^2+\rho^2}$ distributed.

10.13. $.90 \leqslant P(S_n \leqslant 5280) = P(Z \leqslant (5280 - 100n)/50\sqrt{n})$ implies that $(5280 - 100n)/50\sqrt{n} \geqslant 1.28$.

Solve the equation $5280 - 100n = 1.28 \cdot 50\sqrt{n}$, which is a quadratic equation in $\sqrt{n}$, to obtain $n = 49$.

10.15. $n \geqslant 23$

10.17. **(a)** $P(S = 10) = .0318$, approximation $= .0309$

      (b) $P(S = 15) = .1612$, approximation $= .1612$

      (c) $P(S = 20) = .0099$, approximation $= .0111$

10.19. **(a)** .6591; **(b)** .1932

10.21. $.8225 \sqrt{n}$

10.23. $n \geqslant 166$

10.25. **(a)** .8944; **(b)** .9452; **(c)** .4746

10.27. **(a)** N_t is Poisson distributed with parameter $\lambda t = 20t$; N_s is Poisson distributed with parameter $\Lambda = 100$. **(b)** .7088; **(c)** .6318; **(d)** .5762; **(e)** .6046. Part (b) is with the continuity correction: parts (c), (d) and (e) are without the continuity correction.

10.29. **(a)** X_t is Poisson distributed with parameter $100t$. Using the continuity correction: **(b)** $g(19) = .9896$; **(c)** $g(19.5) = .8729$; **(d)** $g(20) = .5040$; **(e)** $g(20.5) = .1379$; **(f)** $g(21) = .0150$.

10.34. **(a)** $f_R(t) = t \exp(-t^2/2)$ for $t > 0$; **(b)** $f_S(t) = (t/\alpha^2) \exp(-t^2/2d^2)$ for $t > 0$

CHAPTER 11

11.1. **(a)** Time until the first failure is exponentially distributed with parameter $1/3 + 1/4 + 1/5 = 47/60$. **(b)** $P(\text{second part wears out first}) = (1/4)/(47/60) = 15/47$.

11.3. Z is concentrated on $(0, 1)$. For $0 < z < 1$, $P(Z > z) = P(T_1 > z$ and $T_2 > z) = P(T_1 > z)P(T_2 > z) = (1 - z)^2$. The distribution and density are $P(Z \leqslant z) = 1 - (1 - z)^2$, $f(z) = 2(1 - z)$ for $0 < z < 1$.

11.5. **(a)** $\Omega_0 = \alpha$, $p_0 = 1$, $q_0 = 0$; **(b)** $\Omega_1 = \beta$, $p_1 = 0$, $q_1 = 1$

11.7. $\Omega_0 = 2\beta$, $p_0 = 1$, $q_0 = 0$; $\Omega_1 = \alpha + \beta$, $p_1 = \beta/(\alpha + \beta)$, $q_1 = \alpha/(\alpha + \beta)$; $\Omega_2 = 2\alpha$, $p_2 = 0$, $q_2 = 1$

11.9. $\Omega_0 = \lambda$, $p_0 = 1$, $q_0 = 0$; $\Omega_1 = \lambda + v$, $p_1 = \lambda/(\lambda + v)$, $q_1 = v/(\lambda + v)$; $\Omega_2 = \lambda + 2v$, $p_2 = \lambda/(\lambda + 2v)$, $q_2 = 2v/(\lambda + 2v)$; $\Omega_3 = 3v$, $p_3 = 0$, $q_3 = 1$

11.11. $\Omega_0 = \lambda$, $p_0 = 1$, $q_0 = 0$; $\Omega_i = \lambda + iv$, $p_i = \lambda/(\lambda + iv)$, $q_i = iv/(\lambda + iv)$ for $0 \leqslant i < N$; $\Omega_N = Nv$, $p_N = 0$, $q_N = 1$

11.13. The body of the program is

```
begin
    readln(A,B,TMAX);
    TIME: = 0.0; SEED: = 0; STATE: = 1;
    while TIME < TMAX do
        begin
            SEED: = (MULT*SEED + ADDR) mod NORM; RND: = SEED/NORM
```

```
              if STATE = 0 then begin
                                STATE: = 1;
                                TIME: = TIME  −  ln(1−RND)/B;
                          end
                      else begin
                                STATE: = 0;
                                TIME: = TIME  −  ln(1−RND)/A;
                          end;
                  writeln(TIME:10:4,STATE);
          end;
    end.
```

11.15. The body of the program is

```
begin
      readln(LAMBDA,NU,QUEUE,TMAX);
      TIME: = 0.0; SEED: = 0;
      while TIME < TMAX do
          begin
              SEED: = (MULT∗SEED + ADDR) mod NORM; RND: = SEED/NORM;
              if QUEUE = 0 then OMEGA: = LAMBDA
                          else if QUEUE = 1 then OMEGA: = LAMBDA+NU
                                      else OMEGA: = LAMBDA+2∗NU;
              TIME: = TIME  −  ln(1−RND)/OMEGA;
              if QUEUE = 0
                  then QUEUE: = 1
                  else begin
                              SEED: = (MULT∗SEED + ADDR) mod NORM;
                              RND: = SEED/NORM;
                              if RND < LAMBDA/OMEGA then QUEUE: = QUEUE + 1
                                              else QUEUE: = QUEUE − 1;
                      end;
              writeln(TIME:10:4,QUEUE);
          end;
      end.
```

11.17. $\phi = (\phi_0, \phi_1) = (\beta/(\alpha + \beta), \alpha/(\alpha + \beta))$

11.19. $\phi = (\phi_0, \phi_1, \phi_2) = ((\alpha/(\alpha + \beta))^2, 2\alpha\beta/(\alpha + \beta)^2, (\beta/(\alpha + \beta))^2)$

11.21. $\phi = (\phi_0, \phi_1, \phi_2, \phi_3) = (1/C, (\lambda/v)/C, (\lambda/v)^2/2C, (\lambda/v)^3/6C)$ where $C = (1 + (\lambda/v) + (\lambda/v)^2/2 + (\lambda/v)^3/6)$.

11.23. $\phi_i = \dfrac{(\lambda/v)^i}{i!} C$, where $C = 1 \bigg/ \displaystyle\sum_{i=0}^{N} (\lambda/v)^i/i!$ for $i = 0, 1, \ldots, N$.

11.25. For the one-server queue the expected length is $\lambda/(\lambda - v) = (\lambda/v)/(1 - (\lambda/v)) = x/(1 - x)$ where $x = \lambda/v$. **(a)** $.9/(1 - .9) = 9$; **(b)** 19; **(c)** 99; **(d)** 999.

11.28. (b) Density function for S_n is $N\delta e^{-\delta t}(1 - e^{-\delta t})^{N-1}$ for $t > 0$.

11.29. Using Problem 5.12

$$E(S_n) = \int_0^\infty P(S_n > t)\, dt$$

$$= \int_0^\infty (1 - (1 - e^{-\delta t})^N)\, dt$$

Therefore

$$E(S_N) - E(S_{N-1}) = \int_0^\infty ((1 - e^{-\delta t})^{N-1} - (1 - e^{-\delta t})^N)\, dt$$

$$= \int_0^\infty (1 - e^{-\delta t})^{N-1} e^{-\delta t}\, dt$$

$$= \frac{1}{\delta} \int_0^1 (1 - u)^{N-1}\, du$$

$$= -\frac{1}{\delta N}(1 - u)^N \Big|_0^1 = \frac{1}{\delta N}$$

where the substitution $u = e^{-\delta t}$ was used to obtain the third equality. $E(S_1) = 1/\delta$ since $S_1 = T_1$ is exp. dist. with par. δ. Thus

$$E(S_2) = E(S_2) - E(S_1) + E(S_1)$$

$$= \frac{1}{2\delta} + \frac{1}{\delta} = \left(1 + \frac{1}{2}\right)\Big/\delta$$

$$E(S_3) = E(S_3) - E(S_2) + E(S_2)$$

$$= \frac{1}{3\delta} + \left(1 + \frac{1}{2}\right)\Big/\delta = \left(1 + \frac{1}{2} + \frac{1}{3}\right)\Big/\delta$$

CHAPTER 12

12.5. $\Pi = \begin{bmatrix} 0 & 1 & 0 & 0 \\ 0 & 0 & 1 & 0 \\ 0 & 1/4 & 1/4 & 1/2 \\ 1/3 & 1/3 & 1/3 & 0 \end{bmatrix}$

12.7. $\Pi^2 = \begin{bmatrix} .52 & .48 \\ .36 & .64 \end{bmatrix}$ $\quad \Pi^3 = \begin{bmatrix} .392 & .608 \\ .456 & .544 \end{bmatrix}$

12.9. $\Pi^2 = \begin{bmatrix} p_0^2 + 1 - p_0 & p_0 p_1 & p_0 p_2 & \cdots & p_0 p_N \\ p_0 & p_1 & p_2 & \cdots & p_N \\ \cdot & \cdot & \cdot & & \cdot \\ p_0 & p_1 & p_2 & \cdots & p_N \end{bmatrix}$

12.11. $\Pi^2 = \begin{bmatrix} 0 & 0 & 1 & 0 \\ 0 & 1/4 & 1/4 & 1/2 \\ 1/6 & 11/48 & 23/48 & 1/8 \\ 0 & 5/12 & 5/12 & 1/6 \end{bmatrix}$

12.15. (a) $\rho^1 = (.1, 0, .9)$, $\rho^2 = (.1, 0, .9)$, $\rho^3 = (.1, 0, .9)$
(b) $\rho^1 = (0, .9, .1)$, $\rho^2 = (.01, .81, .18)$, $\rho^3 = (.019, .729, .252)$
(c) $\rho^1 = (.0667, .3000, .6333)$

12.17. $\rho_j^1 = \sum_{i=0}^{N} \rho_i^0 \, \Pi_{i,j} = \dfrac{1}{N+1} \sum_{i=0}^{N} \Pi_{i,j} = \dfrac{1}{N+1}$. Thus $\rho^2 = \rho^1\Pi = \rho^0$ and in general $\rho^t = \rho^{t-1}\Pi$
$= \rho^0 = (1/(N+1), \ldots, 1/(N+1))$.

12.19. $(3/7, 4/7)$

12.21. $(1/(2 - p_0), p_1/(2 - p_0)\, p_2/(2 - p_0), \ldots, p_N/(2 - p_0))$

12.23. $(2/27, 7/27, 12/27, 6/27)$

12.25. $\Pi = \begin{bmatrix} 0 & 0 & 0 & \cdot & 0 & 1 \\ p & q & 0 & \cdot & 0 & 0 \\ 0 & p & q & \cdot & 0 & 0 \\ \cdot & \cdot & & \cdot & \cdot & \cdot \\ 0 & 0 & 0 & \cdot & p & q \end{bmatrix}$, $\phi_0 = p/(N + p)$, $\phi_i = 1/(N + p)$ for $i = 1, 2, \ldots, N$.

12.27. $(2/55, 3/55, 4/55, 10/55, 36/55)$

12.31. (a) Aperiodic and decomposable
(b) $\{5\} \to \{2, 6\} \to \{0, 1, 3\} \to \{4, 7\} \to \{5\}$; periodic with period 4; indecomposable

12.39. $\tau_0 = 1/\phi_0 = (1 - (b/d)^{N+1})/(1 - (b/d))$ for $b \neq d$. (g) For $b/d = 10$, $\tau_0 = (10^{10} - 1)/9 \cong$
1.111×10^9 seconds $\cong 35.23$ years.

Index